Spurgeon's Vision
for the Church

THE ARMY
OF GOD

Geoffrey Chang

SERIES EDITOR: GEOFFREY CHANG

MENTOR

Copyright © Geoffrey Chang 2024

paperback ISBN 978-1-5271-0873-8
ebook ISBN 978-1-5271-1208-7

10 9 8 7 6 5 4 3 2

Published in 2024
in the
Mentor Imprint
by
Christian Focus Publications Ltd,
Geanies House, Fearn, Ross-shire,
IV20 1TW, Great Britain.

www.christianfocus.com

Cover design by James Amour

Printed and bound by
Bell & Bain, Glasgow

MIX
Paper | Supporting
responsible forestry
FSC
www.fsc.org   FSC® C007785

Copyright © Geoffrey Chang 2024

paperback ISBN 978-1-5271-0873-8
ebook ISBN 978-1-5271-1208-7

10 9 8 7 6 5 4 3 2

Published in 2024
in the
Mentor Imprint
by
Christian Focus Publications Ltd,
Geanies House, Fearn, Ross-shire,
IV20 1TW, Great Britain.

www.christianfocus.com

Cover design by James Amour

Printed and bound by
Bell & Bain, Glasgow

To Baptist churches around the world:
May we recover our ecclesiological heritage.

Contents

Series Preface

Spurgeon's Legacy is a series of historical and theological studies related to the life of Charles Haddon Spurgeon (1834–1892). These volumes move beyond the existing scholarship of previous generations to engage with the latest research on Spurgeon's life and ministry within his Victorian context.

Spurgeon's Legacy will seek to cover a wide range of topics, including his doctrinal convictions, theological controversies, Christian spirituality, pastoral ministry, and philanthropic endeavors, all within the dynamic of his historical context. These topics will be explored from an evangelical perspective with appreciation for his contribution while being careful not to idealize the man or his ministry.

While seeking to be accurate historically, each volume will also have a practical and pastoral aim, bringing fresh insights and applications to church leaders and the broader church. By uncovering aspects of Spurgeon's teaching and ministry, these volumes will shed new light on contemporary issues and challenges facing Christians today.

Geoffrey Chang

Abbreviations

AARM – *An All-Round Ministry: Addresses to Ministers and Students.* London: Passmore & Alabaster, 1900.

Autobiography – *C.H. Spurgeon's Autobiography: Compiled from His Diary, Letters, and Records, by His Wife, and His Private Secretary.* Vols. 1-4. London: Passmore & Alabaster, 1897. Citation will be *Autobiography* [Volume Number]:[Page Number].

Lectures – *Lectures to My Students: Addresses Delivered to the Students of the Pastor's College.* Vols. 1-4. London: Passmore & Alabaster, 1881-1894. Citation will be *Lectures* [Volume Number]:[Page Number].

LS – *The Lost Sermons of C. H. Spurgeon.* Vols. 1-7 Eds. Christian George (Vols. 1-3), Jason Duesing (Vol. 4 & 7), Geoffrey Chang (Vols. 5-7), and Philip Ort (Vol. 7). Nashville, TN: B&H Academic, 2016-2022. Citation will be *LS* [Volume Number]:[Page Number].

MTP – *The Metropolitan Tabernacle Pulpit: Sermons Preached and Revised by C. H. Spurgeon.* Vols. 7-63. Pasadena, TX: Pilgrim Publications, 1970-2006. Citation will be *MTP* [Volume Number]:[Page Number].

NPSP – *The New Park Street Pulpit: Containing Sermons Preached and Revised by the Rev. C. H. Spurgeon, Minister of the Chapel.* Vols. 1-6. Pasadena, TX: Pilgrim Publications, 1975-1991. Citation will be *NPSP* [Volume Number]:[Page Number].

S&T – *The Sword and the Trowel; A Record of Combat with Sin & Labour for the Lord.* 37 vols. London: Passmore & Alabaster, 1865–1902. Citation will be *S&T* [Year]:[Page Number].

Treasury – *The Treasury of David: Containing an Original Exposition of the Book of Psalms; A Collection of Illustrative Extracts from the Whole Range of Literature; A Series of Homiletical Hints Upon Almost Every Verse; And Lists of Writers Upon Each Psalm.* 7 Vols. London: Passmore & Alabaster, 1869-1885. Citation will be *Treasury* [Volume Number]:[Page Number].

Acknowledgments

"But, with so large a number as I have under my charge,
what can one man do?"

Charles Spurgeon recognized that if the church was going to prosper, he could not care for it alone. He needed others alongside him. So it was with this book. The research and writing represented here is the product of many who have come alongside me and supported me in this work. I'm grateful to Jason K. Allen, Jason Duesing, Tom Nettles, and Mark Dever for their encouragement in my work in Spurgeon scholarship; to the trustees at Midwestern Baptist Theological Seminary for the sabbatical to write; to Michael Lawrence and Hinson Baptist Church for their support in my doctoral studies; to Peter Masters, Helen Compston, Jasmine Anigbogu, and Emily Burgoyne for making the archives at the Metropolitan Tabernacle and the Angus Library available for my research; and to my family for persevering with me in this work.

1

Introduction

The figures associated with the ministry of Charles Haddon Spurgeon (1834-92) are staggering. He preached his first sermon at the age of sixteen, not long after his conversion. At seventeen, he was called to be the pastor of Waterbeach Chapel, and in two years the congregation grew from forty to several hundred.[1] In about three years, he had preached nearly 700 times to his congregation and in the surrounding villages.[2] By the time of his departure, the entire village of Waterbeach had been transformed, by his own account.[3] At nineteen, he was called to pastor the historic New Park Street Chapel in London, formerly pastored by leading figures of the Particular Baptists such as Benjamin Keach, John Gill, and John Rippon. Over the course of thirty-eight years, Spurgeon preached on average three times per week,[4] and in some weeks, he preached as many as thirteen

---

1. Wayland notes that the congregation grew from forty to one hundred in the first year. H. L. Wayland, *Charles H. Spurgeon: His Faith and Works* (Philadelphia: American Baptist Publication Society, 1892), 26.

2. The earliest notebooks of Spurgeon's sermons contain over 300 sermon outlines, written and preached during these early years of his ministry. However, their numbering system reveals that he often preached sermons multiple times as he traveled throughout the Cambridgeshire countryside. The final count of his preaching from these notebooks numbers well over 700.

3. *Autobiography* 1:227.

4. Craig Skinner, *Spurgeon & Son: The Forgotten Story of Thomas Spurgeon and His Famous Father, Charles Haddon Spurgeon* (Grand Rapids, MI: Kregel Publications, 1999), 224. There were four corporate gatherings per week at the Metropolitan Tabernacle – Sunday morning, Sunday evening, Monday evening, and Thursday evening – which meant that he preached at least four times a week when healthy, not to mention outside preaching occasions. Skinner's estimate possibly takes into account Spurgeon's seasons of illness.

times.[5] His sermons were sold as weekly pamphlets called the *Penny Pulpit*, with an average circulation of 25,000, but in one case selling as many as 350,000 copies.[6] Each year, his sermons would be collected and published in the *New Park Street Pulpit* and *Metropolitan Tabernacle Pulpit* series, beginning in 1855, through his death in 1892, and only ending in 1917 because of a paper shortage due to the First World War.[7] They would comprise a total of 3,563 sermons in sixty-three volumes.[8] These sermons were sold not only in the British Isles and other English-speaking countries, but also in many other countries around the world, being translated into nearly forty languages, including French, German, Dutch, Swedish, Italian, Arabic, Chinese, Japanese, Russian, Urdu, Spanish, and many others.[9] Spurgeon's publishers estimated over 100 million sermons sold in all.[10]

Spurgeon's ministry was not limited to his own preaching. Beginning with one student in 1855, Spurgeon would go on to found the Pastors' College and train almost 900 preachers, with most of them going on to serve in local churches and as missionaries.[11] According to Michael Nicholls, in the second half of the nineteenth century, "the number of Baptist churches in London doubled and nearly all these were founded under Spurgeonic influence of one kind or another."[12] Spurgeon would also begin the Colportage Association, employing evangelists to go throughout the country selling Christian books and distributing

---

5. *Autobiography* 2:81.

6. Lewis Drummond, *Spurgeon: Prince of Preachers* (Grand Rapids, MI: Kregel Publications, 1992), 324. The sermon that sold 350,000 copies was "Baptismal Regeneration," *MTP* 10:313.

7. C. H. Spurgeon, *C. H. Spurgeon's Sermons Beyond Volume 63*, ed. Terence Crosby (Leominster, UK: Day One Publications, 2009), 11; Skinner, *Spurgeon & Son*, 224.

8. If not for the war shortage, Skinner believes that the total number of sermons published would have approached 10,000. Skinner, *Spurgeon & Son*, 224.

9. *Autobiography* 4:291.

10. Ernest W. Bacon, *Spurgeon: Heir of the Puritans* (Arlington Heights, IL: Christian Liberty Press, 2001), 73.

11. *Autobiography* 4:330.

12. Michael Nicholls, "Mission Yesterday and Today: Charles Haddon Spurgeon 1834-1892," *Baptist Review of Theology* 2, no. 1 (Spring 1992), 39.

tracts, sharing the gospel, holding prayer meetings, and preaching to the poor.[13] In one year, the Colportage Association reported 94 colporteurs engaged in the work, their sales amounting to £8,276, having paid 926,290 visits.[14] In addition to these two, dozens more charitable and evangelistic institutions would be founded during his pastorate at the Metropolitan Tabernacle. At Spurgeon's jubilee celebration, a deacon read a list of sixty-six institutions associated with the church. One of the most significant charitable institutions that Spurgeon founded was the Stockwell Orphanage, begun in 1866. Inspired by the example of George Muller, the orphanage cared for thousands of children through the years.[15]

Much more could be said about Spurgeon's ministry, impact, and popularity, as is evident from his many biographies. Each aspect of his ministry, from his preaching to his publications and to his institutions, is an astonishing story in itself and worthy of examination. However, among the many facets of Spurgeon's ministry, one important facet is sometimes overlooked. Spurgeon was not an itinerant preacher, or writer, or philanthropist. From his arrival in 1854 to his death in 1892, Spurgeon was the pastor of the Metropolitan Tabernacle. He preached weekly and made arrangements for pulpit supply in his absence. He led the weekly prayer meetings. He administered the ordinances of baptism and the Lord's Supper. He examined each membership applicant. He provided leadership to the deacons and elders caring for the church, and under his leadership, the Metropolitan Tabernacle became "the largest church in Christendom."[16] Though the church had greatly diminished to a few dozen prior to his arrival, by the end of his ministry, it had a membership of over 5,000.[17] A total

13. *Autobiography* 3:164.

14. Ibid., 166.

15. Drummond, *Spurgeon*, 420, 430.

16. Eric Hayden, *Highlights in the Life of C. H. Spurgeon* (Pasadena, TX: Pilgrim Publications, 1990), 17.

17. Church Meeting Minutes 1889-1894, Metropolitan Tabernacle, Metropolitan Tabernacle Archives, London, Annual Church Meeting, March 1st 1893.

of 14,692 members were baptized and joined the church under Spurgeon's care.[18]

Spurgeon's Vision for the Church

Widely known as the "Prince of Preachers," much attention has been given to Spurgeon's preaching, publishing ministry, charitable endeavors, and other activities. But undergirding all these ministries is the fact that, for almost forty years, he was quite simply the pastor of a local church. And as the pastor, he had a responsibility not only to preach the gospel but also to lead his church.

But did Spurgeon have a vision for the church? What was Spurgeon's ecclesiology, that is, his understanding of the doctrine of the church? Underneath that overarching question are many other questions about the nature and function of the church: What was Spurgeon's understanding of the universal church and its relation to local churches? Who held authority in the church? What were the historical roots of his ecclesiology? What was his view of local church governance? What was his understanding of the pastoral office? How did he seek to advance his understanding of the church? What role did his ecclesiology play amid the wider context and controversies of his day?

My contention is that Spurgeon most definitely had a vision for the church that was informed by his Reformed heritage and Baptist convictions and rooted in his understanding of Scripture. Even more, Spurgeon promoted and held fast to his vision for the church during a time when Nonconformist ecclesiology was in decline, due to three challenges: ritualism, revivalism, and rationalism. As Spurgeon battled these errors, he held fast to the classic understanding of the church militant, namely, that

---

18. Hayden, *Highlights in the Life of C. H. Spurgeon*, 69. In previous writings, I reported that 13,797 members joined the church under Spurgeon's ministry. I arrived at that number by adding all the reported additions that were reported in the church's annual meeting minutes from 1854-1892. However, the 1892 annual meeting does not contain the additions for 1891 (understandable, given the church's grief over the loss of their pastor), so those numbers are incomplete. Hayden's numbers (14,692) are nearly 900 more than my calculations, far too many to account for the missing year. I'm not sure how Hayden arrived at his number but given that he was a pastor of the Metropolitan Tabernacle, I will assume that his number is correct.

while on earth, the church is to be an army engaged in a fight for the truth.

Ecclesiology since the Reformation

Spurgeon stood downstream from many debates about the nature of the church that were sparked by the Reformation. Late medieval Roman Catholicism had established the church and its elaborate sacramental system as the gatekeeper between man and salvation. But Luther's rediscovery of justification by faith meant that the church also needed to be rediscovered. His primary ecclesiological contribution was that the true church was to be rooted in the gospel. Apart from the gospel, there could be no church. In his Ninety-Five Theses, Luther argued that "the true treasure of the church is the most holy gospel of the glory and grace of God."[19] While theologians of the previous centuries might have agreed with such a statement, Luther redefined terms like "gospel" and "grace" into "something... that many of these [former] theologians would not quite have been able to recognize or acknowledge"[20] and thus also brought a new understanding to the church. In his *Small Catechism*, Luther asked, "Where is this holy Christian Church to be found? This holy Christian Church is to be found *where the Gospel is in use;* for according to God's promise His Word shall not be preached in vain."[21] By focusing the church's very identity on Christ and the salvation found in Him, Luther not only created a basis from which to counteract Rome's ecclesiological abuses, but also paved the way for the Christological emphasis of future Protestant ecclesiology.

The next generation of reformers, led by Calvin and Melanchthon, received Luther's ecclesiological foundation, and built on it. Having established the Christological center, these later reformers "took up the difficult task of determining with some

---

19. Denis R. Janz, ed., *A Reformation Reader: Primary Texts with Introductions* (Philadelphia: Fortress Press, 2008), 88.

20. Jaroslav Pelikan, *Reformation of Church and Dogma (1300-1700)* (Chicago: University of Chicago Press, 1984), 128.

21. Martin Luther, *Dr. Martin Luther's Small Catechism* (St. Louis, MO: Concordia Publishing House, 1971), 134.

precision its circumference,"[22] working towards the purity of the church according to God's Word. Another group, the sixteenth-century Anabaptists, brought a new level of concern for the purity of the church. While this group contained some heretical streams, historians recognize that the evangelical Anabaptists, led by reformers like Balthasar Hubmaier and Menno Simons, stood within the tradition of the Protestant Reformation.[23] Their ecclesiology emphasized separation and purity. The church was a community of regenerated believers, marked off by believers' baptism and the practice of church discipline (or "the ban").[24] Their vision of the church would go on to influence future English Separatism, as well as the Church of the Brethren and English Quakers.[25]

In the English Reformation of the seventeenth century, ecclesiological debates centered on questions of church unity, schism, church governance, church and state, and related issues.[26] Puritanism was initially birthed within the Church of England as a reforming movement, aligned with the continental Reformed churches. As a result, it shared the concerns of Reformed Protestantism in ecclesiology, working towards biblical forms of church government, discipline, and worship.[27] Over the next two centuries, Puritanism would branch out of the Church of England in dissenting streams, represented most prominently by Presbyterians, Independents (or Congregationalists), and Baptists. Though each of these groups largely held the same reformed theology,[28] their understanding and practice of the church varied

---

22. Timothy George, *Theology of the Reformers, 25th Anniversary Edition* (Nashville, TN: B&H Academic, 2013), 243.

23. For example, see William Estep, *The Anabaptist Story: An Introduction to Sixteenth-Century Anabaptism*, 3rd ed. (Grand Rapids, MI: Eerdmans Publishing Co., 1996), 177-99, and George, *Theology of the Reformers*, 267-322.

24. George, *Theology of the Reformers*, 300-13.

25. Ibid., 273-305.

26. Iain H. Murray, *The Reformation of the Church: A Collection of Reformed and Puritan Documents on Church Issues* (Edinburgh: The Banner of Truth Trust, 1997), 7.

27. John Coffey and Paul C. H. Lim, eds. *The Cambridge Companion to Puritanism* (Cambridge: Cambridge University Press, 2008), 2-3.

28. The theological similarities among the English dissenting streams can be seen in their representative statements of faith. See "A Tabular Comparison of the 1646

in the areas of church authority, polity, and ministry. For these differences, the reformers would endure "much mental labor and often physical suffering in contending against religious abuses and setting forth scriptural principles."[29] The beginning of the eighteenth century saw the decline of evangelicalism due to several challenges, most notably the growing rationalism of the Enlightenment, which lead to assaults on the orthodoxy of the churches. Even as dissenters had so recently gained some measure of religious freedom in the Toleration Act of 1689,[30] they were now hesitant to impose creedal tests on their ministers and churches.[31] Some denominations encountered a significant shift in their theology towards Unitarianism, including the English Presbyterians. However, the middle of the century saw a remarkable turning point: the Evangelical Revival. Sparked by the preaching of George Whitefield and John Wesley, evangelicalism experienced a recovery of evangelical theology and gospel preaching for conversion. Large numbers were converted, left the Church of England, and joined either a Methodist or one of the dissenting congregations. By the early nineteenth century, Congregationalists and Baptists had seen the most growth as a result of the revival.

Spurgeon's Ecclesiological Inheritance
Spurgeon stood in theological continuity with the Protestant Reformation, his Puritan predecessors, and the Evangelical Revival. Converted in a Primitive Methodist church, he inherited a passion for preaching the gospel. From his very first sermon to the last one he preached,[32] Spurgeon pointed his hearers to the

---

Westminster Confession of Faith, the 1658 Savoy Declaration of Faith, the 1677/1689 London Baptist Confession of Faith and the 1742 Philadelphia Confession of Faith," Don Lowe and James Anderson, cdli:wiki, https://www.proginosko.com/docs/wcf_sdfo_lbcf.html.

29. Murray, *Reformation of the Church*, 10.

30. Coffey, *The Cambridge Companion to Puritanism*, 93.

31. Jesse Owens, "The Salters' Hall Controversy: Heresy, Subscription, or Both?" *Perichoresis* Vol. 20.1 (2022), 35-52.

32. His very first sermon was from 1 Peter 2:7, "Unto you therefore which believe [Christ] is precious." *Autobiography* 1:201.

saving work of Jesus, calling them to repentance and faith in Him. But beyond gospel preaching, Spurgeon also inherited his predecessors' concern for the purity of the church.[33] Spurgeon's prioritization of the local church can be traced throughout his life. A few weeks after his conversion, he applied for membership at the Congregational church in Newmarket and was accepted into membership on April 4, 1850.[34] For the next forty years until his death, he was a member in good standing in four different local churches.[35] While this church participation could be lost in the background of all his other ministries, Spurgeon's preaching reveals a much higher view of the church. Though his goal was always to preach Christ, Spurgeon understood that salvation in Christ could not be disconnected from the church. Preaching to his congregation in 1877, Spurgeon boldly used Cyprian's metaphor,[36] declaring,

> We love the Church, which is our mother. I do hope that all the members of this church love the whole Church of God, and also have a special affection for that particular part of it in which they were born for God... it would be unnatural not to love the place where we were born into the heavenly family.... We love the Church of God.[37]

Spurgeon's Reformed tradition meant that he was careful never to confuse the church and the gospel. Baptism, membership in the local church, or any other external participation in the church could never be a requirement for salvation. At the same time, he believed that commitment to the church ought to

33. James Leo Garrett, *Baptist Theology: A Four-Century Study* (Macon, GA: Mercer University Press, 2009), 266.

34. *Autobiography* 1:118-21.

35. Spurgeon was a member of the following four churches: April 4, 1850–October 3, 1850: Congregational Church, Newmarket; October 3, 1850–October 1851: St. Andrew's Street Baptist Church, Cambridge; October 1851–April 28, 1854–Waterbeach Chapel; April 28, 1854–January 31, 1892 – New Park Street Chapel / Metropolitan Tabernacle.

36. "He can no longer have God for his Father, who has not the Church for his mother." *Ante-Nicene Fathers*, vol. 5, *Hippolytus, Cyprian, Caius, Novatian, Appendix*, ed. Alexander Roberts and James Donaldson (Peabody, MA: Hendrickson Publishers, 2004), 423.

37. *MTP* 42:477.

characterize every believer. As a Baptist, Spurgeon emphasized the importance of a public profession of faith through baptism. But this was a baptism into Christ,[38] which should lead to ongoing participation in the body of Christ through membership in a local church. Far from being a mere formality, Spurgeon's love for and commitment to the church was an integral part of his vision for the Christian life.

As a pastor, Spurgeon also held convictions from Scripture about how the church was to be ordered. A few years after being called as a pastor to the New Park Street Chapel, he led his congregation to institute the office of elders, because he believed this to be the New Testament practice.[39] He also believed that Scripture taught a congregational form of church government, where the congregation was the final authority of the church in matters of membership, discipline, leadership, and doctrine. He held to the independence of the church, where no extra-ecclesial body could exercise authority over the local church.[40] Not the elders, or deacons, or even Spurgeon himself could unilaterally make decisions in those areas for the rest of the church. At the same time, as the pastor, he was a commanding figure and exercised unmatched influence in his church. Therefore, while Spurgeon held to congregational principles, his polity also recognized the unique role of the pastor and the leadership roles of the elders and deacons.

In his day, Spurgeon recognized several ecclesiological challenges that undermined the orthodoxy of the church and the preaching of the gospel. As a result, his concern was not only for the purity of the church, but that the church would be engaged in the fight for the truth. Perhaps his favorite image for the church was that of an army, the church militant, which can be traced back to the early church fathers.[41] Spurgeon believed

---

38. Cf. 1 Corinthians 12:13.

39. *Autobiography* 3:22-23.

40. *MTP* 7:257.

41. One of the earliest instances of the distinction between the church militant and church triumphant can be found in the *Shepherd of Hermas*, which was written around the first half of the second century. *Ante-Nicene Fathers*, vol. 2, *Fathers of the Second Century: Hermas, Tatian, Athenagoras, Theophilus, and Clement of Alexandria*

the church on earth was always at war, fighting for the defense and spread of the gospel. While his teaching remained focused on defending theological doctrines directly connected to the gospel, this fight also included how churches were to be ordered and guided.[42] Rationalism continued to challenge any doctrinal basis for churches and denominations. Many Baptist churches were moving beyond open communion to open membership, which compromised their distinctive understanding of baptism and of the church. The emphasis on individual salvation from the Evangelical Revival was morphing into a subjective approach to the ordinances, rooted in the experience of the individual rather than the accountability of the church.[43] The Oxford Movement in the Church of England continued to grow in influence, promoting a Roman Catholic view of the church, the sacraments, and the ministry. In these and other challenges, Spurgeon's ecclesiology took on a militant outlook.

Sources and Layout

Theologians have noted how "one's doctrine of the church is integrally related to one's denominational and theological background."[44] For Spurgeon, this was no different. His understanding of the church, his ecclesiology, was informed by his personal and theological background. Therefore, as we explore Spurgeon's understanding of the church, we must connect it with his background and wider theology. But recognizing that he was first and foremost a pastor, we will also emphasize those points of his ecclesiology that connect most directly with the local church. For him, ecclesiology was manifested in the practical

---

(Entire), ed. Alexander Roberts and James Donaldson (Peabody, MA: Hendrickson Publishers, 2004), 43.

42. C. H. Spurgeon, *The Greatest Fight in the World: The Final Manifesto* (Fearn, UK: Christian Focus Publications, 2014).

43. Baptist leaders like John Clifford advocated for this view. See J. H. Y. Briggs, *The English Baptists of the 19th Century* (Didcot, UK: The Baptist Historical Society, 1994), 53. See also Michael Walker, *Baptists at the Table* (Didcot, UK: Baptist Historical Society, 1992), 184-85.

44. Veli-Matti Karkkainen, *An Introduction to Ecclesiology* (Downers Grove, IL: InterVarsity Press, 2002), 231.

outworking of membership and discipline, pastoral ministry, church meetings, worship, and other aspects of day-to-day church life. By connecting Spurgeon's ecclesiology and church polity, and placing it in its wider context, we will examine an important area of Spurgeon's theology and practice.

Spurgeon never systematized his theology, nor did he write a manual of church polity.[45] Therefore, any attempts at systemizing his understanding and ordering of the church will have to rely on his large body of work, including his sermons, books, lectures, and letters. Some of the most important primary sources will be Spurgeon's sixty-three volumes of the *New Park Street Pulpit* and *Metropolitan Tabernacle Pulpit*, his four-volume *Autobiography*, the twenty-seven annual volumes of his monthly magazine, *The Sword and the Trowel*, and the Pastors' College lectures found in the four-volume set, *Lectures to My Students,* and in *An All-Round Ministry*. Other primary sources will include his other books and the recently published *Lost Sermons*,[46] which provide insight into Spurgeon's ecclesiology from his pastorate at Waterbeach.

Unpublished primary works will also be important to this study. The records from the Metropolitan Tabernacle archives are important and seldom accessed sources. These include the Church Meeting Minute Books, Elder Meeting Minute Books, Deacon Minute Books, and the Testimony Books. These books have survived multiple fires, bombings, and church reconstructions and remain accessible to researchers today. Additionally, the collection of Spurgeon-related personal letters and documents at the Angus Library in Regent's Park has been accessed for relevant material.

I have published another book, *Spurgeon the Pastor: Recovering a Biblical and Theological Vision for Ministry,*[47] that focuses

---

45. The closest thing that exists is an article written by James A. Spurgeon, entitled "The Discipline of the Church at the Metropolitan Tabernacle." While an important primary source, this article is not a complete manual of church polity. *S&T* 1869:49-57.

46. C. H. Spurgeon, *The Lost Sermons of C. H. Spurgeon*, 7 vols. (Nashville, TN: B&H Academic, 2016-2022).

47. Geoffrey Chang, *Spurgeon the Pastor: Recovering a Biblical and Theological Vision for Ministry* (Nashville, TN: B&H Publishing, 2022).

on Spurgeon's convictional approach to pastoral ministry. Undoubtedly, there will be some overlap between the contents of that book and the material in here. But in that book, I tried to answer more of the "how" of Spurgeon's pastoral ministry and avoided getting bogged down in church minutes and other details. In this work, I provide more historical and contextual research and focus more strictly on matters of church doctrine.

Having introduced Spurgeon's remarkable impact, his vision for the church, and his theological heritage here, the next chapter will focus on historical context. In particular, we will consider three challenges that contributed to ecclesiological decline among dissenters in the nineteenth-century: revivalism, ritualism, and rationalism. It is against the backdrop that Spurgeon sought to present his vision of the church as the army of God. The following chapter will narrow the lens, giving a brief biographical sketch of Spurgeon's early life, to demonstrate the various influences that shaped his commitment to the church from an early age.

The next six chapters will then present Spurgeon's vision for the church under three headings: his Reformed ecclesiology, his Baptist church polity, and his vision of the Church Militant. In chapters four and five, we will consider how Spurgeon stood squarely in the Reformed tradition in his ecclesiology, as we analyze his view of the local and universal church, the sacraments, the regulative principle, and more. In chapters six and seven, those theological ideas will be given more concrete expression as we examine how Spurgeon implemented his Baptist convictions in church membership and governance. Finally, in chapters eight and nine, we will define Spurgeon's vision for the militant church and show the priority of the church in two of his most important battles: the Baptismal Regeneration Controversy and the Downgrade Controversy. The conclusion will provide a summary of the argument, along with further contemporary reflections and applications.

Preaching in 1870, Spurgeon declared,

> The proper study of the Christian is Christ. Next to that subject
> is the Church. And though I would by no means ever urge you so

to think of the Church as for a moment to put her in comparison with her Lord yet think of her in relation to him. You will not dishonor the sun by remembering that there is a moon, you will not lessen the glory of "the King in his beauty" by remembering that the Queen, his Consort, is "all glorious within." You will not think any the less of Christ for thinking much of his Church.[48]

Spurgeon thought much of Christ's Church. It is our aim to unpack his thought on this important topic.

---

48. *MTP* 60:433.

2

Declining Ecclesiology

In 1869, Spurgeon published an article in *The Sword and the Trowel* entitled, "Discipline of the Church at the Metropolitan Tabernacle." The goal of this article was not to promote a uniform structure of church governance among dissenting churches. However, as he looked at the laxity among churches in their practice of church membership and pastoral oversight, he had little confidence in the discipline of those churches.

> That so few points of agreement should be accepted as a common basis of action, sustaining a sense of confidence in each other's discipline, is little short of a calamity. Mutual confidence arising from known[,] adequate, though it may be at times dissimilar[,] courses of action, leading up to one result, must be a source of blessing to any denomination; and at present we frankly admit, as the result of a somewhat wide observation of the methods of receiving, and the all but uniform want of method in removing names from our church rolls, we have but small faith in ecclesiastical statistics, and what is worse, a limited confidence in letters of commendation from our churches.[1]

Within his own denomination, Spurgeon was concerned about the growing embrace of open membership, which did not require believer's baptism for church membership. While many Baptists celebrated their union with paedobaptists through this practice, promoting a growth in their numbers, Spurgeon believed that it was "eating out the very vitals of the denomination." Open membership would "promote the downfall" of all churches who

---

1. *S&T* 1869:49-50.

practiced it. But his concern was not merely pragmatic. Rather, believer's baptism was a matter of obedience to Christ. As for himself, Spurgeon declared, "he would rather give up his pastorate than admit any man to the church who was not obedient to his Lord's command."[2]

Even more concerning was the growing loss of a theological basis within dissenting churches. Spurgeon once told the story of his brother teaching the *Baptist Confession of Faith* to his congregation in Southampton, which "raised a clamor in the Church." The congregation boasted that they "had no doctrines – no creed; they claimed the glorious liberty of believing anything they liked." Such a view was not uncommon among Baptist churches in the nineteenth century. In his own congregation, Spurgeon re-introduced the *Baptist Confession of Faith* and made it a regular part of their discipleship, so that "it would be difficult to confute the youngest members of their Church on any of the five points. They all loved the old doctrines of grace."[3]

Spurgeon's church background in the Reformed tradition had taught him about the importance of the church.[4] This priority was evident throughout his ministry. Yet all around him, he was surprised to discover that such views of the church were fading among dissenting churches. Why was that? What contributed to this decline? This chapter will trace three sources of ecclesiological decline during Spurgeon's day: the Oxford Movement, the evangelical revivals, and the rising New Theology; or, ritualism, revivalism, and rationalism.[5]

---

2. *MTP* 7:260.

3. *MTP* 7:261.

4. For a study of Spurgeon's background in the Congregational chapel in Colchester under T. W. Davids, see Geoff Chang, "New Insights into the Formative Influence of Spurgeon's Early Years," *Themelios*, Vol. 47, Issue 3.

5. For further study on this topic, see John W. Grant, *Free Churchmanship in England, 1870-1949: With Special Reference to Congregationalism* (London: Independent Press Ltd., 1955). See also P. T. Marsh, *The Victorian Church in Decline: Archbishop Tait and the Church of England 1868-1882* (Pittsburgh, PA: University of Pittsburgh Press, 1969); K. Theodore Hoppen, *The Mid-Victorian Generation 1846-1886* (Oxford: Clarenden Press, 2008); Kenneth Hylson-Smith, *Evangelicals in the Church of England 1734-1984* (Edinburgh: T & T Clark, 1989); L. E. Elliot-Binns, *Religion in the Victorian Era* (Greenwich, CT: The Seabury Press, 1953).

Ritualism

Ritualism arose in the Church of England towards the middle of the nineteenth century, seeking to restore liturgical practices from Roman Catholicism into the Church. With Eucharistic vestments, candles, the eastward facing celebration of Holy Communion, the sign of the cross, the veneration of Mary, and more, this movement began to introduce innovations into parish worship. But behind these liturgical practices were ecclesiological convictions that could be traced back to the Oxford Movement, or Tractarianism, which had begun earlier in the century.[6] These convictions were outlined in a series of tracts known as *Tracts for the Times*, published from 1833-1841.

In these ninety tracts, the Tractarians argued not only for the restoration of Roman liturgical practices, but certain aspects of their ecclesiology. These tracts do not lay out a creed or present a unified doctrinal statement. They do represent a persistent push towards aspects of medieval Roman Catholic ecclesiology, even as they try to maintain a Protestant identity. As these tracts were being published, many suspected that the Oxford Movement was a push for the Church of England to return to the Roman Catholic Church. The movement would encounter a significant setback with the publication of Tract 90 in 1841, when John Henry Newman argued for the compatibility of the Church of England's Thirty-Nine Articles with Roman Catholic doctrine. For this he was publicly denounced, and the tracts came to an end. By 1845, Newman was officially received into the Roman Catholic Church.

The Oxford Movement, however, would continue into the early 1850s under the leadership of E. B. Pusey.[7] The Ritualist emphasis would now be on liturgical reform rather than on doctrinal teaching. But the ecclesiological foundation of the movement was already established. The Tractarian teaching on apostolic

---

6. There is some debate as to the relationship between ritualism and the Oxford Movement, with some recent scholars arguing for discontinuity. However, public perception in the nineteenth century and traditional interpretation since then has been that the two movements were connected. For a brief summary of the debate and the secondary sources involved, see Bennett W. Rogers, *A Tender Lion: The Life, Ministry, and Message of J. C. Ryle* (Grand Rapids, MI: Reformation Heritage Books, 2019), 91-92.

7. Thus, the movement also came to be known as Puseyism.

succession, the meaning of the sacraments, and the role of the clergy linked up nicely with the efforts of the Ritualists.

Apostolic Succession

From Tract 1, the main ecclesiological assertion of the Tractarians was that apostolic succession was what set the Church of England apart from all other churches. Apostolic succession is the belief in an unbroken chain of ordination from present-day bishops, going back through church history, all the way to the apostles. "The Lord JESUS CHRIST gave his Spirit to his Apostles; they in turn laid their hands on those who should succeed them; and these again on others; and so the sacred gift has been handed down to our present Bishops." Tractarians held that the sacred gift of the Spirit had been uniquely conferred on their bishops and all their appointees, as expressed in the Ordination services of the Book of Common Prayer. This was "the real ground on which our authority is built."[8]

Dissenting churches, then, in leaving the Church of England, cut themselves off from the apostolic ministry. In doing so, their ministers had not received a commission from Christ to preach and administer the sacraments.[9] Their ministry was not authorized by Christ. Therefore, while the Tractarians affirmed that the right preaching of the Word and the right administration of the sacraments were the marks of a true church, they also believed that such marks could not exist without apostolic succession. What made these marks "right" was a properly ordained ministry. Therefore, individuals in those churches may well be true believers, but their churches were no true churches.[10]

Accordingly, the sin of dissent was the sin of schism. In separating from the Church of England, dissenters had rejected the authority of the apostles. Unity in the Church could only be recovered, not by agreement in doctrine, but by submission

---

8. *Tracts for the Times; By Members of the University of Oxford.* Vols. I-V 1833-40 (London: J. G. & F. Rivington, 1839-40), Tract 1. Because of the inconsistency of the page numbers in this set, we will only cite the tracts by their number.

9. Tract 15.

10. Tract 4.

to apostolic authority.[11] According to the Tractarians, this unity of submission allowed for the Church to truly be catholic. "Submission to Church authority is the test whether or not we prefer unity, and the edification of CHRIST's body, to private fancies." Rather than giving way to intolerance over ecclesiological or liturgical quibbles, the Church of England allowed for all kinds of groups within its fold, so long as they submitted to apostolic succession. Both Dissenters and Roman Catholic "Papists" (after the Council of Trent), in holding to all their narrow dogmas, had committed schism, banishing themselves from the Church catholic by their rebellion against apostolic authority.[12]

Sacramentarianism

Another feature of Tractarian ecclesiology was a high sacramentarianism. Whereas the Reformation had renewed an emphasis on the preaching of the Word, the Tractarians sought to replace that emphasis with a high view of the sacraments. Tract 32, for example, argues that it is "those two Blessed Ordinances" that "are the standing and definite publication, to every one of us… of the infinite mercies of GOD, as manifested in the Covenant of the Gospel." The writer compares the ordinances to monuments that live on, despite the corruption of false teaching and preaching. Though the church may be corrupted, the ordinances preserve the gospel and will eventually "come forth pure and unsullied, full of sweetness and edifying comfort," like a beautiful ancient statue buried for ages, but now uncovered. These sacraments "will be furnished with all requisites for teaching us those lessons, which the preceding age has been engaged in obliterating."[13] What is striking about this tract is not the valuing of the ordinances, but the absence of preaching alongside the ordinances. Here, the

---

11. "And how did the Apostle endeavour to drive out the spirit of schism? by asserting and enforcing his own authority over them, as the *one* only father whom they had in the Gospel, (though they might choose for themselves ten thousand instructors,) and by sending Timothy to bring them into remembrance of his *ways which were* in CHRIST, as *he taught every where in every Church.* Thus were they to be brought back to the blessed unity of spirit of the One Catholic and Apostolic Church." Tract 21.

12. Tract 61. See also Tract 15 and 45.

13. Tract 32.

ordinances are ultimately able to interpret themselves and do not need the right preaching of the Word to explain their meaning.

While the tracts never deny the importance of faith,[14] their emphasis is on the objective efficacy of the sacraments. The sacraments are the keys of the kingdom in Matthew 16:18-19. Through baptism, "souls are admitted into covenant with God," and through the Lord's Supper, souls are "brought into union with Him." All who reject the sacraments are "cut off from union with Him, from communion with the faithful, and cast out of the Kingdom of Heaven."[15]

With a more objective view of the efficacy of the sacraments, the Tractarians affirmed the language of the Book of Common Prayer which implied baptismal regeneration. Tract 76 provides this definition:

> The Sacrament of Baptism is not a mere *sign* or *promise*, but actually a *means* of grace, an *instrument*, by which, when rightly received, the soul is admitted to the benefits of Christ's Atonement, such as the forgiveness of sin, original and actual, reconciliation to God, a new nature, adoption, citizenship in Christ's kingdom, and the inheritance of heaven,–in a word, Regeneration.[16]

This definition could possibly be interpreted as being consistent with the broader Reformed tradition. It largely depends on the phrase "when rightly received." What does it mean for baptism

---

14. For example, see Tract 26. "If they come to the Holy Sacrament, they must *first examine themselves*, repent of all their sins, turn to God, renew their baptismal vow, and resolve to lead a new life. But this they are resolved not to do. And if they should come to the Sacrament, it would but disturb their quiet, make them uneasy in their minds, and hinder them from enjoying the pleasure they were wont to take in all their sins. And for their part, they had rather displease God than themselves; and neglect their duty rather than leave their sins. And to add sin to sin, and 'treasure up to themselves wrath against the day of wrath, and the revelation of the righteous judgment of God.' This is plainly the case of most of those who live in the neglect of His Holy Commandment. And what can be said to such men? so long as such, they are not fit to come to the Communion. And therefore all that can be said to them, is only to beg of them to consider their condition before it be too late, and repent as soon as they can: lest they die, as they have lived, in sin, and so be punished with 'everlasting destruction from the presence of the Lord, and from the glory of His power.'"

15. Tract 35.

16. Tract 76.

to be "rightly received"? The tract goes on to explain: For adults, it means that "there is no positive obstacle or hindrance to the reception in the recipient, such as impenitence or unbelief." And in the case of infants, as they're not yet capable of sin, they are all "necessarily right recipients of it." Therefore, all infants who receive baptism are indeed regenerated and made citizens of Christ's kingdom.

Similarly, the Tractarians also affirmed the objective nature of the Lord's Supper, which meant a recovery of the Supper as a sacrifice. They rejected the Roman Catholic doctrine of transubstantiation and affirmed Christ's spiritual presence in the Supper, "to be understood in a sacramental and mystic sense; and that no gross and carnal presence of body and blood can be maintained by them." Yet this spiritual presence is the real presence of Christ, "no less true and undoubted than if it were corporal."[17] All this could be viewed as consistent with Reformed tradition. But the Tractarians also taught that the Supper was a sacrifice, providing this definition:

> that "in the Eucharist, an oblation or sacrifice was made by the Church to God, under the form of His creatures of bread and wine, according to our Blessed LORD's holy institution, in memory of His Cross and Passion;"... This commemorative oblation or sacrifice they doubted not to be acceptable to God, who had appointed it; and so to be also a means of bringing down God's favour upon the whole Church.[18]

This "commemorative sacrifice" obtained the remission of sins for the Church and strengthened the soul through communion with God.

The Tractarians never denied the necessity of faith in the sacraments. Rather, partaking in the sacraments, particularly the Lord's Supper, becomes the chief expression of faith for the Christian, or even faith itself. "By eating and drinking frequently of it, we grow by degrees in grace, and in the 'knowledge of our Lord and Saviour JESUS CHRIST,' and still continue steadfast and

17. Tract 27.
18. Tract 81.

active in the true faith and fear of God." For the Christian who is unable to discern any spiritual growth, he can take comfort in knowing that the Lord's Supper strengthens him in the inner man and preserves him from many sins and temptations. So long as the Christian regularly partakes,

> He may rest satisfied in his mind, that he is in the way that CHRIST hath made to Heaven; and thank God for giving him so *many opportunities* of partaking of CHRIST's Body and Blood, and also grace to lay hold of them, to improve them to his own *unspeakable* comfort, such as usually attends the *worthy receiving* of the LORD's *Supper*: whereby we are not *only* put in mind of the great *Sacrifice* which the SON of GOD offered for our sins, but likewise have it actually *communicated* unto us, for our *pardon* and *reconciliation* to the ALMIGHTY GOVERNOR of the world, which is the greatest comfort we can have on this side Heaven.[19]

In other words, the spirituality of the Tractarians centered not on the gospel or on faith, but on participation in the sacraments of the church.

The Role of the Clergy
With this high view of apostolic succession and the sacraments, the Tractarians also naturally held to a fundamental division between the clergy and the laity. These two classes are distinct and yet united, "by the commandment of GOD Himself." Only the clergy have the commission from God, "through regular succession from the Apostles, to preach the gospel, administer the Sacraments, and guide the Church." The clergy also have the unique "power of sending *others* with a divine commission, who in like manner should have the power of sending others, and so on even unto the end." It was through this unbroken chain of successors that Christ's promise to be with the Church until the end of the age was to be fulfilled.[20] What about the laity? They are called "to hear them with attention, receive the Sacraments from their hands, and pay them all dutiful obedience." No lay person

---

19. Tract 26.
20. Tract 15.

has the authority to teach religion, or administer the sacraments, or even "taking care of the souls of other people, unless he has *in some way* been called to undertake the office."[21] The Tractarian vision of ministry centered almost entirely on the clergy, leaving the laity as passive recipients.

With this combination of the lay and clerical divide and apostolic succession, the Tractarians also naturally held to a *de jure* Episcopalianism. Whereas many argued for it pragmatically, the Tractarians believed that Episcopalian church government was commanded in Scripture and, more importantly, practiced by the early church:[22]

> My position then is this; –that the Apostles appointed successors to their ministerial office, and the latter in turn appointed others, and so on to the present day; –and further, that the Apostles and their Successors have in every age committed portions of their power and authority to others, who thus become their delegates, and in a measure their representatives, and are called *Priests* and *Deacons*. The result is an Episcopal system, *because* of the practice of delegation.[23]

The rule of the Church, therefore, was not congregational, nor representative, as with Presbyterianism. Rather, it was to be ruled by bishops, who had received apostolic authority and continued to pass it on down through the ages.

The Effect of Ritualism on Dissenting Ecclesiology

Prior to the Oxford Movement, Nonconformists and Dissenters formed two different attitudes among those outside the Church of England. Nonconformists were willing to tolerate their various disabilities, including their inability to attend university or be buried in the parish churchyard by their own ministers. Even as they separated for their ecclesiological convictions, they respected

---

21. Tract 15.

22. "…let us suppose, *for the sake of argument*, that Episcopacy is in fact not at all mentioned in Scripture: even then it would be our duty to receive it. Why? because the first Christians received it…. If it be a fact, that the earliest Christian communities were universally episcopal, it is a reason for our maintaining Episcopacy; and in proportion to our conviction, is it incumbent on us to maintain it." Tract 45.

23. Tract 7.

the position of the established Church. This was in contrast with the Dissenters who were more active in the political arena, protesting the privileges of the establishment. But as the Oxford Movement gained influence in the mid-1850s and promoted the view that all outside churches were no true churches, Dissent and Nonconformity merged into a unified opposition against the established church.[24]

One result of this controversy among dissenting churches against the Oxford Movement was that it brought matters of ecclesiology to the forefront. However, because these discussions tended to be polemical, they often pushed dissenting ecclesiology beyond its Reformed tradition to lower views of the church. We can see the effects in four ways: minimizing the role of the church in the Christian life, the rejection of liturgical forms, a lower view of the ministry, and more variety in the sacraments.

First, with the Oxford Movement increasingly placing the Church and its sacraments as an intermediary between the individual and Christ, dissenting churches responded by stressing the importance of individual salvation. As one Congregationalist writer expressed,

> They have faith in priests, in sacraments, and the Church, which we altogether abjure. We insist mainly on the relation of the individual soul to Christ, and the blessings to be derived from this personal fellowship; they, on his place in the Church, and the grace which Christ communicates through his appointed channel. We regard man as a free and intelligent agent, accepting his creed on his own responsibility, and by an act of his own mind and will, and coming to Christ by the exercise of his own simple trust in him.[25]

In contrast with the Tractarian emphasis on the sacraments, Congregationalists emphasized the individual's coming to Christ directly. "We tell him that he becomes a member of Christ when he hears His voice, and trusts in His grace, and follows where He leads." Here, the writer has in view not membership

24. Marsh, *The Victorian Church in Declim*, 114-16.

25. "Why do we Dissent?" *The Congregationalist,* Vol. I 1872 (London: Hodder and Stoughton, 1872), 312.

in a visible, local church, but the universal body of Christ that comprehends all true believers. While the Church of England taught a "materialistic" religion, Dissenters "set forth, from first to last, a purely spiritual religion."[26]

Second, as the Ritualists sought to revive the use of medieval liturgical forms, dissenters tended to reject the use of any forms in the worship of the church. Quakers are, perhaps, an extreme example of this as they interpreted the ordinances in purely spiritual terms. But even among Congregationalists and Baptists, corporate prayer now tended to be spontaneous rather than prepared. Dissenting services were marked by contemporary innovations, rather than traditional forms. Elaborate rituals and church calendars gave way to simplicity. As John Clifford wrote, "Baptist have done nothing for the methods and machinery of Christianity, unless it is that they have shown how immeasurably inferior methods and machinery are to intrinsic conviction, personal faith, and passionate devotion to high ideals."[27]

Perhaps the biggest opposition to form came in dissenting opposition to the Tractarian view of the ministry. For dissenters, the best way to combat sacerdotalism was by diminishing the lay-clergy divide, removing the symbols of ministerial authority (dress and titles), and emphasizing the importance of congregational authority. The Reformed tradition rejected the idea that ministers derived their authority from a ceremonial laying on of hands.[28] Rather, among congregational churches, ministerial authority came from the vote of the congregation. Therefore, not just the minister, but any number of people could be authorized by the congregation to preach the Word and administer the sacraments. "The older idea that the ministry is a gift of Christ to the Church was passing away in favour of the notion that it is merely a function of the Church, deriving its powers from the Church."[29]

---

26. Ibid.

27. John Clifford, "The Place of Baptists in the Evolution of British Christianity," *Religious Systems of the World: A Contribution to the Study of Comparative Religion* (London: Swan Sonnenschein & Co., Limited, 1905), 561.

28. For example, see John Calvin, *Institutes*, XIX.iv.

29. Grant, *Free Churchmanship in England*, 157.

This change opened the door for the ministry to be influenced by other spheres, including business and public speaking. R. J. Campbell, a minister who left Congregationalism to join the Church of England, gave this description of his experience of Nonconformity,

> In many churches the minister is regarded as no more than a person whom the rest of the members of a certain religious community choose to appoint and pay to do what they themselves have not time to do, namely look after church affairs and see that they are properly administered. He is to make the church go as they make their business go. To this end he must be a good and attractive speaker, but there is nothing sacrosanct about his pulpit gift any more than about theirs for securing success in any other direction.[30]

Certainly, Campbell's experience should not be taken as universal. But it was widespread enough that he could affirm that "thousands of their own number would acknowledge to be true, and many would think desirable likewise."[31]

As far as the sacramentarianism of the Oxford Movement was concerned, "the net result was to create many varieties of Nonconformist opinion." Rather than a unified position on the Lord's Supper, for example, the conflict created many different positions. The traditional position among Dissenters remained a symbolic or memorial view of the Supper. The High Calvinists pressed towards an objective understanding of the sacraments as a seal or pledge of divine grace, a channel communicating God's grace through participation. New movements, like the social gospel, employed the sacraments to promote their distinctives. And those who held to the New Theology could not find an explanation for why these rituals mattered and relegated them to a secondary place.[32]

---

30. R. J. Campbell, *A Spiritual Pilgrimage* (New York: D. Appleton and Company, 1917), 34.

31. Ibid.

32. Grant, *Free Churchmanship in England*, 162-165.

Revivalism

The Evangelical Revival of the eighteenth century under George Whitefield and John Wesley had its greatest impact in England among dissenting churches. In both Baptist and Congregational churches, ministers began to preach with newfound passion and congregations were awakened to spiritual realities. There was a renewed passion for evangelism, both among preachers and lay people. By the end of the century, the old meeting houses were crowded and many of them had to be enlarged. New churches were planted, and new chapels were erected. Many of the English Calvinistic Methodist congregations planted by Whitefield gradually transitioned to a congregational polity, further adding to dissenting denominations.[33] Out of this growth, new denominational efforts would be undertaken for evangelism, missions, and pastoral training. By the early part of the nineteenth century, however, much of that excitement had waned. Small scale revivals continued in certain areas, particularly among Methodists. But many dissenting churches found themselves once again in decline.

But in the second half of the nineteenth century, two more revivals would come to Britain, both from America. This first was sparked by a weekly noontime prayer meeting begun in New York City in 1857.[34] Soon, with so many attending, the weekly gathering turned into a daily prayer meeting. By the following spring, similar prayer meetings began to sprout throughout the city and in other cities also. Newspapers throughout the English-speaking world reported on the stories of conversion and revival in America. As Spurgeon heard of these revivals, he compared them to what had taken place one hundred years previously under Whitefield: "So marvelous—I had almost said, so miraculous—has been the sudden and instantaneous spread of religion throughout

---

33. R. W. Dale, *History of English Congregationalism* (New York: A. C. Armstrong and Son, 1907), 586.

34. For an account of this revival, see Samuel Prime, *Power of Prayer: The New York Revival of 1858* (Edinburgh: Banner of Truth, 1991) and Roy J. Fish, *When Heaven Touched Earth: The Awakening of 1858 and its Effects on Baptists* (Azle, TX: Need of the Times Publishers, 1996).

the great empire, that it is scarcely possible for us to believe the half of it, even though it should be told us."[35] Soon the revival crossed the Atlantic and reached England. Many revivalists from America began to conduct meetings, but these meetings had now moved beyond the simple New York prayer meetings. They were now characterized much more by emotionalism, spontaneous decisions, and other novel methods.[36]

The second revival started in the 1870s, with D. L Moody's evangelistic preaching tours throughout England. While the 1858 revival did not center on any one figure, this second revival focused on Moody and his distinctive, straightforward, evangelistic preaching. He was accompanied on his tours by Ira Sankey, who led the singing at these meetings, and together they worked to great effect. Tens of thousands attended these meetings and many professed conversion.

One of Moody's primary goals was not only to preach but to raise other missioners to carry on with the work of evangelistic missions. This was one of the lasting effects of this revival. Moody's missions took on a distinctive method, which began to be adopted not only by missioners but also by pastors. R. F. Horton, a Congregationalist minister, found that the most effective aspects of Moody's mission method consisted of "the concentration of effort for the conversion of souls, with much prayer, and nightly appeals, and an inquiry-room in which inquirers could be personally dealt with." In order to encourage a response to his preaching, Horton would often "ask any one in the audience who wished for our prayers, in order to decide for Christ, to hold up the hand."[37] These visible decisions and responses proved the

---

35. For a sermon where Spurgeon addresses the New York Prayer Meeting Revival, see "The Great Revival," *NPSP* 4:161-68.

36. "I have heard of the people crowding in the morning, the afternoon, and the evening, to hear some noted revivalist, and under his preaching some have screamed, have shrieked, have fallen down on the floor, have rolled themselves in convulsions, and afterwards, when he has set a form for penitents, employing one or two decoy ducks to run out from the rest and make a confession of sin, hundreds have come forward, impressed by that one sermon, and declared that they were, there and then, turned from the error of their ways." Ibid.

37. Robert Forman Horton, *An Autobiography* (London: George Allen & Unwin Ltd, 1918), 69-70.

effectiveness of the methods. But Horton noticed that once the evangelistic mission had ended, the multitudes often did not join local churches. So, he experimented with implementing these methods in the church. He writes,

> Why should not every minister be his own missioner? I suggested the question to my Church. In 1886 I undertook, if the Church would help me, to hold a week's mission. I was only thirty-one, and had abundant physical energy. I read carefully Moody's addresses, and tried to get his directness, his fecundity of illustration, and his ardent desire to win souls. My people prayed much, and distributed invitations all round. On the last Sunday night in October the church was thronged; and every night during the week I gave an evangelistic appeal.[38]

In Horton's case, Moody's method would prove to be so successful that it would become a regular ministry of his church. Not only that, but he received invitations from churches all throughout the region and conducted similar missions, employing the same addresses, Bible-readings, and methods in each mission. Over time, the methods of revivalism found their way into evangelical churches. Later in his ministry, Moody himself would shift his meetings from mission halls to churches.[39]

Theologians have distinguished between two different kinds of revival.[40] In the one kind, revival is understood as the surprising work of God through ordinary means to awaken people to spiritual realities. For these revivals, the means employed are no different than the sorts of things the church is always doing, particularly the preaching of the Word and prayer. As people respond to the gospel, they join the church and strengthen the work of the church. Spurgeon was convinced that a genuine revival

---

38. Ibid.

39. James F. Findlay, Jr. *Dwight L. Moody: American Evangelist 1837-1899* (Chicago: The University of Chicago Press, 1969), 304-305.

40. For a modern work distinguishing between revival and revivalism, see Iain Murray, *Revival and Revivalism: The Making and Marring of American Evangelicalism 1750-1858* (Edinburgh: Banner of Truth, 1994), Bebbington notices a similar distinction between spontaneous revivals and planned revivals. See D. W. Bebbington, *Evangelicalism in Modern Britain: A History from the 1730s to the 1980s* (London: Routledge, 2000), 114-17.

was taking place in New York City, and in his own church. The other kind of revival (i.e., revivalism), however, adopts certain methods to produce decisions for Christ and greater commitment to Him. In the nineteenth century, these methods included advance publicity, long nighttime meetings, emotional appeals, inquiry rooms, and many other techniques. As Charles Finney explained, just as the right agricultural techniques will produce a harvest, so the right techniques will produce decisions for Christ.[41] Finney's techniques would prove to be popular among Congregationalists prior to 1850.[42] Even as Spurgeon rejoiced in genuine revivals around him, he also expressed his growing concern for the growth of revivalism.[43]

It would be too simplistic to say that the nineteenth century revivals in Britain were all either revival or revivalism. Throughout the multiple waves of revivals, both dynamics can be found depending on the place, the minister, the people, and many other factors. Nonetheless, these revivals proved to be formative for conservative British evangelicals, even as they did for American evangelicals. The overall effect was that revivalism would come to characterize a generation of conservative British evangelicals, affecting not only their theology, but also their ecclesiology.

The Effect of Revivalism on Dissenting Ecclesiology
What were the effects of revivalism on dissenting ecclesiology? First, revivalism placed an emphasis on individual salvation. The priority of the revival preaching was to bring sinners into union with Christ, without much thought about their union with the church afterwards. The numbers that revivalists were all too

---

41. "The connection between the right use of means for a revival and a revival is as scientifically sure as between the right use of means to raise grain and a crop of wheat. A farmer who knows what he is doing knows how to raise wheat. If he does it right, he will get wheat. A Christian or a preacher who knows what he is doing and does it right will get a revival. The connection is that precise and scientific." Charles G. Finney, *Lectures on the Revival of Religion*, (New York: Leavitt, Lord, & Co., 1835), 29.

42. Bebbington, *Evangelicalism in Modern Britain*, 116.

43. "For any man to assume the title and office of a revivalist, and go about the country, believing that wherever he goes he is the vessel of mercy appointed to convey a revival of religion, is, I think, an assumption far too arrogant for any man who has the slightest degree of modesty." *NPSP* 4:162.

glad to report mostly had to do with individual decisions, not the church.[44] Of course, in a Christianized society like England, the expectation was for new converts to join a church. For those converted under a revival, they usually, by default, joined the church connected with the evangelistic mission.[45] But their interest in that church was based on the evangelical preaching, rather than any of their ecclesiological distinctives. R. W. Dale describes the situation in many churches:

> Evangelical Churchmen passed from the parish church to the Congregational meeting-house because the minister preached "the Gospel" and the clergyman did not. The men and women who had been wholly indifferent to religious truth and duty before their hearts were touched and their consciences awakened by the carpenter who came from the Congregational Church in a neighboring town to preach in a cottage, or in a barn, or on the village-green, became, as a matter of course, members of the Church to which the preacher belonged, and contributed what they could towards building the village Congregational chapel. They heard nothing from the fervent evangelist about the principles of the Congregational polity—they cared nothing about them; they were Congregationalists because it was from a Congregationalist that they had learnt to trust in the infinite mercy of God and to live a Christian life. Nor did the pastors of the larger Churches in the towns care very much about the Congregational idea; their great solicitude was to make men Christians.[46]

This dynamic came to characterize the growth among all Nonconformist denominations that benefited from the revivals. Even while these churches grew in numbers, they were largely populated by those who did not hold to the ecclesiological convictions of previous generations. While the ecclesial forms

44. "What mean these despatches from the battle-field? 'Last night fourteen souls were under conviction, fifteen were justified, and eight received full sanctification.' I am weary of this public bragging, this counting of unhatched chickens, this exhibition of doubtful spoils." *The Soul-Winner,* 13.

45. After his conversion in the Primitive Methodist chapel, Spurgeon briefly considered attending there regularly. *Autobiography* 1:158.

46. R. W. Dale, *History of English Congregationalism* (New York: A. C. Armstrong and Son, 1907), 589.

and practices remained, the meaning and theology of those forms were largely unknown by the members and sometimes forgotten even by the ministers. Dale observes: "It is still one of the characteristics marks of those who may be described as the extreme Evangelicals among us that they believe that evangelical doctrine is everything and that the organized life of a Christian society is of inconsiderable importance. They own no allegiance to the Church to which they happen to belong. They do not recognize its authority."[47]

Unsurprisingly, those ecclesial forms and practices would begin to change without great resistance. The growth of open membership among Baptists towards the second half of the nineteenth century can be attributed, in part, to the priority of the individual over the corporate. Historically, baptism had been understood to be commanded by Christ as the initiating ordinance of Christian discipleship. Therefore, churches have always required baptism for entrance into the church. For Baptists, this meant requiring believer's baptism for all their members, even if they had previously received infant baptism.

But now, with the revivalist emphasis on individual salvation, those who held to open membership believed that any genuine believer, regardless of baptismal status, should be admitted into church membership, opening the door for paedobaptists to join these Baptist churches. At the opening of Westbourne Park Chapel in 1877, pastored by John Clifford, representatives of the Baptist denomination, including Spurgeon, gathered to celebrate the event. The church's Constitution, drawn up by Clifford, made clear their convictions about open membership:

> The Church is Congregational or Independent in its policy; recognizes Jesus Christ as its supreme authority; and takes the principles of the New Testament communities as the expression of His will concerning the basis and conditions of united Christian life. Membership is therefore open to all who are members of "His Body," i.e. to all who confess faith in Christ,

---

47. R. W. Dale, *The Evangelical Revival and Other Sermons: with an Address on the Work of the Christian Ministry in a Period of Theological Decay and Transition* (London: Hodder and Stoughton, 1880), 31.

strive to learn and obey His law, not only in their individual life, but in and by association for mutual help, common worship, and beneficent work.[48]

To be sure, open membership Baptists still affirmed that believer's baptism was the teaching of the New Testament. But because of the priority of individual salvation, every applicant was urged to consider the Lord's will for themselves on this subject, and "the whole question is left to the individual conscience." In other words, the church's official baptismal doctrine became optional, removing the need for unity on this secondary issue. In later years, Clifford would go on to serve as the president of the Baptist Union and promote his open membership views among Baptists in Britain and America.

Another effect of the nineteenth century revivals among evangelicals was the increased emphasis on cooperation between evangelical churches. One expression of this emphasis was in the formation of parachurch societies. A prime example of this comes from the revivals of the previous century and the formation of the London Missionary Society. Formed in 1795 in a gathering of Congregationalists, Churchmen, Presbyterians, and Methodists, this society sought to unite all evangelicals to the task of missions. "The missionaries that the Society sent out, and the Churches they founded, might be Presbyterian, Congregational, or Episcopalian. The directors and their constituents were satisfied if the missionaries and their converts held the Evangelical Faith."[49] This trans-denominational effort set the model for future cooperation.

In the nineteenth century, one of the primary examples of evangelical cooperation was found in the Evangelical Alliance, formed in 1846 as an effort to bring together evangelical churchmen and dissenters in their opposition to the Oxford Movement and the growth of Roman Catholicism in England.[50] Throughout the revivals, this cooperation would only grow, with

---

48. James Marchant, *Dr. John Clifford: Life, Letters, and Reminiscences* (London: Cassell and Company, LTD, 1924), 45.

49. Hale, *History of English Congregationalism*, 601–02.

50. Kenneth Hylson-Smith, *Evangelicals in the Church of England 1734-1984* (Edinburgh: T&T Clark, 1988), 115.

evangelical churchmen playing an important role. Because of their state church context, evangelical churchmen emphasized the unity of the invisible church based on evangelical doctrines, rather than the unity of the visible church.[51] This emphasis came to characterize the revivals, so much so that they came to be associated with the Alliance. As one minister reported on the revival at Newcastle-on-Tyne in 1859 made up of Anglicans, Nonconformists, and Methodists, "The Revival with which this town is favoured is advancing.... All attempts to proselytize are utterly repudiated: hence some designate the work 'the Evangelical Alliance Revival.'"[52]

With the growth of the revivals, new societies would also be founded within denominations, strengthening denominational identity and supplanting the priority of the local church. In his overview of Baptist history, J. M. Cramp highlights the primary contribution of nineteenth century Baptists as the proliferation of all kinds of benevolent societies. He writes:

> This is the age of societies. Designs which would be otherwise impracticable can be carried into effect by combination of effort and division of labour. We have joined other professing Christians in founding and sustaining institutions of general utility, and have borne our full share of the burdens of philanthropy.[53]

These societies included the Baptist Missionary Society, English Baptist Home Missionary Society, Baptist Irish Society, Baptist Highland Mission, Society for Aged or Infirm Baptist Ministers, Baptist Building Fund, Bible Translation Society, and the Baptist Tract Society. For many Baptists, their involvement in these societies competed with their commitment to the local church.

Trans-denominational cooperation can also be seen in the development of evangelical conferences during the nineteenth century. These conferences dovetailed with the revivals in two ways: first, they gave expression to the unity of the invisible

---

1 Ibid., 222.

2 J. Edwin Orr, *The Second Evangelical Awakening*, abridged reprint (NA: Erading Word, 2018), 79.

3 J. M. Cramp, *Baptist History from the Foundation of the Christian Church to the Present Time* (London: Elliot Stock, 1871), 473-74.

church, pulling together evangelicals from every denomination; and second, they emphasized a deepening of the Christian life, which complemented the evangelistic preaching of the missions. The Mildmay Conference, begun in 1870, was to be a conference "for all Christians without regard to office, denomination, or sex."[54] D. L. Moody would be one of their early preachers, and from this conference would arise an emphasis on the power of faith to produce holiness. This emphasis would continue in the Keswick Convention, begun in 1875, with a teaching that differed from Wesleyan perfectionism but still proclaimed a triumphant faith that led to deeper holiness and intimacy with God. Speakers at the Keswick meetings would include Quakers and even Anglican Ritualists.[55]

The emphasis on cooperation also led to not only a minimizing but a condemning of denominational distinctives. One striking expression of this comes through William Robinson, a Baptist minister writing in 1866:

> The divisions of Protestants are their disgrace.... Schism is to be laid to the charge of those who insist on terms of communion offensive to the consciences of their fellow disciples. The Episcopalian who makes the rite of confirmation essential to church membership is a schismatic; as is a Baptist who makes believers' baptism a term of communion; or the Methodist who insists on attendance at class.[56]

Because denominations are schism, Robinson suggests a path forward for Episcopalians, Congregationalists, Baptists, and every other Protestant denomination to be together in a single church. They must agree on four things: 1) the "well-proved piety, wisdom, and aptness to teach" of a minister, 2) that their gathering will include "the communion of saints" and be subject to no other limitation, 3) a common liturgy (if any object to some component of the liturgy, they can simply remain quiet during that portion), and 4) the agreement that everything else be "left to the

---

54. Elliot-Binns, *Religion in the Victorian Era*, 222.

55. Ibid., 225.

56. William Robinson, *Biblical Studies* (London: Longmans, Green, and Co., 1866), 255-56.

consciences of individuals."[57] In other words, Robinson imposes the vision of a parachurch society, like the Evangelical Alliance, on to the visible church. Even while he recognizes that Christians will still hold to distinctive theological and ecclesiological beliefs, he envisions the church as a place where no one conviction will be privileged, and all will be equally tolerated and minimized. Robinson's vision never came to fruition. But his teaching would prove to be popular among fellow ministers. He would be elected the president of the Baptist Union in 1870.

Rationalism

The rationalism of the nineteenth century can be traced back to the Enlightenment of the previous century. The movement sought to abolish all traditions and superstitions of the past in order to apply human reason to solving the world's problems by giving greater human happiness. Rather than speculating about theology or metaphysics, progressive thinkers worked with empirical facts, emphasizing science, exploration, and uncovering new sources of knowledge. These ideals would filter down from the universities to the masses and, according to many historians, would usher in the modern era.

It was in the context of the Enlightenment that rationalism arose within evangelicalism in the nineteenth century. In 1879, one evangelical Cambridge professor gave this definition: "Rationalism may be defined as the abuse and perversion of human reason, in dealing with the claims of Divine Revelation."[58] In other words, rationalism applied Enlightenment ideals to biblical studies by placing human reason above the Scriptures. In areas where biblical doctrine aligned with reason, then Scripture could be properly affirmed and revered. But where biblical teaching conflicted with reason, Scripture either had to be modified or rejected. This led to the questioning or revising of many historic doctrines: creation, sin, substitutionary atonement, the resurrection, and, most of all, eternal judgment. To be sure, conservative evangelicals were

57 Ibid., 259.

58 David W. Bebbington, *The Dominance of Evangelicalism: The Age of Spurgeon and Moody* (Leicester: Inter-Varsity Press, 2001), 111.

not opposed to the proper application of reason. In many ways, their works exemplify the rigorous application of reason that was characteristic of their day.[59] But their concern was an abuse of reason by exalting it above Scripture.

Two challenges arose in the nineteenth century that promoted the rise of rationalism. The first was German higher criticism. Taking advantage of all the advances being made in the study of the past, through geology, the study of religions, archeology, history, anthropology, and other related fields, German biblical scholars sought to implement those advances by looking "behind the text." Rather than interpreting the text itself, scholars sought to discern the socio-historical context of the text, or the psychological state of the authors, to discern the "true" meaning of the text. This approach prioritized the view of Scripture as being primarily, or even entirely, a human document rather than divinely inspired.

The other challenge was the introduction of new scientific theories. Geology was an emerging field of study in the nineteenth century, concerned with the earth's history. Charles Lyell's *Principles of Geology* raised questions about the age of the earth by examining fossils and rock formations. Rather than explaining them through catastrophic events, which had been the widely held view, Lyell argued that the earth was much older than 6,000 years of biblical history. This paved the way for Charles Darwin's *On the Origin of Species*, which sought to explain the diversity of life through the process of natural selection, apart from any divine intervention. Darwin's theory would prove to be influential beyond science. For many people, this firm belief in natural progress would become a kind of philosophical outlook on all of life, including religion. Many Christians believed these theories to be compatible with the teaching of Scripture, though it meant adjusting previously held beliefs.

Spurgeon, however, saw rationalism as an attack on historic Christianity. While he wasn't as vocal on specific scientific

---

59. Bebbington, *The Dominance of Evangelicalism*, 109–37.

theories, like the age of the earth or even evolutionary theory,[60] he was deeply concerned over the diminished views on Scripture that he encountered among evangelicals. This willingness to place reason above Scripture was producing a New Theology, or as he called it, Neology, which was not historic Christianity at all. Writing in 1883, Spurgeon warned his readers,

> The enemy is gathering strength, and mustering his bold forces for fiercer attacks. What doctrine is now left unassailed? What holy thing is regarded as sacred? Truths once regarded as fundamental, are either denied, or else turned inside out till nothing of their essence remains. Holy Scripture is no longer admitted to be the infallible record of revelation, but is made to be a doormat for "thought" to wipe its shoes upon. Every sign of the times warns us of a desperate conflict for all that is precious and vital in our religion.[61]

Rationalism would spread in every denomination. It would have a greater effect among Congregationalists, though Baptists would not escape its influence. For Spurgeon, this battle against rationalism in his own denomination would mark the final years of his life.

The Effect of Rationalism on Dissenting Ecclesiology

One way by which rationalism eroded the ecclesiology of dissenting churches was by challenging any credal basis for churches and church associations. The use of creeds among dissenters, especially Congregationalists, had always been controversial.[62] As those who had left the Church of England, where the Thirty-Nine Articles and the Book of Common Prayer were imposed on all its ministers, dissenters understood that such

---

60. For Spurgeon's response to Darwin's theory of evolution, see my article "A Symbol of the Invisible: Spurgeon and the Animal World," in Geoffrey Chang and C. Anthony Neel, *Andrew Fuller and Charles Spurgeon: A Theology of Animal Life: Reflections in the Eighteenth and Nineteenth Centuries* (Louisville, KY: The Andrew Fuller Center for Baptist Studies, 2021), 24-42.

61. *S&T* 1883, iii.

62. The Salters' Hall Controversy in 1719 is an early example of dissenters wrestling with the use of creeds following the Act of Toleration of 1689. See Jesse F. Owens, "The Salters' Hall Controversy: Heresy, Subscription, or Both?" *Perichoresis* 20.1 (2022), 35-52.

an imposition was meaningless without the minister's voluntary subscription. John Owen, in the preface to the Savoy Declaration, states that when it comes to the imposition of creeds, "whatever is of force or constraint in matters of this nature, causeth them to degenerate from the name and nature of Confessions, and turns them from being Confessions of Faith, into Exactions and Impositions of Faith."[63]

Owen's caution was not an objection to the use of creeds; he still defended their necessity for "[expressing] the substance of the same *common salvation* or *unity of faith*." But in the nineteenth century, this caution against the misuse of creeds changed into an objection against the use of creeds at all. As people and churches wrestled with the questions and doubts of rationalism, many began to move away from doctrines as articulated in the historic creeds. Increasingly, the cry of the day was for toleration rather than dogma. Convictions could still be held on an individual basis, but tolerance of individual convictions trumped any common creed, even the historic creeds of Christianity. Robinson's vision for a church that transcended denominational divisions included members holding to a variety of creeds: "some of its Christian people may receive the Athanasian, and some the Nicene creed; others do not fully approve of either, or may flatter themselves with the notion that they believe both."[64]

In all this, the revolt was not merely against the use of creeds, but "against the whole idea that a Church as such should have common beliefs."[65] The strategy of the New Theology was not to make their teaching the new orthodoxy, but rather to escape from theology altogether by removing credal statements as a source of accountability in churches and associations. Without a theological basis for churches, ethics now became the source of unity. In his vision of the Church of the Future, P. T. Forsyth envisioned the church united around Christian character that comprehended all God's family. The basis for communion was "the saving faith which bound men to God... unsupplemented by 'essential

---

63. John Owen, Preface, *Savoy Declaration*.

64. Robinson, *Biblical Studies*, 258.

65. Grant, *Free Churchmanship in England*, 117.

truths.'"[66] These ideas would spark conflict between conservatives and liberals in the Leicester Conference Controversy in 1877 for the Congregationalists and the Downgrade Controversy in 1887–1888 for the Baptists.[67]

The other effect of rationalism on dissenting ecclesiology was the removal of any Scriptural basis for church polity. Historically, Independents and Presbyterians believed that their particular forms of church government, church officers, membership, discipline, and many other aspects of church polity, were all based on New Testament teaching and example. But by the 1870s, historical criticism caused many to question whether early church practices ought to be binding for all time. Dissenters were glad to employ historical criticism against the Oxford Movement's argument for *de jure* Episcopacy, showing how the New Testament church could not have held such a position. But "with surprising suddenness Nonconformists, especially Congregationalists, decided that they must abandon their claim to be the sole inheritors of apostolic practice."[68] In his lecture to the Congregational Union in 1897, John Brown declared, "We maintain that our Lord has nowhere authoritatively prescribed one definite organization for the Church He instituted."[69] C. A. Scott, a Presbyterian professor of New Testament, took it one step further by arguing that "in the organization and government of the Church... God has left men to the guidance of their reason, sanctified and illumined by the Holy Spirit." Therefore,

> The various forms of Church government which have actually been evolved correspond in fact with the forms of political organization familiar to us—pure democracy, representative democracy, oligarchy, and autocracy. And to none of them can we admit impediment; for none of them can we claim a legitimacy which makes illegitimate the rest. Each type, Congregationalist,

---

66. Hopkins, *Nonconformity's Romantic Generation*, 107-09.

67. For an account of these two controversies, see Mark Hopkins, *Nonconformity's Romantic Generation: Evangelical and Liberal Theologies in Victorian England* (Eugene, OR: Wipf & Stock Publishers, 2004).

68. Grant, *Free Churchmanship in England*, 124-25.

69. John Brown, *Apostolical Succession in the Light of History and Fact* (London: Congregational Union of England and Wales, 1898), 31.

Presbyterian, Anglican, or Papal, has arisen through special emphasis being laid on some one feature in the organization of the primitive Church.[70]

For Scott, all forms of church polity found some biblical justification, and none could be argued as unbiblical. With the biblical supports of church polity removed, ecclesiology now became a matter of expediency rather than conviction. The great concern of the age was to establish the Kingdom of God by improving society and creating a new brotherhood among men. R. J. Campbell, Joseph Parker's successor in London's City Temple, puts it this way:

> The true church of Christ in any and every age consists of those and those only who are trying like their Master to make the world better and gladder and worthier of God.... The church exists to make the world a kingdom of God, and to fill it with His love. No greater mistake could be made than to estimate the church of Jesus by ecclesiastical squabbles and divisions.[71]

According to Campbell's definition, any group of Christians working together for social good might well be considered a church. And, on the other hand, as Fairbairn put it, "churches that do not work for these ends are not churches of Christ's religion."[72] Under the New Theology, churches are defined not by any ontological understanding but primarily by a functional one. Regardless of denominational background, the churches that worked towards this mission "by fittest means, and so to best issues, are the most Christian of churches."[73] This pragmatic spirit was prevalent among all evangelicals but was especially evident among the Baptists.[74]

---

70. C. Anderson Scott, *Evangelical Doctrine – Bible Truth* (London: Hodder and Stoughton, 1901), 256-57.

71. R. J. Campbell, *The New Theology* (New York: The Macmillan Company, 1907), 245-46.

72. A. M. Fairbairn, *Catholicism: Roman and Anglican* (London: Hodder and Stoughton, 1899), 42.

73. Ibid.

74. Bebbington, *The Dominance of Evangelicalism*, 135-36.

Against the backdrop of the church's mission, all debates about church polity and ecclesiology were viewed as mere squabbles and distractions. Churches were to lay aside their differences and partner together for the betterment of society. Associations were to unite with one another to increase effectiveness. By the twentieth century, discussion over matters of polity had largely ceased among dissenters, except when dealing with those in the established church. Some ecclesiastical forms from previous generations remained, but the theology behind them was forgotten. Church membership "was not consciously repudiated but in some quarters it ceased to be understood."[75] Subsequently, membership rolls became inflated as the practice of church discipline faded.[76] Church meetings, once the hallmark of congregationalism, now took on a secular character, devoted to the "business" of the church and devoid of any spiritual understanding.

Conclusion

The decline of ecclesiology among Congregationalists and Baptists in the nineteenth century did not happen all at once. Rather, over the course of the century – from the ritualism of the earlier part, to the revivals in the middle of the century, and to the growing rationalism in the latter half – all these challenges revealed the ecclesiology of dissenters to be much more malleable than that of their predecessors. Even as conservative evangelicals battled for the primary doctrines of the gospel, they were willing to adjust and adapt the secondary doctrines of the church to the cultural influences around them.

In response to the high church ecclesiology of Ritualism, the pendulum swung the other way to a lower view of the church and the ministry. In response to the growth of Revivalism, evangelicals downplayed membership and discipline to maximize numerical growth. And in response to the challenge of Rationalism, denominational distinctives were minimized in favor of an evangelical unity around the gospel. Not many people

---

75. Grant, *Free Churchmanship in England*, 147.

76. "In the Congregationalist literature of the period there is scarcely any mention of the subject." Ibid., 148.

anticipated the effect that these adjustments would have on future generations in their fight to maintain the gospel. This was the context in which Spurgeon sought to advance his vision of the church as the army of God.

3

Ecclesiological Roots

As his fiftieth birthday approached, Spurgeon had the opportunity to reflect on his ministry with the editor of the *Pall Mall Gazette*. In that interview, he stated:

> In theology, I stand where I did when I began preaching, and I stand almost alone. If I ever did such a thing, I could preach my earliest sermons now without change so far as the essential doctrines are concerned. I stand almost exactly where Calvin stood in his maturer years; — not where he stood in his 'Institutes,' which he wrote when quite a young man, but in his later works; that position is taken by few. Even those who occupy Baptist pulpits do not preach exactly the same truths that I preach. They see things differently; and, of course, they preach in their own way.[1]

A few things stand out. First, Spurgeon here acknowledges his indebtedness to Calvin, not simply for the doctrines of grace, but also for his mature theological system as expressed in his later works, including his ecclesiology. Second, Spurgeon notes that many "who occupy Baptist pulpits" had departed from this Reformed theological system in his day. He was "almost alone" in his theology. And third, he notes that these convictions have been with him since his earliest days, when he first began preaching.

Where did Spurgeon's ecclesiological convictions come from? Can we trace their roots not only to when he began preaching, but even before? This chapter will show that Spurgeon's ecclesiological

---

1. "Topics of the Day by Heroes of the Hour: No. XIX. – Fifty Years of My Life, by the Rev. C. H. Spurgeon," *Pall Mall Gazette*, June 19, 1884, 11.

convictions were not a later development, but can be traced back to his childhood, conversion, his early years as a young Christian, and his first pastorate at Waterbeach.

Childhood

Charles Haddon Spurgeon grew up in the Reformed tradition from the time of his birth. He was born on June 19, 1834, into a family belonging to the Independent or Congregationalist church, which traced its heritage through to the English Reformation. Many Congregationalists left the Church of England during the seventeenth century, and by Spurgeon's day they had become a significant dissenting denomination. When ten months old, Spurgeon was sent to live with his grandfather during a busy time, as his father John was starting a new business and his mother Eliza was expecting. His grandfather, James Spurgeon, was the minister of the Independent church in Stambourne, where he served for fifty-four years. One story illustrates James' commitment to his church: at one point in his ministry, having held possession of the chapel and land for over twenty years and discovering that the trustees of the property were dead, James came to legal possession of the properties of the church. His advisers urged him to make a will to pass this property on to his heirs. Instead, James "at once called a meeting of the church and had the property put into trust according to the original wishes of the donor."[2]

What was initially a short stay turned into a much longer arrangement. John Spurgeon soon found himself in financial trouble, and young Charles was forced to stay with his grandfather for several years while his parents sorted out their finances. He would not rejoin his family until he was five years old.[3] And yet, these years would prove to be formative for young Charles. Some of his earliest memories come from living in the home of

---

2. Charles Ray, *The Life of Charles Haddon Spurgeon* (London: Passmore & Alabaster, 1903), 9.

3. For an account of John Spurgeon's financial troubles during these years, Geoff Chang, "New Insights into the Formative Influence of Spurgeon's Early Years," *Themelios*, Vol. 47, Issue 3.

this devoted pastor. From an early age, Spurgeon learned the importance of preaching as he watched his grandfather prepare sermons and was warned not to distract him lest he should be unable to preach, and "then what would happen, if poor people did not learn the way to Heaven?"[4] Together, they would regularly visit Mr. Hopkins, the rector of the local Anglican church, and young Spurgeon would have sugared bread and butter along with tea, while the two ministers discussed evangelistic efforts in their village. Reflecting on those meetings in later years, he appreciated the model of evangelical partnership between an Anglican clergy and a nonconformist minister.[5] As a young boy, Spurgeon attended all the meetings of the church, from corporate worship meetings to congregational meetings, and even to pastoral visits. He was impressed by how thoughtful the members were on biblical and ecclesiastical matters.[6] Spurgeon's early life was shaped around the local church.

Sometime around early 1840, Spurgeon moved back to Colchester to live with his parents. His father had settled his debts and now worked as a merchant clerk for his brother-in-law, Charles Parker Jarvis, who was a coal merchant and prominent leader in the town. Along with his family, young Spurgeon attended Lion Walk Congregational chapel, under a young new pastor, T. W. Davids, who arrived in 1841. Under his leadership, Davids would establish a lay preachers' association, which John would eventually join. When Charles was older, he would sometimes accompany his father to hear him preach.[7] In March of 1850, the congregation at Tollesbury Independent chapel called John Spurgeon to serve as their bi-vocational pastor.

---

4. *Autobiography* 1:16.

5. They partnered together through the local Bible Society, hosting their meetings alternately at the Anglican church and the Congregationalist meeting house. *Autobiography*, 1:19-20.

6. "The old men I talked with, as a little child, were, I am sure, far above all such nonsense; and upon many a Biblical, or political, or ecclesiastical, or moral subject, they would have uttered great and weighty thoughts in their own savory Essex dialect." Ibid., 1:27.

7. "I have a distinct remembrance of a mission-room, where my father frequently preached." Autobiography, 1:43.

Spurgeon's experience at the local Congregational church in Colchester was not nearly as positive as his time in Stambourne. He was impressed with Davids' preaching style. But looking back, he could not remember having heard the gospel preached clearly.[8] Still, the church continued to play a prominent role in Spurgeon's imagination. From Davids, he observed a serious approach to church membership, pastoral care, maintaining accurate membership rolls, and congregational involvement.[9] It appears that Spurgeon learned something of Davids' activism as he and the other children would play church (of course, Spurgeon was the pastor), and as Spurgeon organized a home library, recited hymns with his siblings, wrote a small book, and edited two magazines.[10] At the age of fourteen, Spurgeon was sent to St. Augustine's College, Maidstone, a Church of England school. On one occasion, one of the clergymen challenged Spurgeon's Congregationalist view of infant baptism, demonstrating from Scripture the need for faith and repentance before baptism. For the clergyman, this teaching supported the Church's practice of appointing sponsors for infants being baptized. Spurgeon, after studying the Scriptures for himself, came to the conviction that baptism was only for those who had personally come to faith in Christ. This newfound conviction brought a new resolution: "I resolved, from that moment, that if ever Divine grace should work a change in me, I would be baptized."[11]

In August 1849, Spurgeon moved to Newmarket to attend Newmarket Academy, where he also served as an usher. There, he befriended the cook at the school, Mary King, a strong Calvinist woman who gave him a strong foundation in the doctrines of grace.[12] She also taught him the importance of commitment to the church. On one occasion, when she was complaining about

---

8. Ibid., 1:72-73.

9. For more on Davids' pastoral leadership, see Geoff Chang, "New Insights into the Formative Influence of Spurgeon's Early Years," *Themelios*, Vol. 47, Issue 3.

10. Ray, *The Life of Spurgeon*, 27, 36.

11. *Autobiography*, 1:50.

12. "I do believe that I learnt more from her that I should have learned from any six doctors of divinity of the sort we have nowadays." Ibid., 1:53.

the preaching at her church, Spurgeon asked her why she still bothered going. "Wouldn't it better to stay home?" he wondered. She responded, "Perhaps so... but I like to go out to worship even if I get nothing by going. You see a hen sometimes scratching all over a heap of rubbish to try to find some corn; she does not get any, but it shows that she is looking for it, and using the means to get it, and then, too, the exercise warms her."[13] Spurgeon would remain lifelong friends with Mary and would support her in her old age.

That winter, Spurgeon penned one of his earliest works, "Antichrist and Her Brood; or, Popery Unmasked," for an essay contest. In this unpublished, 295-page, seventeen-chapter handwritten essay, Spurgeon attacks not only Roman Catholicism in general, but particularly its abuse of ecclesiastical authority.[14] Among other things, this essay shows that, at the age of fifteen, Spurgeon was already steeped in Protestantism and his Independent roots. Even before his conversion, Spurgeon was already convinced that the Scriptures are the only proper source of authority in the church.

Conversion

Spurgeon's religious impressions began at an early age. Growing up in church, he came to understand the basic message of the Scriptures and demonstrated an interest in spiritual matters. One of the ways we see this interest is in his early love of books. Living with his grandfather, he had access to his pastoral library and was introduced to Foxe's *Acts and Monuments*, Bunyan's "Pilgrim," and many of the English Puritans. Many of the summers visiting Stambourne were spent exploring those books. He recollects, "Out of that darkened room I fetched those old authors when I was yet a youth and never was I happier than when in their company."[15]

---

13. Ibid.

14. "The Church which withholds the Bible from its members, or takes away from them the genuine Word of God, is guilty of bringing the most dreadful famine upon the minds of men, and will be in a great measure guilty of their blood." Ibid., 1:62.

15. *Autobiography* 1:23.

One of the effects of reading the Puritans was that he was convinced from a young age of his own sinfulness. The discipline of his father and grandfather kept him out of the trouble that was typical for other boys. Even so, beneath that religious exterior, Spurgeon knew the reality of sin in his heart. Though he attended church religiously, this did nothing to ease his guilt.

> I used to feel myself to be a sinner even when I was in the house of God. I thought that, when I sang, I was mocking the Lord with a solemn sound upon a false tongue; and if I prayed, I feared that I was sinning in my prayers, insulting him by uttering confessions which I did not feel, and asking for mercies with a faith that was not true at all, but only another form of unbelief.[16]

He sought to comfort himself by church attendance, listening to sermons, and moral behavior, but none of these disciplines answered Scripture's clear condemnation of those who sin against God. Between the ages of ten and fifteen, Spurgeon suffered doubts, trials, spiritual warfare, and conviction of sin. At one point, in despair, he experimented with an atheistic skepticism, voyaging "to the very verge of the dreary realms of unbelief," but he found it to be a terrifying "nothingness of vacuity," and so he fled back to a world of God and absolute truths.[17] Even so, he was still lost. His experience of the misery of sin before conversion shaped his understanding of the work of the Spirit to bring people to faith in Christ.[18]

In December 1849, an outbreak of fever at the school in Newmarket sent Spurgeon home to Colchester for Christmas. He resolved to make the most of this holiday by visiting every place of worship in the town to find the way of salvation. On Sunday

---

16. *Autobiography* 1:82.

17. *Autobiography* 1:87-88.

18. This experience would shape Spurgeon's approach to his membership interviews, as he sought to discern others' professions of faith. "'Now, sit down,' I say sometimes, when I am seeing an enquirer or a candidate for church-membership, 'and I will tell you what were my feelings when I first sought and found the Savior.' 'Why, sir!' he exclaims, 'that is just how I have felt; but I did not think anyone else had ever gone over the same path that I have trodden.' It is no wonder that, when we have little acquaintance with each other's spiritual experience, our way should seem to be a solitary one; but he who knows much of the dealings of God with poor seeking sinners, is well aware that their experiences are, in the main, very much alike." Ibid., 2:139.

January 6, 1850, on his way to another church, a snowstorm forced Spurgeon to turn in to the Artillery Street Primitive Methodist Chapel, with about a dozen people present.[19] Because the regular minister was unable to make it, a lay preacher preached on Isaiah 45:22, "Look unto me, and be ye saved, all the ends of the earth." Though this inexperienced preacher could hardly get through the sermon, it was the means used by God for Spurgeon's conversion.[20] The unique circumstances surrounding his conversion would shape Spurgeon's ministry and prioritization of the local church in several ways. First, he was converted under the preached Word. This truth convinced Spurgeon of the unique power of preaching. "The books were good, but the man was better. The revealed Word awakened me; but it was the preached Word that saved me; and I must ever attach peculiar value to the hearing of the truth, for by it I received the joy and peace in which my soul delights."[21] Even though he would go on to publish thousands of sermons and books, live preaching would always have a unique place in his mind.

Second, Spurgeon was converted in a chapel of a denomination with which he had no connection. Prior to that Sunday, his main impression of the Primitive Methodists was their loud singing, which made his head ache. But here, God converted him through the preaching of the gospel in one of their chapels. Thinking back to that experience, Spurgeon recognized that many of the chapels he attended during his period of searching were preaching the gospel,[22] regardless of their denominational differences. In future

---

19. There is some debate surrounding the date of Charles' conversion, with advocates for January 6, 1850, January 13, 1850, or perhaps a weekday meeting. John Spurgeon (Charles' father) once also claimed that Charles was converted in December 1850, but this would go against the evidence of Charles' own letters and testimony. For an account of this debate, see Drummond, *Spurgeon*, 124-31. This writer is convinced of January 6, given Charles' own record of that date in his diary. See *Autobiography* 1:129.

20. Ibid., 1:106.

21. Ibid., 1:104.

22. "When, for the first time, I received the gospel to my soul's salvation, I thought that I had never really heard it before, and I began to think that the preachers to whom I had listened had not truly preached it. But, on looking back, I am inclined to believe that I had heard the gospel fully preached many hundreds of times before, and that this was the difference,— that I then heard it as though I heard it not; and when I did hear it, the message may not have been anymore clear in itself than it had

years, he would come to value the unity that evangelical churches shared in the gospel.

Third, although Spurgeon never had an opportunity to meet the uneducated lay preacher, he never forgot how God used that simple sermon to convert him.[23] He would go on to reject the notion that only educated and ordained clergymen were qualified to preach. In his church and college, he was on the lookout for ordinary men who were filled with the Spirit and could proclaim the gospel. The roots of this commitment can be traced to his conversion.

Finally, he was converted in the context of a Lord's Day gathering of a local church. In some ways, this was a surprising turn of events. His hero, John Bunyan, came to discover the gospel while meditating on Scripture and walking alone in a field.[24] As a youth, Spurgeon spent many hours studying and reading on his own.[25] One might have expected that he would have been converted in some solitary manner. Instead, this life-changing conversion took place in the gathering of a local church. Spurgeon was already committed to regular church attendance by this point, and his conversion only solidified that conviction. That evening, Spurgeon attended the Baptist chapel in Colchester and was encouraged in his newfound faith.[26]

Baptism, Membership, and the Lord's Supper

After his conversion, Spurgeon returned to Newmarket and the Congregationalist church he had previously attended. He immediately threw himself into service, but more importantly,

---

been at former times, but the power of the Holy Spirit was present to open my ear, and to guide the message to my heart." *Autobiography* 1:102.

23. There is also a considerable debate concerning the identity of the preacher. While Robert Eaglen, a well-known Primitive Methodist preacher, identified himself as that preacher, Spurgeon did not recognize him upon meeting him, and his life did not quite match up with Spurgeon's own recollection of the man. For a summary of the discussion surrounding this question, see Drummond, *Spurgeon*, 116-24.

24. John Bunyan, *Grace Abounding to the Chief of Sinners* (London: Penguin, 1987), 59.

25. *Autobiography* 1:23, 52.

26. Ray, *The Life of Charles Haddon Spurgeon*, 67.

he now sought church membership. Whereas previously he was content merely to attend, now Spurgeon's desire was to be baptized and admitted to the Lord's Table. In a letter to his mother, Spurgeon wrote as follows:

> I have come to a resolution that, by God's help, I will profess the name of Jesus as soon as possible if I may be admitted into His Church on earth. It is an honor, —no difficulty, — grandfather encourages me to do so, and I hope to do so both as a duty and privilege. I trust that I shall then feel that the bonds of the Lord are upon me, and have a more powerful sense of my duty to walk circumspectly. Conscience has convinced me that it is a duty to be buried with Christ in baptism, although I am sure it constitutes no part of salvation.[27]

Spurgeon's first attempt at joining a church in the spring of 1850 proved to be more difficult than he anticipated. He called on the pastor of the Congregational chapel in Newmarket for a membership interview for four straight days, but was turned away each time. So, Spurgeon wrote him a letter saying if he couldn't get an interview, he "would go down to the church-meeting, and propose myself as a member." This got the pastor's attention. When Spurgeon was finally able to meet with him, "he looked upon me as a strange character."[28] After being proposed for membership, he was disappointed that no one in the congregation seemed interested in getting to know him.[29] Nonetheless, he was admitted into church membership on April 4, 1850. Rejoicing, he wrote to his father a few days later,

> You will be pleased to hear that last Thursday night, I was admitted as a member. Oh that I may henceforth live more for the glory of Him, by whom I feel assured that I shall be everlastingly saved!... Since last Thursday, I have been unwell in body, but I may say that my soul has been almost in Heaven.[30]

---

27. *Autobiography* 1:119.

28. *Autobiography* 1:147.

29. Spurgeon wrote to his father, "At our last church-meeting, I was proposed. No one has been to see me yet." *Autobiography* 1:120.

30. *Autobiography* 1:121.

At this point, Spurgeon faced another dilemma. He had formally become a member of the church and was expected to participate in the Lord's Supper. They accepted him into membership, believing he had been baptized as an infant. Spurgeon, however, no longer believed his infant baptism to be valid, and thus did not think it appropriate to partake at the Table. He wrote to his father,

> Owing to my scruples on account of baptism, I did not sit down at the Lord's table, and cannot in conscience do so until I am baptized. To one who does not see the necessity of baptism, it is perfectly right and proper to partake of this blessed privilege; but were I to do so, I conceive, would be to tumble over the wall, since I feel persuaded it is Christ's appointed way of professing Him.[31]

In *Pilgrim's Progress*, Formalist and Hypocrisy "come tumbling over the wall" rather than entering by the narrow gate.[32] In the same way, Spurgeon considered baptism to be the initiating ordinance and the Lord's Supper as the ongoing ordinance of the church. Those who take the Lord's supper without first being baptized "tumble over the wall" and reject Christ's order. Such an understanding of the biblical sequence of baptism and the Lord's Supper was in line with his Reformed tradition. From these early days, Spurgeon's adoption of believer's baptism influenced not only his understanding of baptism but also of the church.

Spurgeon's decision to be baptized as a believer also created tension with his Congregationalist parents. Letters show that Charles sought his father's permission to be baptized and was kept in suspense for several weeks waiting for an answer. When he finally responded, Charles felt "he [was] rather hard upon me."[33] At one point, his mother exclaimed, "Ah, Charles! I often prayed the Lord to make you a Christian, but I never asked that you might become a Baptist." Spurgeon could not resist giving his famous response, "Ah, mother! the Lord has answered your prayer with

---

31. *Autobiography* 1:121.

32. John Bunyan, *The Pilgrim's Progress*, ed. Roger Sharrock (London: Penguin Books, 1987), 37.

33. *Autobiography* 1:122, 133.

His usual bounty, and given you exceeding abundantly above what you asked or thought."[34]

Eventually, with the help of a fellow student, Spurgeon found a Baptist Church in Isleham, pastored by W. W. Cantlow, a former missionary in Jamaica. With the proper arrangements made, Spurgeon presented himself for baptism on Friday, May 3, 1850. His diary entry records his experience:

> In the afternoon, I was privileged to follow my Lord, and to be buried with Him in baptism. Blest pool! Sweet emblem of my death to all the world! May I, henceforward, live alone for Jesus! Accept my body and soul as a poor sacrifice, tie me unto Thee; in Thy strength I now devote myself to Thy service forever; never may I shrink from owning Thy name![35]

For Spurgeon, the ordinances would always be, first and foremost, a matter of personal communion with Christ, and secondarily, of communion with his people. Spurgeon had already joined the church in Newmarket before his baptism, and so he did not connect his baptism with his church membership in his diary. Rather, his thoughts were fixed entirely on his union with Christ and commitment to him.

As a Baptist, this order of events, first joining a church and then being baptized, would have been considered disorderly. Spurgeon acknowledged this tension even as a young Christian by refusing to participate in the Lord's Supper before his baptism. But in his *Autobiography* written many years later, Spurgeon makes his convictions clear.

> Mr. Stevenson, in *The Rev. C. H. Spurgeon, his Life and Work*, makes it out that I joined the Baptist Church a year before I was baptized; but it was not so. I never dreamed of entering the Church except by Christ's own way; and I wish that all other believers were led to make a serious point of commencing their visible connection with the Church by the ordinance

---

34. Ibid., 1:69.
35. Ibid., 1:135.

which symbolizes death to the world, burial with Christ, and resurrection to newness of life.[36]

Here, Spurgeon rightly denies that he ever joined a Baptist church before his baptism. His first church membership was at a *Congregationalist* church, and they received him based on his conversion and baptism as an infant. Though Spurgeon rejected infant baptism, he understood that he was not upsetting the proper order of the ordinances in the church's view. For his readers, however, Spurgeon made clear that baptism should precede membership, even if this were not the order of his own experience.[37]

Following his baptism, Spurgeon did not join the Baptist church in Isleham but returned to the Congregational church in Newmarket. Spurgeon emphasized this point, underscoring that his decision to be baptized was not based on any human requirement of baptism for membership in a Baptist church. Rather, it was in pure obedience to what he saw in Scripture.[38] On the following Lord's Day, May 5, Spurgeon participated in the Lord's Supper for the first time, "This afternoon, partook of the Lord's supper; a royal feast for me, worthy of a King's son."[39]

Early Ministry and Preaching

After his baptism, Spurgeon began serving in the Sunday school ministry at Newmarket, alongside his tract-distribution ministry. The diary entries of the weeks following his baptism contain all the highs and lows of Spurgeon's spiritual experiences, but a consistent thread is his continued involvement in the church and his growing ministry in it. In the summer of 1850, Spurgeon

---

36. *Autobiography* 1:152-153

37. Spurgeon sometimes would skip his membership at Newmarket Congregational when sharing his testimony. "When I was a boy of fifteen, I believed in the Lord Jesus, was baptized, and joined the Church of Christ; and nothing upon earth would please me more than to hear of other boys having been led to do the same." Ibid., 1:149.

38. "I did not fulfill the outward ordinance to join a party, and to become a Baptist, but to be a Christian after the apostolic fashion; for they, when they believed, were baptized." *Autobiography* 1:154.

39. Ibid., 1:135.

left Newmarket and moved to Cambridge to serve as a tutor in a private school. There, he would be introduced to the Baptist denomination. He found them to be "by far the most respectable denomination in Cambridge."[40]

There were three Baptist chapels in town – St. Andrew's Street, Zion, and Eden. Spurgeon quickly settled on St. Andrew's, likely in part because of their open communion position.[41] As someone coming from the Independent Church, Spurgeon was able to participate at the Lord's table even before becoming a member.[42] By October 2, 1850, Spurgeon had obtained a dismission from the church in Newmarket, and officially joined St. Andrew's Street. But when he joined the church, he found the other members strangely cold, even during the communion service.[43] After the service, he greeted the man who had sat in the same pew, and the man responded by admitting he didn't know who he was. Spurgeon told him that they did know each other, "'for you and I are brothers… when I took the bread and wine, just now, in token of our being one in Christ. I meant it, did not you?'" Despite the implied rebuke, the man laughed, agreed with Spurgeon, and invited him over for tea, and they went on to become life-long friends. This kind of Christian fellowship was not the norm in the church culture of the day.[44]

Spurgeon's ministry at St. Andrew's Street began soon after his arrival in Cambridge. Within a couple of weeks, he took charge of a Sunday school class and began to address the students and teachers as he had before in Newmarket. Before long, people were impressed with his ability to teach, and this drew the attention of

---

40.   *Autobiography* 1:188.

41.   At the time, Zion Chapel also held to open communion, while Eden Chapel held to a strict communion position. See https://eden-cambridge.org/about-us/a-history-of-eden. Accessed 9/29/2023. For a brief history of St. Andrew's Street and its connection to Zion, see Ian Randall, "Changing Spiritual Identity: St. Andrew's Street Baptist Church, Cambridge, from the 1730s to the 1920s." *Journal of European Baptist Studies*, Vol. 22 No. 1 (2022), 179.

42.   Ibid., 1:188-90.

43.   *Autobiography* 1:185.

44.   He would say to Spurgeon later: "I am rather glad you spoke to me, for if you had gone to some of our deacons, I am afraid you would not have received quite as friendly a reply as I have given you." *Autobiography* 1:185-86.

James Vinter, the head of the Lay Preachers' Association. Through a ruse put on by Vinter, Spurgeon found himself preaching his first sermon in a small cottage in Teversham to a small group of villagers gathered for worship. Before this occasion, Spurgeon had taught and lectured publicly in various Sunday school and missionary meetings.[45] This was the first time he *preached*, however, meaning this was the first time he had stood up to exposit Scripture and proclaim the gospel among people "who had come together for worship."[46] Spurgeon's preaching ministry began, not as a self-appointed endeavor, but in connection with the ministry of his local church.

Spurgeon's lay preaching ministry began sometime in January of 1851. For the following spring and summer, he would preach multiple times a week throughout the villages in the surrounding countryside.[47] On October 3, 1851, Spurgeon preached a sermon entitled "Salvation from Sin" from Matthew 1:21 at the Baptist chapel in the village of Waterbeach.[48] The response from this sermon was so favorable that the congregation immediately secured his services for the rest of the month. Even before the month was up, they officially called him as their pastor. At the age of seventeen, Spurgeon agreed to become the bi-vocational pastor of Waterbeach Chapel. During the week, he would continue working as a tutor. On weekday evenings and weekends, he would serve as an itinerant preacher and as a pastor.

The Pastorate at Waterbeach

Though Spurgeon would go on to pastor the largest church in the world and have a famous ministry, he would always look back on his pastorate at Waterbeach with fondness. A Fenland village five miles outside of Cambridge, Waterbeach was known for its wet

---

45. The first record of a public speech by Spurgeon was on September 10, 1849 at a missionary meeting. *Autobiography* 1:55.

46. *NPSP* 5:137.

47. The notes from these earliest sermons can be found in *The Lost Sermons of C. H. Spurgeon*, Vol. 1–7, eds. Christian George, Jason Duesing, Geoffrey Chang, Philip Ort (Nashville, TN: B&H Academic, 2016-2022). Hereafter, this series will be referred to as *LS*.

48. *LS* 1:231.

climate and its association with an illicit still, which resulted in rampant drunkenness. However, over two years, Spurgeon saw a radical transformation in many in the village. "In a short time, the little thatched chapel was crammed, the biggest vagabonds of the village were weeping floods of tears, and those who had been the curse of the parish became its blessing."[49]

Spurgeon's recollections of his time at Waterbeach have all the hallmarks of the ministry of a Baptist pastor.[50] His primary labor was preaching. In addition to the itinerant preaching that he continued to do in villages throughout the week, Spurgeon preached two sermons every Lord's Day, one in the morning and one in the afternoon. A closer look at Spurgeon's sermons from his time at Waterbeach reveals a growing preacher, steeped in Puritan and Baptist theology.[51] These early sermons also reveal a pastors' concern for the order and care of the church, dealing with subjects such as giving to the church,[52] the conversion of sinners in the church,[53] the work of the pastor,[54] church membership,[55] church health,[56] church discipline,[57] church witness,[58] church

---

49. *Autobiography* 1:228.

50. Ibid., 1:227-240, 254-267, 277-302.

51. "Charles continued the practice of borrowing outlines and sermons from other preachers, including John Bunyan, Charles Simeon, Thomas Manton, and Jean Claude. His use of John Gill's commentaries is extensive." *LS* 2:10. The word clouds contained in the *Lost Sermons* volumes give an idea of the broad range of theological topics which Spurgeon covered in these early sermons. See *LS* 1:45, 2:21, 3:20.

52. Sermon 109, "Prove Me Now Herewith," *LS* 2:281-287.

53. Sermon 89, "The Harvest of Souls," *LS* 2:95-97.

54. Sermon 110, "The Minister's Commission," *LS* 2:293-297; Sermon 173, "Who is Sufficient for These Things?" *LS* 3:327-331.

55. Sermon 116, "David in the Cave of Adullam," *LS* 2:349-357; Sermon 322, "Joining a Church," *LS* 6.

56. Sermon 131, "The Church Needs the Spirit," *LS* 2:473-475; Sermon 252, "Spiritual Decline," *LS* 5; Sermon 300, "My Father Is the Husbandman," *LS* 6.

57. Sermon 161, "Making Shipwreck of Faith," *LS* 3:233-239; Sermon 182, "Profane Esau," *LS* 3:449-457; Sermon 219, "The Church is to be Purged," *LS* 4.

58. Sermon 172, "The Church at Antioch," *LS* 3:319-327; Sermon 202, "Salt is Good," *LS* 4.

ordinances,[59] church unity,[60] and more. In these sermons, Spurgeon not only promoted individual faith in Christ but also sought to teach on what it meant to be a church of believers committed to one another.

One of Spurgeon's pastoral challenges during his time at Waterbeach was the influence of hyper-Calvinism in East Anglia, led by Baptists like William Gadsby and John Stevens.[61] Within his church, this often led to battles with "Antinomians,—that is, people who held that, because they believed themselves to be elect, they might live as they liked."[62] In addition to regular preaching on holiness and against immorality, Spurgeon backed up his preaching by carefully limiting the membership of the church to those who gave a credible profession of faith. Spurgeon records at least two instances of church discipline during his two years at Waterbeach, which reveal both his seriousness as a pastor, but also his tenderness.[63] However, an important part of Spurgeon's pastoral care of his flock was walking with them through the pains and difficulties of life. Later in his ministry, Spurgeon would find it harder to provide personal pastoral care for so large a congregation, but he would always look back with

---

59.   Sermon 241, "What Doth Hinder Me to Be Baptized[?]" *LS* 5; Sermon 276, "Baptism," *LS* 5.

60.   Sermon 282, "Walk in Love," *LS* 5.

61.   Robert W. Oliver, *History of the English Calvinistic Baptists 1771-1892: From John Gill to C.H. Spurgeon* (Edinburgh: Banner of Truth, 2006), 313. While Gadsby and other hyper-Calvinists did not necessarily hold to antinomianism, there was a strong correlation between these two positions.

62.   *Autobiography* 1:258.

63.   "While I was Pastor at Waterbeach, a certain young man joined the church. We thought he was a changed character, but there used to be in the village, once a year, a great temptation in the form of a feast; and when the feast came round, this foolish fellow was there in very evil company. He was in the long room of a public house, in the evening, and when I heard what happened, I really felt intense gratitude to the landlady of that place. When she came in, and saw him there, she said, 'Halloa, Jack So-and-so, are you here? Why, you are one of Spurgeon's lot, yet you are here; you ought to be ashamed of yourself. This is not fit company for you. Put him out of the window, boys.' And they did put him out of the window on the Friday night, and we put him out of the door on the Sunday, for we removed his name from our church book" (Ibid., 1:260). The other instance of church discipline is the story of Mr. Charles, who Spurgeon thought was his first convert. This was a case which caused Spurgeon "many bitter tears" (Ibid., 1:238-39. See also *LS* 1:339-41).

fondness to his pastorate at Waterbeach. Thinking back to those days, Spurgeon envisioned himself as Bunyan's Mr. Greatheart, leading "those poor pilgrims on the road to the Celestial City."[64]

By the fall of 1853, word had reached London of the "boy-preacher of the Fens," and an invitation was extended to Spurgeon by one of the deacons to fill the pulpit at the New Park Street Chapel. From these humble beginnings, Spurgeon would soon go on to shape the future of Baptist churches throughout London and around the world.

Conclusion

This brief survey of Spurgeon's birth to his pastorate at Waterbeach reveals an early life steeped in a Reformed understanding of the church and a convictional transition to the Baptist tradition. Raised in the home of a grandfather and a father who served as pastors within the Reformed tradition, the congregational life and structure of the church were ingrained into Spurgeon's understanding from a young age. Even before his conversion, Spurgeon demonstrated zeal for the church, evidenced by his polemic writings against the papacy and his willingness to confront church members who were going astray.[65] When he became convinced about believers' baptism, Spurgeon resolved that he would pursue it, though he was careful to distinguish the church ordinance from his conversion and salvation. Even so, his dramatic conversion would take place in the worship gathering of a local church. As Calvin taught, the church is "the mother of believers," and Spurgeon's faith was conceived and given birth in the church.

Though Spurgeon would eventually leave his Congregational background and join the Baptist denomination, these two

---

64. *Autobiography* 1:240.

65. On one occasion, Spurgeon's grandfather was particularly broken-hearted about a member of his church, "Old Roads," who had relapsed into drinking. Young Charles heard of this and confronted Roads at the pub, saying "What doest thou here, Elijah! sitting with the ungodly, and you a member of a church, and breaking your pastor's heart. I'm ashamed of you! I wouldn't break my pastor's heart, I'm sure." By Roads' own testimony, this rebuke convicted him, resulting in confession and a recommitment to a holy life. *Autobiography* 1:23-24.

traditions shared many similarities in matters of church polity, particularly congregational church polity. In his experience, Spurgeon encountered among the Congregationalists a lax approach to church membership. As a Baptist, Spurgeon sought to promote his conviction not only about believer's baptism, but also regenerate church membership. He would carry this conviction into his pastorate at the New Park Street Chapel.

For Spurgeon, holding to a Reformed ecclesiology meant that his beliefs about the church were grounded in the Scriptures. Though they were secondary to the gospel, they were not beliefs that could be adjusted to suit the changing times. This was the approach to theology that he learned from childhood, and this explains, in part, why his ecclesiology was largely unchanged over the years, even as such views became less common. In the next chapters, we will consider the specifics of Spurgeon's ecclesiological convictions.

4

What is the Church?

The nineteenth-century was an age of activism in Britain. The Industrial Age overturned the limits that had previously been set by class and social rankings and appeared to overturn the very limits of nature. A new generation of industrialists arose to reshape Western society in England and throughout the world. Through their tireless leadership, supported by a growing working and middle class, advancements that couldn't have been imagined by previous generations were made in transportation, agriculture, exploration, communication, and virtually every other facet of society.

But as we've seen in Chapter 2, this energy also spilled over into the religious life of the nineteenth century. For the high Anglicans, this meant advancements in church architecture, liturgy, choral music, religious art, sacramental theology, and much more. Rather than standing by as secularism infiltrated society, the Oxford Movement pushed back with a higher view of the Church and the ministry. And yet for all its energy, its popular effect was doubtful. Spurgeon shared this experience in 1861:

> There was held in Westminster Abbey last Thursday a grand choral festival, at which there were singers from the various choirs of London—St. Page, the Abbey, the Temple; and the Foundling, and some from Windsor beside. Several ecclesiastical dignitaries graced the assembly. Anthem and cantatos, and I know not what else, were performed on a most classic scale. The sermon was preached by a Provost of some college, in which the claims of the Society for the Propagation of the Gospel in Foreign Parts were eloquently advocated, and the whole collection amounted

to seventy pounds— "A very poor result for so sublime a service," said the Times report.[1]

This energy also impacted those of a low church persuasion. Activism was already a distinctive within evangelicalism since its beginnings,[2] but now it was turbo-charged in the cultural progress of the age. Among evangelicals, it resulted in denominational cooperation and the formation of missionary societies, publishing ventures, colleges, and other evangelistic and benevolent institutions. Even though churches continued to be planted and pastored, they were no longer centerstage. The real action was taking place among parachurch institutions. Alongside the multiple revivals of the nineteenth century, many evangelicals saw in these efforts a new age of gospel advancement.

But as the decades rolled on, the hoped-for advancements did not come to fruition. There were still large masses within Victorian society, not to mention the world, that remained unevangelized and outside the reach of the gospel. Societies faced all the same troubles, risks, and inefficiencies as any secular institution. The encroachment of rationalism increasingly redefined evangelism and challenged the basis for cooperation. Beyond these pragmatic considerations, however, Spurgeon saw a theological reason for the ultimate ineffectiveness of societies. God's promises rested, not in societies, but on the local church.

> We have been wondering why our societies have not greater success. I believe the reason is because there is not a single word in the Book of God about anything of the kind. The Church of God is the pillar and ground of the truth, not a society. The Church of God never ought to have delegated to any society whatever, a work which it behooved her to have done herself.[3]

For this reason, even while Spurgeon participated in numerous associational efforts, he understood that his most important

---

1. *MTP* 7:361-62.

2. D. W. Bebbington, *Evangelicalism in Modern Britain: A History from the 1730s to the 1980s* (London: Routledge, 2000), 2-17. For a discussion on the origins of evangelicalism see Michael A. G. Haykin, Kenneth J. Stewart, eds., *The Advent of Evangelicalism: Exploring Historical Continuities* (Nashville: B&H Academic, 2008).

3. *MTP* 7:363

ministry was to his church, and secondarily to other local churches, because it is the church that God has established as the pillar and ground of truth (1 Tim. 3:15).

Amid all these different understandings of the church, from high church Anglicanism to low church evangelicalism, what was Spurgeon's understanding of the church? Could any gathering of Christians be considered a church? How did he shape his people's vision of the church? And how did his ecclesiology fit within the Reformed tradition? We turn now to answering these questions.

Spurgeon's Doctrine of the Church

In 1861, as one of the editors of the *Baptist Messenger*, Spurgeon invited his brother James to contribute an article on "The Church Polity of the New Testament." In later years, Spurgeon would invite James to write a similar article for *The Sword and the Trowel*, describing the polity of the Metropolitan Tabernacle.[4] It appears that Spurgeon found in James an articulate representation of his own ecclesiological views. In the 1861 article, James begins with the many wrong definitions of the word "church" in his day:

> We never find it employed to designate a place of worship. It is quite a question whether places especially devoted to the assembling of Christians were then erected, or even contemplated. Certainly the word "Church" is not applied to them in the Bible. Neither is it ever used to describe the assembly of Apostles, Bishops, and Elders. No countenance is given to the error which confines the word to the assembled priests or office-bearers of the Church. Rome would have us to believe that the hierarchy is the Church, and not the whole body of the faithful. Such, however, is not the teaching of the Scriptures. Neither can we defend the use of the word, when we employ it in expressions like the following – the Lutheran Church, the Church of England.[5]

Spurgeon shared all these same concerns. Living under the shadow of the Church of England, a common use of the term

---

4.   S&T 1869:49, 57.

5.   J. A. Spurgeon, "The Church Polity of the New Testament," *The Baptist Messenger: An Evangelical Treasury and Chronicle of the Churches, For the Year 1861* (London: James Paul, 1861), 37.

"church" was the structure of leadership. In his sermon, "Christ Glorified as the Builder of his Church," Spurgeon states, "It is usual with many Church of England people, to use the term 'church' as specially applying to the bishops, archdeacons, rectors, curates, and so forth.... Now I believe that such a use of the term is not scriptural."[6] Spurgeon also rejected the Episcopal and Presbyterian usage of "church" for the extra-ecclesial structure of the denomination. He was willing to refer to the collection of Anglican churches as the "Church of England," but he understood this to be an unbiblical usage of the term. He was also concerned that such a misuse of the term "church" should not be brought into Baptist or other Dissenting churches, especially as Dissenting denominational structures grew in prominence.[7]

Among evangelicals, a common usage of "church" was to refer to the building in which a congregation met for worship. Two months after the construction of the Metropolitan Tabernacle, Spurgeon declared, "Strangely, but frequently, ['church'] has... been used to designate a mass of bricks and mortar... has actually by the natural debasement of the tongue of priests, come down to mean a building. By no possible construction can it mean any such a thing. A more debasing use of a divine word than that can scarcely be found."[8] Though the congregation had devoted the past three years and so much of their efforts and resources to the construction of the Tabernacle, Spurgeon wanted his people to know that the building was far inferior to their identity as a true church. Because of this conviction, like his Puritan predecessors, Spurgeon was often careful to refer to a church building as a chapel or meeting house,[9] rather than a church.

What then, according to Spurgeon, was a biblical definition of the term "church"? He follows Calvin and the Reformed tradition

---

6. *NPSP* 4:210.

7. "Do not imagine, therefore, when I speak at any time of the church, that I mean the Archbishop of Canterbury, the Bishop of London, and some twenty other dignitaries, and the whole host of ministers. No, nor when I speak of the church do I mean the deacons, the elders, and pastors of the Baptist denomination, or any other." *NPSP* 4:210.

8. *MTP* 7:362.

9. Or a tabernacle, in his case.

by recognizing two definitions of the word, namely the local church and the universal church.[10] Preaching in 1857, Spurgeon provided this definition:

> Any company of Christian men, gathered together in holy bonds of communion for the purpose of receiving God's ordinances, and preaching what they regard to be God's truths, is a church; and the whole of these churches gathered into one, in fact all the true believers in Christ scattered throughout the world, constitute the One true Universal Apostolic Church, built upon a rock, against which the gates of hell shall not prevail.[11]

Likewise, in a sermon preached thirty years later, Spurgeon brings out the same definition:

> A church is a congregation of faithful men—that is to say, of men who are believers in the Lord Jesus, men in whom the Holy Spirit has created faith in Christ, and the new nature of which faith is the sure index. The one church of Jesus Christ is made up of all believers throughout all time. Just as any one church is made up of faithful men, so is the one church of Christ made up of all faithful churches in all lands, and of all faithful men in all ages.[12]

At the time of the Reformation, Roman Catholicism denied the existence of an invisible church and argued that the true church must always be visible, organized with its institutional and leadership structures. Protestants, however, argued that while Scripture does speak of local, visible churches, it also speaks of the church as that invisible body made up of all the elect, not limited by the bounds of any one visible church.[13] In

---

10.   Calvin, *Institutes*, IV:i:7.

11.   *NPSP* 4:210.

12.   *MTP* 33:205. James Spurgeon puts it like this: "We find (the term 'church') used in Scripture in two ways. First, to denote the universal and invisible Church of God, of all time, and of every class and age; which Church he has purchased with his own blood. Its members are the first-born whose names are written in heaven, and who are numbered amongst God's children. Secondly, to describe particular parts of that universal Church – such portions of it as are called together in their militant state on earth, for purposes of mutual comfort, support, and edification." J. A. Spurgeon, "The Church Polity of the New Testament," 27.

13.   For a discussion of this historical distinction, see William Cunningham, *Historical Theology: A Review of the Principal Doctrinal Discussions in the Christian Church Since the Apostolic Age*, Vol. 1 (Edinburgh: Banner of Truth Trust, 1994), 9-20.

these definitions, Spurgeon held to the Reformed distinction between the local and universal church. The visible, local church is a gathering of Christians[14] marked by the preaching of God's truths and the receiving of God's ordinances. The invisible and universal church, on the other hand, is marked by the work of the Holy Spirit, consisting of all true believers from all times and all lands. In describing the invisible church as the "One true Universal Apostolic Church," Spurgeon adopted the language of the Nicene Creed of A.D. 381 to support this understanding of the church.[15]

Both concepts of the visible local church and the universal church would play a prominent role in Spurgeon's preaching and theology. This distinction meant that he always called sinners first to faith in Christ and participation in that universal church. He urged the members of his church not to rest on their membership in the visible church but always to make sure their calling and election into the universal church. Still, Spurgeon's ministry was firmly rooted in the context of a local church. He regularly reminded his congregation of their theological identity as the church of God. Knowing that local churches were a part of the universal body of Christ, this required that all churches be marked by regenerate church membership and ongoing obedience to Christ. Spurgeon's ecclesiology brought a theological focus to his ministry on his local church, but he never lost sight of the wider church. In planting local churches, building associations, partnering with evangelical institutions, Spurgeon worked for the

---

14. Though Spurgeon speaks of a company of Christian "men," he used that term representatively of men and women. His own church took women into membership and allowed them to speak and vote in congregational meetings. For a study on the issue of women and congregationalism during the Victorian era, see Timothy Larsen, *Contested Christianity: The Political and Social Contexts of Victorian Theology* (Waco, TX: Baylor University Press, 2004), 12-20.

15. John H. Leith, ed., *Creeds of the Churches: A Reader in Christian Doctrine from the Bible to the Present* (Louisville, KY: John Knox Press, 1982), 33. The Nicene-Constantinopolitan Creed confesses "one, holy, catholic, and apostolic Church," which have traditionally been recognized as the four marks of the church. Spurgeon here leaves out "holy" and substitutes "universal" for "Catholic." The latter modification was likely to avoid confusion with the Roman Catholic Church. The reason for the former modification is unclear, as Spurgeon certainly believed in the holiness of the universal church.

health of other churches and denominations, giving expression to the reality of the universal church throughout his ministry.

Defining the Local Church

While many identified the church with an organizational hierarchy or a building, Spurgeon believed that a local church was fundamentally an assembly or congregation. He appealed to the meaning of the Greek word *ecclesia* used throughout the New Testament. "*Ecclesia* originally signified assembly; not a mob, but an assembly of persons who were called together on account of their special right to meet for the discussion of certain subjects."[16] Whether as small as three or four, or as large as several thousand, a church was fundamentally an assembly or congregation. But far more important than size was the composition. A church should be made up believers. "Wherever true believers are, there is a part of the church; wherever such men are not, whatever organization may be in existence, there is no church of Jesus Christ."[17] Christians are those called out by the Holy Spirit from the world, and united in the church.[18]

To illustrate its congregational character, Spurgeon frequently compared the church to an army. "If you speak of the army, the whole of the soldiers constitute it; the officers may sometimes be spoken of first and foremost, but still the private soldier is as much a part of the army as the highest officer. And it is so in the church of God, all Christians constitute the church."[19] While Spurgeon recognized the place of officers in the church, the church was not

---

16. *MTP* 7:362. "Any assembly of faithful men is a church. The aggregate of all these assemblies of faithful men make up the one church which Jesus Christ hath redeemed with his most precious blood, and of which he is the sole and only Head." *MTP* 14:613.

17. *MTP* 14:613.

18. *MTP* 7:362. Here Spurgeon connects *ecclesia* with the idea of being called out (*ekkaleo*), which is not an uncommon view. However, some theologians contend that the New Testament writers do not connect those two terms. See Louis Berkhof, *Systematic Theology* (Grand Rapids, MI: Eerdmans, 1996), 555-56.

19. *NPSP* 4:210. "We believe that the Church does not consist alone of the preachers, and deacons, and elders; but that the Church is a company of faithful men and women, banded together according to God's holy rule and ordinance for the propagation of the truth as it is in Jesus." *MTP* 48:196.

made up of the officers alone. Rather, it was the congregation, composed of all the soldiers and the officers together, who made up the church. By the Holy Spirit, they "banded together for the holy purpose of the defence and the propagation of the truth."[20] The congregational character of the church meant that every member of the church was responsible for fighting for the truth.[21]

But would any assembly of Christians constitute a church? Like his Reformed predecessors, Spurgeon held to the two marks of a true church: the right preaching of God's Word and the right observance of God's ordinances. "Any company of Christian men, gathered together in holy bonds of communion for the purpose of receiving God's ordinances, and preaching what they regard to be God's truths, is a church."[22] In other words, the marks of the church required "God's truths." The church must be built on the gospel, the message of salvation. Spurgeon believed that "a true church is based upon eternal truth,"[23] and this was expressed through the preaching and ordinances of the church.

Spurgeon applied these two marks in his sermon, "What the Church Should Be." Foremost was the right preaching of the Word, which ultimately meant faithfulness to the gospel. Regardless of what a congregation may call themselves, "a church is unchurched which is not faithful to the truth."[24] A congregation that failed to hold on to the truth could no longer practice the right preaching of the Word and therefore became "unchurched." As a Protestant, Spurgeon believed that the Roman Catholic Church had rejected the truth and therefore was no true church. At the same time, he was wary of the growing theological liberalism among the churches in England. They were not immune to losing the truth and becoming unchurched. "Alas, any church may thus perish. The apostasy of Rome should be a warning to all

---

20. *MTP* 7:362.

21. "The whole church is to maintain the truth. Dear brethren and sisters, be very zealous for the gospel, the old, old gospel of the grace of God; the doctrine of justification by faith and forgiveness by the atonement. I speak to you who know the truth, for you alone make up the church of God," *MTP* 24:550.

22. *NPSP* 4:210.

23. *MTP* 17:201.

24. *MTP* 24:550.

other churches."[25] Spurgeon would place a Bible and the Baptist Confession of Faith under the cornerstone of the Metropolitan Tabernacle as a symbolic reminder that the church can only exist upon the truth of the Word of God.[26] Amid a world that rejected God's truth, a true church was to be armed with the truth and willing to fight for it. "If the church be a true church, and a holy church, she must be armed: there are so many untrue things and unholy things, that she must be perpetually with her sword in her hand, carrying on combat against them."[27]

Likewise, the right observance of the ordinances was a mark of a true church. "A church ceases to be a church of Christ in proportion also as she alters the ordinances of God. These must be practiced as they were delivered."[28] This did not mean that every church had to practice the ordinances exactly as Spurgeon did. He was willing to fellowship with other Baptists even though there were variations in how they practiced the ordinances.[29] He accepted evangelical paedobaptist churches as true churches, even though he considered infant baptism a serious error. But Spurgeon's concern was for any understanding of the ordinances that contradicted the gospel. "Believers' baptism was thrown to the winds, and then baptismal regeneration must needs be brought in. The Lord's Supper was by far too common, and so the unbloody sacrifice of the mass was devised."[30] In Roman Catholic teaching, baptism and the Lord's Supper were a part of a sacramental system that required them for salvation. Baptism was required for regeneration and the Lord's Supper was viewed as an ongoing sacrifice. For Spurgeon, such views of the sacraments opposed the gospel, resulting in the Roman Catholic Church ceasing to be a

---

25. *MTP* 24:550.

26. *NPSP* 5:351.

27. *NPSP* 5:41.

28. *MTP* 24:551

29. The primary debate was over the question of open versus closed communion, though there were many other differences in communion practice. For a treatment of the various debates surrounding Baptists and the practice of the Lord's Supper, see Michael Walker, *Baptists at the Table* (Didcot, UK: Baptist Historical Society, 1992) 32-81, 121-61.

30. *MTP* 24:551.

true church. But such errors were not limited to Roman Catholics. In his best-selling sermon, "Baptismal Regeneration," preached in 1864, Spurgeon would raise similar concerns against the Church of England for how the liturgy of the church affirmed baptismal regeneration.[31] Though this concern had to do with the Church's liturgy rather than her articles of faith, Spurgeon still believed this was an error serious enough to warrant separation.[32]

Like Calvin, Spurgeon did not see church discipline as a third mark of the church,[33] and did not include it alongside the other marks. Nonetheless, he taught about the vital importance of church discipline. After addressing the danger of being unchurched for failing to preserve the right preaching of the Word and administration of the ordinances, Spurgeon adds,

> Churches also get wrong when they *neglect discipline*, when they admit into their membership persons who do not even profess to be converted; and, I add, when, because of pleasing men, they tolerate in their midst ministers whose teaching is corrupt and full of infidelity.... An unholy, unregenerated church can never be the pillar of the truth. If there be a failure in vital godliness, if humble walking with God be neglected, the church cannot long remain a healthy church of God.[34]

Spurgeon placed church discipline in the category of church order and health. While the loss of the gospel makes a congregation a false church, the lack of church discipline does not unchurch it, but makes it vulnerable to corruption. Subsequently, the loss of discipline harms the church's witness to the gospel. Over time, churches that tolerate a corrupt ministry and accept the

---

31. This controversy will be covered in greater detail in Chapter Four.

32. "Call a man a Baptist, or a Presbyterian, or a Dissenter, or a Churchman, that is nothing to me—if he says that baptism saves the soul, out upon him, out upon him, he states what God never taught, what the Bible never laid down, and what ought never to be maintained by men who profess that the Bible, and the whole Bible, is the religion of Protestants." *MTP* 10:323.

33. Calvin, *Institutes*, IV:xii:1-13. Others in the Reformed tradition included church discipline as a third mark of a true church. Bucer stated, "Where there is no discipline and excommunication there is no Church." Paul D. L. Avis, *The Church in the Theology of the Reformers* (Eugene, OR: Wipf & Stock, 2002), 49.

34. *MTP* 24:552.

unconverted into membership will eventually lose the gospel, and become a false church.[35]

Confessing the One Universal Church

The growth of denominationalism among Protestants in the nineteenth century left many people uneasy at the institutional division and longing for greater visible unity among the churches. Among high Anglicans, this longing for unity extended outside of Protestantism to the Roman Catholic Church and even Eastern Orthodoxy. The Oxford Movement envisioned a reunion of all the major branches of Christianity, with the Anglican Church playing a key role.[36] Yet Spurgeon believed that such a course of action would only lead to a return to the dark ages and the oppression of the papacy. But this desire for unity was not limited to Roman Catholics or high Anglicans. Some Protestant sects and groups, like groups of the Plymouth Brethren or the Campbellites, also claimed to be the one church of God. The unity of the church could only be found within their institution. Against such views, Spurgeon wrote, "The climax of sectarianism is to call your own body *the church of Christ*, and look down upon other believers as sectarians."[37] A proper understanding of the universal church guarded against these errors.

The One Church and the Churches

Amid the seeming division of local churches scattered all over the world, Spurgeon, echoing Calvin,[38] believed that the universal church was a spiritual body which could never be divided.

---

35.   Likewise, Spurgeon placed church polity in this category of church order and health. He believed that Scripture commands that a church should be congregational and led by pastors, elders, and deacons, but he also recognized that other true churches might be ordered in different ways. *MTP* 7:362.

36.   Owen Chadwick, *The Victorian Church, Part One 1829-1859* (London: SCM Press, 1987), 168-172.

37.   *S&T* 1886:517. He goes on, "Those churches which hold the head, Christ Jesus, and are quickened by the Holy Ghost, are all parts of members of Christ's body; or, in other words, they are sections… of the one great church."

38.   "The church is called 'catholic,' or 'universal.' Because there could not be two or three churches unless Christ be torn asunder [cf. I Cor. 1:13]—which cannot happen!" Calvin, *Institutes*, IV:i:2.

There is one spiritual church of God, and there never were two. All the visible churches up and down the world contain within themselves parts of the one church of Jesus Christ, but there were never two bodies of Christ, and there cannot be.... The external church is needful, but it is not the one and indivisible church of Christ.[39]

Spurgeon recognized that among the visible churches, there would be an endless diversity, extending "up and down the world," and throughout all time. Nonetheless, all these churches, insofar as they are faithful to Christ, were united into the "one church of Jesus Christ," the universal church.

This doctrine of the universal church had important implications for local churches. For one, it guarded the independence and freedom of local churches, while at the same time requiring that they all hold to the vital truths of Scripture. We see this dynamic of independence and accountability in the sermon, "The Church of God and the Truth of God."[40]

We may be called by different names; and, according to Scripture, we are to be separated, like sheep, into different folds, yet still there is only one flock and one Shepherd. The independency of Scripture is to be practiced still. Each church is to be separate, having its bishop and its elders governing in the fear of the Lord, without respect of persons, and without being disturbed by the opinion of any other church. But though we are separate churches as to our organization, we are really but one Church, under one Head, the Lord and Bishop of our souls.[41]

The danger of establishing an institutional unity above the local church was that it compromised the "independency of Scripture," where each congregation was to be governed by their leaders, free from the opinions of other churches. The history of religious persecution in the Church of England illustrated this point powerful for Spurgeon. Rather than seeing the diversity of

---

39. *MTP* 29:191.

40. This sermon was preached during the Rivulet Controversy. For an account of that controversy, see *Autobiography* 2:260-69.

41. *MTP* 54:242.

churches as a problem, Spurgeon was grateful for the religious freedom such diversity represented.

At the same time, he believed that belonging to the universal church was only possible as a local church held to the truth. Spurgeon continues: "There are not two churches any more than there are two Gods... there is one Church holding the one Lord, the one faith, and the one baptism. If any hold not the truth, we cannot allow that they belong to 'the church of the living God.'"[42] Only true churches that held to the truth, submitting to the Lordship of Christ in his Word, could be said to belong to the universal church. More than an institutional unity, Spurgeon was concerned that local churches share a theological unity with one another in the truth of the gospel. It was this theological unity between churches that pointed to the unity of the universal church.

But even in that theological unity, the universal church is still invisible in this age. Church associations may arise from that unity, and yet they do not ultimately make the universal church visible. For Spurgeon, it was the invisible nature of the universal church that countered the claims of the Roman Catholic Church or the Plymouth Brethren to be the one church.

> People try to get a visible form of that one Church; but I believe that is utterly impossible. The Church of Rome claims to be that one Church, and we know what sort of a church that is. And, on the other hand, there are certain brethren who profess to be the one assembly of God. Well, I will not say what kind of church they have made; but I believe that all schemes for comprehending all the saints in one visible church must fail. Adam never saw Eve until God had perfectly fashioned her; and you will never see the Church, the Bride of Christ, till she is perfect and complete; and when she is, you will clap your hands with joy at the sight of the exquisite beauty which God shall have given to her ere she is presented to her Heavenly Bridegroom.[43]

---

42. Ibid.

43. *MTP* 48:340. Responding to the claims of the Plymouth Brethren, Spurgeon makes the same point: "We venture to suggest that the church, which is the bride, has not her counterpart on this earth. While Christ who is our life is absent, the life of

Thus, all attempts at equating a visible church with the invisible church in this age flow from an over realized eschatology and result in a church that is vastly inferior to the true Church to be revealed.

Spurgeon's understanding of the universal church prevented him from pursuing any institutional unity that compromised his faith, because he could rest in the unity of the universal church that existed among all faithful churches. At the same time, with churches that held to the gospel, Spurgeon was glad to affirm their unity in the universal church by highlighting their common faith.

The One Church and Individuals

Spurgeon did not limit inclusion in the universal church to local churches; he applied it primarily to Holy Spirit-filled individuals. This unity among genuine believers was rooted in faith in Christ and transcended denomination, class,[44] or church membership. Such unity could even be found with individuals who belonged to false churches,[45] including the Roman Catholic Church,[46] as long as they shared in the same faith. Spurgeon rejected the Roman

the saints is hidden—hid with Christ in God. The new Jerusalem is out of sight. The Epiphany of the church is a feast yet to be celebrated." S&T 1867:121-22.

44.   "Mark you well, that wherever this glory is seen true unity is developed. Suppose I were to find a man, living in the likeness of Christ, with this spiritual glory conspicuous upon him, it may be that he would be poor and illiterate, but what of that? Suppose he is a coalheaver, the glory of his character will be none the less conspicuous amid the dust. Then, let us find another man on whom the same spiritual glory rests, and we will suppose that he is an earl, a supposition which, thank God, is not an impossible one; the glory will be none the more dim because of the good man's honors. The people who are not one with each other are those who are not one with Christ; but once filled with his Spirit we are one of necessity." MTP 25:259.

45.   "I find life in all the churches, in some degree—some good men in all of them. How do I account for this? Why, just in this way—that the oak may be alive, whatever its shape, if it has got the substance. If there be but a holy seed in the church, the church will live; and it is astonishing how the church will live under a thousand errors, if there be but the vital principle in it. You will find good men amongst the denominations that you cannot receive as being sound in faith.... The very best of men found in the worst of churches!" NPSP 3:116.

46.   "For my own part, in reading certain precious works, I have loathed their Romanism, and yet I have had close fellowship with their writers in weeping over sin, in adoring at the foot of the cross, and in rejoicing in the glorious enthronement of our Lord. Blood is thicker than water, and no fellowship is more inevitable and sincere than fellowship in the precious blood, and in the risen life of our Lord Jesus Christ." MTP 58:151.

Catholic Church as a false church, but this did not mean having to write off all Catholics. He believed there were individual Catholics who held to the biblical gospel, and he believed himself to be united with them, and all other true believers, in the universal church.

At the same time, Spurgeon recognized that there were many hypocrites within the visible church, even his own local church, who did not genuinely possess faith in Christ. Though they professed the same faith and shared membership in the church with him, Spurgeon boldly declared that they did not share in the unity of the universal church.

> We know that they are not all Israel who are of Israel, and that the visible Church is not identical with that Church which Christ loved, and for which he gave himself. There is a Church invisible, and this is the center, and life of the Church visible; what the wheat is to the chaff and heap upon the threshing floor, such are these living Christians amongst the mass of professors in the world. There is a distinction which we cannot see.[47]

Because the universal church was invisible, there was no need to talk about the marks of the universal church. Rather, Spurgeon shifted his concern to his hearers, that they would embrace a saving faith in Christ, the only mark of membership in the universal church.[48] In Spurgeon's mind, belonging to the invisible church was far more important than any membership in a visible church. Therefore, even to his own church members, Spurgeon did not hesitate to preach the gospel and call any false professors to faith in Christ.

Biblical Images of the Church

When Spurgeon read his Bible, he followed the example of the apostles, who understood that all Scripture pointed to Jesus Christ and his redeeming work.[49] This would be the priority of

---

47. *MTP* 11:255.

48. "I would to God we were all members of his Church. There is only one token of membership which is infallible, and that is, saving faith in Christ." Ibid.

49. In his sermon "The Exodus," Spurgeon defends a typological reading of Scripture: "It is our firm conviction and increasing belief, that the historical books of

all of Spurgeon's ministry: to preach Christ and to make him known from the Scriptures.[50] But next to Christ, Spurgeon loved to study and preach on the church. "You will not think any the less of Christ for thinking much of his Church."[51] Spurgeon did not see ecclesiology as competing with Christology. Rather, a proper study of the church in relation to Christ will only lead to a greater understanding of his glory in his love for his church. While he taught on the more abstract theological concepts of the church, Spurgeon wanted to bring his congregation's understanding of the church to life. To that end, he found in the many images of the church throughout Scripture a rich source of ecclesiological reflection.

The Covenant People of God

The foundation of the church lies in the eternal purposes of God. Like Calvin, Spurgeon believed that Christ sealed the salvation of his church by offering himself as surety before the creation of the world. "Having covenanted to be the surety of the elect, and having determined to fulfill every stipulation of that covenant, he from all eternity delighted to survey the purchase of his blood, and rejoiced to view his Church in the purpose and decree, as already by him delivered from sin and exalted to glory and happiness."[52]

Scripture were intended to teach us by types and figures spiritual things. We believe that every portion of Scripture history is not only a faithful transcript of what did actually happen, but also a shadow of what happens spiritually in the dealings of God with his people, or in the dispensations of his grace towards the world at large. We do not look upon the historical books of Scripture as being mere rolls of history, such as profane authors might have written, but we regard them as being most true and infallible records of the past, and also most bright and glorious foreshadowings of the future, or else most wondrous metaphors and marvellous illustrations of things which are verily received among us, and most truly felt in the Christian heart." *NPSP* 2:9.

50.   Quoting an older minister, Spurgeon once claimed, "Don't you know young man that from every town, and every village, and every little hamlet in England, wherever it may be, there is a road to London?... and so from every text in Scripture, there is a road to the metropolis of the Scriptures, that is Christ.... I have never yet found a text that had not got a road to Christ in it, and if I ever do find one that has not a road to Christ in it, I will make one. I will go over hedge and ditch but I would get at my Master, for the sermon cannot do any good unless there is a savor of Christ in it." *NPSP* 5:432.

51.   *MTP* 60:431.

52.   *S&T* 1865:229.

The church's security rested in the Son's covenant with the Father. Regardless of what she may encounter in this life, she is safe.

The history of the people of God began with Adam and Eve.[53] As the first human community, Spurgeon believed they were redeemed and chosen by God, and saw them as a type of "the church of God." Though they fell and were cast out of the garden, they received God's promises of gracious salvation and lived in the world by faith in his Word;[54] this is how God's people have lived ever since. Spurgeon rejected a dispensational reading of Scripture for creating too much discontinuity between the Church and the Old Testament people of God. Responding to an article that promoted such a view, Spurgeon wrote, "Do not, we beseech you, be cajoled by any appeal to 'God's dispensational arrangements,' knowing that, however various they may have been, his covenant has endured the same through them all."[55] He did not ignore developments at various points in redemptive history, but saw these changes as an advancement of the people of God in knowledge, privilege, and worship.[56] Yet these advancements do not negate the overarching covenant under which all of God's people existed. Nor do these advancements ever usher in perfection, until the return of Christ. Until then, God's covenant people live by faith.

> Difference of dispensation does not involve a difference of covenant; and it is according to the covenant of grace that all spiritual blessings are bestowed. So far as dispensations reach they indicate degrees of knowledge, degrees of privilege, and variety in the ordinances of worship. The unity of the faith is not affected by these, as we are taught in the eleventh chapter of the epistle to the Hebrews. The faithful of every age concur in

---

53. "When the church left Paradise, I say, for I believe that Adam and Eve were in the church of God, for I believe that both of them were redeemed souls, chosen of God, and precious. I see God give the promise to them before they leave the garden, and they go out from the garden, the church of God. Since that time, what a path has the church had to tread, but how faithfully has Jehovah led the way." *NPSP* 5:90.

54. Cf. Genesis 3:15.

55. *S&T* 1867:120.

56. "It is a mere trust that Abel was not circumcised, that Noah did not observe the Passover, and Abraham was not baptized." Ibid., 120-21.

looking for one city, and that city is identically the same with the New Jerusalem described in the Apocalypse as "a bride adorned for her husband." Surely, beloved brethren, you ought not to stumble at the anachronism of comprising Abraham, David, and others, in the fellowship of the Church![57]

This understanding of God's covenant people meant that Spurgeon could draw lessons from Israel's history and apply them to the church. From God's promises to bless[58] and protect[59] Israel, to Israel's struggles,[60] to all the rest of God's dealings with Israel, Scripture tells the story of the church, because it tells the story of the people of God.

The Temple of God

Following Paul's teaching in the New Testament, Spurgeon understood that the church was the fulfillment of Solomon's temple. God no longer dwelled in a building, but in the church, his people. In his sermon, "Prayer for the Church," Spurgeon declares, "There is still a temple upon the earth, but it is a temple not made with hands—a temple reared, not by human masons, and hewers of stone, and carpenters, and other artificers, but built by God himself. This temple is the Church of God."[61] Likewise, in "What the Church Should Be," Spurgeon recognizes that the dwelling of the omnipresent God is in the church. "True hearts view the entire universe as a temple wherein everyone speaks

---

57. Ibid., 120-21.

58. "It is God the everlasting Jehovah speaking: he says, 'I will make them "blessing."'" None of us can bless others unless God has first blessed us. We need divine workmanship. 'I will make them a blessing by helping them, and by constraining them.' God makes his people a blessing by helping them.... And so it is with God's people. If they will go through their lives, wherever they have been made a blessing, they will find that God seems to have thrust them into the vineyard." *NPSP* 1:214-15.

59. "As Jerusalem is fortressed by the mountains, so are God's people castled in the covenant, fortressed in the Omnipotence of God, and therefore they are impregnably secure. We shall thus understand the text, and endeavor this morning to work out the great thought of the security of God's people in the arms of Jehovah their Lord." *NPSP* 3:429.

60. "The present times are, in many respects, similar to those of Haggai. History certainly repeats itself within the church of God as well as outside of it; and therefore the messages of God need to be repeated also." *MTP* 32:482.

61. *MTP* 48:339.

of the glory of God. Yet there is a shrine and a temple, but it is living and spiritual: the called out assembly, the church of the living God is the special abode of Deity."[62] To be sure, every local church will contain unbelievers in whom God does not dwell. But if a visible church contains genuine believers who hold to God's Word, they are the fulfillment of the temple of God.[63]

This was a marvelous truth that Spurgeon wanted his people to grasp. God dwelled not in a shrine or mountain, but in and with his people.

> If you would find God, he dwelleth on every hill-top, and in every valley, God is everywhere in creation; but if you want a special display of him, if you would know what is the secret place of the tabernacle of the Most High, the inner chamber of divinity, you must go where you find the church of true believers, for it is here he makes his continual residence known—in the hearts of the humble and contrite, who tremble at his word.[64]

God's clearest manifestation was not in nature or in cathedrals, but among his people, gathered for worship as a church.

> In holy communion—in the breaking of bread, and in the pouring out of wine, in holy baptism—in the immersion of believers into the Lord Jesus Christ, in the preaching of the Word, in the constant declaration of the great salvation of Jesus, in the lifting up of the cross, in the high exalting of him that died upon it, in the preaching of the Covenant, in the declaration of the grace of God—here is he to be seen, here is his name written in brighter letters and in clearer lines than elsewhere the wide world o'er. Hence his church is said to be his temple.[65]

Yet the dwelling of God was not limited to the church's gatherings. Rather, in the heart of every individual believer out in the world,

---

62. *MTP* 24:542.

63. "There is only one Church of our Lord Jesus Christ. 'Which church is that?' again asks someone. None of them all; but there are some people, in all the visible churches, who belong to the one sanctuary of God.... You cannot say of any part, or of the whole of what is called the visible church, that it is the sanctuary of God; it is a sort of shell in which the real Church of God is encased, and which it helps, perhaps, to preserve, but which it also certainly disfigures." *MTP* 48:339-40.

64. *NPSP* 4:210.

65. *NPSP* 4:211.

God dwells. In the godly woman in the workhouse, or the humble farmer behind the plow, or the holy woman who lives sacrificially, "that is where God dwells."[66] Spurgeon is careful not to call any individual a "church." Nonetheless, he recognizes that the imagery of temple extends to the individual believer and affirms that God dwells in his people.[67]

The church, as the temple of God, also meant that the church was the only place where God could be rightly worshiped. Again, in saying this, Spurgeon did not mean that God could only be worshiped at certain times or places. Rather, the church is the congregation of *believers* and only those who believe in Christ can worship God acceptably.

> No acceptable service can be offered to Christ except by his church. Only those who believe in Christ can offer songs, and prayers, and praises, that shall be received of God. Whatever ordinances you attend to, who are without Christ in your hearts, you do belie that ordinance and prostitute it—you do not honor God therein.[68]

If the church is the temple of God, then Christ is the only altar, and Christians are now the fulfillment of the priesthood, "chosen out of the world to be clothed in white robes to minister at his altar."[69] Apart from this temple, no sacrifice of worship will be accepted, regardless of tradition or ceremonies.[70]

Finally, the temple in the Old Testament was the place where God reigned and sent forth his Word in power. Spurgeon saw this fulfilled in the church sending out evangelists and missionaries in the power of the Holy Spirit.

---

66.   *MTP* 48:342.

67.   Cf. 1 Corinthians 6:19.

68.   *NPSP* 4:211.

69.   Ibid.

70.   "A number of us may meet together, and call ourselves Christians, and think that we are worshipping God; but, unless we are really regenerate, and the Spirit of God is in us, there is no true worship. You cannot offer acceptable worship to God by forms, or ceremonies, or the sweetest music, or even in the simplest style of worship in the plainest meeting-house, or by sitting still, and saying nothing, as the members of the Society of Friends do, unless you worship God, who is a Spirit, in spirit and in truth." *MTP* 48:342.

The temple at Jerusalem was also the throne of Jehovah's power. It was out of Zion that he sent forth his rod; and from that sacred shrine that he spoke, by his ancient prophets, the Word that was full of power. Who could stand against him when he was angry, and spoke in his fury out of his holy place? And Christ's power, through the Holy Ghost, still goes forth from his Church.... The living waters flowed forth from Jerusalem. Light, and instruction, and the oracles of God, went forth from Jerusalem of old; and they must go forth from the Church of God, which is among men to this day.[71]

Here in the mission of the church, Spurgeon did not miss an opportunity to connect the temple to the militant church. As God's dwelling was under attack by false teaching and persecution, Spurgeon called on God's people to defend the church.

The church is God's home, will he not defend it? Will he suffer his own house to be sacked and stormed? Shall the hearth of divinity be stained with the blood of his children? Shall it be that the church is overthrown, and her battlements stormed, her peaceful habitations given up to fire and sword? No, never, not while God hath a heart of love, and while he calleth his people his own house and his habitation.[72]

The church as the temple of God was a theological truth that Spurgeon preached to move his congregation towards greater zeal for the gospel and the church. Rather than being passive or allowing the church to be overrun by false teaching and sin, Christians are to demonstrate God's power because he dwells in their midst.[73]

---

71. Ibid.

72. *NPSP* 5:344.

73. While Spurgeon loved the New Testament association of the temple with the church, when it came time to name his new church building in 1861, he did not call it a "temple," but a "tabernacle." In doing so, he wanted to remind people that they were still sojourning in a fallen world and looking forward to the building of the true temple of the universal church, which would be finished with the return of Christ. "We believe this building to be temporary, and only meant for the time that we are in the wilderness without a visible King. Our prayer is, 'Thy kingdom come.' We firmly believe in the real and personal reign of our Lord Jesus Christ, for which we do devoutly wait. That is the reason why it is called a tabernacle, not a temple. We have not here the King in person, the Divine Solomon; till he come, we call it a tabernacle still." *MTP* 6:361-62. More

The Body of Christ

Another image of the church Spurgeon frequently preached on was that of the body of Christ.[74] Like the others, this image conveys the glory of the church in her relation to Christ. In his sermon on Colossians 1:18, "The Head of the Church," Spurgeon marvels at how Paul honors Christ as "the image of the invisible God" and the Creator of all. And then "in the same breath the Son of God is styled... 'the head of the body, the church.' We dare not, therefore, think slightly of this title."[75] Just as the risen Christ is not ashamed to be the head of the church, but glories in his headship, so Christians ought to honor the church and glorify their Head. Once again, Spurgeon clarifies that this image applies not only to the universal church, but also local churches: "Any assembly of faithful men is a church. The aggregate of all these assemblies of faithful men make up the one church which Jesus Christ hath redeemed with his most precious blood, and of which he is the sole and only Head."[76]

Spurgeon used this image of the body of Christ to teach his people about the church's relationship with Christ, their head. It is only through Christ's representative headship over his body that his people are saved. "God has been pleased to deal with mankind as a community, and his great covenant transactions have been with men in a body, and not with separate individuals."[77] Though Spurgeon believed that a person could only be saved by coming to faith in Christ individually, nonetheless their salvation was also a corporate reality. One can only be saved if he is united to Christ's body and included in his covenant of grace. Salvation is a corporate reality through the representative headship of Christ.

In this image, Spurgeon also saw the importance of remaining in Christ. "Separation from Christ is spiritual death." Part of what this means is living in obedience to the Head. "The whole fabric

---

practically, Spurgeon might have avoided naming his church a "temple" because Joseph Parker, the famous Congregationalist preacher, already pastored London's City Temple.

74. Cf. Romans 12:4-5; 1 Corinthians 12:12-27; Colossians 1:18.

75. *MTP* 14:613.

76. *MTP* 14:613.

77. Ibid.

of the church actuated by his life, being filled with his Spirit, most readily concedes to him that in all things he shall have the pre-eminence... in so far as they are spiritual men, so far doth Jesus rule them as the head governeth all the members of the body."[78] In essence, the life of Christ in his Body is the indwelling of the Spirit in his members. But this life must be expressed in the church's obedience to the Head in all things. And in that obedience, the church recognizes that her glory is not in her activity, but in Christ. Even as the chief beauty of a person lies in his head, so it is with the church. "In Jesus Christ all the beauty of the church is summed up. What were all his church without him?"[79]

This image also carries implications for how Christians are to treat one another as members of one body. Spurgeon applied the body of Christ to the universal church, calling people to see their union with all those who were united to Christ. "Some friends talk about exclusive communion; but it is impossible to practice such a thing, for all true communion is with Christ the Head, and also with all the rest of the members, just as, in the body, every member communicates with every other member."[80] Spurgeon took issue with the strict communion Baptists, who refused to commune with paedobaptists. While he understood their objection, he also sought to give expression to the unbreakable unity of the universal church. Despite the divisions that exist among visible churches, they all make up one body, all shared in one Head, and so should fellowship with one another. For Spurgeon, this abstract idea was given expression in his practice of open communion, that is, welcoming paedobaptist visitors to the Table.

Spurgeon also applied this point within the local church. Every true church is also an expression of the body of Christ. So Spurgeon could say to his people:

> What art thou doing, my brother, what art thou doing, my sister, to promote the glory of God in his sanctuary? All the

---

78, Ibid 614

79. *MTP* 14:614-15.

80. *MTP* 48:340.

living members of the body of Christ contribute something to the general welfare of the whole body. The little finger would be missed if it were cut off, and there is not a tiny valve near the heart, nor a minute vessel anywhere in the human system, which could be taken away without inflicting an injury upon the whole body.[81]

As members of the body of Christ, each person has their work to contribute, no matter how small. Service in the church indicates that they belong to the body. Inactivity reflects that they have no portion in Christ. Spurgeon knew there were many temptations to envying and despising one another, especially in such an active and prominent church as his, which drew people from all kinds of backgrounds. But once again, this image of the body reminded the members of their unity despite their differences.

It is a great blessing when the members of the church do not thrust one another, but every one goeth in his own path. There are different orders of workers, and these must cooperate.... We are like the different members of the body, and the eye must not say to the foot, 'I have no need of thee,' neither must the hand say to the ear, 'I have no need of thee.'[82]

The themes of the headship of Christ, service, and unity in the body overlapped with his vision of the church as an army. By preaching on the body of Christ, Spurgeon strengthened his people's faithfulness to Christ and to one another.

The Bride of Christ

Another biblical image that Spurgeon used to help his people understand their identity as a church was that of Bride of Christ. In his sermon on Ephesians 5:25-27, "A Glorious Church," Spurgeon uses this image to explain the nature of Christ's love for the church.[83] Rather than a general and universal love, Christ loves the church with a particular and exclusive love.

---

81   Ibid.

82.   *MTP* 52:106.

83.   Spurgeon also preached many sermons from the Song of Solomon, where he followed the Puritan practice of seeing the book as a type of Christ's love for the

We perceive that Christ did not love the world in the sense in which the term "loved" is here meant. We see here that Christ gave himself not for the world, but for it, that is the Church. In the sense in which he is said here to give himself, he did so for none except his chosen people, the Church; his one, special, and particular object of affection.[84]

This is not to say that the church is any better or different from the world. Like the rest of the world, the church was lost in sin. Christ did not set his love on the church on account of its beauty. [85] Rather, it was by his particular, electing love that the church was made beautiful.

> I see the Church of God, not as a fair maid decorated for the marriage-day with jewels, and carrying herself right gloriously both in her person and her apparel; but I see her as a helpless child, neglected by her parents, cast out, unwashed, unclothed, left uncared for, and covered with her filth and blood. No eye pities her, no arm comes to bring her salvation. But the eye of the Lord Jesus looks upon that infant, and straightway love beams forth from that eye, and speaks from that lip, and acts through that hand; he says, "Live!" and the helpless infant is cared for: she is nurtured; she is decked with dainty apparel; she is fed, and clothed, and sustained, and made comely through the comeliness of him who chose her at the first. Thus it is that strong love moved the grace of God, and the Church found that Christ gave himself for it.[86]

Far from being merely sentimental, Christ's effectual love for the church as bride reveals the sovereign power of God in salvation:

---

church. For example, see No. 282 "Christ's Estimate of His People", No. 338 "Love to Jesus," and No. 364 "The Shulamites Choice Prayer."

84. *MTP* 11:255.

85. "Are you and I members of that Church? Ah, then, we are compelled to confess that in us by nature dwelt all manner of concupiscence, vileness, and an evil heart of unbelief, ever prone to depart from the living God and to rebel against the Most High." Ibid., 256.

86. *MTP* 11:257.

God's unconditional election and Christ's effectual atonement for his people.[87]

Yet, Spurgeon does not leave this meditation in the theological realm; he seeks to bring it home to his hearers in terms they can understand. Spurgeon's spirituality is "thoroughly Christocentric, with an overriding stress on communion with Christ"[88] and here is a biblical image that supports such spirituality. As a good husband, Christ loves the church with a particular love. This love is constant, and it is passionate:

> A husband loves his wife with a hearty love, with a love that is true and intense. It is not mere lip-service. He does not merely speak, but he acts; he is ready to provide for her wants; he will defend her character; he will vindicate her honor; because his heart is set upon her. It is not merely with the eye that he delighteth now and then to glance upon her, but his soul hath her continually in his remembrance; she has a mansion in his heart from whence she can never be cast away. She has become a portion of himself; she is a member of his body, she is part of his flesh and of his bones; and so is the Church to Christ for ever, an eternal spouse.[89]

Death will not separate the church from Christ's love but will continue into eternity. "A husband loves his wife with an enduring love; it never will die out: he says, 'Till death us do part will I cherish thee;' but Christ will not even let death part his love to his people."[90] Today, the church is despised and surrounded by enemies. But the day is coming when his Bride will be revealed in all her glory, "the favourite of heaven, the peculiar treasure of Christ—his regalia, the crown of his head, the bracelet of his arm,

---

87. "Now what is this Church which Jesus Christ loved, if it be not the entire company of the elect? As many as the Father gave him from before the foundation of the world, whose names were written in the Lamb's Book of Life before the stars began to shine." *MTP* 11:255.

88. Peter J. Morden, *Communion with Christ and His People: The Spirituality of C. H. Spurgeon* (Eugene, OR: Pickwick Publications, 2013), 14.

89. *MTP* 11:258.

90. Ibid.

the breastplate of his heart, the very center and core of his own love."[91] She will be united with her Husband forever.

If this is how Christ has loved the church, then how should we respond? She should honor him and remain committed to him as her Husband. She should look forward "with sacred expectation" for the marriage day when she is reunited with him. And she should joyfully live under his loving authority.

> Jesus Christ ruleth in his church, not as a despotic lord, compelling and constraining his subject bride against her will, but as a husband well-beloved, obtaining obedience voluntarily from the heart of the beloved one, being in all things so admired and had in esteem as to win an undisputed pre-eminence."[92]

Spurgeon himself sought to model this kind of trust in Christ to his people. In the last sermon he ever preached at the Tabernacle, he concluded by pointing his people to Christ, the loving husband, the captain of his army.[93]

The Church as Mother

The image of the church as a mother traces back to the early church fathers. The Roman Catholic Church used that image to communicate the belief that salvation could only be found through the sacraments of the church, dispensed by a priestly hierarchy. Spurgeon rejected such an understanding of the church, but he did not hesitate to affirm the image itself. In a sermon on Isaiah 49:20-21 entitled "The Church is a Mother," Spurgeon declared: "The Church is a mother; she always did stand in that relationship to all her members. Take each member of the Church individually, he is a child; take us altogether, we make up the mother, the Church."[94] In some of the other images

---

91. *MTP* 11:258.

92. Ibid.

93. "He is the most magnanimous of captains. There never was his like among the choicest of princes…. If there is anything that is gracious, generous, kind, and tender, yea lavish and super abundant in love, you always find it in him. These forty years and more have I served him, blessed be his name! and I have had nothing but love from him. I would be glad to continue yet another forty years in the same dear service here below if so it pleased him." *MTP* 37:324.

94. *MTP* 48:194.

(for example, the temple of God), Spurgeon was able to apply the image both corporately and individually. But here, Spurgeon makes clear that only the congregation corporately makes up the mother, the church.

Individually, each believer is a child of the family of God, cared for by the mother, the church. Additionally, because of the intimate nature of this image, Spurgeon did not use it to refer to the universal church, but kept it focused on the local church, particularly the congregation. While the Church of England or Roman Catholic Church sought to apply its concept of motherhood through its extensive hierarchical structures, Spurgeon believed that it was only in the congregational life of the local church that the church could be a mother for her children.

This mother-child relationship began at conversion:

> The Church is a mother because it is her privilege to bring forth into the world the spiritual children of the Lord Jesus Christ... through God's using the Church, her ministers, her children, her works, her sufferings, her prayers—through making these the means of the increase of his spiritual kingdom, she proves her right to take to herself the title of mother.[95]

Only God, by the Holy Spirit, can bring about conversion. Yet, God has chosen to use the means of the church to bring sinners into his family. This sermon was preached in the spring of 1860, when many were being converted in the church. Spurgeon himself was converted through the ministry of a church.[96] Yet even those not converted in the church had to acknowledge that it was "through the church's instrumentality the Bible itself has been preserved to us, and by her the gospel has been preached to every age." Therefore, "[the church] is our mother and we love her."[97]

---

95. Ibid.

96. Preaching in 1872, Spurgeon reflected, "By the Holy Spirit we were begotten unto newness of life, but it was in the church, and through the preaching of the word there that we were brought into the light of life. We owe our conversion, the most of us, to some earnest teacher of the truth in the church of God, or to some of those godly works which were written by Christian men." *MTP* 18:92.

97. Ibid.

Because the church is the Christian's mother, the church is the place where a Christian grows and is nurtured. Primarily, this means that the church is responsible for feeding her children "the unadulterated milk of the Word." Through her ministers, her teachers, her classes, the children are to feed on the church's doctrine and ordinances "to supply all their spiritual wants by feeding their understandings, their affections, their hearts."[98] Rather than outsourcing this teaching to schools or other parachurch agencies, every faithful church will seek to train up those given to her.

> Why should we, the Church of Christ, give up our children when we first taught them to speak in Christ's name, to be trained and to be taught by others? No, by every motherly feeling that remains within the bosom of Christ's Church, let us see her children brought up at her own knees, dandled there in her own lap, and not give up the work of training her sons and daughters to others.[99]

The church is also the place where the weak are comforted. "Alas! in the Church's family, there are always some sickly ones, not only sick in body, but sick in spirit. And never does the Church appear so truly a mother as she does to these. Over these she will be, if she is what she should be, peculiarly watchful and jealous."[100] For all those suffering due to illness, cast down by grief, weighed down by temptation, or wandering away from Christ, the church has a responsibility to walk with them in their troubles and point them to the Savior. For all these, the church will double her care and attention, imitating the example of Christ.

Over time, however, a church will not be content merely to coddle her children. Spurgeon saw too many churches "that seem to do nothing whatever in the way of training up the young in their midst," and so the people remain inactive and perhaps even unconverted. But "true nursing churches" train up their children

---

98. *MTP* 48:194-95.

99. *MTP* 7:365.

100. *MTP* 48:195.

for war. Here, the image of the church as mother intersects with the militant church.

The church receives them into her arms, and she takes them to be hers, to be trained up for future deeds of usefulness. She trains up some of her sons to be captains in the Lord's host. She puts the sword of the Spirit into their hands, and bids them to use it in fighting their Master's battles. She trains up others of her sons and daughters to teach still younger ones and these she puts into her schools. She trains up all her children, some by one means and some by another. She says to some, "Go abroad, my children, and labor for your Lord in his far-off fields, and extend his kingdom wherever you can."[101]

> But even as she sends out her children, the church continues her care. As her children engage in the battle of life, it is the church that inspires them with love and advice, sustaining them in any difficulties.[102]

In all these exhortations, Spurgeon understood that the congregation is responsible for fulfilling these tasks. This is not primarily the job of the preachers or the deacons or the elders. Rather it is the church, made up of the entire "company of faithful men and women" that is responsible for carrying out this role of the church as a mother.

> Every time I give the right hand of fellowship to a new member, especially to those just brought in from the world, I think I hear Christ's voice speaking to me, and saying, "Take these children, and nurse them for me, and I will give thee thy wages." I say this is said to me, but I mean it is said to the entire Church—I merely speak, of course, as the representative of the body. We have, whenever members are given to us, a great charge, under God, to nurse them for him, and, instrumentally, to advance them in the road to heaven... the Church, then—by which I mean the great company and body of the faithful—that Church is a nursing mother.[103]

---

101. Ibid.
102. *MTP* 7:365.
103. *MTP* 48:196.

Given this understanding of the church, it would be impossible for Spurgeon to conceive of any faithful approach to the Christian life which did not find its home in the church. From beginning to end, a Christian belonged to the family of the church.

Other Biblical Images

Spurgeon drew from many other biblical images in his teaching about the church. The church is the flock of God, purchased by the blood of their shepherd.[104] Though Christ's sheep were once scattered, they have heard the voice of their shepherd and have been brought together in one flock.[105] Now, pastors are called to feed God's flock faithfully from his Word.[106]

The church is the pillar of truth, a steadfast and immovable pedestal upholding and proclaiming the truth of Scripture throughout the ages.[107] During times of persecution, the church goes underground and becomes the ground of truth, maintaining the truth within its heart.[108] And yet, through history, the church has also been a pillar for the truth, upholding it and proclaiming it for all to hear.

Perhaps Spurgeon's favorite biblical image of the church is that of the army of God.[109] In this image, Spurgeon is not advocating

---

104. "We alone are the flock of God which he hath redeemed with his own blood. Hence man cost God more than the whole universe beside." *MTP* 26:470.

105. "There never was but one Shepherd of the sheep yet, even Christ Jesus; and there never was but one flock of God yet, and there never will be. There is one spiritual church of God, and there never were two." *MTP* 29:191.

106. "You, my brethren, elders and deacons, when you accepted office, you knew what the church meant. She expected holiness and zeal of you. The Holy Ghost made you overseers that you might feed the flock of God. Your office proves your obligation. You are practically under a vow. Has that vow been performed? Have you performed it in Zion unto the Lord?" *MTP* 17:669.

107. "The church stands steadfast and unmoveable as a pillar of truth fixed on its base. If you find not truth anywhere else, you will find it in the church of the living God." *MTP* 24:548.

108. "When the Church stands boldly out, and preaches the Word, it is the pillar of the truth; when it is hidden in the Roman catacombs, and cannot proclaim the Savior's name to the world, still there lives the truth deep in the hearts of believers, and they are then the ground of the truth." *MTP* 54:248.

109. One of the passages that Spurgeon frequently quotes in connection with this image is Song of Solomon 6:4, 10, which he connects typologically with the revealing of the Church Triumphant: "Who is she that looketh forth

physical conflict. Rather, he understands the church to be engaged in a spiritual struggle:

> The Church of Christ is continually represented under the figure of an army; yet its Captain is the Prince of Peace; its object is the establishment of peace, and its soldiers are men of a peaceful disposition. The spirit of war is at the extremely opposite point to the spirit of the gospel. Yet nevertheless, the church on earth is, and until the second advent must be, the church militant, the church armed, the church warring, the church conquering.[110]

This will be studied in greater detail in a later chapter, but as has already been shown, the image of the militant church gave an active and outward emphasis to Spurgeon's understanding of the church.

Conclusion

As a preacher who loved to use engaging and memorable imagery in his sermons, these biblical images provided rich illustrations for teaching his congregation what it meant to be a church. Spurgeon's Reformed ecclesiology did not remain abstract but was brought to life through his use of the various biblical images of the church. Though God's redemption must be individually received, it involved a glorious, corporate reality of being united to a people, the Body of Christ, the Temple of God. Christian discipleship cannot be properly understood apart from the local church.

Spurgeon held to the Protestant marks of the local church and distinguished between the visible and invisible church. At times in his preaching, he blurred the line between the visible and invisible church. But this perhaps reflected his conviction that the local church is an expression of the universal church. When it came to the local church, his emphasis was on its congregational character. Just as an army is not made up only of the officers, but of the whole company of soldiers, so in the church the entire

---

as the morning, fair as the moon, clear as the sun, and terrible as an army with banners?"

110. *NPSP* 5:89.

congregation constituted the church. Similarly, in the universal church, all the various evangelical denominations assembled under Christ's rule and under their own distinctive banners in the fight for the truth.

However, these theological concepts which arose out of the Reformation were not his main concern in his teaching about the church. Rather, as a preacher, Spurgeon's ecclesiological teaching came to life in the numerous biblical images of the church. Whether in the image of the church as the temple, or as the body of Christ, or as the people of God, or as one of many other images, Spurgeon sought to bring Scripture's teaching on the church to life, not through abstract theological concepts, but in painting compelling pictures of the corporate nature of the Christian life.[111] His favorite image of the church was an army. In joining the church, Spurgeon reminded his people that they were in a fight against the spiritual forces of darkness for the cause of the gospel. Through these images, Spurgeon called his people to love and fight for the church.

---

111   "I think that, if necessary, I should have been glad to go on pilgrimage alone, as Christian went; but I should have liked much better to have gone with Christiana, and Mercy, and the children, and with Mr. Greatheart, and old Father Honest, and all that noble party of pilgrims who went together to the Celestial City." *MTP* 53:379.

5

Regulative Principle

Sundays were busy at the Metropolitan Tabernacle. As the congregation grew, so did the various ministries and activities of the church. In 1873, the Tabernacle printed the following Sunday schedule:

> Service commences – Morning at 10:45. Evening at 6:30. Persons holding Tickets are admitted by side entrance until five minutes before each Service, after which the doors are opened to the Public. Sabbath Prayer Meetings, Morning, 9:30; Evening, 8:15.... The Lord's Supper every Sabbath Evening, except on the Second Sabbath in the Month, when it is held after the Morning Service.... Sunday Schools at Tabernacle and Manchester Hall, commence at 9:15 a.m. and 2:30 p.m. Ragged School, Burdett Street, 6:30 p.m. Catechumenical Classes at Tabernacle, and Almshouse Schoolroom, Walworth Road, 3 p.m.... Special Service for Children at 6:30 every Lord's-day; also Service for Deaf and Dumb, Morning 11, Evening 6:30.[1]

Sundays were consecrated for the service of God, both in worship and in ministry. From morning to evening, both in private and public, the members of the church committed themselves to the corporate gatherings of the church and to serving their community in different ways. But the most important activity each Sunday was the gathering of the church. The Sunday morning worship at 10:45 AM and the Sunday evening worship at 6:30 PM are listed first because these were the gatherings that all members were expected to participate in. Surrounding those

---

1. "Metropolitan Tabernacle Directory," *Spurgeon Almanack*, 1873.

gatherings were congregational prayer meetings, one at 9:30 AM before the morning service, and one at 8:45 PM following the evening service. Both meetings prayed for God's blessing upon the day, knowing that apart from His gracious work, it was all in vain. The Tabernacle also held morning and evening services for the deaf and dumb at 11 AM and 6:30 PM. These services were much smaller, and though they were connected to the church, the deaf and dumb gathered separately because of their inability to participate in the main service. Finally, in addition to gathering for worship, the congregation devoted themselves to ministry, particularly to children. After a lunch break, many members returned to the church or went out into different neighborhoods to serve in Sunday Schools, Ragged Schools, catechumenical classes for the youth, and more. After supper, most of the congregation gathered for worship again. There would normally be more visitors in the evening, and members sought to welcome them and get to know them. Additionally, many of the college students went out to their mission stations to lead evening services, while some members helped to lead an evening worship service geared towards children.

Sundays were busy for the members of the church, but undoubtedly, they were even more full for the pastor. He usually arrived early on Sundays to finalize the details of the services (which he planned), preached and led both morning and evening services, had many pastoral conversations, met with visitors in his vestry, and more. But in all this, Spurgeon loved the gatherings of the church. These sabbath gatherings were work, but they were a joyful, holy kind of work. And these gatherings pointed him not to the futile work of this life, but to the eternal rest that awaits all the saints. Reflecting on these sabbath gatherings, Spurgeon once penned a poem, which begins,

Behold, the glorious Sabbath morn,
Its calm and peaceful rest.
A holy joy begins at dawn
To make us mortals blest.

Sweet time to leave our earthly cares
And meet the Sabbath's Lord;
Forget our trials, pass our snares,
To feast upon his word.[2]

In these gatherings, the church received comfort for their trials, strength to face their snares, and a view of the "purchas'd mansion" above in "that land of joy, so wondrous fair, A place prepar'd by thee." Though Spurgeon was the preacher and the service leader, he found a way to also participate in the services so that he was also a recipient of these joys.

The key to all these blessings in the church's gatherings lay not in the people, but in "the Sabbath's Lord," as they met with him and feasted "upon his word." In other words, these corporate gatherings were an expression of his benevolent rule over his people. In this chapter, we will consider Spurgeon's view of the corporate gatherings of the church. How did the reign of Christ relate to the church's gatherings? How did this belief shape how Spurgeon organized those meetings? What did the church do when they gathered? What did Spurgeon believe about the ordinances?

A Church Ordered by God's Word

While Luther acknowledged that the Word preceded the church and gave existence to the church, it was Calvin who built on that foundation and sought to order the church entirely according to the Word. Reformed ecclesiology looks to Scripture to determine the order and worship of the church because this is what best expresses the lordship of Christ in the church.[3] Because of this emphasis on God's Word, Reformed worship looked very different from the Lutheran tradition. While Luther permitted practices that Scripture did not forbid, and therefore kept many of the forms of Roman Catholic worship, Reformed churches implemented the regulative principle, which grounded their worship in what

---

2. C. H. Spurgeon, *Christ Our All: Poems for the Christian Pilgrim* (Nashville: B&H Academic, 2024), 193.

3. Calvin, *Institutes*, IV:iii:1.

was mandated by Scripture, either by command or example.[4] Reformed worship, as a result, was marked by simplicity, focusing on prayer, Scripture reading, congregational singing, preaching, and the sacraments. Every other aspect of worship was evaluated according to the standard of God's Word, from the architecture of the building to the posture in worship, the use of liturgies, and more. The center of Christian worship was no longer the sacraments, but the preaching of the Word. Additionally, the pastor now played a vital role in the life of the church as he faithfully represented Christ's rule and fed the congregation from his Word. All these ideas permeated Spurgeon's thinking and would be evident in his pastoral ministry.

Christ's Reign over the Church

The starting point, then, for understanding Spurgeon's approach to the church's gatherings is in his unshakeable conviction that it is Christ who reigns over the church by his Word, not the preferences of men. Here, as a dissenter, Spurgeon departed from Calvin in a significant way. Calvin believed that the magistracy was ordained by God and should serve faithfully under God's authority, even exercising coercive force to promote piety in the church.[5] For Spurgeon, however, the existence of a state church meant that ungodly earthly authorities exercised authority in the Church, sometimes in contradiction to the rule of Christ. Amid the growing ritualism and rationalism within the Church of England and wider society,[6] Spurgeon held to the supreme rule of Christ in his Word over the church. In the sermon, "The Head of the Church," Spurgeon declared:

---

4.   J. Ligon Duncan III, et al., eds. *Give Praise to God: A Vision for Reforming Worship* (Phillipsburg, NJ: P&R Publishing, 2003), 21-24.

5.   Calvin, *Institutes*, IV:xx:9.

6.   The debate over the existence of the state church would only increase with the emancipation of the Roman Catholics from civil liberties in 1829 and the election of Charles Bradlaugh, an avowed atheist, to Parliament in 1880. Christians in England wrestled with what it would mean for the Church to be ruled by a Parliament containing Roman Catholics and atheists. See Owen Chadwick, *The Victorian Church: Part One 1829-1859* (London: SCM Press, 1997), 7-24, and Owen Chadwick, *The Victorian Church: Part Two 1860-1891* (London: SCM Press, 1997), 112-50.

Christ is the Head of his church as King in Zion. In the midst of the church of God the supreme government is vested in the person of Christ.... I know no subject which it is more necessary to insist upon in these eventful times. Let Jesus be owned as the only Head of the church, and the way out of the present political debate which agitates our nation is clear enough.[7]

In a time when debates about historical criticism, science and the role of reason, the rise of Catholicism, and the role of government threatened to overturn churches, Spurgeon believed that here was a truth that settled all those debates: Jesus Christ is the head of the church, and therefore his Word must reign. By his sacrificial death and resurrection, and by God's decree, Jesus Christ reigns over the church.[8]

At the same time, Spurgeon was careful to define the church: "The church is the kingdom of God among men. It is purely spiritual, comprehending only spiritual men, and existing only for spiritual objects. And who is its King? None but Jesus."[9] In other words, Spurgeon was not advocating a return to theonomy, but instead saw a clear separation between the kingdom of Christ and the kingdom of this world.[10] The church was to be made up only of regenerate, spiritual believers, called out of the world, and living "for spiritual objects." This is not to say that Christians should not be engaged in the world and obedient to earthly authorities. But the church, "the kingdom of God among men," was to be ruled by Christ alone, which meant a rejection of any other authority in the church. "Kings and princes and parliaments have no lawful jurisdiction over the church of Jesus Christ... it beseems not the best of monarchs to claim those royal prerogatives which God

---

7. *MTP* 14:616.

8. Ibid., 620-21.

9. Ibid., 616.

10. "Leave the Lord to rule in the kingdom of mind and spirit, and let Caesar keep his kingdom of civil government; let the state do its work and never interfere with the church, and let the church do her work and never interfere with, or be interfered with, by the state. The two kingdoms are separate and distinct. Broad lines of demarcation are always drawn, throughout the whole of the New Testament, between the spiritual and the temporal power, and the mischief is when men cannot see this. Christ is the head of the church, not any one who represents the state." Ibid.

has given to his only begotten Son. Jesus alone is the Head of his spiritual kingdom, the church."[11]

In saying this, Spurgeon believed that the Church of England was a compromised church because of its connection with the state. But this would be true of any alliance with any earthly influence that compromised the church's allegiance to Christ. To live properly under the rule of Christ, a church could not be under any other human authority. Independency, then, was not about the congregation's freedom from all restraints, but about their freedom to live under the Lordship of Christ. State churches forfeited this freedom and suffered for it.[12]

The Reign of Christ in the Church's Doctrine and Ministry

The rule of Christ over the church meant that he alone could determine its doctrines and teachings according to the Scriptures.[13] "The church is not her own head, she has no right to act upon her own judgment, apart from the statutes of her King; she must come to the Book—everything is there for her."[14] While believers should respect the judgment of ancient church councils, they were not to bow before them. No matter how many good men gathered together to affirm a particular dogma, "if the dogma was not authorized long before they decided it—if it was not written in the Book, the decision of the learned council amounts to nothing."[15]

---

11. *MTP* 14:616.

12. "Some churches have not learned this lesson, but are held in leash like dogs by their masters; they crouch down at the feet of the state to eat the crumbs which fall from Mammon's table; and if they are cuffed and beaten by the powers that be, well do they deserve it; and I would almost pray that the whip may fall upon them yet more heavily, till they learn to appreciate liberty, and are willing to take off the dog collar of the State, and be free from human domination." Ibid.

13. Spurgeon believed this to be true not only for a church's doctrine, but its polity also. "Now the church of God hath no power whatever to make laws for herself, since she is not her own head; and no one has any right to make laws for her, for no one is her head but Christ. Christ alone is the law-maker of the church and no rule or regulation in the Christian church standeth for anything unless in its spirit at least it hath the mind of Christ to support and back it up." Ibid. The following chapter will examine Spurgeon's approach to church polity in more depth.

14. *MTP* 14:623.

15. Ibid., 617.

This was true not only for the ancient church councils, but also for Luther, Calvin, and all other Reformed traditions.

> To Christians it is nothing to say that certain doctrines are taught in books of common prayer, or of conference discipline, or of systematic theology; to us it is of small account that either Presbytery, or the Episcopacy, or Independency, have put their stamp upon a certain form of teaching. Authority is no more to us than the snap of a man's finger, unless the truth thus commended derives certainty from the testimony of Jesus Christ himself, who is the Head of his body the church.[16]

In saying this, Spurgeon did not deny the importance of the ancient creeds. He himself was widely read in historical theology and often appealed to teachers who came before him. Rather, his point was that these creeds or teachings were only valid and instructive insofar as they were faithful to the teaching of Scripture.

When creeds and confessions properly reflected the teaching of Scripture, far from being a threat to the reign of Christ, they became an expression of the church's allegiance to Christ and his Word. Against those who held to a "broad" view of the church, allowing people of various theological convictions to be a part of the church, Spurgeon believed that each church should make clear what it believed. In his sermon, "The Church as She Should Be," Spurgeon compares the church's doctrinal statement to a banner that an army carries, signifying the rule of her King:

> The church unfurls her ensign to the breeze that all may know whose she is and whom she serves. This is of the utmost importance at this present, when crafty men are endeavoring to palm off their inventions. Every Christian church should know what it believes, and publicly avow what it maintains. It is our duty to make a clear and distinct declaration of our principles, that our members may know to what intent they have come together, and that the world also may know what we mean.[17]

---

16. Ibid.

17. *MTP* 17:194.

Spurgeon believed that creeds were critical for making clear a church's doctrines and denied that a church could exist without any doctrines. Part of the work of the Spirit in the church is to instill theological convictions.[18] Spurgeon's congregation held to the Baptist Confession of Faith of 1689. Though it had fallen out of use over the years, Spurgeon had it republished in 1855 and made it cheaply available to his congregation. Writing to his church, Spurgeon clarified the proper use of creeds:

> To The Church In New Park Street, Among Whom It Is My Delight To Minister,
>
> Dearly-beloved,
> This ancient document is a most excellent epitome of the things most surely believed among us. By the preserving hand of the Triune Jehovah, we have been kept faithful to the great points of our glorious gospel, and we feel more resolved perpetually to abide by them.
>
> This little volume is not issued as an authoritative rule, or code of faith, whereby you are to be lettered, but as an assistance to you in controversy, a confirmation in faith, and a means of edification in righteousness. Here, the younger members of our church will have a Body of Divinity in small compass, and by means of the Scriptural proofs, will be ready to give a reason for the hope that is in them.
>
> Be not ashamed of your faith; remember it is the ancient gospel of martyrs, confessors, Reformers, and saints. Above all, it is the truth of God, against which the gates of hell cannot prevail.
>
> Let your lives adorn your faith, let your example recommend your creed. Above all, live in Christ Jesus, and walk in Him, giving credence to no teaching but that which is manifestly approved of Him, and owned by the Holy Spirit. Cleave fast to the Word of God, which is here mapped out to you. May

---

18. "He (Mr. Spurgeon) denied that there could be a Church without doctrines.... Those who did not insist upon Christ's truth were not a Church at all, but a mixed multitude of Israel and Egypt, ready to rebel at all times. Churches would get on very well without creeds so long as they were dead, but when they were alive and had the energy of the Spirit among them, they would find that creedless men were like dead limbs and would have to be cut off." *MTP* 7:261.

our Father, who is in Heaven, smile on us as ever! Brethren, pray for —

Your affectionate Minister, C. H. SPURGEON.[19]

Here, Spurgeon is careful to clarify that the Confession was not authoritative in itself but rather "an assistance... in controversy, a confirmation in faith, and a means of edification in righteousness." Insofar as it was a faithful representation of the true faith, the ancient gospel, and the truth of God, the Baptist Confession of Faith was a faithful and useful tool for the church. At times, Spurgeon provided copies of the Confession of Faith to young Christians who joined church.[20] Small groups sometimes studied the Confession, along with a revised Westminster Shorter Catechism. Speaking in 1861, Spurgeon expressed pride in the fact that some of the youngest members of his church could defend the five points of the doctrines of grace because of their use of this creed.[21]

While some churches rejected the use of creeds as sectarian or bigoted, Spurgeon saw such objections as a battle against the truth. His conviction was that all people believed in some creed, whether they wrote it down or not. It was the duty of Christians to "unfurl the old primitive standard, the all-victorious standard of the cross of Christ."[22] While antiquity alone did not validate any creed or the use of creeds, Spurgeon believed that these battles over the church's doctrine could be traced through history to the early church. In holding fast to the Baptist Confession, Spurgeon's church stood in line with the long tradition of historic Christian orthodoxy, Protestantism, and, more recently, Baptist convictions.

If Christ reigns over the church, then what is the role of the church? While remaining distinct from the world, the church's task is to represent Christ before the world. Therefore, the church wields not an inherent authority, but a *delegated* and *ministerial*

---

19. *Autobiography* 2:160-61.

20. Hannah Wyncoll, ed., *Wonders of Grace: Original Testimonies of Converts during Spurgeon's Early Years* (London: The Wakeman Trust, 2016), 47.

21. *MTP* 7:261.

22. Ibid.

authority. "The church's power is twofold. It is a power to testify to the world what Christ has revealed. She is set as a witness, and she must act as such. She has, next, a ministerial power, by which she carries out the will of Christ, and doeth his bidding as Christ's servant and minister."[23] According to the Master's command, the church is to testify to the world what Christ has revealed and to carry out his will in the world as his minister. In doing so, the church may speak and act with the authority of the King, insofar as she accurately represents his Word and will. However, as the church interacts with the world, her authority is never coercive; it is only declarative, making known the will of the King. As soon as a church strays from this ministerial role, seeking to establish her own authority, she has begun to stray from Christ's rule and has no real power behind her.[24]

The Reign of Christ through His Spirit

Though Christ is the risen king and the visible church remains here on earth, Spurgeon did not envision his rule over the church as a distant reality, mediated merely through a book. Rather, through the Spirit, the spiritual presence of the King rested within the church.

> It is by the working of the Spirit of God that Christ's presence in the church is manifested; and we are to expect no other presence than that: we have the spiritual divine presence of the second person of the blessed Trinity, and the presence of Christ Jesus also in the power of his representative on earth, the Holy Ghost. This presence, not a bodily but a spiritual presence, is the glory of the church of God.[25]

The presence of Christ by the Spirit did not dwell in the church in some general abstract way. Rather, the Spirit dwelt in the hearts of his people. Here was the link between Christ's supreme rule

---

23. *MTP* 14:623-24.

24. "So a church met together to consult how to carry out the Master's will, how to enforce his laws, does rightly; but a church meeting to make new laws, or a church meeting to rule according to its own judgment and opinion, imagining that its decision will have weight, has made a mistake, and placed itself in a false position." Ibid., 624.

25. *MTP* 18:86.

over the church and the congregational rule of the church. As a community of spiritual men and women, Christ dwelt in the church and exercised his reign through his Spirit-filled people.

> Christ is not only the legislator of the church, and has left to us his Statute-book, sufficient to guide us in every dilemma, but he is also the living administrator in the church. He is not here, it is true, but as monarchs often administrate through lieutenants, so the Lord Jesus administereth through his ever living Spirit, who dwells in the hearts of his people.[26]

Practically, this meant that in the church, true believers filled with the Holy Spirit should regularly gather together, pray humbly for Christ's guidance, and look to his Word for "plain directions as to their course of action." Throughout Spurgeon's ministry, his church prayed for direction regarding church building projects, the election of church leaders, new ministry endeavors, and more. In these situations, Spurgeon believed that a church could be confident that "though they be many minds, they shall be led as one man to choose that course of action which shall be after the mind of Christ."[27]

However, in this Spirit-led congregationalism, Spurgeon did not envision a leaderless mass. Through the Holy Spirit, Christ reigned over the church by appointing and gifting leaders. It was the risen Christ who gave to the early church gifts of apostles, teachers, preachers, and evangelists, and Spurgeon believed that Christ would continue to do so until the end of the age. While the Spirit of God remained, the church should never fear that gospel preachers would be stamped out. Spurgeon once told of a Welsh pastor who lamented the lack of great preachers as in previous generations. Spurgeon responded:

> So in England we have neither Wesley nor Whitefield, nor any of their order; yet, as with God is the residue of the Spirit, he can fetch out from some chimney-corner another Christmas Evans, or find in our Sunday-school another George Whitefield, who shall declare the gospel with the Holy Ghost sent down from

---

26. *MTP* 14:618.
27. Ibid., 619.

heaven.... Have faith in God through our Lord Jesus Christ! When he ascended on high he led captivity captive, and received gifts for men. He then gave apostles, teachers, preachers, and evangelists, and he can do the like again.[28]

By his Spirit, Christ will always provide ministers for his people and empower his church for ministry. And so, the Spirit-filled church, led by Spirit-gifted elders and deacons, exercises its authority under the reign of Christ.

The Reign of Christ in the Church's Gatherings

For the Christian, the worship of God is not limited to church gatherings but overflows into every aspect of life. Singing, prayer, and Scripture reading are a part of the Christian life and should take place in the world[29] and in the home.[30] At the same time, Spurgeon believed that something unique happened in the gatherings of the church. There, Christians met together to worship their Lord, experiencing a foretaste of the heavenly assembly to come.

> To forsake the assembling of ourselves together would involve the loss of one of the dearest Christian privileges, for the worship of the church below is the vestibule of the adoration of heaven. If ever heaven comes down to earth it is in the communion of saints. Our Lord's table is oftentimes glory anticipated. The prayer meeting often seems to be held close to Jerusalem's city wall; it stands in a sort of border land between the celestial and the terrestrial; it is a house and yet a gate, fruition and expectation in one, the house of God and the very gate of heaven. Church

---

28. *MTP* 32:488.

29. "Whatever your trade and calling may be, if you cannot sing aloud, you can sing in your hearts while your hands are busy; you can ring out the praises of God as well to the sound of the hammer on the anvil as to the peal of the organ; your feet at the sewing machine may beat time to a sacred tune; you can as well praise God while you crack your whip as when you sing to a Psalm tune. Why not? If the heart be right you can mount up to the heavens from any place or labor." *MTP* 16:69.

30. "I agree with Matthew Henry when he says, 'They that pray in the family do well; they that pray and read the Scriptures do better; but they that pray, and read, and sing do best of all.' There is a completeness in that kind of family worship which is much to be desired." *MTP* 32:290.

fellowship is meant by our Lord Jesus to be the table upon which the daintiest meats of the banquet of grace are served up.[31]

To be sure, this did not mean that church gatherings should be accompanied by ecstatic visions or heavenly experiences. Rather, the heavenly joys of church gatherings could only be experienced by faith. There is still an expectation and anticipation for Christians as they await that final gathering of the universal church. Even so, here on earth, we attain a glimpse, a foretaste of that heavenly reality in the local church.

Spurgeon rejected any revivalist attempts at manipulating emotions and saw strange, physical contortions as "mere human excitement,"[32] or perhaps even evidence of demonic activity.[33] Instead, God's Word should always order the gatherings of God's people. But in the hearing of God's Word, in the singing of God's praises, in the offering of prayers, these Sabbath gatherings were a time of great joy for those who knew God's grace. Quoting the hymn "Jerusalem My Happy Home," Spurgeon declared,

> There is no verse which gives you a better idea of heaven as a place than that
>
> "Where congregations ne'er break up,
> And Sabbaths have no end."

---

31. *S&T* 1868:339-340.

32. "It is neither decent nor orderly for people to dance under the sermon, nor howl, nor scream, while the gospel is being preached to them, and therefore it is not the Spirit's work at all, but mere human excitement." *NPSP* 4:166.

33. "In the old revivals in America a hundred years ago, commonly called 'the great awakening,' there were many strange things, such as continual shrieks and screams, and knockings, and twitchings, under the services. We cannot call that the work of the Spirit.... Now, if in any revival you see any of these strange contortions of the body always distinguish between things that differ. The Holy Spirit's work is with the mind, not with the body in that way. It is not the will of God that such things should disgrace the proceedings. I believe that such things are the result of Satanic malice. The devil sees that there is a great deal of good doing; 'Now,' says he, 'I'll spoil it all. I'll put my hoof in there, and do a world of mischief.'" *NPSP* 4:166. Though Spurgeon rejected revivalistic manipulation, he did believe that people could respond to preaching with great emotion through the work of the Spirit. See *Autobiography* 2:95.

Gracious souls love the place where God's honor dwelleth, and the assembling of themselves together is always a blessed thing to them.[34]

In connecting the gathering of the church to heaven, Spurgeon taught his people that their worship services were a visible expression of the kingdom of Christ, an in-breaking of Christ's rule on earth. For all eternity, God's people will worship him, and yet even now, gracious souls had the opportunity to participate in that worship.

Regulative Principle

If worship gatherings are an expression of Christ's reign on earth, then these gatherings must be ruled by the Word of Christ. Like the Reformers before him, Spurgeon held to the regulative principle. Though Spurgeon never used that term, he consistently taught that the worship of the church ought to be ruled entirely by Christ according to his Word.

Christ alone is the law-maker of the church and no rule or regulation in the Christian church standeth for anything unless in its spirit at least it hath the mind of Christ to support and back it up…. When we meet together in church-meeting we cannot make laws for the Lord's kingdom; we dare not attempt it. Such necessary regulations as may be made for carrying out our Lord's commands, to meet for worship, and to proclaim the gospel, are commendable, because they are acts needful to obedience to his highest laws; but even these minor details are not tolerable if they clearly violate the spirit and mind of Jesus Christ. He has rather given us spiritual guides rather than legal rubrics and fettering liturgies, and he has left us at liberty to follow the directions of his own free Spirit.[35]

For Spurgeon, the regulative principle included every part of the church's life. All that the church did should follow "the spirit and mind of Jesus Christ" as revealed in his Word. However, this principle did not nullify the need for the church to seek the

---

34. *MTP* 10:451.

35. *MTP* 14:617-18.

Spirit's leading. There were areas of the church's activity and mission where Scripture might be less clear, so the church needed to depend on the guidance of the Spirit. Even as the worship of the church was not to be ruled by "legal rubrics and fettering liturgies," Christians should exercise their freedom in the Spirit. Nonetheless, Christ reigns over his church and the church is to follow Christ's will in its worship and in all other matters.

While Spurgeon did not preach explicitly on the regulative principle, he did apply it in several ways. First and foremost, he taught that true worship could only be offered by a believer through faith in Christ. "Only those who believe in Christ can offer songs, and prayers, and praises, that shall be received of God. Whatever ordinances you attend to, who are without Christ in your hearts, you do belie that ordinance and prostitute it—you do not honor God therein."[36] While this was not an emphasis of the Reformers in their teaching on the regulative principle, this was in line with a Protestant understanding of the necessity of faith. Only those who trusted in Christ could offer acceptable worship to God. Apart from faith in Christ, any external form of worship was only superstition.

Second, Spurgeon rejected any practices not found in Scripture. Roman Catholicism, and increasingly the Church of England, was filled with many such practices: crossing the forehead with holy water, requiring certain forms of church architecture, the use of certain flowers and vestments and rubrics, the keeping of religious holidays, and many other such practices.[37] All of these Spurgeon believed offensive to God, because such practices could not be found in God's Word but rested on human ideas.

Third, Spurgeon rejected any alteration of the outward forms of worship handed down in Scripture. While the outward forms of religion were not to be equated with spiritual life, nonetheless Spurgeon believed that God commanded certain forms, and they were to be honored. This was a principle taught throughout the Old Testament. For Christians, these forms were particularly important in the ordinances

---

36. *NPSP* 4:211.
37. *NPSP* 4:173.

It is quite certain, in the first place, that the form of religion must never be altered.... His two great ordinances of Baptism and the Lord's Supper are sent for us from on high. I dare not alter either of them. I should think it a high sin and treason against heaven if, believing that baptism signifieth immersion, and immersion only, I should pretend to administer it by sprinkling; or, believing that baptism appertaineth to believers only, I should consider myself a criminal in the sight of God if I should give it to any but those who believe. Even so with the Lord's Supper. Believing that it consists of bread and wine, I hold it to be highly blasphemous in the Church of Rome to withhold the cup from the people; and knowing that this ordinance was intended for the Lord's people only, I consider it an act of high treason against the Majesty of Heaven, when any are admitted to the Lord's Supper who have not made a profession of their faith and of their repentance, and who do not declare themselves to be the true children of God.[38]

In other words, administering baptism by immersion only to believers, or the bread and cup to those who have publicly professed faith, Spurgeon considered these forms a matter of obedience to Christ. Dissenters tended to downplay the importance of rituals and forms. But for Spurgeon, where Scripture prescribed forms, he dared not alter them, but sought to follow them faithfully.

Fourth, though he defended a simple worship liturgy, he understood that the human heart could turn any form into a point of pride. Among Dissenters, he encountered many who would bristle at any change to their meeting space or their style of music.

You know it is quite as easy for a man to trust in ceremonials, when they are severely simple, as for a man to rely upon them when they are gorgeous and superb. A man may as much trust in the simple ordinance of immersion and the breaking of bread, as another may trust in the high mass and in the prayers of priests.[39]

Even while Spurgeon promoted a simple liturgy, he did not want to create a new ceremony that his people relied on for acceptable worship to God. This would be a misapplication of the regulative

38. *NPSP* 4:170.
39. *NPSP* 4:173-74.

principle. Though Spurgeon promoted a consistent and simple liturgy, he called the congregation to worship by faith rather than by form.

Corporate Worship at the Metropolitan Tabernacle

At the ceremony of the laying of the first stone of a new building in 1859, a history and account of the church was read by Deacon B. W. Carr. Amid the ecclesiological innovations of their day, the New Park Street Chapel was distinguished by its consistency of faith and practice from the very beginning.[40] This was true not only for the church's theology and polity, but also its corporate worship: "The services of religion have been conducted without any peculiarity or innovation. No musical or aesthetic accompaniments have ever been used. The weapons of our warfare are not carnal, but they are mighty."[41]

The services that Spurgeon led always consisted of three elements: prayer, congregational singing, and the ministry of the Word. These elements would also make up the small worship services that he led while traveling, and special services that he led, like the Fast-Day Service in 1857, with over 23,000 in attendance. As one professor recorded after attending a Sunday service at the Surrey Gardens Music Hall, "The service was like the Presbyterian,--psalms, prayer, expounding a Psalm, and a sermon."[42]

Those three basic elements would take on different forms, however. There would typically be an opening prayer and a pastoral prayer. For the congregational singing, Spurgeon picked a variety of hymns and psalms, depending on the themes of the

---

40. "Owning but one rule of faith—the pure unadulterated Scriptures; recognizing the order of government or discipline no other standard than the example and precept of the apostles as contained in the New Testament, without alloy of tradition or modification, under fresh phases of secular estate, the old creed has been endorsed by each successive generation of believers, and is held intact by those, who this day are gathered to transmit the testimony they have received to a posterity yet unborn. No novelty whatever led to the distinctness of our communion." *NPSP* 5:268.

41. Ibid.

42. Charles C. F. Greville, Esq., *The Greville Memoirs: A Journal of the Reign of King George IV, King William IV, and Queen Victoria*, Vol. 8 (London: Longmans, Green and Co., 1911), 85.

service. The ministry of the Word would involve a Scripture reading and exposition (which varied in length and text), and a forty-five-minute sermon. The ordinances of baptism and the Lord's Supper were also regularly observed, but not at every gathering of the church. The entire service then concluded with a benediction.

While the elements of prayer, singing, and Word ministry were fixed in Tabernacle worship, Spurgeon deliberately varied their order from time to time. Speaking to his students, he encouraged them to "to vary the order of service as much as possible. Whatever the free Spirit moves us to do, that let us do at once."[43] In saying this, Spurgeon was not advocating for the invention of any new elements in worship. This would have been a rejection of the regulative principle. Rather, he advocated for variety in the forms of the elements of worship. This could mean varying the length and content of prayers, breaking up the singing of the hymns, varying the number of hymns, changing the order of service, and many other variations.[44] Spurgeon once even commended a pastor for preaching the sermon at the commencement of the service in order that the latecomers might be able to participate in prayer.[45] In his own practice, however, Spurgeon always saved the sermon for the end of the service, as hearing from God in the preaching of the Word was the climax of worship.

While there could be variations, Spurgeon also encouraged his students to bring unity to the service by ordering it around a single theme. Typically, this would be a theme that flowed from the sermon text.[46] Spurgeon would pick hymns and Scripture readings that were in line with the sermon text. Through his

---

43. *Lectures* 1:68.

44. In his visit to the Metropolitan Tabernacle in 1868, Justin D. Fulton reports the following order of service: Opening prayer, hymn, Scripture reading, pastoral prayer, hymn, and sermon. Justin D. Fulton, *Spurgeon Our Ally* (Brooklyn, NY: The Pauline Propaganda, 1923), 220-23.

45. *Lectures* 1:68. This author is not aware of any instance where Spurgeon followed this example.

46. Hence there is not the wide distinction to be drawn between preaching and prayer that some would have us admit; for the one part of the service softly blends into the other, and the sermon frequently inspires the prayer and the hymn." *Lectures* 1:53-54.

prayers, he would seek to blend the themes of the hymns into the themes of the exposition and sermon.[47]

For example, on Sunday evening, July 8, 1888, Spurgeon preached a sermon, "Pardon for the Greatest Guilt," from the story of Manasseh in 2 Chronicles 33.[48] That evening the congregation sang, hymn 201, "Thy Mercy My God", hymn 202, "Great God of Wonders," and hymn 568, "Depth of Mercy." For his Scripture expositions prior to the sermon, Spurgeon read and commented on 2 Chronicles 33:1-20, giving the wider context of Manasseh's story, as well as Isaiah 1:2-19, as an illustration of Israel's stubbornness and God's forgiveness. Clearly, the entire service was organized around the theme of God's forgiveness even for sinners.

Spurgeon did not pay much attention to the liturgical calendar. Like the Puritans before him, Spurgeon rejected any superstitious or Roman Catholic understanding of Christmas.[49] But as a Victorian and a Christian, he also loved Christmas, both as a cultural holiday and as a theological celebration of the incarnation.

> I wish there were ten or a dozen Christmas-days in the year; for there is work enough in the world, and a little more rest would not hurt laboring people. Christmas-day is really a boon to us, particularly as it enables us to assemble round the family hearth and meet our friends once more. Still, although we do not fall exactly in the track of other people, I see no harm in thinking of the incarnation and birth of the Lord Jesus.[50]

---

47. "There is a way of taking a line of prayer, if the Holy Spirit; shall guide you therein, which will make the service all of a piece, and harmonize with the hymns and discourse. It is very useful to maintain unity in the service where you can; not slavishly, but wisely, so that the effect is one." Ibid., 69.

48. *MTP* 40:433-44.

49. "We have no superstitious regard for times and seasons. Certainly we do not believe in the present ecclesiastical arrangement called *Christmas*. First, because we do not believe in the mass at all, but abhor it, whether it be sung in Latin or in English; and secondly, because we find no Scriptural warrant whatever for observing any day as the birthday of the Savior; and consequently, its observance is a superstition, because not of divine authority." *MTP* 17:697.

50. *NPSP* 2:25.

Christmas services, however, were just like any other Sunday. There was no special adornment or different liturgy. As one paper reported on Christmas Sunday at the Tabernacle in 1870, "At the Metropolitan Tabernacle on Sunday there were no outward signs of Christmas."[51] Given the cultural attention on the holiday, Spurgeon didn't mind preaching on the Nativity during Christmas, but sometimes, he would be just as happy to preach on another text. For example, on Christmas Sunday, 1874, he preached on the infallibility of Scripture, from Matthew 4:4.[52] But the following Christmas, 1875, he preached on Immanuel, God with us, from Matthew 1:23.[53] Not only that, but Spurgeon did not limit himself to only preaching on the Nativity during Christmas. Sometimes, the congregation would be delighted to hear a sermon on the Incarnation in the middle of the year, accompanied by readings and carols on the birth of Christ.[54]

In all these practices, Spurgeon sought to maintain his people's attention, promote their solemnity, and prevent distractions. While keeping the elements of his liturgy simple, Spurgeon found infinite variety in the themes and doctrines of Scripture, and he took advantage of all the forms of prayer, singing, and Word ministry to bring out the treasures of Christ for his people. Spurgeon's goal in corporate worship was the edification of the church and the right worship of God.

Corporate Prayer

While Nonconformists had a reputation of minimizing prayer for the preaching of the Word,[55] Spurgeon rejected such an idea

---

51. "Christmas Day at the Metropolitan Tabernacle," *South London Press*, Dec. 31, 1870, 10.

52. *MTP* 20:697.

53. *MTP* 21:709.

54. For example, see "The True Tabernacle, and its Glory of Grace and Peace," preached on September 27, 1885. *MTP* 31:529. One of the hymns sung in this service was Hymn 256, "Hark, the Herald Angels Sing," and one of the Scripture readings was from John 1:1–18.

55. "It has sometimes been the boast of Episcopalians that Churchmen go to their churches to pray and worship God, but that Dissenters merely assemble to hear sermons." Ibid., 53.

and believed that corporate prayer was "one of the most weighty, useful, honorable parts of the service, and that it ought to be even more considered than the sermon."[56] At times, it was in leading his congregation in prayer that Spurgeon felt closest to heaven, almost forgetting his surroundings.

Many times he testified that, when leading the great congregation in prayer, he was so rapt in adoration, and so completely absorbed in the supplication or thanksgiving he was presenting that he forgot all his surroundings and even felt a measure of regret, upon closing his petition, and opening his eyes, to find that he was still in the flesh, in the company of men of like passions with himself, instead of being in the immediate presence of the Most High, sharing in the higher worship of the holy angels and the spirits of just men made perfect.[57] Others have testified to similar experiences in listening to Spurgeon pray.[58]

The opening prayer of the service reminded the congregation that the primary orientation of their worship was towards God. Typically, there would be a loud buzz throughout the auditorium as the large congregation took their seats.[59] Then, at the scheduled time, Spurgeon would ascend the stairs to the platform along with the other church officers, and as they took their seats the congregation grew quiet. There would be a pause for prayer. Spurgeon encouraged his students not to be afraid to let people sit in reflective silence for two or even five minutes. "Solemn silence makes noble worship."[60] Then Spurgeon would rise and begin the service with the simple phrase, "Brethren, let us pray."

---

56. Ibid.

57. *Autobiography* 4:71.

58. Visiting in 1868, Fulton reported: "His prayer was greater to me than his sermon. In his sermon he talked with men. In his prayer he communed with God." Justin D. Fulton, *Spurgeon Our Ally*, 222. Many of these prayers were recorded and published. See C. H. Spurgeon, *C. H. Spurgeon's Prayers* (Pasadena, TX: Pilgrim Publications, 1990).

59. "Fancy a congregation, consisting of ten thousand souls, streaming into the hall, mounting the galleries, humming, buzzing, and swarming,--a mighty hive of bees,--eager to secure at first the best places, and at last, any place at all." *Autobiography* 2:247-48.

60. *Lectures* 1:69.

Some Nonconformist churches had implemented creative "preliminaries" before the sermon, meant to warm-up the congregation, including various choir anthems, instrumentals, and lessons.[61] Spurgeon saw these innovations as a distraction from the worship of God. Far more fitting was to open the service with a prayer, acknowledging God's gracious reign and requesting his work in the hearts of his people.[62]

The second prayer in the worship service was the pastoral prayer,[63] which was typically longer, blending the themes of praise, confession, thanksgiving, and supplication. Spurgeon instructed his students to let the Lord alone be the object of their prayers. Yet these prayers reveal that Spurgeon never forgot about his congregation. His role was to lead them in corporate prayer and bring their requests before God. The record of his corporate prayers shows that Spurgeon always prayed in the first-person plural, in order that the congregation might be able to pray along with him and participate in his praises and requests. While Spurgeon was careful not to "go into every minute detail of the circumstances of the congregation,"[64] his prayers reveal a pastor's concern for his congregation. While he could not pray specifically for every individual in such a large congregation, he could still pray for their particular needs. On one occasion, Spurgeon prayed,

> Now this morning, we would bring before Thee all Thy saints, and ask Thee to attend to their trials and troubles. Some we know here are afflicted in person, others are afflicted in their dear friends; some are afflicted in their temporal estate, and are

---

61. "On one occasion, when Mr. Spurgeon was to preach in a Nonconformist 'church' where the service was of a very elaborate character, someone else had been asked to conduct 'the preliminaries.' The preacher remained in the vestry until the voluntary, the lessons, the prayers, and the anthem were finished, then entering the pulpit, he said, 'Now, brethren, let us pray;' and the tone in which the last word was uttered indicated plainly enough what he thought of all that had gone before." *Autobiography* 3:347.

62. "The first prayer was short and general in character, but very devout. No fooling here, we are met to worship God." Fulton, *Spurgeon Our Ally,* 220.

63. "We come a second time to Thee in public worship this morning, with the same prayer with which we commenced." Spurgeon, *The Pastor in Prayer,* 131.

64. *Lectures* 1:61.

brought into sore distress. Lord, we do not know the trials of all Thy people, but Thou dost; for Thou art the Head, and the pains of all the members are centered in Thee. Help all Thy people even to the end.[65]

In addition to praying for practical needs, Spurgeon also regularly led his congregation in a confession of sin. As before, these confessions would not be so specific as to highlight an individual's sin but were general enough that everyone could participate. For example, on another occasion, Spurgeon prayed:

And now, Lord, Thou wilt listen to us while we confess before Thee how unworthy we have been of all Thy goodness; for we are a sinful generation, even as our fathers were. We have sinned times without number, and even those of us who are Thy people, and have been born into Thy house, we have even more than others to mourn over our sin, for Thou hast made us more sensible of it, and we have sinned against greater light, which we do sorrowfully confess. Our sins of pride, of unbelief, of hasty judgment of Thy providence, our neglect of searching into Thy mind in the Word, our neglect of possessing Thy mind in our daily life, our transgressions and our shortcomings make against us a great list of accusations.[66]

Even though he was their pastor, he did not hesitate to include himself in these prayers of confession and supplication, identifying with the struggles of his people. Indeed, these corporate prayers became an important way Spurgeon exercised his pastoral care over his congregation.

In addition to the prayers offered in the worship service, Spurgeon's congregation also gathered regularly on Monday evenings for a congregational prayer meeting. According to Spurgeon, here was the secret to the power of the church. "Prayer is the power, which brings God's blessing down upon all our work."[67] While Spurgeon did not track attendance at these prayer meetings, he saw habitual and willful neglect of these meetings by members as worthy of condemnation and likely an indication of a

---

65. Spurgeon, *The Pastor in Prayer*, 87.

66. Ibid., 53.

67. *MTP* 48:347.

poor private prayer life.[68] The reason these prayer meetings were so vital was because the church was not a machine. It was never meant to exist independently of God. The church's strength and life were to be found in God. Spurgeon feared any dependence on structures and good practices, no matter how Scriptural or proper, would only lead to disaster. "The Church of God was never meant to be an automaton.... The Church was meant to be a living thing, a living person, and as the person cannot be supported, if life be absent, or if food be kept back, or if breath be suspended, so should it be with the Church."[69]

The prayer meeting was held in the main auditorium, which would largely be filled. After a hymn and Scripture reading with commentary, one of the deacons read a list of requests for prayer from all the various ministries of the church, both local and abroad. Then various church officers and members of the church, along with Spurgeon, led in prayer for those items. The congregation participated in these prayers, voicing their amens.

Additionally, several hundred in the congregation met prior to the Thursday night service for prayer devoted to their pastor,[70] and another group held a morning prayer meeting during the week.[71] Spurgeon believed that "his success had been due under God to the prayers of his Church. No mere preaching could do what had been done, but it was the prayer which had done it."[72] For all the conversions and ministries that flowed out of the Metropolitan Tabernacle, Spurgeon believed this to be the work of God through the faithful prayers of the congregation.

---

68. *MTP* 18:95-96.

69. *MTP* 7:366.

70. "Every Thursday night, before the service, there is a prayer-meeting at 6 o'clock, in which a few friends gather specially to pray that their Pastor may be helped to preach; and tonight I suppose there were three or four hundred gathered together with that object, and it is real praying, let me tell you—short, deep, earnest cries to God for a blessing; and the preacher cannot help preaching when he is prayed for like that." *MTP* 46:443.

71. "There were two or three things which had made that Church strong. One of these was its prayerfulness. A morning prayer-meeting had been established some four or five years ago as the result of a sermon which he preached, and it was still continued, and he hoped it would never be given up." *MTP* 7:261.

72. Ibid.

Congregational Singing

"Soldiers march best to battle when the trumpet and drum excite them with enlivening strains…. it is an excellent thing when Christian men know how to sing as well as to work, and mingle holy music with holy service."[73] A Christian's song was not only a declaration of praise to God but also something that strengthened and enlivened him towards action. Spurgeon saw his church not only as an army, but as a singing army.[74]

As the pastor, Spurgeon planned all the congregational singing. He arrived early before the service and selected the hymns,[75] working with the precentor, or song leader, on which tunes would be best adapted to them and to the congregation's singing.[76] The precentor stood on the platform and held a staff that helped the congregation to sing together, in tempo. As one on the platform, with a prominent leadership position, the precentor had to be a member of the church who was "unimpeachable in character."[77]

The singing at the Metropolitan Tabernacle was performed without any instrumentation.[78] Before each hymn, Spurgeon would sometimes read through the entire hymn, so that the congregation could consider what they were about to sing and

---

73. *MTP* 16:69.

74. *MTP* 51:85.

75. *Autobiography* 4:70-71.

76. The hymns were printed without tunes, only the lyrics. The congregation learned the tunes separately from the hymns. "The tunes used at the Tabernacle are chiefly taken from the 'Union Tune Book.' A few come from the 'Bristol Tune Book,' and three or four from 'Hymns Ancient and Modern.' A new tune is not introduced unless it has become popular in the schools and classes connected with the place; then it is tried in the service, and if it goes well it is permanently placed on the list, if not, it is dropped at once." J. Spencer Curwen, *Studies in Worship-Music, Chiefly as Regards Congregational Singing* (London: J. Curwen & Sons, 1880), 208.

77. On one occasion, William Hale was under investigation for church discipline, and as a result he was not allowed to serve as precentor any longer. "Our Pastor however informed the meeting that he would not be allowed to conduct the singing again, since it was of the utmost importance that a person in so prominent a position should be unimpeachable in character." "Church Meeting March 9th, 1863," *MB 1861-1866*.

78. "The first hymn was sung with a will. No chanting or piping organ, no choir to attract attention, but one grand purpose to glorify our Christ." Fulton, *Spurgeon Our Ally*, 200.

sing intelligently.[79] On one occasion, a visitor claims to have been converted listening to Spurgeon line out Wesley's hymn, "Jesus, Lover of My Soul."[80] Then, following the precentor, the congregation would rise to sing their praises to God, "as only a Tabernacle audience of six thousand people could sing it."[81] One writer visiting in 1880 gives the following report:

> As the people stood up the precentor advanced from the back of the platform and started the melody with a clear voice. Like a giant that needs a moment to arouse himself the congregation allowed a note or two to pass before they entered in full strength. Then the heavy tide of sound streamed forth from every part of the building. Many churches have more cultivated congregational singing than Mr. Spurgeon's, but, from the numbers engaged, no other singing touches the heart with such an indefinable pleasure, and makes the frame glow with such a sense of worshipful sympathy.[82]

To aid in the singing, Spurgeon provided his church with their own hymn book. Prior to 1866, the church used two different hymnals, "Dr. Rippon's Selection" and "Dr. Watts' Psalms and Hymns." However, watching visitors fumble with multiple hymnals, Spurgeon decided that the church needed their own. For many Christians in the nineteenth century, the church hymnbook was "the only book of divinity with which they were acquainted."[83] Knowing this, in 1866 Spurgeon himself compiled a hymnal, *Our Own Hymn Book*, seeking to give expression to the church's theological convictions and priorities.[84] Demonstrating his belief

---

79. "But why should the hymns be read twice through? It may help some illiterate people to understand the words, and Mr. Spurgeon's energetic reading may infuse the devotional spirit of the poet among the congregation; but nearly all the hymns are so well known, that these considerations must be of little practical worth." Curwen, *Studies in Worship-Music*, 209.

80. *Autobiography* 4:33.

81. *Autobiography* 4:22.

82. Curwen, *Studies in Worship-Music*, 208.

83. J. H. Y. Briggs, *The English Baptists of the 19th Century* (Didcot, UK: The Baptist Historical Society, 1994), 36-37.

84. C. H. Spurgeon, *Our Own Hymn Book: A Collection of Psalms and Hymns for Public, Social, and Private Worship* (London: Passmore and Alabaster, 1869).

in the universal church, Spurgeon drew widely, both in terms of geography and church tradition.[85] These hymns contained a wide range of theological subjects, as well as a variety of moods and tones, from joyful praise to penitential songs.[86] In particular, Spurgeon highlighted four distinctives in this hymnal: first, the use of the original works of the authors, as much as possible, as opposed to abridgements or edited works; second, hymns that addressed overlooked theological doctrines, like the doctrines of sovereign grace, or the personal return of Christ; third, hymns suitable for particular events in the life of the church,[87] such as seasons of spiritual revival or prayer meetings; and fourth, the psalms of David.[88]

While Spurgeon prioritized the content of what was sung, he was also concerned that the hymns all be "in forms suitable for congregational singing."[89] In other words, it was not enough for a hymn to be theologically correct. The congregation had to be able to sing it. Writing to the various song leaders, Spurgeon reminds them:

> O sweet singer of Israel, remember that the song is not for your glory, but for the honor of the Lord, who inhabiteth the praises of Israel; therefore, select not anthems and tunes in which your skilfulness will be manifest, but such as will aid the people to magnify the Lord with their thanksgivings. The people come together not to see you as a songster, but to praise the Lord in

---

85. "The area of our researches has been as wide as the bounds of existing religious literature, American and British, Protestant and Romish, ancient and modern. Whatever may be thought of our taste we have used it without prejudice; and a good hymn has not been rejected because of the character of its author, or the heresies of the church in whose hymnal it first occurred; so long as the language and the spirit commended the hymn to our heart we included it, and believe that we have enriched our collection thereby." C. H. Spurgeon, *Our Own Hymn Book*, vi-vii.

86. Spurgeon emphasized the need to have a variety of songs and tunes which Christians can sing in all seasons of life. "Remember, beloved, that the same Savior, who will accept the joyful shoutings of the strong, will also receive the plaintive notes of the weak and weeping." *MTP* 52:176.

87. A majority of the hymns that Spurgeon composed were written for important occasions in the life of the church, including baptisms, communion, and the calling of church officers.

88. Spurgeon, *Our Own Hymn Book*, viii-ix.

89. Ibid., ix.

the beauty of holiness. Remember also, that you are not set to sing for yourself only, but to be a leader of others, many of whom know nothing of music; therefore, choose such tunes as can be learned and followed by all, that none in the assembly may be compelled to be silent while the Lord is extolled.[90]

To facilitate congregational singing, the precentor should pick tunes appropriate to the words and containing thoughtful variety. Music was not in itself spiritual. However, spiritual praise could be given "suitable embodiment" through the appropriate use of music. In leading the congregation, the precentor should also pay attention to the tempo, not dragging a song that needs energy, nor treating a solemn hymn as a jig. "Be wise enough to strike the fitting pace each time, and by your vigorous leadership inspire the congregation to follow *en masse*." Spurgeon also encouraged song leaders to train the congregation to sing, providing classes for young and old to learn how to read musical notation and memorize some tunes. In all this, "one of your great objects should be to induce all the congregation to join in the singing."[91]

The priority of congregational singing is why Spurgeon refused to use instrumentation. Many churches had resorted to using instruments to help the singing, but Spurgeon believed this only weakened the singing. He preferred the sound of human voices to any instrument:

> As for instrumental music, I fear that it often destroys the singing of the congregation, and detracts from the spirituality and simplicity of worship. If I could crowd a house twenty times as big as this by the fine music which some churches delight in, God forbid I should touch it.[92]

Some churches also resorted to using choirs or special singers to enhance or even replace congregational singing, but Spurgeon rejected this practice. Not all church members were skilled singers, but he believed that the most important factor

---

90. *S&T* 1870:277.

91. *S&T* 1870:277-78.

92. *MTP* 14:141.

in a congregation's singing was not their musical skill, but their hearts.[93]

The Ministry of the Word

The Reformed tradition placed the greatest emphasis in corporate worship on the ministry of the Word. Spurgeon shared this priority and taught his students that preaching was the pastor's most important battle: "Often have I said to my brethren that the pulpit is the Thermopylae of Christendom: there the fight will be lost or won. To us ministers the maintenance of our power in the pulpit should be our great concern, we must occupy that spiritual watch-tower with our hearts and minds awake and in full vigor."[94] Spurgeon believed that it was the faithful and Spirit-filled preaching of the Word week after week in churches throughout the land that defeated error and preserved the unity of the church.[95]

The services at the Tabernacle would typically have two forms of the ministry of the Word. The first was the Scripture reading combined with comments, also known as Scripture expositions. Here, Spurgeon would read from a longer passage of Scripture, usually a chapter, which was in some way connected to his sermon text. As he read, he would provide commentary at the end of the paragraph, but only as needed to help his people understand the

---

93. "If you cannot sing artistically, never mind, you will be right enough if you sing from the heart, and pay attention to it, and do not drawl out like a musical machine that has been set therefore runs on mechanically. With a little care the heart brings the art, and the heart desiring to praise will by-and-by train the voice to time and tune." *MTP* 14:141. Curwen's critique of the singing at the Metropolitan Tabernacle was that it was largely untrained, though he did commend the congregation for their religious and spiritual singing. See Curwen, *Studies in Worship-Music*, 209-10.

94. *Lectures* 2:146.

95. "The chief business of a captain is to know how to handle his vessel, nothing can compensate for deficiency there, and so our pulpits must be our main care, or all will go awry. Dogs often fight because the supply of bones is scanty, and congregations frequently quarrel because they do not get sufficient spiritual meat to keep them happy and peaceful. The ostensible ground of dissatisfaction may be something else, but nine times out of ten deficiency in their rations is at the bottom of the mutinies which occur in our churches." Ibid.

passage.[96] The goal of this practice was to expose his people to the wider context of Scripture. Apart from a Christian's responsibility for Bible study, Spurgeon believed it was the pastor's responsibility to teach his congregation how to read their Bibles in context.

> The present plan of preaching from short texts, together with the great neglect of commenting publicly upon the Word is very unsatisfactory. We cannot expect to deliver much of the teaching of Holy Scripture by picking out verse by verse, and holding these up at random.[97]

Therefore, while Spurgeon typically preached on shorter texts, he saw his preaching and the Scripture expositions as working together. The expositions taught his people about the importance of biblical context when studying any passage. By implementing the regular practice of Scripture reading and commentary, Spurgeon believed that the people could continue to grow in their understanding of Scripture, even while he adopted varied preaching forms.[98]

Spurgeon instructed his students to read from both the Old and New Testaments, and not to avoid difficult passages. "We must make sure in our public expositions that obscure and involved sentences are explained. To overleap difficulties, and only expound what is already clear, is to make commenting

---

96. "When reading short psalms, or connected passages of the other books, do not split up the author's utterances by interjecting your notes. Read the paragraph through, and then go over it again with your explanations; breaking it up as you may think fit at the second reading. No one would dream of dividing a stanza of a poet with an explanatory remark; it would be treason to common sense to do so: sound judgment will forbid your thus marring the word of God. Better far never to comment than to cut and carve the utterances of inspiration, and obscure their meaning by impertinently thrusting in untimely remarks of your own." *Lectures* 4:31.

97. Ibid., 22. Spurgeon continues: "It would be an astounding absurdity if our friends used our private letters in this fashion, and interpreted them by short sentences disconnected and taken away from the context. Such expositors would make us out to say in every letter all we ever thought of, and a great many things besides far enough from our minds; while the real intent of our epistles would probably escape attention." Ibid.

98. "Since topical preaching, hortatory preaching, experimental preaching, and so on—all exceedingly useful in their way—have almost pushed proper expository preaching out of place, there is the more need that we should, when we read passages of Holy Writ, habitually give running comments upon them." *Lectures* 4:22.

ridiculous."[99] The passages which troubled them were likely also the ones that troubled the congregation and the pastor had to be ready to explain those difficulties. At the same time, commenting should not become a mere academic exercise. Rather, the pastor should apply the Scripture text to his hearers. "The chief part of your commenting, however, should consist in applying the truth to the hearts of your hearers... it is of little service to supply men with information unless we urge upon them the practical inferences therefrom."[100]

In modeling regular Scripture reading and commenting, Spurgeon believed that the pastor not only taught his people the Scriptures but trained them in how to read their Bibles for themselves. Therefore, he warned his students about fanciful interpretations or novel theologies drawn from one solitary text. Scripture had to be read in light of the rest of Scripture. Though his students were trained in Hebrew and Greek, he warned them against needlessly amending the Authorized Version translation. "It is unwise to be making every old lady distrust the only Bible she can get at, or what is more likely, mistrust you for falling out with her cherished treasure. Correct where correction must be for truth's sake, but never for the vainglorious display of your critical ability."[101] The corporate Scripture reading was never meant to be a replacement for personal Bible reading, but rather to equip the people to read their Bibles for themselves.[102]

The main form of the ministry of the Word, however, was the sermon. Spurgeon believed that the sermon was the climax of the service. Responding to those who would pit the other elements of the service against preaching, Spurgeon responded:

> If the observation be meant to imply that the hearing of sermons is not worshipping God, it is founded on a gross mistake, for

---

99. Ibid., 28.

100. Ibid., 29.

101. *Lectures* 4:31.

102. To aid in family worship and private devotions, Spurgeon published *The Interpreter*, which is a running commentary on the entire Bible. See C. H. Spurgeon, *The Interpreter, or, Scripture for Family Worship: Being Selected Passages of the Word of God for Every Morning and Evening Throughout the year, Accompanied by a Running Comment and Suitable Hymns* (London: Passmore & Alabaster, n.d.).

rightly to listen to the gospel is one of the noblest parts of the adoration of the Most High. It is a mental exercise, when rightly performed, in which all the faculties of the spiritual man are called into devotional action.[103]

Spurgeon typically preached for forty-five minutes.[104] He normally only preached on a verse or two, and his goal in the sermon was to exposit that text of Scripture. Spurgeon typically avoided topical sermons. Speaking to his students, Spurgeon commended expositional preaching:

> Brethren, if you are in the habit of keeping to the precise sense of the Scripture before you, I will further recommend you to hold to the *ipsissima verba*, the very words of the Holy Ghost; for, although in many cases topical sermons are not only allowable, but very proper, those sermons which expound the exact words of the Holy Spirit are the most useful and the most agreeable to the major part of our congregations. They love to have the words themselves explained and expounded.[105]

At the same time, some sermons tended to be more devotional, especially on Sunday evenings or Monday nights. In those sermons, Spurgeon might use a text to launch into a devotional meditation on a related subject. Even so, Spurgeon was careful to briefly explain the text in its original context, before transitioning to his meditation.

The goal of Spurgeon's preaching was to communicate the meaning of God's Word to his congregation. He rejected any use of rhetoric which made the plain meaning of Scripture more confusing. Rather, his practice and instruction to his students were to preach in such a way "that the people may not merely hear, but know" God's Word for themselves.[106] At the same time, sermons should not be simplistic or shallow. Rather, the whole counsel of Scripture was to be preached including God's sovereignty and

---

103.   *Lectures* 1:53.

104.   *S&T* 1872:150.

105.   *Lectures* 1:75-76.

106.   Ibid., 72. The majority of Spurgeon's *Lectures to my Students* are instructions for communicating God's Word clearly and powerfully, through illustrations, anecdotes, the proper use of the voice, the use of commentaries, and more.

the doctrines of Calvinism. However, these doctrines should not merely be preached as theological abstractions, but once again, the preacher's task was to connect and apply these doctrines to the lives of the people.[107]

Spurgeon understood that preaching alone was not sufficient to accomplish anything. Only the Holy Spirit was the effectual cause for any spiritual life and blessing. However, in God's sovereignty, preaching was the appointed instrumental cause that the Holy Spirit used to accomplish his purposes.[108] This was true when it came to the salvation of the lost. The preaching of the gospel was God's "ordained means for the gathering in of the elect."[109] Therefore, Spurgeon believed that every sermon needed to proclaim the message of salvation in Jesus Christ and call people to repentance and faith in him. There was no shortage of preaching in Spurgeon's day, and yet he lamented how little gospel there was in so many sermons.[110] Apart from gospel preaching, the lost would not be saved.

Yet preaching was not only for the unconverted. It was also how the Holy Spirit awakened God's people.[111] Preaching mobilized the congregation for action.

> The great weapon of the Christian religion has been the public preaching of the Word, nor would I disparage it, but it will never evangelise the nations unless there be attendant with it

---

107. "The sublimest views of divine sovereignty have a practical bearing, and are not, as some think, mere metaphysical subtleties; the distinctive utterances of Calvinism have their bearing upon every-day life and ordinary experience, and if you hold such views, or the opposite, you have no dispensation permitting you to conceal your beliefs." Ibid., 77.

108. "But while [the Spirit] is the only actual cause, yet there are instrumental causes; and the main instrumental cause of a great revival must be the bold, faithful, fearless preaching of the truth as it is in Jesus." *NPSP* 4:163.

109. *NPSP* 1:Preface.

110. "It is to be lamented that there are so many who are considered not to be bad preachers who scarcely ever mention Christ's name, and are very loose concerning atonement by his precious blood. You will hear people say they have gone to such and such a chapel, and whatever the sermon might have been about it certainly was not about the gospel. Oh may that cease to be the case! May our pulpits ring with the name of Jesus; may Christ be lifted up, and his precious blood be the daily theme of the ministry!" *MTP* 12:694.

111. *NPSP* 4:163.

a constant reiteration of the truth preached, till it flow through innumerable little conduits into every circle of society.[112]

As the Word awakens people, these people would now "gossip" about the gospel wherever they went, speaking it to their neighbors, sharing it at their workplaces, and proclaiming it in their homes.

> The waking up of Christian life throughout the entire body of the Church of God, and the enlisting of the entire life of the Christian Church in the cause of Christ is an enterprise to be consummated by the individual agency of each, and the general action of all who seek the glory of God and the welfare of man.[113]

Spurgeon envisioned his entire congregation, men, women, and children, awakened to the gospel and enlisted in the service of the cause of Christ, all through the power of the preaching of the Word.

Church Ordinances

Against Roman Catholic teaching, the Reformers taught that Christ commanded only two ordinances: baptism and the Lord's Supper. These were the ordinances that were practiced from the time of the early church and were handed down by the church through the ages. Like the rest of the Protestant world, Spurgeon also held to this view and regularly observed these two ordinances in his local church.

Spurgeon's theological understanding of the ordinances reflects his Reformed tradition. First, he believed that God's Word governed the practice of the ordinances. While Spurgeon believed that faith was central to the right practice of the ordinances, he rejected the spiritualizing of the Quakers, who rejected all outward forms of the ordinances. Rather, it was a matter of obedience to Scripture to use the proper outward forms of the ordinances.[114]

---

112. *MTP* 60:152-53.

113. *MTP* 60:153.

114. "The very fact that the baptism mentioned in the Scripture is a baptism which one man can administer to another, is sufficient to prove that in this baptism

The reason outward forms mattered was because these symbols pointed to theological realities. In his own practice of baptism, Spurgeon immersed exclusively and did not consider pouring or sprinkling a proper act of baptism.[115] One of the more unique features of the new Metropolitan Tabernacle was the massive marble baptistry, still an uncommon sight in most Baptist churches. Likewise, in the Lord's Supper, Spurgeon believed that the Roman Catholic Church's use of an altar, withholding of the cup from the laity, the practice of kneeling, and other such additions turned the Lord's Supper into "an unscriptural celebration."[116] Proper observance of the ordinances meant following the regulative principle and obeying the clear instructions of Scripture.

Second, Spurgeon believed that the ordinances were distinct from salvation. Baptists were often accused of making too much of their understanding of baptism. But Spurgeon believed that if anyone was in danger of making too much of baptism, it was those in the Oxford Movement, who held to baptismal regeneration and the Lord's Supper as a sacrifice. On the contrary, Baptists understood that both baptism and the Lord's Supper was subordinate to the doctrines of salvation. A performance of the ordinances could not save anyone.[117] This distinction can be seen in the Baptist convictions that saving faith must

---

there is some outward, visible, material rite, ceremony, or ordinance which Christian people are to observe. Thus far, with the exception of the Society of Friends, I believe we are all agreed that the ordinance of baptism does imply the use and application of water in some way or other." *MTP* 7:265. This sermon was preached by Hugh Stowell Brown at the Metropolitan Tabernacle as a part of the opening services of the new building in the spring of 1861. Brown's teaching on baptism in this sermon would have been representative of Spurgeon's position.

115. "The majority of Christian people believe that so far as the outward rite is concerned, the conditions of the ordinance are fulfilled when water, in however small a quantity, is poured or sprinkled upon the candidate; we, on the other hand, believe that the outward conditions of the ordinance are not fulfilled unless the candidate be wholly immersed in water." *MTP* 7:265-66.

116. *MTP* 54:409.

117. "The ordinance of baptism is held by us in most thorough and lowly subordination to the Deity of the Lord Jesus Christ, to the work of atonement by his sacrifice and death, to the influence and the indwelling of the Divine Spirit, to the necessity of repentance and of faith, to the importance of a life of personal holiness, and to every other great principle of the holy faith which we profess." *MTP* 7:271-72.

precede baptism.[118] For Spurgeon, the issue in baptism according to Scripture was not age but faith.[119] Baptism was "the outward expression of the inward faith. He who believes in Christ with his heart confesses his faith before God and before the Church of God by being baptized."[120] Those who refused to be baptized should have little reason for confidence in the sincerity of their profession of faith. Similarly, Spurgeon rejected any meritorious approach to the Lord's Supper apart from faith in Christ. Those who did so only brought judgment upon themselves. This is how Spurgeon interpreted Paul's warning not to eat or drink unworthily. "He who shall come to the outward and visible sign of Christ's presence, and shall eat of the bread in order to obtain money by being a member of the church, knowing himself to be a hypocrite, or who shall do it jestingly, trifling with the ordinance; such a person would be eating and drinking unworthily, and he will be condemned."[121]

Finally, Spurgeon believed that by faith, a believer could enjoy spiritual communion with Christ in the ordinances. Against the Roman Catholic understanding of transubstantiation, Spurgeon denied that Christ was "actually present in his flesh and blood" in the elements of the Lord's Supper. Such an understanding denied the real humanity of Christ, seated at the right hand of God.[122] Instead, in the tradition of Calvin and against a bare memorialist view of the Lord's Supper, Spurgeon believed "in the real presence of Christ which is spiritual, and yet certain."[123] By calling it a spiritual presence, Spurgeon did not diminish its reality. Rather, for those who were spiritual, their fellowship with Christ was a

---

118. "First, let me remind you that our Savior's words teach us that baptism follows faith: 'He that believeth and is baptized.' Never neglect the order of things in the Bible." *MTP* 39:605.

119. "And here let me observe that the very common notion that we were in the habit of practicing adult baptism is utterly a mistake. We do not contend for the baptism of adults; we contend for the baptism of believers. Show us a child however young, who believes in Christ, and we gladly accept him." *MTP* 7:266.

120. *MTP* 39:606.

121. *MTP* 54:617.

122. *MTP* 18:85.

123. Spurgeon, *Till He Come*, 149.

spiritual fellowship and they grasped "the true and real presence of Jesus with his people" by faith. One of the few hymns that Spurgeon wrote was a communion hymn celebrating the presence of Christ in the Supper:

Amidst us our Beloved stands,
And bids us view His pierced hands;
Points to His wounded feet and sides,
Blest emblems of the Crucified.

What food luxurious loads the board,
When at His table sits the Lord!
The wine how rich, the bread how sweet,
When Jesus deigns the guests to meet![124]

In many of his Lord's Supper meditations, Spurgeon's repeated theme was communion with Christ, because he wanted to guard his people against merely participating in the outward form while missing out on Christ.[125] Likewise, Spurgeon taught that baptism pictured the believer's union with Christ, both theologically and experientially. In the notice sent out to baptism candidates, the leaders of the church prayed, "May it be a holy and joyful season with you, and may you have much fellowship with the Lord Jesus in his death, burial, and resurrection."[126] Baptism set forth both a representative and a realized union with Christ of the believer, and this was to be lived out in the Christian life.[127] This was, after

---

124. C. H. Spurgeon, *Our Own Hymn Book: A Collection of Psalms and Hymns for Public, Social, and Private Worship* (London: Passmore and Alabaster, 1869), 573.

125. A collection of these communion meditations can be found in C. H. Spurgeon, *"Till He Come": Communion Meditations and Addresses* (Pasadena, TX: Pilgrim, 1971).

126. Baptism Notice, *Spurgeon Memorabilia*, Metropolitan Tabernacle Archives, London.

127. "Baptism sets forth the death, burial, and resurrection of Christ, and our participation therein. Its teaching is twofold. First, think of our representative union with Christ, so that when he died and was buried it was on our behalf, and we were thus buried with him. This will give you the teaching of baptism so far as it sets forth a creed. We declare in baptism that we believe in the death of Jesus, and desire to partake in all the merit of it. But there is a second equally important matter, and that is our realized union with Christ which is set forth in baptism, not so much as a doctrine of our creed as a matter of our experience. There is a manner of dying, or being buried,

all, Spurgeon's own experience of baptism.[128] At the heart of these ordinances was the believer's communion with Christ.[129]

Baptism and the Church

Spurgeon believed that baptism was an ordinance of the church. It was not to be practiced independently, but under the authority of the church. Spurgeon only baptized in the context of the gathering of the church. Baptism services were normally held on Thursday evenings at the Metropolitan Tabernacle. The service opened with prayer, a hymn, and a brief baptismal devotion from the pastor.[130] Then baptism candidates came forward and were baptized by the pastor. With so many joining the church, sometimes there were dozens of baptisms taking place during these services. These baptismal services were public affairs, attended by the congregation of the Metropolitan Tabernacle, as well as visitors and guests. These baptismal services could sometimes bring public scorn, especially from paedobaptist visitors.[131] One Presbyterian paper mocked how filthy the baptismal waters became as more people were baptized.[132] But for these new believers, here was an opportunity for them to identify with Christ unashamedly. "Why, I have seen persons come to the pool of baptism, fearing, shaking,

---

of rising, and of living in Christ which must be displayed in each one of us if we are indeed members of the body of Christ." *MTP* 27:618.

128.   Spurgeon wrote in his diary on May 3, 1850 on the day of his baptism: "Started with Mr. Cantlow at eleven, reached Isleham at one o'clock. In the afternoon, I was privileged to follow my Lord, and to be buried with Him in baptism. Blest pool! Sweet emblem of my death to all the world! May I, henceforward, live alone for Jesus! Accept my body and soul as a poor sacrifice, tie me unto Thee; in Thy strength I now devote myself to Thy service forever; never may I shrink from owning Thy name!" *Autobiography* 1:135.

129.   For a more extensive study of Spurgeon's spirituality in the ordinances, see Morden, *Communion with Christ and His People*, 77-105, 165-89.

130.   For an example of a baptismal devotional given at a baptism service, see "Communion with Christ: A Baptizing Sermon," *MTP* 46:145-52.

131.   "Both these ordinances bring a cross with them to some degree, especially the first. I was noting, when reading the life of good Andrew Fuller, that, after he had been baptized, some of the young men in the village were wont to mock him, asking him how he liked being dipped, and such like questions which are common enough nowadays. I could but notice that the scoff of a hundred years ago is just the scoff of today." *Autobiography* 1:150.

132.   *The British and Foreign Evangelical Review*, Vol. XV, 1866, 204-05.

and trembling: but I have not found it so with the majority of those who have been baptized in this place. They seem proud to own their Master.... I have rejoiced to see the boldness of the young converts, I have heard of them fighting with the antagonists of the truth."[133]

Baptism symbolized the Christian's union, not only with Christ but with his people.[134] Because baptism was the seal of one's covenant with Christ, it also marked a covenant relationship with the church. This relationship was pictured in church membership. Spurgeon always held baptism and church membership together.[135] For a convert to be baptized at the Metropolitan Tabernacle, he first had to go through the membership process. Only after having been interviewed by the elders and approved by the congregation for membership, was a convert eligible for baptism. Spurgeon did not hold formal baptismal classes for those requesting baptism. Rather, the membership process mainly sought to discern whether there was a credible profession of faith. Then, membership in the church brought the needed accountability for that profession. Since baptism and church membership were linked, Spurgeon could say that baptism was "necessary to the very existence of the Church of God."[136] Apart from this public profession of faith, the people of God would remain hidden, and the kingdom of Christ could not advance in this world. But through baptism, the disciples of Christ could be publicly known and bear witness to their King.

Spurgeon rejected the movement among Baptist churches to remove believers' baptism as a prerequisite for church

---

133. *NPSP* 2:75.

134. "We make with God, after conversion, a covenant of gratitude; we come to him sensible of what he has done for us, and we devote ourselves to him. We set our seal to that covenant when in baptism we are united with his church." *NPSP* 5:417.

135. "The gospel commission which we have received is this—'Go ye into all the world and preach the gospel to every creature. He that believeth and is baptised shall be saved.' That is the message as we find it, we did not insert the clause concerning baptism, neither dare we leave it out, or advise you to neglect it. I give you the very words of the Savior. Do not, therefore, divide the gospel command in order to throw half of it behind your back, but both believe and avow your belief, and be added to the church." *MTP* 20:208.

136. *MTP* 39:607.

membership. While Spurgeon allowed paedobaptist visitors to partake of the Lord's Table (open communion), he remained strict on believer's baptism when it came to church membership (strict or closed membership). In 1867, Spurgeon responded through an article in *The Sword and the Trowel* to the movement within the Congregational Union to create a new union of Baptist and Congregationalist churches (called "Union Churches"), which refused to divide over the issue of baptism and church membership. These churches would be able to accept into membership both paedobaptists and credobaptists alike, allowing each member to adopt their own understanding of baptism. Spurgeon believed such a scheme to be "traitorous to Christ and his Word." For the sake of greater size and influence, open membership compromised the church's obedience to Christ's commands.[137] Though they still held to the primary articles of the faith, Spurgeon was concerned that such an attitude towards clear commands from God's Word would be "merely the beginning of the end, a stepping-stone to something more." If pastors were willing to ignore these commands about the church, then it was only a matter of time before they would also begin to compromise the gospel. Though these open membership Baptist churches saw growth in numbers, Spurgeon believed they "were eating out the very vitals of the denomination... and [were] its real weakness."[138] In this compromise, they lost the distinctiveness of what it meant to be a Baptist church.

The Lord's Supper and the Church

Spurgeon also had a strong corporate understanding of the Lord's Supper. The primary context in which Spurgeon observed the Lord's Supper was in the gathering of the church. When he first arrived at the New Park Street Chapel, the congregation observed the Lord's Supper on the first Sunday of the month, at the conclusion of a Sunday evening service. Over time, the congregation would increase that practice to twice a month, and then eventually to a weekly observance. In the element of the

---

137. *S&T* 1867:326.

138. *MTP* 7:260.

loaf,[139] in the use of a table,[140] in the acts of giving and receiving,[141] the Lord's Supper was filled with symbols of the church's unity and fellowship with one another. In his sermon, "Christ and his Table Companions," Spurgeon reminded his congregation that the table symbolized their equality in the church and the rejection of any clericalism. More than that, table fellowship indicated their faithfulness to one another, brotherly affection, and confidence in each other's sincerity. Here was a picture of the spiritual reality that the church was a family gathered around the family table for a spiritual meal.[142] As an expression of their unity and care for one another, the church often took up a benevolence offering after communion to care for the poor in their midst.[143] At the conclusion of their celebration, following the example of Christ and the disciples, the church often sang a hymn, yet another picture of their unity in Christ.[144]

While Spurgeon believed that the proper, and perhaps even primary, context for the Lord's Supper was the local church, he also believed it was an ordinance of the universal church. He believed that genuine Christians existed outside of his local church and beyond his Baptist denomination, and that through Christ, in the universal church, they also participated in spiritual communion with one another. This affected Spurgeon's practice of the Lord's Supper in two ways.

First, Spurgeon practiced open communion, meaning he allowed members of paedobaptist churches, who had not been baptized upon their profession of faith, to participate in the Lord's Supper. Though the New Park Street Chapel had practiced

---

139. "The word 'loaf' helps to bring out more clearly the idea of unity intended to be set forth by the apostle." *MTP* 58:145.

140. "For what expresses fellowship better than surrounding a table, and eating and drinking together?" *MTP* 54:409.

141. Spurgeon, *Till He Come*, 118-19.

142. *MTP* 54:409.

143. "Indeed, at the Lord's supper, which is the embodiment of communion, we have ever been wont to make a special contribution for the poor of the flock, and we believe that in the collection there is as true and real an element of communion as in the partaking of the bread and wine." Spurgeon, *Till He Come*, 118.

144. *MTP* 52:176-177.

strict communion from their earliest days, in 1839, under the leadership of Joseph Angus, the congregation adopted open communion as their practice.[145] Prior to his pastoral calling to that church,[146] Spurgeon wrote to his father telling them of their open communion practice and confiding that he was "not quite settled about it."[147] However, by the time Spurgeon was settled into the pastorate at New Park Street, he was settled in his open communion position.

His primary reasoning for this practice was simply his belief that the universal church was broader than his credobaptist convictions. In the sermon "The Holy Spirit and the One Church," Spurgeon declared:

> At the Lord's table I always invite all Churches to come and sit down and commune with us. If any man were to tell me that I am separate from the Episcopalian, the Presbyterian, or the Methodist, I would tell him he did not know me, for I love them with a pure heart fervently, and I am not separate from them. I may hold different views from them, and in that point truly I may be said to be separate; but I am not separate in heart, I will work with them—I will work with them heartily.... Oh, how my heart loves the doctrine of the one church. The nearer I get to my Master in prayer and communion, the closer am I knit to all his

145. Annual Church Meeting Minutes January 17, 1839, *Church Meeting Minutes 1808–1854 Tooley Street & Carter Lane*. Metropolitan Tabernacle Archives, London. The motion is recorded thus: "It is Resolved that this Church will hereafter admit to the Communion of the Lord's Supper persons professing repentance towards God and faith in & obedience to our Lord Jesus Christ although such persons may not have been baptized by immersion." The vote passed 45-27 after much discussion.

146. It's not clear what Spurgeon's communion practice at Waterbeach would have been. Spurgeon's account shows that the church was influenced by the hyper-Calvinism of the East Anglia Baptists (see *Autobiography* 1:258) and those churches practiced strict-communion. But Spurgeon was previously a member of St. Andrew's Baptist Church which practiced open communion. Unfortunately, no records remain of Waterbeach's communion practice in those days.

147. "They are open communion Baptists but like myself they do not admit unbaptized persons into the Church, but only allow members of Paedobaptist churches to sit down at the Lord's table. – This may be right or wrong. Some of them like the Strict way best & I am sure I never quarrel with them for I think they have quite as much Scripture on their side as the open ones. I seldom bring up the question for it is a knotty one but I see they are like me not quite settled about it." *C.H. Spurgeon – Letters to his Father and Mother – 1850-84*. Spurgeon Collection, Regent's Park College, Oxford.

disciples. The more I see of my own errors and failings, the more ready am I to deal gently with them that I believe to be erring. The pulse of Christ's body is communion; and woe to the church that seeks to cure the ills of Christ's body by stopping its pulse. I think it sin to refuse to commune with anyone who is a member of the Church of our Lord Jesus Christ.[148]

Spurgeon so identified the fellowship of the Lord's Supper with the spiritual communion that exists among believers that he feared barring a true believer more than any risks associated with admitting the unbaptized.[149] However, in saying this, Spurgeon was not careless about those admitted to the table. He still required those paedobaptist visitors to be members of other evangelical churches, where they had been baptized according to their understanding and were members in good standing.[150] All such visitors were welcome to participate in the Lord's Supper with his congregation, provided that they had previously been interviewed by one of the elders and received a ticket that granted them temporary access to the Table.[151]

---

148. *NPSP* 4:23-24.

149. "Dear to our hearts is that great article of the Nicene Creed, the 'Communion of Saints.' I believe not in the communion of Episcopalians. I do not believe in the communion of Baptists. I dare not sit with them exclusively. I think I should be almost strict communicant enough not to sit with them at all, because I should say, 'This is not the communion of saints, it is the communion of Baptists.' Whosoever loves the Lord Jesus Christ in verity and truth hath a hearty welcome, and is not only permitted, but invited to communion with the Church of Christ." *NPSP* 5:353.

150. While Spurgeon did not require believers' baptism for participation in the Lord's Supper at his church, he did teach that baptism (however one understood it from the Bible), and therefore church membership, was a prerequisite to the Lord's Supper. See *Autobiography* 1:148.

151. In August of 1856, the congregation at the New Park Street Chapel passed the following motion:
It having been reported to our Pastor and the Deacons that certain unworthy persons having partaken of the Lord's Supper without their knowledge and consent, and that others whom they believe to be Christians but still are walking disorderly by not joining a Christian Church have also been partakers in this divine ordinance.
To prevent therefore such unworthy persons from approaching the Lord's Table; and also to discountenance any disorderly conduct in Christians the following resolutions were unanimously agreed to:
1st, That tickets be given to all individuals who enjoy trans-communion with us
2nd, These tickets to be collected before the Lord's Supper with those of the Members

Second, Spurgeon did not limit his practice of the Lord's Supper only to the local church but was willing to practice it in other contexts. He regularly took the Lord's Supper in smaller settings with his elders, or other groups in the church and encouraged the members of his church to do the same. He also participated in communion services with ministers of other churches during meetings of the London Baptist Association. This practice of private communion can be seen particularly in Spurgeon's practice of the Lord's Supper in his gatherings in Mentone, France. Spurgeon regularly spent extended time away in the warm climate of Mentone during the winter season and to recuperate his health. Over time, a group of believers gathered around him from various denominational backgrounds, and Spurgeon led them in worship services, including the celebration of the Lord's Supper. Spurgeon never individualized the Lord's Supper but always emphasized the corporate realities of the Lord's Supper and their common fellowship in Christ.[152] Nonetheless, Spurgeon recognized that this gathering of believers was not a local church. Instead, once again, he appealed to the universal church:

> We hear much discourse upon "the Unity of the Church" as a thing to be desired, and we may heartily agree with it; but it would be well also to remember that in the true Church of Christ real union already exists. Our Lord prayed for those whom the Father had given Him, that they might be one, and the Father granted the prayer: the Lord's own people are one. In this room we have an example of how closely we are united in Christ. Some of you are more at home in this assembly, taken out of all churches, than you are in the churches to which you nominally belong. Our union in one body as Episcopalians, Baptists, Presbyterians, or Independents, is not the thing which our Lord prayed for; but our union in Himself. That union we do at this moment enjoy; and therefore do we eat of one bread,

3rd, That no person receive more than three consecutive monthly tickets but to be questioned as to the rightness of their position and dealt with accordingly

See Monthly Church Meeting August 13th, 1856, *Church Minute Minutes 1854–1861 New Park Street*. Metropolitan Tabernacle Archives, London.

152. Spurgeon, *Till He Come*, 112.

and drink of one cup, and are baptized into one Spirit, at His feet who is to each one of us, and so to all of us, altogether lovely.[153]

Even though these various friends formally belonged to other local churches (though some nominally), Spurgeon believed that they were united "in the true Church of Christ." Presumably, Spurgeon personally knew every single person in the room in these intimate gatherings and could vouch for the credibility of their profession of faith. Therefore, he believed that the Lord's Supper was a fitting expression of their union in the universal church.

Does this practice of private communion (i.e. communion apart from the gathering of the church) reveal a decline in Spurgeon's ecclesiology? Certainly, it was out of step with his Reformed tradition, which always tied the Lord's Supper with the discipline and gathering of the local church. In his practice of open communion, Spurgeon continued to tie the ordinances to the local church by requiring membership in good standing in an evangelical church. But in his practice of private communion, those links were seemingly severed. Spurgeon's appeal to the universal church was a noble attempt to bring theological justification to his practice. But in the end, it represents a significant departure from Reformed practice. Such a practice pits the reality of the universal church against the discipline and authority given to the local church. It also confuses the covenant meal associated with the universal church. The Lord's Supper is the covenant meal, not of the universal church, but of the local church. On that final day, when Christ returns and the universal church gathers for the very first time, we will feast with him, not a symbolic meal of bread and wine, but in the wedding banquet of the Lamb.

Conclusion

The previous two chapters have presented Spurgeon's ecclesiology, rooted in the Reformed tradition and shaped by his vision of the church militant. Spurgeon never published a manual of church polity or a systematic ecclesiology, as some of his predecessors

---

153. Ibid., 113.

had.[154] Nonetheless, when one surveys his vast body of published work and how much of it was focused on the doctrine of the church, it exceeds the writings of his predecessors. Spurgeon held to a reformed ecclesiology, which manifested itself throughout his preaching and ministry. Though his main passion was always to preach the message of salvation in Jesus Christ, he believed that the church was Christ's bride. Therefore, he also loved to preach about the church.

The martial image of the church affected how Spurgeon ordered his church. He believed that Christ's reign over the church was best displayed through its obedience to his Word. Christ was the church's King and Captain, and his rule was expressed through his Word. Spurgeon grounded the identity of the church in its understanding of the gospel and required this theological unity in all the members of his church. Likewise, the worship of the church was to be ordered by the instructions of its Captain. Holding to the regulative principle of the Reformed tradition, Spurgeon only allowed in the worship of the church what was expressly commanded in Scripture. Through the preaching of the Word, the ordinances, the songs, and the prayers of the church, the congregation of the Metropolitan Tabernacle was strengthened and mobilized for service in the city of London and throughout the world.

Spurgeon's Reformed heritage shaped his understanding of the church, preserving both a clear distinction and connection between the gospel and the church. Salvation existed apart from the church. At the same time, the church upheld and defended the gospel. Therefore, the church was not to be ordered by human imagination, but by the Word of God. This was true not only to the church's public worship, but also to its polity. Spurgeon's approach to church membership, authority, and discipline stood within his Baptist tradition. Yet for Spurgeon, this polity was also colored by his view of the church militant. The church, the army

---

154. For example, see Benjamin Keach, "The Glory of a True Church and its Discipline Displayed (1697)," in *Polity*, ed. Mark Dever (Washington DC: Nine Marks Ministries, 2001), 63-91, and John Gill, *A Complete Body of Doctrinal and Practical Divinity; or, a System of Evangelical Truths, Deduced from the Sacred Scriptures,* Vol. III (London: W. Winterbotham, 1796).

of God, should "follow the New Testament church order" so that God's people might be "fully armed, and drilled, and trained... to wage war for King Jesus."[155] It is to Spurgeon's approach to church order that we turn to next.

---

155. *MTP* 50:249.

6

Regenerate Church Membership

Spurgeon had accepted an invitation to speak at a meeting of Welsh churches in London held on October 17, 1866. Due to the industrial revolution, there had been a steady flow of Welsh immigrants into urban centers like London, and the number of Welsh-speaking churches were growing throughout the city. Spurgeon had an affection for the Welsh. He himself had preached in Wales to crowds of tens of thousands during his fundraising campaigns for the Metropolitan Tabernacle. He loved the stories of the Welsh revival that took place in the previous century. He admired preachers like Christmas Evans and others who preached with "Welsh fire." Though he could not speak the dialect, Spurgeon thought it sounded so beautiful that "it must have been the language of Paradise."

But on this occasion, while he spoke on the importance of preaching in the life of the church, Spurgeon concluded his address with a heartfelt plea: a greater attention to membership and discipline.

> May I ask you, with the deepest affection and respect, to see as much as ever you can to the discipline of the Church? We do not complain of our churches as they might exist, but we have to complain that sometimes Welshmen in London are very different from Welshmen among the hills; that, although they may be very useful members of their own churches, they do succumb very terribly to the temptations of London. Whether or not this indicates that there must be some of them unconverted,

or whether they are simply backsliders, I leave to my brethren to judge. But we must be very scrupulous about our membership.[1]

With the city came all kinds of new temptations, and the Welshmen had acquired something of a reputation for drunkenness and other vices. Though these Welsh-speaking churches became an important source of community for new immigrants, Spurgeon did not want them to compromise their Christian identity simply for their shared Welsh culture. Rather, he urged these believers to maintain the discipline of their churches by working for a regenerate church membership, that is, admitting only those who were converted and excommunicating any who were backsliding. Even for immigrant churches, insofar as they were a true church of Jesus Christ, it was true conversion that ultimately mattered, not any cultural or ethnic identity.

Spurgeon knew this was not an easy rebuke to hear. But he also believed that the health and witness of the Welsh churches, and all other churches, depended on their faithfulness in this matter. In his own congregation, amid all his other responsibilities, Spurgeon labored to live out his conviction that the church should be a regenerate body, made up only of believers. It is this important conviction that we will now consider.

Baptist Polity and Regenerate Church Membership

Spurgeon traced his theological heritage back to Calvin and the Reformed tradition. At the same time, he was a Baptist, holding to believer's baptism. Though the Reformed tradition embraced paedobaptism, the tradition itself also taught about the rule of Christ in the church through his Word. Therefore, each congregation had to order itself ultimately according to Christ's Word, even when it conflicted with church tradition. Influenced by Anabaptist thought,[2] and beginning in the late sixteenth century,

---

1. G. H. Pike, *The Life and Work of Charles Haddon Spurgeon*, Vol. 3 (London: Cassell & Company Ltd, 1892), 182.

2. The Anabaptists' convictions on regenerate church membership and congregational polity can be found particularly in their teaching on baptism, church discipline, and the pastorate. For example, see The Schleitheim Confession of 1527, John H. Leith, ed., *Creeds of the Churches: A Reader in Christian Doctrine from the Bible to the Present*, 3rd ed. (Louisville, KY: John Knox Press, 1982), 284-87; Walter

some English Separatists began to examine the issue of baptism and, over time, adopted believer's baptism. These early Baptists, as they began to be called, were adamant that they were not Anabaptists, but that they stood in the same stream of Reformed theology as the Congregationalist and Presbyterian churches. But their belief in believer's baptism had greater ecclesiological implications than simply the proper subjects of baptism.

From their earliest days, the Baptist practice of believers' baptism led to an understanding of the church that was distinct from other Separatists. Baptists believed that the church should be composed only of believers. Such an understanding can be traced back to John Smyth, whose discovery of believers' baptism led him to the view that "the church of Christ is a company of the faithful; baptized after confession of sin and of faith, endowed with the power of Christ."[3] This conviction meant that churches that practiced infant baptism were corrupted by "the falsity not of their ministry but of their constitution (membership)."[4] As Particular Baptists became established in England in the following decades, they also declared their belief in regenerate church membership. The London Confession of 1644 makes clear that the church is only to receive those who have been "called and separated from the world, by the word and Spirit of God, to the visible profession of faith of the Gospel, being baptized into that faith, and joined to the Lord, and each other, by mutual agreement."[5]

Baptists recognized that no church in this age could be perfectly pure. The existence of indwelling sin meant that there would always be the danger of hypocrisy in the church. Therefore, church discipline took on renewed importance among Baptists. Even so, Baptists understood that this did not change their responsibility to baptize and admit into membership only

Klaassen, ed., *Anabaptism in Outline: Selected Primary Source* (Waterloo, ON: Herald Press, 1981), 101-39, 162-231.

3.   John Smyth, "Short Confession of Faith in XX Articles (1609)," in William Lumpkin, *Baptist Confessions of Faith* (Valley Forge, PA: Judson Press, 1969), 101.

4.   Stephen Wright, *The Early English Baptists, 1603–1649* (Woodbridge, UK: Boydell Press, 2006), 35.

5.   "London Confession, 1644," in Lumpkin, *Baptist Confessions of Faith*, 165.

those who gave evidence of a credible profession of faith. The Second London Confession, published in 1677, puts it this way: "The Members of these Churches are Saints by calling, visibly manifesting and evidencing (in and by their profession and walking) their obedience unto that call of Christ."[6] As a result of this conviction, Baptist churches not only practiced believer's baptism, but they took their membership practices seriously, implementing church covenants, membership interviews, regular church meetings, pastoral accountability, and more.

Church Membership in England in the Nineteenth Century

As we have already seen, however, by the nineteenth century, many of these ecclesiological convictions were falling away. But that's not to say that Christianity was in decline. Though secularism grew significantly throughout Victorian England, statistics also show a rise in church-attendance and involvement during that period.[7] However, as Spurgeon observed the religious expansion of his day, he found little encouragement. Writing in 1856, he stated:

> In going up and down this land, I am obliged to come to this conclusion, that throughout the churches there are multitudes who have "a name to live and are dead." Religion has become fashionable. The shopkeeper could scarcely succeed in a respectable business if he were not united with a church. It is reckoned to be reputable and honorable to attend a place of worship, and hence men are made religious in shoals.[8]

Spurgeon saw this as a problem, not only in the Church of England, but among Dissenting churches also.[9] In many places, joining the church was simply a matter of applying for membership, without any spiritual examination. In a culture where every English

---

6. Lumpkin, 286. One of the signers of the Second London Confession was Benjamin Keach, pastor of the church at Horsleydown, Southwark, which would eventually become the Metropolitan Tabernacle. Ibid., 239.

7. Owen Chadwick, *The Victorian Church, Pt. 2 1860–1901* (London: SCM Press, 1997), 220-24.

8. *NPSP* 2:113-14.

9. "Take our churches at large—there is no lack of names, but there is a lack of life. Else, how is it that our prayer meetings are so badly attended?" Ibid. 114.

citizen was considered a Christian, people were wary of drawing lines of division or distinction. Therefore, the church growth strategy of his day was simple: minimize the distinction between the church and the world.

> They say, "Do not let us draw any hard and fast lines. A great many good people attend our services who may not be quite decided, but still their opinion should be consulted, and their vote should be taken upon the choice of a minister, and there should be entertainments and amusements, in which they can assist."[10]

Many churches had so lost the practice of church membership that simply attending the church would count one as being a part of that church, even to the point of determining the liturgy or voting on a minister! In such an environment, pastors who attempted to impose any kind of accountability on such "members" would soon find themselves embattled.

> He may do as he pleases; he may sin with impunity; and if his minister should hint to him that his conduct is inconsistent, he will make a storm in the church, and say the minister was personal, and insulted him. Reproof is thrown away upon him. Is he not a member of the church? Has he not been so for years? Who shall dare to say that he is unholy?[11]

Though these churches might see some growth, Spurgeon believed that the loss of regenerate church membership blurred the distinction between the church and the world. They would ultimately lead to the church's downfall, not her prosperity. "The theory seems to be, that it is well to have a broad gangway from the church to the world: if this be carried out, the result will be that the nominal church will use that gangway to go over to the world, but it will not be used in the other direction."[12]

The loss of regenerate church membership would ultimately have theological consequences. With the rise of liberal theology in the church, Spurgeon saw less and less about the church's

---

10. *MTP* 33.212.

11. *NPSP* 2:387.

12. *MTP* 33:212.

beliefs and morality that was distinct from the world.[13] As a result, "many professors play at being Christians; they are not real in their church-membership, not in very deed separate from sinners, or devoted to the service of God."[14] As one pastor lamented to Spurgeon during the height of the Downgrade Controversy, "People are just taken into membership without ever being questioned respecting a spiritual change. It is quite enough that they express a wish to attend the chapel.... You will not be surprised that that church has long ago given up Prayer Meetings."[15] Spurgeon attributed the nominalism of his day to the decline of theological orthodoxy as unconverted members began to question the inspiration of Scripture and the doctrines of sin, eternal punishment, and more. Amid all this decline, Spurgeon was committed to maintaining distinct lines of church membership at the Metropolitan Tabernacle.

Spurgeon's Teaching on Church Membership

Spurgeon rejected the association of a church with a building or an authority structure, maintaining that the church was the assembly of God's people, gathered under the preaching of God's Word and administration of the ordinances. However, any given service drew numerous visitors, coming from all kinds of religious backgrounds. How could he know who belonged to his church? This is what church membership was for: making clear the distinction between the church and the world.

> Touching all the members of this select assembly there is an eternal purpose which is the original reason of their being called, and to each of them there is an effectual calling whereby they actually gather into the church; then, also, there is a hedging

---

13. "A divine of the modern school is of opinion that the lines have faded considerably between what is known as the church and the world, arising from a mutual movement towards each other; we cannot look upon this fact with the complacency which he manifests, but we are compelled to observe and lament it." *S&T* 1873:3.

14. Ibid.

15. "Letter from Rev. W. H. Burton," *Spurgeon Memorabilia*, Metropolitan Tabernacle Archives. Burton notes how many evangelical churches even tolerated Unitarianism among their members.

and fencing about of this church, by which it is maintained as a separate body, distinct from all the rest of mankind.[16]

God's eternal purpose of salvation called people into the universal church. But beyond this, Spurgeon believed that every Christian was also called to "actually gather into the church," by committing themselves to local churches. Then, within each church, there was to be "a hedging and fencing" in the membership of the church, making it "a separate body, distinct from all the rest of mankind."

This theme of being distinct from the world began in the Old Testament, as Israel was given circumcision and other ceremonial laws that distinguished her from the surrounding nations.[17] With the coming of Christ, this distinction from the world was no longer to be found in ethnic Israel, but among Christ's followers, those who had been baptized and partook of the Lord's Supper. Through the ordinances, the church made visible those whom they affirmed to be members of Christ, and thus members of his Body. Church membership was the pattern that the apostles set in the New Testament,[18] and it should be the pattern of discipleship for every Christian. In joining the church, the Christian gives not only of his time, or money, or presence, but he gives of himself to the church. "In the whole force and weight of his influence, personality, and ability, so far as God shall help him, he is to give up to the Church."[19]

Spurgeon was careful not to equate conversion with joining the church. Even while calling his hearers to be baptized and join the church, he warned them that such ceremonies could not save.

> Your admission into the church by infant sprinkling, your admission into the church by confirmation, your admission into the church by the right hand of fellowship, or your admission into the church by believers' immersion, all go for nothing unless you have been admitted into union with Christ. Your sitting at

---

16. *MTP* 24:542.

17. *NPSP* 2:15-16

18. "Now, our text tells us of one old custom in the apostles' days. Those who became Christians first gave themselves to the Lord, and then they gave themselves to the Church, according to God's will." *MTP* 60:289.

19. Ibid., 293.

the Lord's table, your coming often to holy communion, your being found regularly occupying your place in public worship, your joining in the solemn hymn, your bending with others in earnest prayers—these things are all nothing, and less than nothing and mockery, unless your heart has been renewed. Unless you have the Spirit of Christ you are none of his.[20]

At the same time, Spurgeon did not hesitate to hold salvation and church membership closely together.[21] He believed that joining the visible church was an expression of the Christian's participation in the invisible church. In his article, "Confessing Christ" in *The Sword & the Trowel*, Spurgeon reminds his readers, "This spiritual household exists visibly in the world, with an organization to provide for its welfare, look out for its interests, and help on its work. If you are a child of God, you will wish to be recognized as such by entering his visible fold; you will wish to be seen and found there. It is your first and highest duty, as well as privilege."[22]

Spurgeon believed that someone could be a true Christian without joining a church.[23] But such prolonged behavior undermined the existence of visible churches and the importance of the ordinances.[24] Even more, it called into question the genuineness of such a profession of faith.

Now, I know there are some who say "Well, I hope I have given myself to the Lord, but I do not intend to give myself to any church, because ... I can be a Christian without it." Now, are

---

20. *MTP* 15:178.

21. "If you are not born again, if you are not a partaker of the Spirit, if you are not reconciled to God, if your sins be not forgiven, if you are not this day a living member of the living church of Christ, all the curses that are written in this book belong to you, and that part of them in particular which it will be my solemn business to thunder out this morning." *NPSP* 5:442.

22. *S&T* 1873:37.

23. "Oh, if you should look to Jesus this day, it may not be registered in our church-book, and we may not hear of it; but still it will be registered in the courts of heaven, and they will set all the bells of the New Jerusalem a-ringing, and all the harps of angels will take a fresh lease of music as soon as they know that you are born again." *MTP* 54:620.

24. "Well, suppose everybody else did the same, suppose all Christians in the world said, 'I shall not join the Church.' Why there would be no visible Church, there would be no ordinances. That would be a very bad thing, and yet, one doing it—what is right for one is right for all—why should not all of us do it?" *MTP* 60:295.

you quite clear about that? You can be as good a Christian by
disobedience to your Lord's commands as by being obedient?[25]

Through membership in the local church, the invisible church
was made a visible reality in this world, and one's profession of
faith received the affirmation of the church.

If the church was an army, then church membership was how
a Christian enlisted in the fight. To refuse to join a church was
like a "craven... soldier who shirks his proper place on the field
of battle." These soldiers could use all kinds of excuses to explain
why they refused to join the church,[26] but in the end, none of
these excuses justified their refusal to declare their allegiance
to Christ. Spurgeon exhorted his hearers, "Act then according
to your duty, and if you be a Christian, join with Christians; if
you love the Master, love the servants; if you love the Captain,
unite with the army, and join that regiment of it which you
think cleaves closest to the Master's word."[27] Spurgeon's call was
not for Christians to join his church, or even to join a Baptist
church. Rather, he urged them to join a gospel-preaching church
that aligned most closely to their biblical convictions, whether
Presbyterian, Methodist, Independent, Strict Baptist, or any of
the other evangelical churches.

> If you are a Christian, you should unite with other Christians.
> I believe, brethren and sisters, that it is the duty of all converts to
> test the various sections of the professing church by the Word of
> God, and then to cast in their lot with that part which holds the
> truth most fully and clearly; and, having conscientiously done
> that, to rally with the hosts of God in the great battle against

---

25. Ibid.
    "There has been a great deal said in these latter days about being simply a Christian
and not joining any particular church—a piece of cant mostly, and in all cases a
mistake. In the name of unity this system is preached up, and yet it is clear to all that
it is the reverse of unity, and is calculated to put an end to all visible church fellowship."
MTP 20:208.

26. For Spurgeon's answers to objections about church membership, see *MTP*
60:295-98, and *S&T* 1873:37-39.

27. *MTP* 20:208.

wrong. Oh, you converts, who have never joined the church, what are you at?[28]

Spurgeon did not intend people to search endlessly for a perfect church, because no such church existed. Those who were looking for a perfect church must be perfect themselves and should "go to heaven, and join the Church there, for certainly you are not fit to join it on earth, and would be quite out of place."[29] Rather, he called Christians to test churches according to the Word of God and "to cast in their lot" with the group that they believed was most faithful to the biblical model. Only by joining a church did Christians join in "the great battle against wrong." Apart from joining a church, a Christian acted independently as a mercenary.

Duties of Church Membership

Far from simply being a formality or a name on a membership roll, Spurgeon believed that membership in the church brought with it certain duties. More specifically, church membership was bound by a church covenant:

> Some such vow we made, too, when we united ourselves to the church of God. There was an understood compact between us and the church, that we would serve it, that we would seek to honor Christ by holy living, increase the church by propagating the faith, seek its unity, its comfort, by our own love and sympathy with the members. We had no right to join with the church if we did not mean to give ourselves up to it, under Christ, to aid in its prosperity and increase. There was a stipulation made, and a covenant understood, when we entered into communion and league with our brethren in Christ.[30]

Church covenants had been a vital part of Baptist church life since the seventeenth century, "reminding church members of the moral and spiritual duties and privileges to which they had initially committed themselves in uniting with a church."[31]

---

28. *MTP* 50:245.

29. *MTP* 60:296.

30. *MTP* 17:669.

31. Charles W. Deweese, *Baptist Church Covenants* (Nashville, TN: Broadman Press, 1990), 32.

However, by the nineteenth century, their usage had declined among Baptists.[32] This appears to have been the case with the Metropolitan Tabernacle. Their official church covenant was *The Solemn Covenant* (also known as *Keach's Church Covenant*) adopted in 1689.[33] But by Spurgeon's day, this covenant was more of "an understood compact," rather than an explicit and active document. In all of Spurgeon's sermons, writings, and church meeting minutes, there is no reference to the covenant.

Nonetheless, Spurgeon makes clear that the covenant understanding of membership was not lost. In joining the church, each member made a covenant with one another to carry out certain duties. The various commitments Spurgeon lists reflect the vows expressed in *The Solemn Covenant*. Even if the official church covenant was no longer being used in the life of the church, Spurgeon carried on a covenantal understanding of church membership, with its duties and responsibilities.

In his sermon, "Joining the Church," Spurgeon outlined four duties of membership.[34] The first duty was "consistency of character," or holy living.[35] Church membership now meant that Christ's and the church's reputation was attached to the Christian's life. Many in the community would be looking more closely at their conduct and character. "If you make no profession of religion, and live as you like—you shall answer for that at the last great day. But if you join a Christian Church, take heed how you live, for your actions may become doubly watched, and will be doubly sinful if you fall into inconsistency."[36] Those who had

---

32. Ibid., 35-36.

33. Mark E. Dever, ed., *Polity: Biblical Arguments on How to Conduct Church Life* (Washington, DC: Nine Marks Ministries, 2001), 90-91. According to a conversation this author had with Peter Masters in the summer of 2017, the pastor at the Metropolitan Tabernacle, *The Solemn Covenant* continues to be the official covenant of the church.

34. For another sermon where Spurgeon outlines the responsibilities of membership, see "Additions to the Church." *MTP* 20:206-16.

35. Cf. Article 1 of *The Solemn Covenant*, "We do promise and engage to walk in all holiness, godliness, humility, and brotherly love, as much as in us lieth to render our communion delightful to God, comfortable to ourselves, and lovely to the rest of the Lord's people." Dever, *Polity*, 90.

36. *MTP* 60:293.

no interest in changing their moral conduct should not consider joining the church.

The second duty Spurgeon gave was "attendance upon the means of grace."[37] First and foremost, this meant attending corporate worship on Sundays. But in a nominally Christian society, Spurgeon was also particularly concerned that his people gather during the week to pray as a church and sit under the Word together. "Any hypocrite comes on a Sunday, but they do not, to my knowledge, all of them come on Monday to the prayer-meeting, nor all to the week-night service on a Thursday."[38] Spurgeon understood that this was not possible for some members, given the distance or their work schedules. However, for the rest, he saw weeknight participation in the life of the church as part of their commitment to the church. Additionally, church membership granted access to the Lord's Table. Though attending communion was a duty, it was also one of the highest privileges of the Christian life.[39] It was the duty of the Christian to grow through the means of grace, and faithful attendance at the Table was one of those means.

Third, it was the duty of all church members "to aid and comfort one another."[40] They were to "comfort those that mourn, help those who are poor, and, in general, we ought to watch for each other's interests, seeing that in the church we are all members of one family... let your brethren and your sisters have the most and

---

37. Cf. Articles 3 & 7 of *The Solemn Covenant*, "We do promise in a special manner to pray for one another, and for the glory and increase of this church, and for the presence of God in it, and the pouring forth of His Spirit on it, and His protection over it to His glory.... We do promise to meet together on Lord's Days, and at other times, as the Lord shall give us opportunities, to serve and glorify God in the way of His worship, to edify one another, and to contrive the good of His church." Dever, *Polity*, 91.

38. *MTP* 60:294.

39. "The Lord's table is spread once every month, and it is free to all God's children, but you never approach it. Why is that? It is your banquet." *NPSP* 1:68.

40. Cf. Articles 4 and 5 of *The Solemn Covenant*, "We do promise to bear one another's burdens, to cleave to one another, and to have a fellow-feeling with one another, in all conditions both outward and inward, as God in His providence shall cast any of us into.,,,, We do promise to bear with one another's weaknesses, failings, and infirmities, with much tenderness, not discovering them to any without the church, nor any within, unless according to Christ's rule, and the order of the Gospel provided in that case." Dever, *Polity*, 91.

best of what you can give."[41] Certainly, this involved providing practical help for those in need in the church. Just as one should prioritize the needs of their family, so the Christian prioritizes the needs of fellow church members over the poor of the world. But even more important was the spiritual care that they were to exercise over one another. At times, love required admonition. Church members should not be petty or uncharitable, but in wisdom and love they ought to help one another against the deceitfulness of sin.

Let us endeavor, if the Lord is keeping us by his grace, to "exhort one another daily." We are not to scold one another daily, nor to suspect one another daily, nor to pick holes in one another's coats daily; but when we see a manifest fault in a brother, we are bound to tell him of it in love; and when we do not see any fault of commission, but the brother is evidently growing lax and cold, it is well to stir him up to greater zeal by a loving exhortation. Wisely said, a word may save a soul from declension and sin. A good fire may need a little stirring. The best of believers may grow better by the communications of his friends.[42]

Finally, each member was "to give himself to the church in the sense of doing his share in all church work." This was a constant theme in Spurgeon's preaching. He did not want church members merely to profess the right doctrine and attend on Sundays. Rather, he wanted a working church. Just a soldier who joined an army had a role to fill, so should it be with every member of the church.

> What odd notions people have of joining the church. Many a young man joins a rifle corps. There he is! When he joins the church, where is he? We have the distinguished honor of having the names of many young gentlemen on our books. But where are they? What are they doing? They think it enough that they have joined the church; and they don't think that anything more is required. When they join a literary institute, or anything of that kind, they do so for the purpose of doing something, and obtaining an advantage from it; and I say to such young men,

---

41. *MTP* 60:294.
42. *MTP* 36:108.

"Do you believe the Christian church to be a farce? If you do so, we could even dispense with your names; if you do not believe the Christian church is a farce, then show that you don't by working so far as you can in the cause of Christ."[43]

Though Spurgeon saw tremendous membership growth in his day, he believed that without a proportionate increase in activity and service, such growth was worthless.[44] More than a full membership roll, Spurgeon wanted an active membership where his people covenanted with one another and joined together in the mission of the church.

Joining the Church

The membership numbers associated with Spurgeon's ministry in London are staggering.[45] When Spurgeon first preached at the New Park Street Chapel on December 18, 1853, there were only a few dozen people present in a room that seated 1,200. Membership was likely between two and three hundred.[46] The earliest official membership records available after Spurgeon's arrival put the membership of the church at 313 at the end of 1854, eight months after his arrival.[47] Over the next thirty-eight

---

43. Charles H. Spurgeon, *Speeches at Home and Abroad* (Pasadena, TX: Pilgrim Publications, 1974), 60.

44. "Our churches are increasing at a great rate. There are an immense number of Christians now alive; but I think I would rather have the one hundred and twenty men that were in the upper chamber at the day of Pentecost, than I would have the whole lot of you. I do think those one hundred and twenty men had got more blood in them, more divine Christian blood and zeal, than as many millions of such poor creatures as we are. Why, in those days every member of the church was a missionary. The women did not preach, it is true; but they did what is better than preaching, they lived out the Gospel; and all the men had something to say. They did not leave it as you do to your minister serving God by proxy; they did not set deacons up, and leave them to do all God's work while they folded their arms. Oh! no; all Christ's soldiers went to battle. There was no drafting out one or two of them, and then leaving the others to tarry at home and share the spoil. No, every one fought, and great was the victory." *NPSP* 4:352.

45. See Table 1 for the reported additions in the Annual Meeting Minutes found in the Metropolitan Tabernacle *Minute Books*.

46. Drummond, *Spurgeon*, 189.

47. Charles H. Spurgeon, *The Metropolitan Tabernacle: Its History and Work* (Pasadena, TX: Pilgrim Publications, 1990), 82.

years, Spurgeon would take 14,692 people into membership.[48] Of that number, 10,063 (seventy-three percent) were taken into membership through baptism, 2,764 (twenty percent) were taken into membership through a letter of dismission from another church, and 949 (seven percent) were received by profession. On average, the church brought roughly 400 people into membership each year, though this number could be as high as 571 in one year (in 1872). Naturally, not all 14,692 remained. In a city like London, people were constantly on the move. In some years, the church took in hundreds of new members and still saw a net decrease in membership.[49] Nonetheless, by the end of Spurgeon's ministry in 1892, the membership of the Metropolitan Tabernacle was 5,313.

Conversions in the Church

Spurgeon's commitment to regenerate church membership meant that if the church were to grow, it must see conversions. Spurgeon did not want to fill the church with the nominally Christian. Nor did he want to fill the church with professing Christians from other churches who were drawn by the novelty of the young preacher. He was not fighting against other churches or evangelical denominations but against the kingdom of Satan. Of course, such membership additions by transfer were inevitable, but Spurgeon would consider it shameful if they made up the majority of his congregation.

> I should reckon it to be a burning disgrace if it could be said, "The large church under that man's pastoral care is composed of members whom he has stolen away from other Christian churches." No, but I value beyond all price the godless, the careless, who are brought out from the world into communion with Christ. These are true prizes, not stealthily removed from friendly shores, but captured at the edge of the sword from an enemy's dominions.... To recruit one regiment from another is

---

48. The following numbers are based on the reported additions in the Annual Meeting Minutes found in the Metropolitan Tabernacle *Minute Books*. Hereafter, these *Minute Books* will be referred to as *MB*.

49. In 1883, the church took four hundred and forty-nine people into membership and saw a net decrease of seventy members.

no real strengthening of the army; to bring in fresh men should be the aim of all.[50]

Spurgeon found new converts to be some of the best members of the church, bringing fresh zeal and warmth to the rest of the congregation.[51] Far from resenting new converts, Spurgeon taught his church to pray for them and welcome them into the church with open arms. The fact that most members entered the church by baptism shows that Spurgeon's labors for conversions did not go unrewarded.

At the same time, with all the new converts coming forward, Spurgeon felt the pressure of a growing congregation and a lack of space to meet. If these converts were not able to gather with the church for lack of space, then he could not responsibly bring them into church membership and disciple them. In that case, Spurgeon believed he could not in good conscience remain a pastor and should become a traveling evangelist. It was Spurgeon's commitment to church membership that ultimately convinced him to erect a new building.[52]

The primary evangelistic activity of the church was the gathering of the church, where the gospel was preached regularly. However, the preaching was merely the beginning. Following the service, Spurgeon wanted his congregation to be on the lookout for any who might be under conviction of sin. Rather than directing such people to an elder or the pastor, Spurgeon encouraged his people to follow up with them directly and press the gospel home, a kind of "hand to hand battling" in the pews.

> Every believer should be doubly on the alert in watching for souls. None in that congregation should be able to say, "We attended that place, but no one spoke to us." There should be much hand to hand battling with unbelievers, for this mode of

---

50. *MTP* 15:90.

51. "No church can be healthy without the constant infusion of fresh blood. Unless there are new converts, you cannot see the church built up. They often help to keep the old members warm and zealous... therefore, she ought to have every preparation for their reception. There should always be an arrangement in every church to afford a welcome to the coming ones." *MTP* 46:437-38.

52. *Autobiography* 2:313.

wrestling with sin is greatly blest, and it is the duty of all who are themselves partakers of the divine life. If all members of the church became seekers of souls they would, with God's blessing, all become winners of souls. This would yield a season of increase such as our present experience has not enabled us to realize.[53]

Over time, the members of the Metropolitan Tabernacle developed a reputation for greeting visitors and talking about the effect of the sermon on their souls. Some visitors found this annoying.[54] But many visitors were convicted by those conversations. Some asked to meet with the pastor, and Spurgeon set aside time after the service and during the week to meet with visitors. Some came as enquirers, to ask further questions about the gospel and the state of their souls. Others came as converts, ready to share about how they had been saved. Spurgeon's preaching was so fruitful that he often was unable to meet with all those who were coming to see him.[55] On one occasion, Spurgeon met with so many visitors that he neglected to eat all day and only discovered this oversight late into the night.[56]

What was Spurgeon's method of tracking conversions? In future years, Spurgeon's successors at the Tabernacle would adopt Moody's use of inquiry rooms to promote decisions and measure results. [57] During his ministry, Spurgeon tolerated the use of inquiry rooms in the church's mission stations and evangelistic events but never at the expense of properly examining

---

53. *S&T* 1872:441.

54. "I do not think any sermon ought to be preached without each one of you Christian people saying, 'I wonder whether God has blessed the message to this stranger who has been sitting next to me. I will put a gentle question to him, and see if I can find out.' I have known some hearers to be annoyed at such a question being put to them by an earnest brother. Do not be annoyed, dear friend, if you can help it, because you are very likely to be treated in that way again. It is our custom to do it here, so you will have to put up with it; and the only way to get over the annoyance is to give your heart to Christ, and settle the matter once for all." *MTP* 46:438.

55. "Souls are being saved. I have more enquirers than I can attend to. From six to seven o'clock on Monday and Thursday evenings, I spend in my vestry; I give but brief interviews then, and have to send many away without being able to see them." *Autobiography* 4:98.

56. *Autobiography* 2.137.

57. Iain Murray, *The Forgotten Spurgeon* (Edinburgh: The Banner of Truth Trust, 2002), 219-21.

each profession of faith.[58] Spurgeon rejected any attempts at revivalism or manipulating people for quick decisions. Though on certain days, he could not meet with all those who came to him, he trusted that if their conviction were genuine, they would persevere. Those who professed conversion were not counted but encouraged towards membership in the church.[59] The only counting of converts was in the membership reports of the church, published once a year at the church's annual meeting.

The Membership Process at the Metropolitan Tabernacle

Spurgeon did not believe it was possible to have a perfectly regenerate church membership here on earth. Part of the struggle of the church militant was the reality of the ongoing battle against indwelling sin.[60] While this battle continued, the church would always have to deal with the existence of false professors within her membership. Nonetheless, Spurgeon was committed to the principle of regenerate church membership, namely, that the church should only accept into its membership those who, as far as we can tell, have been regenerated by the Holy Spirit and are trusting in Christ alone for their salvation. One of the primary ways Spurgeon promoted this principle was through the rigorous membership process in his church.

Writing in 1869, Spurgeon published an article in *The Sword and the Trowel* by his brother James, entitled "The Discipline of the Church at the Metropolitan Tabernacle." Here James

58. "What mean these despatches from the battle-field? 'Last night, fourteen souls were under conviction, fifteen were justified, and eight received full sanctification.' I am weary of this public bragging, this counting of unhatched chickens, this exhibition of doubtful spoils.... Enquiry-rooms are all very well; but if they lead to idle boastings, they will grieve the Holy Spirit, and work abounding evil." Charles H. Spurgeon, *The Soul-Winner, or How to Lead Sinners to the Savior* (Pasadena, TX: Pilgrim Publications, 2007), 15.

59. "After each sermon, announce that inquirers will be immediately seen, and encourage them to stay behind. Also publish frequently the way of joining the church, and urge secret believers to confess their Lord. Let no one say, 'I wish to be baptized, but do not know where to apply.' Keep the church agencies above board, and make plain paths for the feet of seekers." *S&T* 1872:440.

60. "We leave the imperfect church on earth, but we claim membership with the perfect church in heaven. The church militant must know us no more, but of the church triumphant we shall be happy members." *MTP* 12:646.

Spurgeon outlines the membership process for joining the church in six steps.[61]

Step 1 – Elder Interview

> All persons anxious to join our church are requested to apply personally upon any Wednesday evening, between six and nine o'clock, to the elders, two or more of whom attend in rotation every week for the purpose of seeing inquirers. When satisfied, the case is entered by the elder in one of a set of books provided for the purpose, and a card is given bearing a corresponding number to the page of the book in which particulars of the candidate's experience are recorded.[62]

The first step in the membership process was a membership interview with one of the elders. Records of these membership interviews can still be found in the Testimony Books that reside in the Metropolitan Tabernacle Archives in London. An entry was normally one page, but it could be as short as a few sentences[63] or as long as several pages.[64] At the top, left corner of the page is the date, and the applicant's name and address. The main portion of the page contains the applicant's testimony, written out by the elder. These testimonies vary widely, with applicants coming from all kinds of backgrounds and undergoing all kinds of experiences in their conversion.[65] For approved applicants, the elder records that a card was given to the applicant.[66] This card contained the

61. This section is adapted from my article: Geoff Chang, "Membership at Metropolitan Tabernacle: Church Polity with Charles Spurgeon," https://www.desiringgod.org/articles/membership-at-metropolitan-tabernacle, accessed 11/28/2023.

62. C. H. Spurgeon, *The Sword and the Trowel; A Record of Combat with Sin & Labour for the Lord.* 1865–1897 (London: Passmore & Alabaster), 1869:53.

63. "Entry 1353," *Testimony Book 1201-1600,* Metropolitan Tabernacle Archives.

64. "Entry 1304-1306," *Testimony Book 1201-1600,* Metropolitan Tabernacle Archives.

65. Many of these testimonies have been published in *Wonders of Grace.* Hannah Wyncoll, ed., *Wonders of Grace: Original Testimonies of Converts during Spurgeon's Early Years* (London: The Wakeman Trust, 2016).

66. "A record is made by the Elder of the result of that interview in what is called the Inquirers' Book. If satisfied with the candidate, he gives a card, which qualifies for

corresponding number on the corner of the page so that the applicant's testimony could be easily found.

In each interview, the elders were looking for two things: a clear understanding of the gospel and evidence of spiritual change. For example, in an interview with James Melbourn, the elder records, "He has frequently heard Mr. Spurgeon and prefers his preaching to any he ever heard. I don't think he has the faintest idea of the Gospel." However, Melbourn is "sober, honest, industrious, and willing to join a church." The elder is "astonished how any man could sit under our pastor's ministry one Lord's Day and be so entirely ignorant of his own ignorance of the Gospel."[67] Despite his evident moral life, the elder is not convinced that Melbourn understands the gospel. So rather than rushing him through the membership process, the elder refers him to a Bible class, where he can study the Scriptures further and come to a saving knowledge of Christ.

But more than simply an intellectual understanding, conversion produces a change of life. In hearing their testimony, the elders also looked for evidence of genuine repentance and faith. For Emma Wilcox, the elder records how she previously was "fond of the gaieties of the world," including "theatres, concerts and driving out on Sundays." But after one particular sermon, "a decided change has taken place. No Sunday rides, no ballroom, no playhouse now, old things have passed away, all things have become new. Wishes to show her love to Jesus by meeting with his people and desires to be baptized."[68] Here was evidence of both a turning away from worldliness and a turning to Christ in faith. And so, the elder happily gave her a card for the next step.

Step 2 – Pastor Interview

Once a month, or oftener when required, the junior pastor appoints a day to see the persons thus approved of by the elders.

---

direct intercourse with Mr. Spurgeon, who devotes a fixed portion of his time to that office." *S&T* 1865:31.

67.   Hannah Wyncoll, ed., *Wonders of Grace: Original Testimonies of Converts during Spurgeon's Early Years* (London: The Wakeman Trust, 2016), 70.

68.   *Wonders*, 86.

When the applicant arrived to meet with the pastor for the second step of the membership process, the card would be given to the pastor ahead of time so that he could review the testimony. In this meeting, the pastor would attempt to discern the sincerity of the applicant's profession of faith, asking further questions focusing on the nature of their faith in Christ.[69] If the pastor was satisfied, he would write on the applicant's page, "Proposed," indicating his willingness to bring the application before the congregation and propose a messenger for the following step.

For approximately the first fifteen years of his ministry, Spurgeon interviewed every candidate for membership. By 1869, Spurgeon's brother James had been called to be his co-pastor, and he largely took over this task for the remaining years. Even so, Spurgeon didn't entirely drop this responsibility. Writing in 1884, he declared:

> Oh, brothers, on that day on which I lately saw forty persons one by one, and listened to their experience and proposed them to the church, I felt as weary as ever a man did in reaping the heaviest harvest. I did not merely give them a few words as enquirers, but examined them as candidates with my best judgment.[70]

As busy as he was, Spurgeon did not leave the membership process entirely in his elders' hands, but he felt a sense of responsibility as the lead pastor to meet briefly with each candidate personally.

Spurgeon trusted his elders' judgments, and I have yet to come across a case where he goes against an elder's recommendation. Yet, he does not hesitate to express his concerns and cautions. For one candidate, Spurgeon writes in the margin, "This young man's moral character must be seen into with care. He is but a

---

69. "There is nothing we want to know of a person coming before the church, except this. Dost thou believe on the Lord Jesus Christ? Hast thou had pardon from his hands? Hast thou had union with his person? Dost thou hold communion with him day by day? Is he thy hope, thy stay, thy refuge, thy trust? If so, then thou mayest come in." *NPSP* 2:80.

70. C. H. Spurgeon, *The Metropolitan Tabernacle Pulpit*, Vol. 30 (London: Passmore & Alabaster, 1884), 310. He continued, "I thought that if I had many days of that sort I must die, but I also wished it might be my lot to die in that fashion. Having so many coming to confess Christ my mind was crushed beneath the weight of blessing, but I would gladly be overwhelmed again."

young man & I fear has many temptations…. I have no reason to suspect, but only advise." For another candidate, he writes, "Another difficult case, requiring a diligent investigation. I think delay would be advisable." At times, Spurgeon's comments deal with the care of the candidate, "Ought to have the Confession of Faith. Messenger to get her one."[71] Church membership was important enough for multiple elders to be involved in the membership process, and this step guaranteed that at least two elders would examine every candidate.

Steps 3 & 4: Congregational appointment of a visitor & visitor inquiry

> If the pastor is satisfied, he nominates an elder or church member as visitor, and at the next church meeting asks the church to send him to enquire as to the moral character and repute of the candidate.

If an applicant passed the first two steps, the third step would be for an elder to give a brief introduction of the applicant's testimony at the next members' meeting and then nominate a member of the church to be a visitor or messenger. The congregation would then vote to commission the visitor, typically an elder or deacon, to go on behalf of the church and "enquire as to the moral character and repute of the candidate." This would involve visiting the candidate's place of work, home, or neighborhood and asking questions about the candidate: Do you know this applicant? Did you know he is a Christian? Did you know he was looking to be baptized and join the Metropolitan Tabernacle? What do you know about his character? What is he like at work? How does he treat his family? And so on. Often, these messengers drew their questions from the applicant's interview.[72]

This is what Spurgeon was referring to in his comments when he mentioned making "diligent investigation" and seeing into the applicant's moral character with care. On one occasion, Spurgeon

---

71. *Wonders*, 47.

72. Elder Thomas Moor cautions a messenger in his notes regarding an applicant, "Note: she is excessively nervous and needs gentle enquiry." Wyncoll, *Wonders of Grace*, 22.

commented on a particularly confused applicant, Jonathan Cook, who served with the police:

> This man is in a muddle & seems to me to be rather loose in his head. This is perhaps the reason why he has not been promoted in the police service. I do not think he will be any great credit to us & should not be sorry if the messenger declines to recommend him. He has evidently overcome swearing & I think drunkenness, & it may turn out that he is a simple, silly but genuine man, however I beg the messenger to make *very* diligent enquiry for I fear he is weak in the head & not very sound in the heart. I cannot judge, *character* must decide.[73]

Based on these comments, it is likely that the messenger would have visited the police station to talk with Cook's fellow policemen about his behavior, including his swearing and drunkenness. Another visit to his home to inquire about these matters would likely also have been in order. As it turns out, it appears from the *Testimony Books* that Cook was never proposed for membership.

Most applicants were more straightforward. However, for some, the elders recognized that judging one's profession of faith based on two interviews could still prove difficult. This step allowed the church to get a sense of the person's ongoing reputation in their community and get further evidence of a credible profession of faith. And undoubtedly, it created evangelistic opportunities for the applicant, as their neighbors heard about their profession.

Step 5: Congregational vote

If all went well with the enquiry, the next step would be taken.

> If the visitor be satisfied he requests the candidate to attend with him at the following or next convenient church meeting, to come before the church and reply to such questions as may be put from the chair, mainly with a view to elicit expressions of his trust in the Lord Jesus, and hope of salvation through his blood, and any such facts of his spiritual history as may convince the church of the genuineness of the case.... After the statement before the church, the candidate withdraws, the visitor gives in his report, and the vote of the church is taken.

---

73. *Wonders*, 80-81.

If the messenger were satisfied with his inquiry, he would invite the applicant to attend the next church meeting along with him.[74] During the meeting, the messenger would give a report on their inquiry. Then the meeting chair, usually Spurgeon, would interview the candidate briefly, usually asking for some kind of statement about their trust in Christ, as well as highlighting parts of their testimony. Spurgeon would sometimes ask members of the church to speak, for example, a Sunday school teacher or the member who shared the gospel with them, and give their affirmation of the applicant's conversion. On one occasion, in the age before women's suffrage, a student asked Spurgeon if it was advisable for women to speak in a church-meeting. Spurgeon answered:

> Suppose there is a candidate before the church, and I know that one of the female members can testify to his Christian character, I should not hesitate to say, "Our Sister Brown knows this young man; would she like to tell us anything about him?" I think it would be most seemly if she should reply, "Yes, dear friends, he is a very admirable young man; I am especially grateful to him for he has been the means of the conversion of my husband." It would be a very great pity for anybody beside Mrs. Brown to give such a testimony as that.[75]

In other words, church membership was ultimately a decision of the congregation. For a person to join a church, this involved not only the elders and the pastor but also the entire congregation, as they commissioned messengers, heard the applicant's profession of faith, and heard one another's testimonies about the individual. All this would then culminate in a congregational vote to bring the person into membership, expressing not only their approval but their covenant commitment to the new member.

---

74. At times, a messenger would decline to bring a report. "Brother Cornish reported that he must decline to bring forward the case of William Hacker, to whom he was appointed messenger. Dec. 9th 1861." "Church Meeting February 13th, 1862," *MB 1861–1866*.

75. *Sword*, 1897:255.

Step 6: Ordinances

The applicant would not become a member until they were baptized and partook of the Lord's Supper, where they officially received "the right hand of fellowship."

> When the candidate has professed his faith by immersion, which is administered by the junior pastor after a week-day service, he is received by the pastor at the first monthly communion, when the right hand of fellowship is given to him in the name of the church, and his name is entered on the roll of members.[76]

This is ultimately what church membership consists of, according to the New Testament. Church membership is made up of those who have been baptized upon their profession of faith and give expression to an ongoing profession of faith through their participation in the Lord's Supper. In other words, membership in the church signifies the theological reality of the believer's union with Christ and his people, as depicted by the ordinances of the church. By making baptism and the Lord's Supper the final step of the membership process, the church reminded these applicants that church membership was rooted in theological truths.

Six weeks after being proposed, the meeting minutes on August 31, 1863 record, "Benjamin Walker [along with others] ... came before the Church and gave satisfactory accounts of the Lord's dealings with their souls and the messengers reports being favourable it is agreed that they be received into communion with this Church after baptism."[77] That fall, Walker would be baptized at the Metropolitan Tabernacle and would participate in the Lord's Supper on November 1, 1863, receiving the right-hand of fellowship.[78] The entire membership process, beginning with the initial elder interview, took almost eleven months for Mr. Walker. Though not all membership applications took that long, the length itself was part of the rigor of the membership process,

---

76. *S&T* 1869:53-54.

77. "Church Meeting held after the Prayer Meeting Aug 31st[, 1863]," *MB 1861-1866*.

78. "The following persons having been previously baptized were this evening received as members in full communion with this Church =... Benjamin Walker." "Lord's Day November 1st, 1863," Ibid.

promoting a regenerate church membership, especially during times when many applicants were coming forward.

This membership process was consistently followed throughout Spurgeon's ministry, with few exceptions.[79] The *Church Meeting Minutes* of the Metropolitan Tabernacle from 1854 to 1892 reveal this rigorous approach of church membership, bringing thousands of people through this six-step membership process. In each of these steps, the membership application could stop at any point, as often was the case. Not every applicant joined the church. The elder who performed the first interview might decide that the applicant was still unconverted and recommend the applicant to join a Bible class instead. Or the messenger, after visiting the applicant's home and workplace, might decide not to bring his name forward. In one case, the messenger not being present at the meeting meant that the applicant could not be voted on by the congregation.[80] Individuals in the congregation might also speak during step five and raise new questions about an applicant's profession of faith.[81] Even in the final step, an applicant could decide they did not want to join the church after all.[82]

---

79. There are occasional exceptions made in this process. For example, at the church meeting on October 2, 1861, the minutes record, "Charles W. Smith, a student for the ministry, under the care of our pastor, was proposed as a candidate for church fellowship, and it is agreed that he be allowed to give his testimony to the Church the same evening, and before the close of the meeting he came before the Church and gave a highly satisfactory statement, and it is agreed that he be received as a member in full communion with this Church." In this case, the congregation decided to vote on Charles W. Smith at the same meeting he was proposed. The reason for this is likely because he was one of Spurgeon's students and was living with Spurgeon or another member of the church. Since the church already had ample evidence of a consistent conduct, they were able to skip the visitor enquiry. *MB* 1861-1866.

80. If the messenger was not present at the meeting to give a report, then the applicant could not be voted on by the congregation. On June 18, 1861, the minutes record, "Sarah Fortmann also came before the Church and gave a satisfactory statement, but the messenger, Brother Cornish, not being present she could not be received into the Church." *MB* 1861-1866.

81. At the church meeting on October 28, 1861, the minutes record, "Thomas Ebenezer Mansfield also came before the Church but a demurrer being raised by two sisters it is agreed that the case be deferred for further investigation." *MB* 1861-1866.

82. This was the case on September 8, 1862, where the church meeting minutes record, "Brother G. Moore called attention to the minute relating to the dismission of Martha Cornock, Church Meeting February 10th and reported that it was not Miss Cornock's intention to be baptized at present and that she had again united herself

Some visitors who were interested in joining the church objected to this rigorous membership process. Spurgeon nevertheless believed that the strictness of the process filtered out those of nominal faith. In certain cases, the lengthy process served to remove applicants that the elders considered doubtful or had mistakenly accepted. Yet those who were willing to undergo this extensive examination demonstrated greater sincerity in their profession of faith and commitment to the church.[83] Such a rigorous membership process further highlights how astonishing it was that 14,692 individuals joined the church during Spurgeon's ministry. These were not casual members, but at one point in time, they were all serious in their commitment to the church.

Letters of Dismission and Membership Transfers

This membership process applied both to unbaptized converts and any baptized believers who did not belong to any church. The former were added to the church by baptism. The latter joined the church by their profession of faith. A third category of additions were those who came to the Metropolitan Tabernacle bearing a letter of dismission from their previous church. For many churches, the historic practice was that these letters allowed the bearers to join a church without having to go through the membership process. This was particularly the case for those coming from Baptist churches that shared the same doctrinal and ecclesiological convictions.

Spurgeon, however, viewed things differently. He was aware that the membership process in many other churches was not

---

with the Church at Wolton under Edge & consequently is not to be rece'd into our fellowship." *MB* 1861-1866.

83. "We have never yet found it tend to keep members out of our midst, while we have known it of service in detecting a mistake or satisfying a doubt previously entertained. We deny that it keeps away any worth having. Surely if their Christianity cannot stand before a body of believers, and speak amongst loving sympathizing hearts, it is as well to ask if it be the cross-bearing public confessing faith of the Bible? This is no matter of flesh and blood, but of faith and grace, and we should be sorry to give place to the weakness and shrinking of the flesh, so as to insult the omnipotence of grace, by deeming it unable to endure so much as the telling in the gates of Zion what great things God has done for the soul." *S&T* 1869:53-54.

nearly as rigorous as his.[84] Some churches were willing to grant letters of dismission even when the applicant had not attended their church for years.

> In dealing with such as are members of other churches, we have been by sad experience compelled to exercise more caution than at first seemed needful. The plan we adopt is to have the person seen by an elder, who enters particulars in the transfer book. If there appears to be any difficulty, an interview is arranged with one of the pastors, who investigates the case on its own merits, as alas! he has discovered that membership with some churches is not always a guarantee even of morality. Some churches retain a name upon their books for years after the person has ceased to commune; and frequently when he has passed away from all knowledge of or connection with the church, it will nevertheless grant a transfer as if all were satisfactory. We record this with mingled shame and sorrow.[85]

Therefore, every applicant at the Metropolitan Tabernacle had to go through an interview process, even when bearing a letter of dismission, with few exceptions.[86]

However, those who did bear a letter did not have to be proposed to the congregation, and messengers were not appointed, skipping steps three and four. Rather, after meeting with the pastor for approval, at the following church meeting they would be voted on for membership based on the letter of dismission. For example, at the church meeting on June 18, 1861, the minutes record, "Letters were read from the Church in Regent St. Lambeth dismissing Edward Harris and Emily Harris to our fellowship... and it is

---

84. "Ah! my hearers, in this age it is a very easy thing to make a profession of religion: many churches receive candidates into their fellowship without examination at all; I have had such come to me, and I have told them, 'I must treat you just the same as if you came from the world,' because they said, 'I never saw the minister, I wrote a note to the Church, and they took me in.'" *NPSP* 4:35. This was similar to Spurgeon's own experience at the Congregationalist church in Newmarket. *Autobiography* 1:120.

85. *S&T* 1869:54.

86. Rare exceptions can be found, however. In place of a testimony, Mr. Roe records the following entry in the *Testimony Books* regarding an applicant, "Member of Mr. R Langford's, Baptist Colchester, wishes to unite with the Church in this place. To write for dismissal." "Entry 1205," *Testimony Book 1201-1600*, Metropolitan Tabernacle Archives.

agreed that they be received as members in full communion with this Church, having been previously baptized."[87]

Promoting Meaningful Membership

Bringing someone through the membership process and into membership was only the beginning of the story. Once they joined, Spurgeon believed the church had a responsibility before God to care for them and walk with them on the journey to heaven. At the end of the membership process, during a communion service, new members would join the pastor before the congregation and "receive the right-hand of fellowship," where they were officially welcomed into church membership. Spurgeon saw this act as a representative action on behalf of the whole congregation.

> Every time I give the right hand of fellowship to a new member, especially to those just brought in from the world, I think I hear Christ's voice speaking to me, and saying, 'Take these children, and nurse them for me, and I will give thee thy wages.' I say this is said to me, but I mean it is said to the entire Church—I merely speak, of course, as the representative of the body. We have, whenever members are given to us, a great charge, under God, to nurse them for him, and, instrumentally, to advance them in the road to heaven.[88]

The church was not merely a place for new members to enjoy the comforts of church fellowship. Rather, if the church was made up of regenerate believers, then they should be expected to grow spiritually and advance in Christian service. Like Christian in the House Beautiful,[89] the church was to be an armory where Christians were strengthened and equipped for spiritual battle.[90] Certainly, the pastor's labors in those efforts were crucial. However, in a church that size, Spurgeon knew that he could not

---

87. "Church Meeting June 18th, 1861," *MB* 1861-1866.

88. *MTP* 48:196.

89. Bunyan, *Pilgrim's Progress*, 49.

90. In one of his earliest sermons, Spurgeon lists one of the "Privileges to be enjoyed" in joining a church as "Strength and Preparation from the armoury." See Sermon 322, "Joining a Church," *LS* 6.

care for the church apart from the labors of the congregation. It took the entire church to do the work of the church.[91]

> No two pastors can possibly watch over this vast assembly of four thousand five hundred professed believers. Let the watching be done by all the members: by the officers of the church first, and then by every individual.... Guide them and cheer them on. Help their weakness, bear with their ignorance and impetuosity, and correct their mistakes. I charge you, my beloved sisters, be nursing mothers in the church, and you, my brethren, be fathers to these young people, that they may be enabled by your help through God's Spirit to hold on their way. It is an evil thing to receive members, and never care for them afterwards. Among so many some must escape our supervision, but if all the members of the church were watchful this could not be; each would have some one to care for him, each one would have a friend to whom to tell his troubles and his cares. Watch over the church, then, I pray you.[92]

Maintaining an Accurate Membership

One of the challenges that Spurgeon faced in having such a large church was in maintaining an accurate account of membership. Speaking to the Pastors' College Conference, he once lamented how poorly some churches maintained their membership rolls.

> I would urge upon the resolve to have no church unless it be a real one. The fact is, that too frequently religious statistics are shockingly false.... Let us not keep names on our books when they are only names. Certain of the good old people like to keep them there, and cannot bear to have them removed; but when you do not know where the individuals are, nor what they are, how can you count them? They are gone to America, or Australia, or to heaven, but as far as your roll is concerned they

---

91. One of the ways the church promoted spiritual growth and relationships was through smaller Bible classes and societies where people could study the Scriptures and serve alongside other members of the church in smaller settings. For a list of many of these groups, see C. H. Spurgeon, *The Metropolitan Tabernacle: Its History and Work* (Pasadena, TX: Pilgrim Publications, 1990), 2:7-8.

92. *MTP* 20:215-16.

are with you still. Is this a right thing? It may not be possible to be absolutely accurate, but let us aim at it.[93]

The *Minute Books* reveal Spurgeon's commitment to maintaining an accurate membership roll.[94] In the membership numbers reported at each annual meeting, over thirty-eight years, the Metropolitan Tabernacle removed 9,281 people from membership, sixty-seven percent of those brought into membership. This means for two out of every three members who were received into membership, the church not only had to take them through a rigorous membership process, but also go through the process of removing them. Of all those removals, 1,497 (sixteen percent) were deaths, 3,798 (forty-one percent) received letters of dismission to other churches, 279 (three percent) emigrated to another country, 1155 (twelve percent) joined other churches, 2,299 (twenty-five percent) were removed for non-attendance, and 253 (three percent) were removed by exclusion, including cases of church discipline.[95]

In maintaining an accurate membership roll and removing people from membership, Spurgeon did not believe this was a cause for grieving.[96] Rather, he encouraged his people to see God at work to sanctify his people. In the case of deaths, though the loss was at times felt deeply by the church and by the leaders, Spurgeon used these instances as a reminder for those who remained to redouble their efforts:

> Now that so many saints have gone home, there are so many the fewer on earth to praise the Lord. O you who have recently

---

93. C. H. Spurgeon, *The Greatest Fight in the World* (Fearn, UK: Christian Focus, 2014), 92.

94. See Table 2 for the reported removals in the Annual Meeting Minutes found in the Metropolitan Tabernacle *Minute Books.*

95. Some of the exclusions were not cases of church discipline, but withdrawals. According to Keach, withdrawals are still a form of church censure, though distinct from excommunication, and are to be reserved for the disorderly. "But if after all due Endeavors used he is not reclaimed, but continues as a disorderly Person, the Church must withdraw from him.... This is not a delivering up to Satan, Excommunicating or dismembering the Person; for this sort are still to be owned as Members, tho disorderly ones. Dever, *Polity*, 72. In the case of the Metropolitan Tabernacle, withdrawals did result in a removal from membership.

96. Except in cases of church discipline, which will be discussed below.

come into the church, you who have been baptized for the dead to fill up the gaps in our ranks, be you earnest, with your loud hosannahs, to bless and magnify the name of the Lord. Brethren, let us take a blessed revenge on death; and if he takes from our numbers, let us, as God helps us, increase the real efficiency of the church, by each of us endeavoring to become double what we formerly were in the service of our Master.... if some of the troops have fought the good fight, and exchanged the sword and shield for the palm-branch and the harp, let us who are left pray with all our might unto the Lord God of hosts to strengthen us in this day of battle, that we may not go till we have finished our part of the fight.[97]

Likewise, when it came to those who left the church to join another church, Spurgeon encouraged his congregation to see this as a sending out of their workers. In many cases, as members went on to join other, smaller churches, they could take the many things they learned at the Tabernacle and use it to bless other congregations.

Often, the removal of a Christian out of a particular place is in order that he may be more helpful to another community than he is in his present position. I have frequently seen brethren, who were just ordinary members of this church, good, useful people, but they did not attain to any very great prominence; yet, in another place, they have been exceedingly useful. I go into the country to preach, and the deacon shakes hands with me, and as I look at him, I say, "Ah! I recollect you." "Well, sir," he replies, "I moved away from London, some years ago, and the Lord has been pleased to put me here, so that I may help this little cause. It has been strengthened, I hope, by my coming;" and I find the brother greatly developed by being transplanted.[98]

Even when members emigrated to another country, likely never to be seen again, Spurgeon considered this a great blessing and saw this as an opportunity for these brothers and sisters to work for the

---

97. *MTP* 39:4.
98. *MTP* 46:434-35.

spread of the gospel in foreign lands.[99] Considering the thousands of former members of the Metropolitan Tabernacle who went on to join other churches and live in other parts of the world, it is hard to estimate the extent of the influence of Spurgeon's ministry. Naturally, as an affectionate pastor, Spurgeon did feel the sadness of the loss of loved ones from his congregation.[100] But as the leader of his church army, he helped his people see the bigger picture of the spread of the gospel.

In a church so large, how did Spurgeon maintain an accurate membership? One of the primary methods was the use of communion tickets. At the beginning of each year, each member received a perforated communion card containing numbered tickets. At each communion service once a month, the tickets were checked, indicating the attendance of each member at the communion. Those who were absent for more than three months were visited by an elder or sent a letter from the church.[101] The labor that went into tracking members can be seen in the *Elders Minute Books* contained in the Metropolitan Tabernacle Archives. The elders met together frequently, at least once a month, usually

---

99. "For my part, I thank God for the many whom we lose by emigration. I am glad that some friends have gone to America. What would the United States have been, at this moment, if it had not been for 'the men of the Mayflower' in the olden times, and the many pilgrim fathers and pilgrim sons who have since gone across the Atlantic to be as salt in that part of the earth? Look still further away to Australia, so largely peopled by those who are of our race. What a mercy that it is so! Would you have those lands given up to Romanism, or to Mohammedanism, or to Paganism? God forbid! Salt ought not to be kept in a box; it is meant to be rubbed into the meat, and Christians are intended to be scattered all over the carcass of this world, to salt it all, and act with purifying and preserving power in every place." *MTP* 46:434-35.

100. "We have lost our children; we have lost many simply from the fact of their having to remove to a distance; in this way, our congregations are necessarily scattered. Some of those who used to sit under our ministry Sabbath by Sabbath, who came up with our great company, and kept holy day, cannot now be seen in our midst. And I, if you do not, feel this as bereavement; I cannot bear to miss the face of a single one from the members of the church. There is a sort of sacred bond of union that binds all together; and I do not like any one to go away, except it is, now and then, when some grow dissatisfied, and then I feel it is better for them to go somewhere else—it is certainly not worse for their minister. But those who have been loving, tender children have had to leave the church—those who have striven for her good. It is a sad thing to see them separated from us, and that has happened to this church over and over again." *MTP* 48:197-98.

101. *S&T* 1869:54.

on Mondays before the prayer meeting. The primary business of these meetings was to track non-attending members, though occasionally, they discussed other business concerning the life of the church.

The work that went into tracking members can be seen in the case of Anne Coppings, #380.[102] At the elders' meeting on Monday, June 12, 1876, with both Charles and James Spurgeon present, her name was raised as someone who had not attended in a long time. The book records, "380 Coppings, Anne E. / White / No Report."[103] Coppings had been assigned to elder White to visit, but it appears White was kept from his duties as he is not listed as present at any elder meetings that summer or fall. For all the elder meetings through October, the same record is made for Coppings, "No Report." Then, at the elders' meeting on October 2, 1876, elder Marshall was assigned to the case.[104] At the meeting in the following week, there is still "No Report" for Coppings.[105] But a discussion is shown in the minutes immediately following about the need for more elders and for action taken towards elders who were not fulfilling their duties.

> Some conversation took place with reference to the names of Brethren mentioned as suitable for Elders, agreed that a meeting be called when both Pastors can be present. It is also agreed to request the Pastor to take into consideration the advisability of taking action in reference to the Brethren who have not fulfilled their office during the past year.[106]

Clearly, the elders were troubled that no action was taken in pursuing this non-attending member for so long. Whatever happened with elder White, the elders wanted to make sure that this problem was addressed. Finally, at the first elders' meeting

---

102. The number which accompanies each member name in the *Elder Minute Book* was likely the number of the members' communion card.

103. "Elders Meeting Monday June 12 [1876]," *Elders Minutes 1876-1881*, Metropolitan Tabernacle Archives.

104. "Elders Meeting Monday Oct. 2, 1876," *Elders Minutes 1876-1881*, Metropolitan Tabernacle Archives.

105. "Elders Meeting Monday Oct. 9 [1876]," Ibid.

106. "Elders Meeting Monday Oct. 9 [1876]," *Elders Minutes 1876-1881*.

in November, Marshall reported that he had been in touch with Coppings' mother and learned that she has moved to Hastings, but her address was not known.[107] At this point, knowing that Coppings was no longer in London, her name was not raised at the next elders' meeting. The Coppings' case reveals that member care at the Metropolitan Tabernacle was laborious and, at times, complicated. Here, the elders had to deal with a delinquent elder, a member who moved away without notifying anyone in the church, and in the end, no way to get in touch with her. The elders did not remove her from membership right away, in case there was something that they missed. But in time, Coppings was likely removed from membership for non-attendance.[108]

Not all cases were this complicated. Sometimes an investigation resulted in the bittersweet discovery that a member had died, or "gone to heaven."[109] In such cases, the congregation was notified and the person was removed from membership automatically. If the elders discovered that these members had joined other churches, letters were granted and they were removed from membership.[110] Spurgeon did not believe that Christians should be members of multiple churches but desired them to be committed to one church.

In many cases, the enquiry would result in an explanation for the member's non-attendance. These reasons would vary: distance,[111] a difficult work schedule,[112] having missed the

---

107. "Elders Meeting Monday Nov. 6th[, 1876]," *Elders Minutes 1876-1881*.

108. "Many varieties of circumstances may thus render absence no sin; but surely only for sin, removal to another church, or utter failure to find out a brother's whereabouts after earnest searching, ought we to erase a name from the roll of our membership." *S&T* 1872:198. In this case, Coppings likely fell in that third category. Unfortunately, I was not able to find the church meeting motion where Coppings was removed from membership.

109. This was the report for Elija Evans (10) in "Elders Meeting Monday June 12th [1876]," *Elders Minutes 1876-1881*, Metropolitan Tabernacle Archives.

110. "131 Newton, Mary Ann. Joined another church. Name to be removed." "Elders Meeting Monday June 26th [1876]," *Elders Minutes 1876-1881*, Metropolitan Tabernacle Archives.

111. "27 White, George / Dunn / Distance, attends as often as he can, has not turned in his cards," in "Elders Meeting Monday June 19th [1876]," Ibid.

112. "31 Hambling, Charles, Verdun – has attended Dr. Parkers – works at Field Lane R School, promised to attend more regular." "Elders Meeting Monday June 26th

communion service,[113] simply forgetting to bring the communion card,[114] illness,[115] and more. In cases of non-attendance due to hardship rather than sin, Spurgeon did not recommend their removal, but encouraged his elders to patiently care for these members:

> If a sheep has strayed let us seek it; to disown it in a hurry is not the Master's method. Ours is to be the labor and the care, for we are overseers of the flock of Christ to the end that all may be presented faultless before God. One month's absence from the house of God is, in some cases, a deadly sign of a profession renounced, while in others a long absence is an affliction to be sympathized with, and not a crime to be capitally punished.[116]

His desire to keep an accurate membership roll did not mean that he neglected to care for sheep that were struggling to attend. Rather, if the elder's visit uncovered areas of need in the lives of their people, they would work patiently with them to encourage their participation and to provide care for them in their absence. Since each elder was assigned a particular district, he would likely work with other members in that district to provide care. The 2,299 reported cases of removal for non-attendance were not hasty removals; the elders only took that step if they believed that those members were beyond the care of the church.

Church Discipline

Though Spurgeon did not think that the church should ultimately grieve the loss of members due to deaths or dismissals to other churches, he did consider church discipline a different situation.

> But there is another source of decrease over which we must greatly grieve, and that is, the backsliding of many professors.

[1876]," Ibid.

113. "34 Irwin, Maria, Croker, Distance, has attended Tabernacle, but not communion, hopes to come in future." Ibid.

114. "608 Leary, Maria / Rowang / Case is more hopeful to have her cards." "Elders Meeting Monday June 19th [1876]," Ibid.

115. "4 Palliversa, Eliza. Ward. Ill health suffers from Erysipelas. Would only be too glad to attend." "Elders Meeting Monday July 3rd [1876]," Ibid.

116. *S&T* 1872:198.

Over this decrease I mourn even more than over another, grievous as that is, namely, the sifting process by which the chaff is removed from the wheat. For, when the saints backslide, they are still God's people, although their power for good, their influence, their help to the Church of God is gone until they are brought back, and that is very lamentable. Churches lose much, if not in number, yet certainly in strength, in fervor, in power of prayer, by the declining in grace of some who once did run well, but who have been hindered. Pray much, dear friends, that God would keep all who are members with us from growing cold.[117]

Spurgeon distinguished between the backsliding of genuine professors and the removal of those who proved to be no genuine believers at all.[118] In either case, the action of the church should be to confront these wandering members and bring them through a process of discipline. Spurgeon did not relish confronting and rebuking sinners. At the same time, he did not believe church purity could be compromised for growth. "When we rebuke sharply, we would be anxious lest the rebuke should fall where it is not needed, and should bruise and hurt the feelings of any who God hath chosen. But on the other hand, we have no wish to see the church multiplied at the expense of its purity."[119]

Because of Spurgeon's commitment to regenerate church membership, he considered church discipline crucial to the health of a church.[120] To maintain hypocrites in the membership

---

117. *MTP* 46:435-36.

118. "As for that other decrease over which we mourn—the sifting by which the chaff is separated from the wheat—how sadly true it still is, as the beloved apostle wrote, 'They went out from us, but they were not of us; for if they had been of us, they would no doubt have continued with us: but they went out, that they might be made manifest that they were not all of us.' There is a separating process always going on in the professing church, and the most effectual fan of all is a faithful ministry. After a while, some of our hearers do not like what we say; it is too personal, too cutting, too searching. They want to listen to that kind of preaching which will allow them to go on comfortably in their sins, and to keep up a name to live even while they are dead." *MTP* 46:436.

119. *NPSP* 4:17.

120. "Ah! sirs, the church is not pure; the church is not perfect; we have scabbed sheep in the flock. In our own little communion, now and then, we find them out, and then comes the dread sentence of excommunication, by which they are cut off from our fellowship." *NPSP* 2:386-87.

of the church would result in great harm and loss to the church. Church discipline existed for the unity and protection of the church. Spurgeon warned his congregation, "I do not care about all the adversaries outside; our greatest cause of fear is from the crafty 'wolves in sheep's clothing,' that devour the flock. It is against such that we would denounce in holy wrath the solemn sentence of divine indignation, and for such we would shed our bitterest tears of sorrow."[121] In particular, Spurgeon observed how these wolves fostered mistrust and division within the church, complaining and finding fault with those who were seeking to follow Christ.[122] But perhaps even more grievously, these erring members brought shame to the cause of Christ by their behavior.

> If any man in the street were to pelt me with mud, I believe I should thank him for the honor, if I knew him to be a bad character, and knew that he hated me for righteousness sake. But if one who called himself a Christian should injure the cause with the filthiness of his own licentious behavior. Ah! that were more injurious than the stakes of Smithfield, or the racks of the Tower.[123]

Though the elders sought to care for their members and intervene before they engaged in any scandalous sin, this was not always possible.[124] In those cases, the only remaining action was to excommunicate them from the church, making clear the church's disapproval of such behavior. Church discipline mattered not only for the protection of the church but the vindication of Christ's reputation in the world.

---

121. Ibid., 389.

122. "Again: nothing divides the church more. I have seen many divisions in journeying through the country, and I believe almost every division may be traced to a deficiency of piety on the part of some of the members. We should be more one, if it were not for cants that creep into our midst. We should be more loving to each other, more tender-hearted, more kind, but that these men, so deceptive, coming into our midst, render us suspicious." NPSP 2:389.

123. Ibid.

124. "There are many of whom we are not aware, who creep like snakes along the grass, and are not discovered till they inflict a grievous wound upon religion, and do damage to our great and glorious cause." Ibid., 387.

The process of church discipline could begin in many different ways. A case could be brought to the elders' attention by a member of the church. Or news about a members' involvement in a scandalous sin could hit the press. In many cases, the discovery resulted from the elders' inquiry into a case of non-attendance. However a discipline case began, the elders were always involved in the investigation. Spurgeon reminded his congregation:

> If you know of any case of open sin, let the elders of the church be informed, and it will be dealt with tenderly and firmly. In so large a church as this there may be cases of evil living not known to the overseers of the flock; but we invite the co-operation of all in maintaining the purity of the entire body, and we trust that we have it.[125]

The *Elder Minutes* reveal their regular discussions regarding cases of discipline. Multiple elders were usually involved in a particular case so that multiple witnesses could be established. If the case were serious enough, this would lead to a recommendation to the congregation for discipline. Depending on the seriousness of the case, the elders could notify the congregation of the case at varying points of the investigation.

An example of the discipline process can be seen in the case of John Moakes. At the meeting on June 12, 1876, elder Dunn "reported unfavorably upon this case" and elders Cockrell and Pearce were assigned to visit Moakes.[126] At the following meeting, their report confirmed Dunn's report, and the elders agreed for his "name to be removed for conduct inconsistent with his profession."[127] On June 29, 1876, at the church meeting, the congregation approved the following motion, "John Moakes [along with one other], having been guilty of conduct inconsistent with their profession, it is agreed that their names be removed from our Church Books."[128]

---

125. *MTP* 34:455.

126. "Elders Meeting Monday June 12th [1876]," *Elders Minutes 1876-1881*, Metropolitan Tabernacle Archives.

127. "Elders Meeting Monday June 19th [1876]," Ibid.

128. "Church Meeting held after the Lecture June 29th, 1876," *MB 1871-1876*.

Most cases followed the example of the Moakes' case, where multiple church meetings were called before the excommunication vote took place. Usually, there was at least two meetings: one to present the case and to appoint messengers, and another to present the messengers' findings and to vote. However, in particularly scandalous cases, the elders could also lead the church to vote at the same meeting where the charges are first presented. In such a case, there would be sufficient testimony from other members so that there was no need for further messengers. The minutes record at least one such case:

> Our Pastor stated that he had several times heard various charges against Mary Ann Meagre and had requested our elder Phillips to watch the case and that it was really so bad that he advised instant excommunication. Our Brother Phillips having frequently seen Mary Ann Meagre at the request of the pastor and having long watched her conduct reported various cases of gross inconsistency and immorality on her part, and his statements being supported by other members of the Church it is agreed that she be forthwith excommunicated from the fellowship of the Church.[129]

As can be seen in these cases, the minutes do not always record the exact charges raised. It is not always clear how much detail was shared with the congregation before their vote. In some instances, the elders called on the congregation to trust their leaders.

When details of cases under discipline are kept from the church, the fact is openly stated, and leave asked for the maintenance of such public reticence; while any member is informed, that if dissatisfied, the pastor will give him the reasons why the elders have advised the removal of the offender, and their motive in not giving details of the sin. When it would be for the injury of good morals, or expose the pastor to a suit-at-law, the officers ask the confidence of the church, and request it to adopt their verdict in the case without hearing detailed information; this is cheerfully accorded in every case, and much evil thus averted.[130]

---

129. "Church Meeting September 24th 1861," *MB* 1861-1866.

130. *S&T* 1869:55.

The minutes, however, record the general nature of the charges. Discipline cases during the first seven years of Spurgeon's ministry involved instances of embezzlement,[131] abandonment,[132] financial and sexual impropriety,[133] adultery,[134] lasciviousness,[135] lying,[136] neglect of religious duties,[137] repeated thefts,[138] immorality,[139] and spousal abuse.[140]

On some particularly painful occasions, the elders led the congregation in disciplining officers in the church who had fallen into scandalous sin. One example of this is the case of elder Mead.

This was a very sorrowful evening to all assembled. Our Pastor announced to the Church the mournful news that our Brother

---

131. "Church Meeting July 10th, 1855," *MB 1854-1861*.

132. "Church Meeting March 11th, 1857," Ibid.

133. "The same Messengers Brethren Low and Olney also reported in the case of our Brother James Woods (Secretary to our Building Fund & Missionary) on which it was – Resolved – That our Brother James Woods having been found guilty of irregular conduct in money matters and improper conduct with a female, that he be no longer a member of this Church and that his name be erased from our church book until it shall please God to give him repentance." Church Meeting March 11th, 1857," *MB 1854-1861*.

134. In one case, this adultery involved two members of the church. "Our Brother William Catchpole having confessed to the sin of adultery (with next case) be withdrawn from and cease to be a Member of this Church until it shall please God to give him repentance.... Our Sister Mary Ann Kimber being charged with immoral conduct, Brethren Low and Olney are requested to enquire into the case and report thereon at the next meeting." Ibid.

135. "Our brother Moore reported to the Church the mournful history of William Woodman, who had sorely backslidden and fallen into lasciviousness and afterwards in a fit of remorse had attempted to destroy himself by taking poison. Amid many tears and supplications it was resolved that William Woodman be excommunicated from the fellowship of this Church until God shall grant him repentance." "Church Meeting February 1st, 1858," Ibid.

136. "Church Meeting February 17th, 1858," Ibid.

137. "Church Meeting August 12th, 1858," Ibid. See also "Church Meeting January 31st, 1859," Ibid.

138. "Church Meeting July 13th, 1859," Ibid.

139. "Church Meeting October 10th, 1859," Ibid. See also "Church Meeting March 22nd, 1860," Ibid.; "Church Meeting August 6th, 1860," Ibid.

140. "Brethren Low and Olney the messengers appointed to enquire into the case of our Brother Thomas Golding reported, that they considered the charges brought against him of repeated acts of cruelty to his late wife had been fully proved Whereupon it is agreed that Thomas Golding be excommunicated from the fellowship of this Church until it shall please God to grant him repentance." "Church Meeting November 22nd, 1860," Ibid.

and Elder Mead had fallen into gross sin, and Brethren Cook and Olney stated that they had visited him and found him in a truly wretched & hardened state having for some time past indulged in the sin of drunkenness. It is, therefore, agreed that he be at once put away from the office of the eldership, and that brethren Thomas Moor and Roe be appointed messengers to visit him, with the special object of endeavoring to lead him to repentance.[141]

Four weeks later, this report was given,

Our pastor stated that the case of William Mead had been fully & patiently investigated and although some hope had at first been entertained of his sincere repentance further disclosures proved his conduct to be even worse than was reported and it was evident that in addition to lust & drunkenness he had been guilty of falsehood & hypocrisy. It is therefore agreed that he be forthwith solemnly excommunicated from the fellowship of this Church.[142]

Though necessary, church discipline was a "sorrowful" affair for the entire church, leading to many tears.

The language in the church minutes reveals what lay behind the discipline. Members were "excommunicated from the fellowship of this Church until it shall please God to grant [them] repentance." In other words, by their persistent sin, these fallen members no longer demonstrated the repentance of a genuine Christian. Therefore, the congregation could no longer affirm their profession of faith by allowing them to participate in the communion of the church. At the same time, even as the church removed them from membership, they prayed that God would grant them repentance and restore them to their fellowship. Spurgeon urged his people to continue to pray for those who had been excommunicated.[143] A true Christian could not ultimately

---

141. "Church Meeting March 3rd, 1862," *MB 1861-1866*

142. "Church Meeting March 31st, 1862," Ibid.

143. "On the other hand, there are some even among the grossest backsliders who have the vital spark in them. They are the people of God; they are God's sheep, even though they have sadly gone astray, and for these our prayers must be constant, incessant, fervent, believing. 'O Lord, save thy people.'" *MTP* 13:483-84.

fall away, nor could they persist in sin, but must be called back to Christ.[144]

In joy, the church saw many restored to their fellowship after falling away and being disciplined.[145] The *Minute Books* annual meeting membership reports record twenty-one members who were restored to membership during Spurgeon's years. Here was yet another purpose of church discipline: to awaken backsliding members and bring them to repentance. Through all the trials and temptations of life, church membership was a means of grace for preserving the faith of its members.

Writing in 1865, Spurgeon reflected on how relatively few cases of discipline his church encountered thus far and attributed this to the work of God:

> Out of the vast numbers who have been added to this Church, how few, happily, how few has God permitted to fall into gross sin or outward backsliding! We have not built a wall which the foxes have broken down. Our ministry has not nourished gourds, which come up in a night and perish in a night, but in the midst of temptations sore, and trials many, all the defections which we have had to mourn over have been but as the small dust of the balance compared with the many who have been kept by the power of divine grace. If the Lord has done all this for us, shall we not delight to honor him?[146]

Spurgeon knew of churches that were committed to regenerate church membership, but they were sloppy in their membership

---

144. "Backslider, you were once a jewel in the church; you were put down in the book as a church-member, but from the casket of the church Satan stole you. Ah, but you did not belong to him, and he cannot keep you! You have agreed to be his, but your agreement does not stand for anything. You did not belong to yourself, and so you could not give yourself away. Christ has the first and only valid claim to you, and will yet obtain his rights by the omnipotence of his grace." *MTP* 52:31.

145. One example of this is William Catchpole. "William Catchpole came before the Church and professed his deep and unfeigned repentance of the sin for which he was excommunicated and his hope that the Lord had restored to him the light of his countenance, and Brother Moore, having stated that he had thoroughly investigated the case and could with confidence recommend him, our Pastor also informing the Church that no persons had offered any objection and that the offended brother was willing that he should be received, it is therefore agreed that he be restored to membership with this Church." "Church Meeting September 5th, 1861," *MB 1861-1866.*

146. *S&T* 1865:6.

process, resulting in an excessive number of church discipline cases.[147] But his commitment to regenerate church membership included the dual commitment of maintaining a careful membership process, while also diligently practicing church discipline. As a result, he saw relatively few cases of discipline. As was noted earlier, two hundred and fifty-three members were removed by exclusion during Spurgeon's ministry. Though each discipline case was a painful occasion for the church, it is still worth noting that this was less than two percent of all the members that were taken into membership.[148]

Conclusion

As a Baptist, Spurgeon was committed to the principle of regenerate church membership. This is made evident through his teaching and the record of the *Church Meeting Minutes* at the Metropolitan Tabernacle. Through the careful maintenance of the membership of the church, the presence and witness of the church was made distinct from the world. The church militant here on earth will never be perfect. Within the church, there will always be hypocrites and backsliders, deceiving others and even themselves by their false profession of faith. Nonetheless, Spurgeon believed the church should do her best in evaluating professions of faith and only bringing into membership those who were truly converted. But having brought them into membership, Spurgeon continued to uphold regenerate church membership by expecting his members to grow spiritually and serve the cause of Christ. Those who refused to do so were entreated and pursued. In cases of serious unrepentant sin, they were excommunicated from the church. But such cases were the minority. Spurgeon's

---

147. "I know a church which excommunicated eighty members in twelve months, for disorderly conduct and forsaking the truth, and they had taken in a hundred or so the year before, from some great spasm, which had been occasioned by one of those spurious revivalists, who came about making a great noise, and doing no good whatever, but scorching and burning up the ground, where other men might have sown the good seed of the kingdom." *NPSP* 2:76.

148. The actual percentage is even smaller as the above figure does not take into account those who were already members when Spurgeon arrived and the fact that some of those exclusions included were withdrawals, which are different from excommunications.

commitment to regenerate church membership ensured that the majority of those who joined the church were true soldiers of Christ, prepared for battle.

> So, brethren, in the church of God there must be discipline—the discipline not only of admission and of dismission in receiving the converts and rejecting the hypocrites, but the discipline of marshalling the troops to the service of Christ in the holy war in which we are engaged.[149]

---

149.   *MTP* 17:195.

7

Elder and Deacon-Led Congregationalism

To celebrate the construction of the Metropolitan Tabernacle in the spring of 1861, the congregation held a series of public meetings in the new building. The first meeting was with neighboring churches in the area, held on March 27, 1861. Here was an opportunity for these nearby churches to express their prayers and support of Spurgeon and his ministry, and for Spurgeon to express his gratitude and commitment to work with them in gospel ministry.[1] One week later, there was a meeting with fellow London Baptist churches. Here, Spurgeon opened the meeting by declaring that "this chapel belongs not to me nor to my Church specially, but to all the Baptist denomination" and urged for the advancement of Baptist convictions throughout the land.[2] Then the following night, representatives from various evangelical denominations and churches gathered together in the Tabernacle "to testify to the essential union of the Church."[3] Though Spurgeon was a convinced Baptist, he was eager to express his union with other evangelical denominations and work alongside them in the gospel. In all these meetings, it was clear that Spurgeon did not see his ministry operating apart from others. No matter how large his church became, the Metropolitan Tabernacle did not exist alone, but in association with other evangelical churches.

1. *MTP* 7:193.
2. Ibid., 225.
3. Ibid., 234.

But there was one final meeting. On Monday evening, April 8, 1861, the congregation of the Metropolitan Tabernacle gathered for a meeting of their own church, "designed to set forth the independency, harmony, and family character of each Church."[4] At the opening of the meeting, Spurgeon gave the following remarks:

> We have met together during the last two weeks as a part of the Baptist denomination, and as a portion of the one great Church of the Lord Jesus Christ. We have endeavored to give expression to our firm faith in the unity of all the faithful in Christ... now tonight, the one thought is to be this, that the Church of Christ meeting here is within itself a family, that it is whole and entire and needs nothing from without to make it complete. We do not, for instance, need to appeal to a synod, or to a general assembly. We do not look up to one minister called a bishop, or to some other person called an archbishop. The Church has its own bishop or pastor; it has its own presbytery or elders; it has its own deaconship, and is not therefore dependent on any other, but should every other Church become extinct its organization would not be marred. I take it, so far as I have read Scripture, that a modified form of Episcopalian Presbyterian Independency is the Scriptural method of Church government; at any rate, no other form of government would have worked in so large a Church as this. You have found it necessary to have one who shall be the overseer of the Church under God. You have found it needful to gather a presbytery around him, that they may be with him the pastors of the flock. You believe it also to be exceedingly needful that the Church should maintain its congregational principles, and yet be ever ready to enter into Presbyterian alliance with any other Church, not for its government, but for mutual assistance to be rendered and to be received.[5]

While "Presbyterian alliances" were important, Spurgeon believed each church was itself a family, a whole, and not dependent on any other church or association for its existence. This was true particularly when it came to the government of the church. No

4. *MTP* 7:257.
5. Ibid.

synod, bishop, or general assembly was to govern over a local church, but each church was to be governed from within, by its appointed leaders, maintaining "congregational principles." Spurgeon called his form of church government "a modified form of Episcopalian Presbyterian Independency." He saw aspects of Episcopal church government in his polity, particularly in the role of the bishop (*episkopos*), or pastor, of the Church. Like the Presbyterians, the church had called a plurality of elders to serve alongside the pastor. But despite those modifications, the Tabernacle held to the Independency, or congregationalism, of the church. The congregation was the final authority in the church.

Spurgeon believed that this modified congregationalism was needful for managing a church that size. But more importantly, Spurgeon believed this was "the Scriptural method of Church government." Ultimately, he did not follow this polity because it was practical, but because he believed this was the pattern set by the apostles.[6] Here, at the beginning of a new chapter of their history, Spurgeon reminded his congregation of their independent standing before God and their responsibility to carry on the ministry of the gospel. In this chapter, we will consider Spurgeon's view of congregational church polity and how this polity related to his vision for the church militant.

Congregational Polity

Except for his teaching on church discipline, Calvin paid relatively little attention to the structure of the congregation. Instead, his focus was on the leaders of the church. He identified four offices in the church: deacon, teaching elder (or teacher), ruling elder, and pastor. Whoever refused Christ's provision of these officers "[was] striving for the undoing or rather the ruin and destruction of the church."[7] Groups within the Reformed stream, like the English Baptists, would vary from Calvin in their structure of the

---

6.   "This form of Church government has risen out of the peculiar circumstances of a rapid increase, and is, we believe, in harmony with that which in similar circumstances existed in the primitive Churches." *S&T* 1865:31.

7.   *Institutes*, IV:iii:2.

church, but they would inherit his commitment to ordering the church according to God's Word.

Church polity refers to a church's ordering and authority structure. From the very beginning, Baptists have held to a congregational polity,[8] which places the authority of the church in the congregation, especially in matters related to the church's doctrine, membership, discipline, and leadership. Final authority in these matters did not reside in the denomination, government, a bishop, a board of elders, synods, or any other organization. For example, the London Confession (1644) highlights the congregational rule of each church in the calling of pastors. "That being thus joined, every Church has power given them from Christ for their well-being, to choose to themselves meet persons into the office of Pastors, Teachers, Elders, Deacons, being qualified according to the Word."[9] Similarly, the congregation should also exercise authority in matters of membership and church discipline. "Christ has likewise given power to his whole Church to receive in and cast out, by way of Excommunication, any members; and this power is given to every particular Congregation, and not one particular person, either member or Officer, but the whole."[10] Though Baptists affirmed the important biblical role of pastors and deacons in churches, the final authority for the most fundamental matters resided in the congregation. Yet congregational polity did not negate the importance of cooperation and counsel among Baptist churches.[11]

---

8.   English Baptists can trace their origins to English Separatism, which "drew a line between [civil authority] powers in society at large and their power with regard to local churches." Anthony Chute, Nathan A. Finn, Michael A. G. Haykin, *The Baptist Story: From Sect to Global Movement* (Nashville, TN: B&H Academic, 2015), 14-16. Matthew Bingham argues the logic of congregational ecclesiology "had the unintended consequence of eroding the logic upon which paedobaptism rested." *Orthodox Radicals: Baptist Identity in the English Reformation* (Oxford: Oxford University Press, 2019), 73-74.

9.   Lumpkin, *Baptist Confessions of Faith*, 166.

10.   Ibid., 168.

11.   "Although the particular Congregations be distinct and several Bodies, every one a compact and knit Citie in it selfe; yet are they all to walk by one and the same Rule, and by all meanes convenient to have the counsel and help of one another in all needful affaires of the Church, as members of one body in the common faith under Christ their onely head." Ibid., 168-69.

These early Baptist confessions represented some of the earliest efforts among Baptists to associate together for doctrinal clarity. From there, Baptists would go on to cooperate in church planting, pastoral training, social causes, missions, and more.

Spurgeon's Teaching on Congregationalism

The foundation of congregational polity lay in the lordship of Christ over the church. Because Christ alone ruled the church, no other person or group of persons should ever exercise authority over it.[12] Rather, every church, led by the Spirit, had the freedom to follow Christ's reign, as reflected in the Scriptures. While many churches turned to various books or councils or traditions for direction on how their churches were to be ordered, Spurgeon believed that the Scriptures were a sufficient guide.

> To us it is of small account that either Presbytery, or the Episcopacy, or Independency, have put their stamp upon a certain form of teaching. Authority is no more to us than the snap of a man's finger, unless the truth thus commended derives certainty from the testimony of Jesus Christ himself, who is the Head of his body the church.[13]

In other words, the regulative principle applied not only to the corporate worship of the church but also to the polity of the church.

Christ alone could make laws for the church, and therefore, it was the duty of the congregation to follow those laws.[14] At the heart of Christ's ordering of the church was a congregational polity, where the congregation exercised authority in all the most important matters. In his sermon, "The Church – Conservative

---

12. "Jesus Christ had been the official teacher of his saints whilst on earth. They called no man Rabbi except Christ. They sat at no men's feet to learn their doctrines; but they had them direct from the lips of him who 'spake as never man spake.' 'And now,' says he, 'when I am gone, where shall you find the great infallible teacher? Shall I set you up a Pope at Rome, to whom you shall go, and who shall be your infallible oracle? Shall I give you the councils of the church to be held to decide all knotty points?' Christ said no such thing." *NPSP* 1:34.

13. *MTP* 14:617.

14. *MTP* 14:617-18.

and Aggressive," Spurgeon lays out Christ's design for the order of the church:

> To our minds, the Scripture seems very explicit as to how this Church should be ordered. We believe that every Church member should have equal rights and privileges; that there is no power in Church officers to execute anything unless they have the full authorization of the members of the Church. We believe, however, that the Church should choose its pastor, and having chosen him, that they should love him and respect him for his work's sake; that with him should be associated the deacons of the Church to take the oversight of pecuniary matters; and the elders of the Church to assist in all the works of the pastorate in the fear of God, being overseers of the flock. Such a Church we believe to be scripturally ordered; and if it abide in the faith, rooted, and grounded, and settled, such a Church may expect the benediction of heaven, and so it shall become the pillar and ground of the truth.[15]

Here, Spurgeon makes clear that every church member "should have equal rights and privileges." No church officer carries more votes in church matters than any member of the congregation. Rather, church officers can only act as representatives of the congregation's authority and are elected by the congregation. But these offices also have distinct responsibilities. The pastor and the elders are to labor together for the spiritual care of the flock, and the deacons are to give attention to financial and other practical matters. Undoubtedly, this required leadership in their spheres of delegated authority. Yet ultimately, it is the members of the church who are to exercise authority in the church. Spurgeon believed that this was not merely a pragmatic solution to ordering a large church, but the "very explicit" teaching of Scripture. Here was a biblical model for how churches should be ordered.

In all this, Spurgeon did not see this structure as replacing the church's need to rely on the Spirit. What characterized the polity of the apostles was not primarily an organizational structure, but

---

15. *MTP* 7:362.

the presence of the Spirit empowering all that the church did.[16] The last thing Spurgeon wanted was for pastors to think that having a right structure meant that the church could function like a machine, without prayer or dependence on the Spirit.

> "We have got a machinery," said a brother to me once, "we have got a machinery in our Church which will go on just as well, whatever the characters of the members may be." "Then," I said to him, "depend upon it, yours is not that which God has ordained." For it seems to me that the most Scriptural system of Church government is that which requires the most prayer, the most faith, and the most piety, to keep it going.[17]

Church order without the presence of the Spirit resembled a well-ordered cemetery: organized but without life. But the kind of order that Spurgeon wanted was that of a company of soldiers, assembled under Christ and armed for war.[18] Congregationalism was not a process to mindlessly carry out, but a means of promoting the activity and involvement of the congregation in the work of the church in dependence on the Spirit.

Church Meetings

At a special church meeting on April 19, 1854, the congregation of the New Park Street Chapel passed the following resolution:

> It was resolved unanimously, that while as members of this Church we desire to record, with devout & fervent gratitude to God, our estimation of the Revd. C. H. Spurgeon's services during the period of his labours amongst us, we regard the

---

16. "The church of God is well organised. Perhaps never in the history of the world has the church of God been so potent in its organizations and possessions as it is now; but it wants the first fire, the pristine zeal and energy which the apostles and their immediate successors had." *MTP* 13:486.

17. *MTP* 7:366.

18. "The true church is an organised whole; and life, true spiritual life, wherever it is paramount in the church, without rules and rubrics, is quite sure to create order and arrangement. Order without life reminds us of the rows of graves in a cemetery, all numbered and entered in the register: order with life reminds us of the long lines of fruit trees in Italy, festooned with fruitful vines. Sunday school teachers, bear ye the banner of the folded lamb; sick visitors, follow the ensign of the open hand; preachers, rally to the token of the uplifted brazen serpent; and all of you, according to your sacred calling, gather to the name of Jesus, armed for the war." *MTP* 17:196.

extraordinary increase in the attendance upon the means of grace both on Lord's days and week evenings, combined with the manifest fact that his Ministry has secured the general approbation of the Members, as an encouraging token that our heavenly Father has directed his way towards us in answer to the many prayers we have offered up for a suitable Pastor.

And as there are several inquirers desirous of joining our fellowship we consider it prudent to secure as early as possible his permanent settlement with us.

We therefore beg to tender our Brother the Revd. C. H. Spurgeon a most cordial and affectional invitation forthwith to become Pastor of this Church, and we pray that the result of his services may be owned of God with an outpouring of the Holy Spirit and a revival of religion in our midst that it may be fruitful in the conversion of sinners & the edification of those who believe.[19]

They were notified on May 5, 1854, of Spurgeon's acceptance of this call,[20] and in less than two weeks, on May 17, 1854, Spurgeon presided over his first church meeting as pastor of the New Park Street Chapel.[21]

What was the purpose of these church meetings? As a church, the congregation discussed and approved resolutions dealing with property, finances, church officers, and more. But the vast majority of the business had to do with church membership. As Spurgeon's popularity grew, more and more people were converted and sought membership at his church, which required more church meetings. Before Spurgeon's arrival in 1854, the church held meetings once a month. But by the fall of 1855, the congregation began meeting twice a month to receive all the visitors applying for membership. In the following year, the congregation held thirty church meetings, almost twice the number as the previous year. The move to the Metropolitan Tabernacle in 1861 brought an increase in membership applications, more than doubling the number from previous years. As a result, the number of

---

19. "Special adjourned Church Meeting Wednesday 19th April 1854," *MB 1808-1854*.

20. "Special Church Meeting 5th May 1854," Ibid.

21. See Table 3 for the number of church meetings during Spurgeon's ministry recorded in the Metropolitan Tabernacle *Minute Books*.

church meetings that year also increased to forty-four. Over the next thirty years, there would only be four years where the congregation had fewer than forty church meetings.[22] In two years, the congregation met more than eighty times.[23]

To begin with, the church held its monthly church meetings on Wednesday evenings. But as they grew more frequent, to accommodate Spurgeon's busy schedule,[24] the church began holding church meetings on Monday evenings, before and after the prayer meeting, and on Thursday evenings, before and after the Bible study. In other words, rather than having one monthly meeting, have more frequent, shorter meetings, taking advantage of those nights when the church was already gathering. This allowed the church to hold at least eight church meetings a month, without having to assemble on any additional evenings.

Spurgeon's chairing of these meetings gives a glimpse of his pastoral involvement in the church. Throughout his ministry (May 1854–January 1892), the church held 1,862 church meetings. In the first nine years of his ministry (1854-1862), Spurgeon attended and chaired every church meeting, 267 meetings in all. It was, after all, the custom of the church to have the pastor chair church meetings. During these early years, Spurgeon was in the prime and energy of youth. But this would have been a massive pastoral load for any individual, and no prior pastor dealt with the level of growth that Spurgeon saw.

As his ministry and responsibilities grew, his health began to suffer, and Spurgeon had to lean on others. Beginning in 1863, Spurgeon began to allow deacons and elders to chair the church meetings, giving many of them a turn. Also, in the previous year, the church recognized John Collins to fill the office of Teacher in the church,[25] and in 1863, he also began to preside at church meetings to relieve Spurgeon. Collins and other Teachers would eventually be called away to other pastorates, but in 1868, the

---

22. These years were 1885, 1886, 1887, and 1891.

23. In 1864, the church held eighty-one church meetings. In 1866, the church held eighty-three church meetings.

24. For an example of Spurgeon's full weekly schedule, see *Autobiography* 2:102.

25. "Church Meeting November 24th, 1862," *MB 1861-1866*.

church called Spurgeon's brother James to serve as Assistant Pastor. James would chair most church meetings during his years at the Tabernacle. Towards the end of Spurgeon's years, the elders and the pastors would divide chairing of church meetings more or less evenly.

What would have been the effect of these church meetings on the life of the church? Most of Spurgeon's biographers recount at length the vast gatherings of thousands each Lord's Day, many of them visitors and guests. This was especially the case during the first seven years, when the congregation met at Exeter Hall and the Surrey Gardens Music Hall. But the weekday meetings of the church, particularly the church meetings, were an opportunity for the congregation to gather as a church family. For all the attention and controversy that often surrounded their pastor,[26] these meetings were a regular reminder to the congregation that they were not a spectacle or a show, but a church.

Church meetings among Baptist churches in Spurgeon's day had a bad reputation. Often, they were poorly led and organized,[27] resulting in "a sort of ecclesiastical bear-garden."[28] But this was not the case for Spurgeon's church. With so many young converts, Spurgeon was particularly concerned that church meetings display the love and warmth of the church. He once charged his congregation,

> Let us have no surly tempers in our midst, no cold hearts, and no divisions, because, when these young converts come among us, they will be frightened if they find us full of evil passions, and with little or no love to Christ.... I would like, sometimes, to say to those who have noisy church-meetings, or who display a party

---

26. For a collection of articles about the controversy from the first seven years of his ministry, see *Autobiography* 2:33-61.

27. Responding to a question about whether or not pastors should allow members to raise new subjects in a church meeting without prior notification, Spurgeon writes, "Surely, common sense alone is needed to form a judgment upon this point. Would such a thing be borne with any but an assembly of idiots? The men of the world have needed no enlightenment upon so simple a matter; hath not nature herself taught them how to act? This folly which we fear is committed in some churches, is but another illustration of our Lord's saying, 'The children of this world are in their generation wiser than the children of light.'" *S&T* 1872:135-36.

28. *MTP* 7:261.

spirit, 'Hush; be quiet, for the sake of these new-comers. Do not let them be hurt in their feelings, and injured in their minds.'[29]

One entry provides a glimpse into the nature of these meetings. On Friday, May 18, 1860, commencing at two p.m., the Minute Books records forty-two membership candidates who came before the church to be received into membership.[30] Assuming an efficient use of time, giving ten minutes for each membership interview, report, and congregational vote, this meeting could have easily lasted more than seven hours. And yet, written beneath the meeting minutes in Spurgeon's handwriting, a note reads, "This most blessed meeting lasted till a late hour at night. Bless the Lord."[31] In other words, the lateness of the meeting was an indication not so much of inefficiency, but of God's blessing upon the church through the conversion of sinners. As the chairman, Spurgeon used these church meetings for the edification of his congregation. He loved listening to testimonies of God's grace,[32] and with hundreds of people coming forward for membership, each testimony was a reminder to the congregation of God's power and faithfulness to transform lives through the gospel.

More than simply dealing with business, church meetings were an important part of the life of the church. Sunday worship services were devoted to the corporate worship of God and represented the evangelistic mission of the church. Thursday Bible studies provided a midweek gathering around God's Word. Monday prayer meetings reminded the congregation of their dependence on God to work in the lives of people. And church meetings were a joyful reminder of their identity as a church. In their unity of mind, evident in their church meetings, Spurgeon saw the church moving as a phalanx, knit together as one against the spiritual forces of evil, displaying the power of God in their midst.

---

29.   *MTP* 48:476.

30.   "Church Meeting May 18th, 1860," *MB 1854-1861*.

31.   "Church Meeting May 18th, 1860," *MB 1854-1861*.

32.   *Autobiography* 2:137.

Here is the secret of strength. Split us into fractions and we are conquered; unite us into a steady phalanx, and we become invincible, knit us together as one man, and Satan himself can never rend us asunder.... I could not but wonder at our Church Meeting on Wednesday, how all seemed to fly as a cloud. No sooner was a thing proposed than the whole church seemed without a dissentient opinion to be carried along irresistibly by one thought that possessed its bosom. It is very seldom you see a church really united: but God has united us.[33]

Congregationalism and Church Membership

The main reason for the increase in church meetings during Spurgeon's pastorate was due to his commitment to the congregation's involvement in bringing people into church membership. Although membership applications grew, the church refused to take any shortcuts in their membership process. Certainly, it would have been much more efficient for the elders to approve people into membership directly. After all, they were the ones who interviewed and examined each applicant, and the congregation only acted on their recommendation. But Spurgeon remained committed to congregationalism when it came to church membership. Rather than changing the process, the church increased the number of church meetings and continued to require congregational involvement in bringing each individual into membership.

As was previously shown, the congregation voted at least twice in every membership application: first, in appointing a messenger to visit each applicant; and second, in voting an applicant into membership.[34] As a final additional step, each applicant would not officially become a member until after they received the right hand of fellowship at the Lord's Table. Undoubtedly, the elders and pastor played an important role in the membership process. The congregation was largely dependent on these church leaders for all the preliminary work of hearing and examining testimonies. If the pastor or the messenger was not pleased with what they

---

33. *NPSP* 2:75.

34. *S&T* 1869:53-54.

discovered, they could decide not to bring a candidate forward to the congregation.[35] At the same time, for the membership process to move forward, the congregation had to be involved. While the congregation entrusted the task of examining membership candidates to their leaders and followed their recommendations, the vote reveals that the congregation took ultimate responsibility for each new member. Membership, pictured ultimately at the Lord's table, was not anything that the elders or deacons could bestow apart from the congregation. Congregationalism gave expression to this commitment.

Congregationalism extended not only to the receiving of members but also to the removal of members. Membership in the church meant accountability to the church. Except in the case of deaths, which are ultimately an act of God, there was no way for a member of the church to escape accountability to the congregation. The *Minute Books* reveal that all removals required a congregational vote, from the removal of inactive members for non-attendance to every dismissal to another church, to every case of church discipline. This is not to say that the church should be wrongly territorial or possessive of their membership. Spurgeon taught his congregation to dismiss their members graciously and prayerfully as they went on to labor in other spheres.[36] And yet, in each vote to remove someone, the congregation held each member accountable in their departure. In cases of discipline, congregationalism brought greater weight to each case, as scandalous sins were made public to the church. With each vote, excommunication expressed the view not only of a few leaders, but of the entire congregation.

At the Metropolitan Tabernacle, congregationalism on the front-end of church membership expressed the commitment of the entire church to one another. Congregationalism on the back-end of church membership made accountability to that commitment possible.

---

35. This author is not aware of any membership application where the congregation overruled a messenger or pastor's decision not to bring someone forward for membership.

36. *MTP* 46:434-435.

Congregationalism and Church Leadership

Spurgeon was a firm congregationalist, firmly holding to the authority of the congregation in the life of the church. In addition to all matters related to membership additions and removals, the congregation voted on many other issues. A survey of the first seven years of church meetings after Spurgeon's arrival shows the congregation voting on deacons, elders, building projects, the method for fencing the Lord's Table, the appointing of committees, the sending of messengers to associational meetings, the tabling of motions, the collection of special offerings, the provision of benevolence for needy members, public statements about the ministry of the church and their pastor, gifts to other churches, and special seasons of prayer. In each of these decisions, church leaders played an important role in leading the congregation and recommending these motions to them. Spurgeon did not see the teaching of Scripture on the role of leaders in the church as incompatible with the congregational authority of the church. Rather, in holding to "a modified form of Episcopalian Presbyterian Independency," Spurgeon understood that church leaders were vital to the proper functioning of congregational polity.

Referring to the practice of plural elders, Wills writes that "by 1820 most churches had dropped the practice."[37] This was Spurgeon's own experience as he was the only pastor during his time at Waterbeach and upon his arrival in London, serving alongside his deacons.[38] Baptist churches of Spurgeon's day rarely appointed elders for fear that such an office would conflict with the authority of the congregation.[39] John Gill, one of Spurgeon's

---

37. Greg Wills, "The Church: Baptists and Their Churches in the Eighteenth and Nineteenth Centuries," in *Polity: Biblical Arguments on How to Conduct Church Life* (Washington, DC: Nine Marks Ministries, 2001), 34.

38. One explanation that Spurgeon heard for the removal of a plurality of elders was the combining of deacons and elders into the diaconal office. "They were told in Baptist and Independent Churches that the deacons were elders as well, but he wished to know by what law the two offices had been amalgamated." *MTP* 7:260.

39. Shawn D. Wright, "Baptists and a Plurality of Elders," in *Shepherding God's Flock: Biblical Leadership in the New Testament and Beyond,* ed. Benjamin L. Merkle and Thomas R. Schreiner (Grand Rapids, MI: Kregel Publications, 2014), 255-67.

predecessors, had argued against the necessity of a plurality of elders.[40] But in spite of these trends, Spurgeon believed that it was the combined efforts of elders and deacons that made the ministry of his church possible, and he hoped other Baptist churches would follow the New Testament pattern.[41]

The office of deacon was well-established when Spurgeon arrived in 1854. At the Tabernacle, the deacons were men who were elected by the congregation to lifetime terms. Spurgeon approved of this arrangement as this provided stability and consistency for the congregation, even amid pastoral transitions.[42] The office of a deacon was a difficult position. Therefore, Spurgeon believed these men were to be chosen according to their character more than anything else.[43] Though Spurgeon would go on to establish the office of elders in the church, he never minimized the importance of deacons.

> Deprive the church of her deacons, and she would be bereaved
> of her most valiant sons; their loss would be the shaking of the

---

40. Ibid., 274-276. Spurgeon writes concerning Gill, "It was thought desirable that some younger minister should be found to act as co-pastor. To this, the Doctor gave a very decided answer in the negative, asserting 'that Christ gives *pastors*, is certain; but that he gives *co-pastors*, is not so certain.' He even went the length of comparing a church with a co-pastor to a woman who should marry another man while her first husband lived, and call him co-husband. Great men are not always wise." *Autobiography* 1:310.

41. "He could only say that it would have been utterly impossible for that Church to have existed, except as a mere sham and huge pretence, if it had not been for the Scriptural and most expedient office of the eldership. He blessed God for his deacons, and they worked very hard; but when they had both the temporal and spiritual conduct of the Church's work, it was too much for them, and he saw at once, that if the elders took the spiritual, and the deacons the temporal conduct of affairs, the work would be much more efficiently performed. He believed his elders had uniformly commanded the respect, the esteem, and the love of the Church, and he personally felt extremely grateful to them for what they had done. He only wished other Baptist Churches would follow their example in this matter, and he was sure that both the Churches and the minister would find the good effects of such a course." *MTP* 7:260.

42. "Our brethren in the deacon's work are not so migratory as our ministers; they are frequently born to Christ in the churches in which they live and die; they cannot readily remove when evil days becloud the church, but remain chained to the oar to bear the odium of discontent and the sorrow of decay." *S&T* 1868:244.

43. "Much ought to be taken into consideration in estimating the character of men sustaining office in the church, for many difficulties may be incidental to the position, and this may mitigate the severity with which we ought to judge the men." Ibid.

pillars of our spiritual house, and would cause a desolation on every side. Thanks be to God such a calamity is not likely to befall us, for the great Head of the church in mercy to her, will always raise up a succession of faithful men, who will use the office well, and earn unto themselves a good degree and much boldness in the faith.[44]

Writing in 1869, James Spurgeon described the role of deacons at the Tabernacle in this way: "Their duties are to care for the ministry, and help the poor of the church, to regulate the finances and take charge of the church's property, seeing to the order and comfort of all worshipping in the place."[45] Given the massive financial and administrative coordination required to run the Metropolitan Tabernacle,[46] Spurgeon's appreciation of his deacons is understandable. While it was the congregation that approved decisions about the finances, property, and ministry of the church, it was the deacons, under the leadership of the pastor, who implemented those decisions in an orderly and efficient manner.

When Spurgeon first arrived, the deacons were responsible for the pastoral, as well as the temporal, care of the church. With hundreds applying for membership each year, along with other cases of discipline and member care, this soon became too heavy a responsibility. So, in the annual meeting of 1859, the Minute Books record the following:

> Our pastor in accordance with a previous notice then stated the necessity that had long been felt by the Church for the appointement of certain brethren to the office of Elders to watch over the spiritual affairs of the Church. Our pastor pointed out the Scripture warrant for such an office and quoted the several

---

44. S&T 1868:243-44.

45. S&T 1869:52.

46. Glimpses into the work of the deacons can be seen in the *Deacons Meeting Minutes*. For example, at the Deacons Meeting on April 2, 1861, the deacons arranged for the presence of six policemen during these first meetings at the Metropolitan Tabernacle in order to preserve order and safety, and they approved a plan for the regular cleaning of the new chapel. "Minutes of Deacons Meeting held at the Metropolitan Tabernacle, April 2nd, 1861," *Deacons Meetings 1861-1882*, Metropolitan Tabernacle Archives.

passages relative to the ordaining of Elders, Titus I 5, Acts XIV 23, the qualifications of Elders, 1 Timothy III 1-7, Titus I 5-9, the duty of Elders, Acts XX 28 to 35, 1 Timothy V 17 James V 14, mention made of Elders, Acts XI 30, XV 4 6 23 XVI 4 1 Timothy IV 14. Whereupon it was resolved that the Church having heard the statement made by its pastor respecting the office of the eldership desires to elect a certain number to serve the church in the office for one year. It being understood that these brethren are to attend to the spiritual affairs of the Church and not to the temporal matters which appertain to the deacons only.

These minutes reveal the carefulness with which Spurgeon undertook this change. First, Spurgeon made a biblical case for this office. Rather than pushing for this change, his strategy was to teach on the passages in the New Testament that dealt with elders. As the congregation became convinced of the practice, they began to push for this change themselves.[47] The motion above reflects the biblical grounding of this change.

Second, elders would only hold one-year terms, reflecting their accountability to the congregation. Unlike the deacons who held lifetime terms, these elders had to be approved yearly, and this allowed the congregation to remove an elder easily if anything should go wrong. However, most elders would go on to serve for life, being re-elected year by year.[48]

Finally, there was a careful separation of spiritual and temporal responsibilities, with elders only being given spiritual responsibilities.[49] The deacons continued to oversee building projects, properties, and the finances of the church, while the elders would be devoted entirely to the spiritual care of the flock.[50]

Spurgeon published this description of the work of the elders:

---

47. "I did not force the question upon them, I only showed them that it was Scriptural, and then of course they wanted to carry it into effect." *Autobiography* 3:22.

48. *S&T* 1869:52.

49. The deacons and elders functioned as two separate boards, and their work did not overlap. The elders gave spiritual oversight, but they did not manage the deacons. For a story illustrating this dynamic, see *Autobiography* 3:23.

50. Some deacons would serve simultaneously as elders. For example, in the first class of elders, Deacons Low, Olney, W. Olney, and Moore were also nominated to serve as elders. See "Annual Church Meeting January 12th, 1859," *MB 1854-1861*.

The seeing of inquirers, the visiting of candidates for church membership, the seeking out of absentees, the caring for the sick and troubled, the conducting of prayer-meetings, catechumen and Bible-classes for the young men—these and other needed offices our brethren the elders discharge for the church. One elder is maintained by the church for the especial purpose of visiting our sick poor, and looking after the church roll, that this may be done regularly and efficiently.[51]

In addition to their pastoral work, the yearly election of elders at the annual meeting raised the profile of the elders. Spurgeon always brought the congregation a list of recommended men to serve as elders. He believed an open election was one of the worst methods for electing church leaders, tending towards disunity and the election of unqualified men.[52] Instead, Spurgeon consulted with the existing officers on all the nominations, and together they agreed on the names to bring forward. He was always on the lookout "for those who have proved their fitness for office by the work they have accomplished in their private capacity."[53] Every single elder nomination had to be approved by a congregational vote, and the congregation generally approved all of their leaders' recommendations.

Spurgeon would often be the one to approach members about serving as elders. One occasion, he reported back to the elders on those conversations.

Dear friends,

In reference to brethren whom I was to see about the eldership, I have to report as follows:

Brother Bantick is very grateful for the good opinion of the brethren & would gladly do all in his power but business so occupies him that he cannot fulfill the duties of the office & therefore declines.

---

51. *S&T* 1869:53.

52. "In my opinion, the very worst mode of selection is to print the names of all the male members, and then vote for a certain number by ballot. I know of one case in which a very old man was within two or three votes of being elected simply because his name began with A, and therefore was put at the top of the list of candidates." *Autobiography* 3:23.

53. Ibid.

Brother Hayles had a stroke of paralysis on the brain a few days ago & therefore cannot be expected to undertake the work.

Brother S. Johnson cannot take Wednesday evening work as it is his class night, but in any other way, he will act with us & I believe he will be a most efficient worker. We may heartily recommend him to the Church.

Brother Stubbs can undertake the work & is quite willing to do so. He will, I trust, prove to be a helpful brother.

Brother Woolacott in the kindest manner declines on account of the distance at which he resides & his business engagements.

Brother Wigney to my great regret feels that his class demands all his time & that he could not fulfill elder's duties.

We have these, dear brethren, need to look round again.

Yours ever truly,

C. H. Spurgeon.[54]

Clearly, each of these men were actively involved in the ministry of the church. For some, it was their ministries that prevented them from serving. They also took seriously the responsibilities of the office and many of them declined to serve. Spurgeon's conclusion is striking, "We have these, dear brethren, need to look round again." As gifted as he was, he knew he could not lead the church alone, or even with a small band of elders. He needed more men working alongside him in the spiritual care of the congregation.

By introducing elders in 1859, Spurgeon prepared the church for the even greater growth that would come when the congregation moved to the Metropolitan Tabernacle in 1861. Spurgeon declared that "it would have been utterly impossible for that Church to have existed, except as a mere sham and huge pretence, if it had not been for the Scriptural and most expedient office of the eldership." Without the faithful ministry of his elders, Spurgeon believed it would have been impossible to care pastorally for a congregation so large.[55] If there were a third element of his polity that he would have highlighted, it would have been the plurality

---

54. "Letter to the Elders," J. T. Dunn Collection, Spurgeon Library Archives, Midwestern Baptist Theological Seminary.

55. *MTP* 7:261; *S&T* 2:148.

of elders.[56] And yet, even in this, he was careful not to take away any of the congregation's authority. Rather, in the elders' pastoral labors, the congregation saw a model of how they were to work for the good of the church.[57]

Congregationalism and the Pastor

As the pastor of the church, Spurgeon understood his unique position. At the heart of his role was the task of "constantly ministering to them the Word of life" and modeling a life of total devotion to Christ. In the pastoral role, Spurgeon's vision of the militant church came to life. By his preaching and example, the church was mobilized.

> The battle is to be fought, brethren. It is to be fought by Christ's army, not by hirelings. What are you and I to do! I must stand at the end of the line and wave my sword, and say, "Come on, comrades!" And you, with steady step advancing, with firm bold front maintaining every inch of the ground you take, and at last—rushing in one tremendous phalanx straightway to the thick of the fight—you must carry every thing before you, and win the crown for King Jesus.[58]

But even while rousing his congregation to action, Spurgeon did not forget his responsibility to shepherd his people individually. In this, the pastor was another one of the elders of the church, responsible for the spiritual care of his people.[59] Yet as the elder

---

56. A plurality of elders was the first of several of "peculiarities which he supposed were not to be found in any other Church, at least in England" that Spurgeon listed during the opening services of the Tabernacle. *MTP* 7:260.

57. "Especially should each of us endeavor to behave himself aright in the house of God if we know that we are looked up to and imitated ... especially all deacons, elders, and preachers, should pray the Lord that they may know how they may behave themselves in the house of God, lest inadvertently their misbehaviour should be injurious to the weaker sort." *MTP* 24:541.

58. *MTP* 7:367-368.

59. Biblically, Spurgeon understood that the terms overseer (or bishop), elder, and pastor were used interchangeably in the New Testament and he himself used those terms interchangeably. For example, in speaking to his students about pastoral calling, he stated: "All are not called to labor in word and doctrine, or to be elders, or to exercise the office of a bishop; nor should all aspire to such works, since the gifts necessary are nowhere promised to all; but those should addict themselves to such important engagements who feel, like the apostle, that they have 'received this ministry.' (2 Cor. 4:1.) No man

primarily responsible for preaching God's Word, the pastor played a unique role. Like Mr. Great-heart in Bunyan's story, Spurgeon saw himself personally and tenderly leading his flock to the Celestial City, even as he fought off dragons and giants to clear the way.[60] Spurgeon's vision for the faithful pastor was that of a warrior-shepherd.

Inherent in this role, the pastor was to be a leader of the church. Spurgeon believed that congregations should follow the command of their pastors, like soldiers following their commanders:

> It has been truly said that, if the members of our churches were in a right condition of heart, the work of the pastor towards them would be no more difficult than that of a commanding officer to his troops. A general, or a captain, has never to study eloquence; he has simply to give the word of command tersely and plainly, and himself to lead the way.[61]

For an organization as massive as the Metropolitan Tabernacle with many separate institutions under it, it was Spurgeon's strong pastoral leadership that unified it all. James Spurgeon described it this way:

> The discipline of the church thus emanates from a common center, acting through recognized division of labor. All meetings and institutions are subject to the influence, and when required, to the action of the Pastorate. It would be, at least, unseemly to have a hydra-headed band of Christians. Sunday-school, college, orphanage, almshouses, psalmody, are all under the supervision of a common headship, so as to prevent almost inevitable confusion, if not conflict, as the result of divided action. The leader of the church should surely lead the church's work. Strife without measure has arisen from rival authorities disputing about the boundaries of their little empires. The spirit of peace has kept us from this evil, but a judicious arrangement has been helpful in producing the result. There are still Diotrephes in the present age—men loving to have the pre-eminence—but it is the

---

may intrude into the sheepfold as an under-shepherd; he must have an eye to the chief Shepherd, and wait his beck and command." *Lectures* 1:19.

60. *Autobiography* 2:131.

61. *MTP* 39:1.

duty of the minister to magnify his office, and rule even these, which is best done not by assertions of power or complaints of want of influence, but by possessing such personal weight of piety and prudence, zeal, godliness, gentleness, and forbearance, as will inevitably place him in the front in course of time.[62]

As a result of this vision, Spurgeon bore a heavy role in the church. He was a *de facto* member of every committee in the church.[63] The elders and deacons served on separate boards, and Spurgeon participated in the work of both boards, as well as the board of trustees, who were responsible for the property of the church. When the church was bursting at the seams, it was Spurgeon's vision that drove the construction of the Metropolitan Tabernacle. To help alleviate Spurgeon's load, the church called his brother James to serve as assistant pastor or co-pastor in 1868.[64] At the same time, the congregation made it very clear that James' position was secondary to Spurgeon's and took nothing away from his role as the pastor of the church.[65]

Many during Spurgeon's day commented on his strong leadership at the Tabernacle. One historian outlines the grumbling among those who "detected Papal authority in the manner in which Spurgeon wielded power."[66] Even more sympathetic biographers recognize that "Spurgeon took a quite authoritative

---

62.   *S&T* 1869:51.

63.   C.H. Spurgeon, *The Metropolitan Tabernacle: Its History and Work* (Pasadena, TX: Pilgrim Publications, 1990), 2:27-28.

64.   Though Spurgeon's pastoral load decreased with James' calling as assistant pastor, he remained involved in the pastoral work of the church when his health permitted. Speaking in 1884, Spurgeon declared, "Oh, brothers, on that day on which I lately saw forty persons one by one, and listened to their experience and proposed them to the church, I felt as weary as ever a man did in reaping the heaviest harvest. I did not merely give them a few words as enquirers, but examined them as candidates with my best judgment. I thought that if I had many days of that sort I must die, but I also wished it might be my lot to die in that fashion. Having so many coming to confess Christ my mind was crushed beneath the weight of blessing, but I would gladly be overwhelmed again." *MTP* 30:310.

65.   "Special Church Meeting convened by Special notice and held Jan. 9th, 1868," *MB 1866-1871*.

66.   Patricia S. Kruppa, "Charles Haddon Spurgeon: A Preacher's Progress" (PhD diss., Columbia University, 1968), 133-35.

approach."[67] Here is something of the "Episcopalian" element of the Spurgeon's "modified form of Episcopalian Presbyterian Independency."[68] In order to lead such a large church, Spurgeon had to exercise a tremendous amount of governance over his church. But how was Spurgeon's leadership intersecting with his commitment to congregationalism?

First, Spurgeon's position as the pastor of the Metropolitan Tabernacle was made possible only by a congregational vote. He did not appoint himself as pastor of the New Park Street Chapel, nor did the officers, or any denominational official. Rather, it was the congregation at the New Park Street Chapel that had been hearing him preach throughout the spring of 1854 and that had extended the call to him.[69] This was not just a matter of procedure, but Spurgeon understood that his authority and ministry was preceded by the congregation's call. He once said to his students,

> The signs and marks of a true bishop are laid down in the Word for the guidance of the church; and if in following such guidance the brethren see not in us the qualifications, and do not elect us to office, it is plain enough that however well we may evangelize, the office of the pastor is not for us. Churches are not all wise, neither do they all judge in the power of the Holy Ghost, but many of them judge after the flesh; yet I had sooner accept the opinion of a company of the Lord's people than my own upon so personal a subject as my own gifts and graces. At any rate, whether you value the verdict of the church or no, one thing is certain, that none of you can be pastors without the loving consent of the flock.[70]

Though he would go on to have a tremendous ministry, Spurgeon never accepted any extra-ecclesial ordination or honorary

---

67. Drummond, *Spurgeon*, 208.

68. *MTP* 7:257.

69. "Special Adjourned Church Meeting 19th April, 1854," Church Meeting Minutes 1808-1854.

70. *Lectures* 1:30.

academic degrees. Rather, his influential ministry took place under the pastoral calling of this congregation.[71]

Second, as has already been discussed, Spurgeon's vision for his ministry was not that he would labor alone, but that in his example, the other church officers would join him in that work. As Spurgeon's load expanded, he did not hesitate to lean on the other officers of the church, whether it was presiding at church meetings, leading prayer meetings, meeting with enquirers, visiting classes, meeting with Sunday School teachers and volunteers, caring for the students of the College, and more.[72] Among his fellow leaders, there was a collegial spirit as they labored in the ministry together. Though Spurgeon was called "the Governor," which he found ironic, this was a nickname given in brotherly love, and all the other deacons had their nicknames as well.

> All my church-officers are in a very real sense my brethren in Christ. In talking to or about one another, we have no stately modes of address. I am called 'the Governor,' I suppose, because I do not attempt to govern; and the deacons are known among us as 'Brother William,' 'Uncle Tom,' 'Dear Old Joe,' 'Prince Charlie,' 'Son of Ali,' and so on.[73]

One of the more encouraging signs of health in the church was that during times of Spurgeon's sickness and extended absence, the ministry did not falter, but the congregation rallied in greater devotion to prayer and support of the elders.[74] In other words, the members of the church loved their pastor, but they were also glad to follow their elders and deacons.

---

71. Spurgeon saw the call of the congregation as an authoritative and sufficient external call to ministry. Writing to one of the deacons after he accepted the call, Spurgeon stated, "I believe in the glorious principle of Independency. Every church has a right to choose its own minister; and if so, certainly it needs no assistance from others in appointing him to the office. You, yourselves, have chosen me; and what matters it if the whole world dislikes the choice? They cannot invalidate it; nor can they give it more force." *Autobiography* 1:357.

72. For examples of ways the church officers labored alongside Spurgeon, see the list of church events published in *The Sword and the Trowel. S&T* 1866:91; 1867:174-76.

73. *Autobiography* 3:20.

74. S&T 1877:145-49.

Finally, Spurgeon's relationship with his congregation was one marked by affection and trust, not dictatorial authority. The congregation's love for their pastor was made public through congregational statements in their church meetings. Three months after calling him, the congregation passed the following motion:

> Resolved—That we desire as a Church to record our devout and grateful acknowledgements to our Heavenly Father for the success that has attended the ministry of our esteemed Pastor, and we consider it important at as early a period as possible that increased accommodation should be provided for the numbers that flock to the Chapel on Lord's days.[75]

On October 19, 1856, following the disaster at the Music Hall of the Royal Surrey Gardens,[76] the congregation passed a public statement stating the facts of the event, defending their pastor from any wrongdoing, thanking God for preserving his life, raising him out of his deep discouragement, and restoring him to the ministry.[77] Likewise, in the fall of 1858, Spurgeon became seriously ill and was unable to preach for almost three months. The congregation passed the following statement on his first church meeting back:

> Whereupon it was resolved, that we desire as a church to record our devout and heartfelt thanks to our Heavenly Father for sustaining our Beloved Pastor during his indisposition and restoring him again to the Church in the enjoyment of health and we earnestly pray that his recovery may be marked by increasing success in the ingathering of souls to Christ and in building up his people in the knowledge and truths of the Gospel.[78]

Where did this love come from? Given that Spurgeon personally baptized so many of the members of the church,[79] he undoubtedly

---

75. "Adjourned Church Meeting 30th August 1854," *MB 1854-1861.*

76. *Autobiography* 2:195-220.

77. "Church Meeting October 19th, 1856," *MB 1854-1861.*

78. "Monthly Church Meeting November 24th, 1858," *MB 1854-1861.*

79. G. Holden Pike, *The Life and Work of Charles Haddon Spurgeon, Volumes 1–2* (Edinburgh: Banner of Truth Trust, 1991), 1:290.

played a formative role in the conversion and spiritual growth of most of his congregation, and this formed an affectionate bond between them. As the one who regularly preached God's Word to them, the members of the church were deeply aware of how God had used Spurgeon to awaken them to the glory of Christ. As a result, they were deeply grateful for his ministry and full of affection for their pastor. As one biographer writes, "It must be granted that Spurgeon took a quite authoritative approach.... Yet, his leadership in the church was always tempered with genuine love. He won his leadership stance through real Christian love and service to his people; he did not just assume it."[80]

As a result of this love,[81] the congregation was willing to trust Spurgeon's leadership. As he and the elders brought recommendations to the congregation, they always sought to be transparent whenever possible.[82] But in certain cases, especially when dealing with discipline, the congregation was asked to trust their elders.[83] Even when they did not know all the information, they trusted their leaders and were willing to approve their recommendations. In both of these cases, Spurgeon did not lead as an autocrat but sought to shepherd his congregation with openness and honesty.

---

80. Drummond, *Spurgeon*, 208.

81. For more examples of the pastors' love for his congregation and vice-versa, see *Autobiography* 3:241-56.

82. "In all our business the aim is to have everything done openly and aboveboard, so that no one may complain of the existence of a clique, or the suppression of the true state of affairs. We occasionally ask the unquestioning confidence of the church in its officers in cases delicate and undesirable to be published, but otherwise we consult the church in everything, and report progress as often as possible in all matters still pending and unsettled. Nothing, we are persuaded, is so sure to create suspicion and destroy confidence as attempts at secret diplomacy, or mere official action." *S&T* 1869:55.

83. "When details of cases under discipline are kept from the church, the fact is openly stated, and leave asked for the maintenance of such public reticence; while any member is informed, that if dissatisfied, the pastor will give him the reasons why the elders have advised the removal of the offender, and their motive in not giving details of the sin. When it would be for the injury of good morals, or expose the pastor to a suit-at-law, the officers ask the confidence of the church, and request it to adopt their verdict in the case without hearing detailed information; this is cheerfully accorded in every case, and much evil thus averted." Ibid.

Congregationalism and Church Institutions

Over sixty Bible Classes, benevolent ministries, Sunday Schools, mission stations, and other organizations were formed out of the Metropolitan Tabernacle during Spurgeon's ministry. Three of the most prominent institutions established by the church were the Pastor's College, the Colportage Association, and the Stockwell Orphanage.[84] Spurgeon was the clear leader of all three of these ministries. They had each "originated under his influence, he had planned its form of organization and had overseen its growth, and his word was supreme in all its affairs."[85] At the same time, these three ministries were associated with the Metropolitan Tabernacle. How did the congregationalism of the church shape her relationship with these three institutions?

The Colportage Association and the Stockwell Orphanage

The Colportage Association began in September 1866 in response to an article in *The Sword and the Trowel* decrying the growth of the Oxford Movement in the Church of England.[86] In it, Spurgeon called for evangelicals to respond by employing men to go throughout the land, distributing good Christian books and tracts. A member of the Metropolitan Tabernacle was willing to give generously towards the start of such an association, and so under Spurgeon's leadership, a committee was formed, and the association began. This work grew rapidly and continuously. Because they were primarily engaged in book distribution, the colporteurs were recruited from all evangelical denominations. But their work expanded beyond books. They traveled throughout the land as home missionaries, sharing the gospel, holding prayer meetings, and preaching to the poor.[87] In 1878, the Colportage Association reported ninety-four colporteurs engaged in the work, their sales amounting to £8,276, having paid 926,290 visits.[88]

---

84. *Autobiography* 3:125-80.

85. Arnold A. Dallimore, *Spurgeon: A Biography* (Carlisle, UK: Banner of Truth Trust, 2014), 154.

86. *S&T* 1866:339-45.

87. *Autobiography* 3:164.

88. Ibid., 166.

The Stockwell Orphanage began when Anne Hillyard, the widow of a clergyman of the Church of England, read that same article in *The Sword and the Trowel*. Spurgeon called for the formation of evangelical schools for children to counteract the Oxford Movement, and this struck a chord for Hillyard. Through her generous gift of £20,000, the orphanage was founded. Within a month, Spurgeon purchased land for the project in Stockwell, a district not far from the Tabernacle. This decisive action proved risky, because Hillyard's gift was tied up in railroad bonds, which still had two years left before maturity,[89] but Spurgeon did not want to wait given the pressing need of orphans. Through his visionary leadership, donors came forward (many of them associated with the Tabernacle) and contributed to the construction of several orphan homes. Eventually, the rest of the orphanage was constructed, including a headmaster's house, a dining hall, a gymnasium, and an infirmary. By 1878, five hundred and twenty-seven orphans coming from a variety of denominational backgrounds had found a home at Stockwell.[90]

While Spurgeon played a key role in the leadership of the Colportage Association and the Stockwell Orphanage, the Minute Books do not reveal any congregational involvement in the formation of those institutions.[91] There is no mention of the Colportage Association in any of the meeting minutes during its formation.[92] The first mention of the Stockwell Orphanage is in the Annual Church Meeting on January 23, 1868. There, the church passes the following resolution:

---

89. *S&T* 1:313.

90. *Autobiography* 3:177.

91. Though perhaps the Minute Books contain a record of Spurgeon's first exposure to the idea of colporteurs. Speaking of his visit to a small Baptist church in Paris in late 1861, he shared with the congregation, "The church is composed chiefly of converted Roman Catholics, and they are exerting themselves to their utmost to spread the truths of the gospel, their chief agency being the colporteurs, who visit the houses with religious tracts, etc., but they have been much crippled by the stoppage of supplies from America consequent on the present war." "Church Meeting 5th Jan 1862," *MB 1861-1866*.

92. The work of the colporteurs began November 1866. *S&T* 1867:376-77.

Resolved—That on a review of the very wonderful display of the Lord's goodness connected with the founding of the Stockwell Orphanage the Church desires to have a record of the circumstances connected with that institution preserved in its books, with a view of the new buildings; it sympathizes thoroughly with Mrs. Hillyard, the Pastor and the other trustees in their desire to promote the good of poor fatherless children and pledges itself to aid the work as far as possible by its efforts and prayers.[93]

By this point, the orphanage was operating, and the congregation was glad to express their support of the work. But this was not a motion to establish the work. Although both the colporteurs and the orphanage were significant institutions connected with the church, they were not established and ordered by the congregation. Spurgeon's leadership in these institutions was not subject to the congregationalism of the church, but the church supported their pastor in his involvement in those ministries.

The Pastors' College

The Pastors' College was a different matter, however. Before 1861, Spurgeon trained up men for the ministry on his own initiative. One by one, he took men under his wing, arranging tutors for them, equipping them to preach, and then sending them out. By 1861, he had trained and sent out seven ministers and was supporting and training sixteen more, but the burden and cost were becoming too much for him to bear alone. So, on Sunday, May 19, 1861, Spurgeon shared with the congregation his vision for pastoral training and took up a special offering to support the work.[94] But the congregation would do more than give an offering. The minutes for July 1, 1861 record the following motion:

Our Pastor having told the Church of his Institution for educating young ministers, and having informed them that several were now settled in country charges and laboring with great success, it was unanimously agreed,—That this Church rejoices very greatly in the labors of our Pastor in training young men for the

---

93. "Annual Church Meeting 23rd Jan 1868," *MB 1866-1871*.

94. *Autobiography* 3:125-26.

ministry and desires that a record of his successful & laborious efforts should be entered in the church-books—Hitherto, this good work has been rather a private effort than one in which the Church has had a share, but the Church hereby adopts it as part of its own system of evangelical labors, promises its pecuniary aid, and its constant and earnest prayers.[95]

In this motion, the congregation pledges not only to support the work of their pastor but to "[adopt] it as part of its own system of evangelical labors." No longer would this be the private effort of the pastor, but now the Pastors' College would be an official ministry of the church, supported by the giving and prayers of the members.

The College has now become the most important of all the Institutions connected with the Church at the Metropolitan Tabernacle. The place which it once held in the heart of the pastor alone, it now holds in the hearts of the elders and deacons with him. It is indeed a part of the whole Church.[96]

At times, the college was even referred to as "The Metropolitan Tabernacle College."[97] The close connection between the church and the college is evident in the Annual Meeting Minutes of the church after 1861, as an extensive report on the college is included among the other reports of the church.

The clear association between the church and the Pastors' College became part of Spurgeon's pastoral training strategy. In addition to its theological framework and educational philosophy, Spurgeon emphasized the college's ecclesial context as one of its most important distinctives:

The relation of the College to a large and active Church, by which it is principally sustained, and which takes a lively interest in its welfare, is one special means of its prosperity. The intercourse of the Students with the Members of the Church contributes much to their social and their spiritual welfare. The officers of the Church cheer them by their kindness and aid them by

---

95. For example, see "Church Meeting 1st July 1861," *MB 1861-1866*.

96. *S&T* 1865:218.

97. *S&T* 1866:41.

their counsel. A familiarity with Church discipline is acquired, and with all the appliances by which a flourishing Church is sustained and enlarged, which is treasured up for future use, and supplies what has hitherto often proved to be a serious deficiency in a College education for the pastoral office.[98]

More than supporting the ministry of the Pastors' College, the congregation provided the context for the training, showing students how a flourishing church operated. Spurgeon writes:

At the Pastors' College our brethren can not only meet, as they do every day, for prayer by themselves, but they can unite daily in the prayer-meetings of the church, and can assist in earnest efforts of all sorts. Through living in the midst of a church which, despite its faults, is a truly living, intensely earnest, working organization, they gain enlarged ideas, and form practical habits. Even to see church management and church work upon a large scale, and to share in the prayers and sympathies of a large community of Christian people, must be a stimulus to right-minded men, Our circumstances are peculiarly helpful, and we are grateful to have our institution so happily surrounded by them. The College is recognized by the Tabernacle church as an integral part of its operations, and supported and loved as such.[99]

The church was also a training ground for the students. Rather than being removed from normal congregational life, students were immersed in the life of an active church. Spurgeon expected his students to test their ministerial calling by serving actively in the church.[100]

Brethren, we have no right to thrust a brother into the ministry until he has first given evidence of his own conversion, and has also given proof not only of being a good average worker but something more. If he cannot labor in the church before he pretends to be a minister, he is good for nothing. If he cannot whilst he is a private member of the church perform all the duties of that position with zeal and energy, and if he is not evidently a consecrated man whilst he is a private Christian, certainly you

98   S&T 1966:107 98

99.   S&T 1871:226.

100.   MTP 12:412-13.

do not feel the guidance of God's Holy Spirit to bid him enter the ministry.[101]

All students in the Pastors' College either joined the church or were already members of the church. The Minute Books contain several instances of marginalia highlighting students of the college as they joined the church.[102] This involvement meant not only discipleship but also accountability. At least on one occasion, a student of the college, having confessed to "gross inconsistency of conduct," had his name "withdrawn from the Church books."[103]

Likewise, the tutors of the college were not simply scholars, but at times also elders in the church.[104] They not only taught the students but pastored them, giving them a vision for godliness and leadership in the church. Many of the students would live with certain families in the church, where they would see a well-ordered Christian home.[105] The congregation as a whole understood these students to be a part of their ministry and were delighted to invest in them, not only financially, but relationally.

> But with regard to [the College students] we have in our midst, why there is nothing that any of you would not cheerfully do for them. As soon as there is a new face seen among them, some of the elders of the Church are sure to get him into their houses, are sure to speak kindly with him till I fall into another difficulty. Sometimes my friends take them away too much, are too kind to them, get them away from their studies in order to be with them, when they ought rather to be sticking fast by their books. I find no lack of sympathy, and I know the men are happier; and I believe they have greater motives to be holy, because they are more watched, more observed by the members of the Church.[106]

---

101. *S&T* 1865:218.

102. For example, see "Church Meeting November 13th, 1861," *MB 1861-1866* and "Church Meeting December 9th, 1861," Ibid.

103. "Church Meeting October 19th, 1865," Ibid.

104. The congregation called Brother Archibald Fergusson, a tutor of the College, as Elder, "to represent that institution" among the officers of the church. "Church Meeting May 25th, 1863," Ibid.

105. *S&T* 1866:135.

106. *MTP* 7:365-66.

As these students participated in the worship, ministry, and discipline of a healthy church, they gained a vision for a robust congregational life, "treasured up for future use." By this association between the Metropolitan Tabernacle and the Pastors' College, Spurgeon sought to address an ecclesiological deficiency in the training of pastors in his day.

Given these dynamics, what can be learned about the church's congregationalism in relation to these three institutions? First, congregational authority would only be tied to distinctively Baptist institutions. Both the Stockwell Orphanage and the Colportage Association were broadly evangelical. The orphanage took in children from all kinds of religious backgrounds and employed a paedobaptist as the headmaster.[107] Likewise, the Colportage Association initially only sent out Baptist colporteurs, but within a year, they decided to have an "undenominational basis," with the only requirement being that these were men of godly character, holding firmly to evangelical convictions.[108] These ministries did not actually belong to any church, but to the boards that governed them. Because Spurgeon was instrumental in their founding and ongoing leadership, the Tabernacle was supportive of them in their prayers, volunteers, and giving, but they did not exercise any authority over them. The Pastors' College, however, was different. Through its association with the Metropolitan Tabernacle, the Pastors' College trained men in the Baptist distinctives of the church.[109] Spurgeon's vision was to raise up ministers to start Baptist churches "of like faith and order."[110] This was an institution that was tied to the denominational convictions of the church. This connected the institution more tightly with the church, allowing them to play an active role in the institution, from its official formation to its regular support and oversight.

---

107. Ibid.

108. *Autobiography* 3:162.

109. At one point, Spurgeon appointed a Congregationalist to serve as Principal of the Pastors' College, and another to serve as a lecturer, but the Baptist convictions of the school remained. *Autobiography* 3.177.

110. "Church Meeting April 10th, 1861," *MB 1861-1866*; "Church Meeting April 14th, 1862," Ibid.

Second, congregational authority only extended to institutions established by the church. Because the church did not formally establish the orphanage and the Colportage Association, Spurgeon's leadership of those institutions did not conflict with the authority of the congregation. The ideas for these ministries did not arise from the congregation, nor from Spurgeon himself. Rather, individuals came to him with the vision and the funding, and after prayerful consideration, Spurgeon took it on. In other words, these organizations were ultimately para-church organizations. Because of their connection to Spurgeon, they were supported by the Metropolitan Tabernacle, but they were not a part of the church.

Spurgeon had the vision for the Pastors' College and led in its formation and organization. And once the congregation adopted it, they were in charge. Beginning in 1865, the congregation passed the following resolution at every Annual Meeting:

> Resolved—That we desire as a Church to record our gratitude to God for that abundant measure of success which has attended the Pastors' College during the past year and we hereby express our hearty sympathy with our beloved pastor in this noble work to which we believe our gracious Lord has called him.[111]

While this was a record of thanksgiving, it also expressed ongoing support of the pastor in the leadership of the Pastors' College. In other words, in this annual resolution, the congregation affirmed the delegated authority of their pastor in the leadership of this ministry.

Many more institutions would arise out of the Metropolitan Tabernacle. But only these three were founded and led by Spurgeon in this way. And only the Pastors' College would be owned by the congregation in this unique way. The many other societies, Sunday School classes, Bible Classes, mission stations, and more would be connected to the church, but they would be grassroots endeavors of church members and college students.[112]

---

111. "Annual Meeting January 25th, 1865," *MB 1861-1866*.

112. During Spurgeon's Jubilee celebration, J.W. Harrald read a list of sixty-six institutions associated with the Metropolitan Tabernacle. Of those, five were charities for the poor, two were for pastoral training, two were for supporting pastors, nineteen

The congregational nature of these ministries can be seen, as members of the church followed the example of their pastor and initiated new ministries.

Congregationalism and Church Planting

According to one historian, in the second half of the nineteenth century, Spurgeon's students planted one hundred and eighty-seven churches, doubling the number of Baptist churches in London.[113] "Students were sent out to new areas or existing churches, normally at the command of 'the guv'nor.'... It was his enterprising, imaginative, powerful and generous vigour which inspired many to venture out in Christ's name at a propitious time of revival activity."[114] This active work of church planting was, in part, driven from necessity. As the church membership continued to grow, how could the church continue to accommodate visitors who needed to hear the gospel? One answer lay in pastoral training and church planting.[115] As new churches were planted by Spurgeon's students, they not only evangelized the area, but they recruited members from the Metropolitan Tabernacle who lived nearby to join the work. Often, this meant that some church plants could begin with a sizeable congregation at the outset, creating more space at the mother church.

But with so many churches planted by the Metropolitan Tabernacle, did Spurgeon exercise an "Episcopalian" authority over those church plants? Or did he preserve "congregational principles" in those churches? The Minute Books provide insight into these questions.

---

were for discipleship and Bible classes, twenty-nine were evangelistic missions, and nine were Sunday Schools. See C. H. Spurgeon, *The Metropolitan Tabernacle: Its History and Work* (Pasadena, TX: Pilgrim Publications, 1990), 2:7-8.

113. Michael Nicholls, *C. H. Spurgeon: The Pastor Evangelist* (Didcot, UK: Baptist Historical Society, 1992), 99. For a list of the one hundred and eighty-seven churches, see Ibid., 175-77.

114. Michael Nicholls, "Spurgeon as a Church Planter," *Baptist Review of Theology* 2.1 (Spring 1992); 39.

115. Pike, *The Life and Work of C. H. Spurgeon*, Vol. 3, 75.

Church Planting Process

From the beginning, the goal of the Pastors' College was "not only to train students, but to found churches."[116] As much as he emphasized the importance of evangelism, Spurgeon recognized more churches were needed to disciple and care for new converts. "No amount of occasional evangelistic services will ever render needless the abiding work of organized Christianity; in fact, in proportion as special efforts are of use, our churches will become the more necessary. The larger the harvest, the more need of barns."[117] There were at least four steps in the church planting process at the Metropolitan Tabernacle, as shown in the church minute books.

1. Preaching Stations and Local Evangelism

The first step was to send a college graduate to a location with little or no evangelical presence and establish a preaching station, usually "in a hall or other hired building,"[118] in a location that did not have a Baptist chapel nearby. Alongside these services, these pioneers would also hold open-air services, distribute tracts, visit hospitals, and seek to share the gospel with people in the community. This was arduous and difficult work. *The Sword and the Trowel* provides this description:

> Few of our readers can understand the difficulties of a young village minister in starting a new effort. He goes down to a village, hitherto untried by, say, that portion of the Baptist denomination which aims to be aggressive. A room is hired. Three persons dissatisfied perhaps with the high sentiments and low practices of "Rehoboth" chapel are his only supporters. The unodorous traditions of the unpeaceful clique that has given the public such unpleasant notions of what Baptists are, are dead against him. The Congregational minister looks shy upon his impertinence in poaching near his manor. The high minister comes down low enough to preach against "the boy's" Arminianism, charges the young people who wish to hear him with having "itching

---

116.   *S&T* 1878:240.
117.   Ibid., 238-39.
118.   *S&T* 1878:238.

ears," though he probably has imparted the disease by his incapacity to understand the young. The student is called one of "Spurgeon's cubs."[119]

These endeavors, however, had the effect of toughening the students and knitting them together in their hardships. The students would have a strong support network from the various evangelistic societies of the Tabernacle and the other college graduates.[120] Over time, many of these preaching stations would slowly begin to gather converts.

2. Baptism and Membership at the Metropolitan Tabernacle

Since these preaching stations were not yet churches and new converts needed to be baptized, the next step was to bring them into membership at the Metropolitan Tabernacle. Sometimes this would mean taking converts through a typical membership process, including membership interviews, sending messengers, a full report given at a church meeting, a congregational vote, baptism, and a communion service. In cases where converts were coming from a distance, accommodations could be made, either in sending elders out for interviews or scheduling baptismal and communion services at more convenient times.

3. Dismissal Requested to Form a Church

Once there were enough converts to form a church, they sent a letter to the Metropolitan Tabernacle, recounting the work that God has done in that area, expressing their desire to form a church, and asking for dismissal from membership for that purpose. This letter was read to the congregation at a church meeting, and they voted to approve the dismissals and to appoint elders to help that group form a church of like faith and order. At this point, the newly-formed church would call their pastor and church officers, and partake of the Lord's Supper together as a sign of their covenant. In the early years, the congregation at the Tabernacle would approve the gift of a communion service,

---

119. *S&T* 1869:260-61.

120. Nicholls, "Spurgeon as a Church Planter," 42.

that is, a set of silver engraved communion platters, pitcher, and common cups, for many of the new churches.[121]

4. Association and Support

Once the churches were formed, they remained in association with the Metropolitan Tabernacle. Letters were exchanged, dismissing members and sharing about the progress of the work. Many of these churches joined the London Baptist Association and gave financial support to the Pastors' College, though there was no condition laid on the churches to do so. Spurgeon often helped fundraise on behalf of these churches for the construction of a new chapel.[122]

The Story of Two Church Plants

The Minute Books contain the minutes related to the formation of many of the churches planted by the Metropolitan Tabernacle. The earlier accounts go into greater detail, describing not only the process, but the joy of the congregation in seeing the expanding work. As the work progresses and more churches are planted, the minutes become more efficient, recording only the most pertinent information.[123] While the process for church planting generally followed the four-step process listed previously, sometimes there were variations.

One of the earliest preaching stations was in a meeting house in the Old Bailey, in the heart of London, led by a student of the college, Alfred Searle.[124] By July 1861, the work had grown sufficiently for the congregation to appoint elders to inquire into the work.[125] Their positive report led to a special church meeting to hear several applications for membership. Over the next six months, several converts would join the Metropolitan Tabernacle so that by April 14, 1862, the sixteen members from Old Bailey

---

121. "Church Meeting November 17th, 1862," *MB 1861-1866*; "Church Meeting December 2nd, 1862," *MB 1861-1866*.

122. Nicholls, "Spurgeon as a Church Planter," 44-46.

123. The joy nevertheless remains evident in the accounts of the church plants and revitalizations in *The Sword and the Trowel*. *S&T* 1878:237-70.

124. *S&T* 1878:264.

125. "Church Meeting July 15th, 1861," *MB 1861-1866*.

sent a letter recounting the work in their area and requesting letters of dismission so that they might form a new church. The Minute Books read:

> The Church gave a very hearty response to this letter, rejoicing that God had been so gracious to the dear brethren, and unanimously agreed to their dismissal from our fellowship and formation into a distinct church as they desired. After their dismissal they agreed that Brethren Searle and Rawlings should be their delegates to answer as to their faith & order. These answers being in every respect satisfactory, acknowledging that they held the doctrines of grace as set forth in the Baptist confession of faith, acknowledging also that the church order and discipline as established among us, were such as they purposed to adhere to, our pastor caused several of them to join together with the right hand of fellowship and pronounced them a distinct Church. They then elected Brother Searle as their pastor, Brethren Rawlings and Edwards deacons, and Pauter and Brame elders. After which the two Churches sat down to the Lord's table and in loving communion partook of the Lord's supper.[126]

Later that summer, the church at Old Bailey would send a gracious letter expressing their gratitude to God for the Metropolitan Tabernacle and thanking them for the generous gift of the communion service.[127]

Another work happening during this time was in Cheam, a small village in Surrey, where two students, Frost and Jackson, had set up a preaching station in a cottage.[128] For eighteen months, they labored in that area, and by February 1862, several people had been converted. Two elders were appointed by the church to inquire into new converts, and they reported back their encouragement about the work.[129] Then on May 13, 1862, the church gathered for a special meeting to hear about the work at Cheam. Six converts came forward and testified to the work

---

126. "Church Meeting April 14th, 1862," *MB 1861-1866*.

127. "Church Meeting August 21st, 1862," Ibid.

128. For a brief account of this work, see *S&T* 1878:250.

129. "Church Meeting February 17th, 1862," *MB 1861-1866*.

of grace in their lives, and the congregation voted to accept them into membership. That evening, these converts were baptized by the pastor, and in order "to spare them another journey to London," they received the right hand of fellowship as they took the Lord's supper in the vestry with the church officers and a few others.[130]

But being so far away from London, this little group of believers was unable to regularly attend the services and participate in the Lord's Table. So at a church meeting on July 7, 1862, Spurgeon read a letter from the six members at Cheam, asking for "dismission in order that we may constitute a Church of like faith and order with yourselves and walk in all the commandments of the Lord blameless. At present we cannot attend on the ordinances of God's house which we feel to be a duty we owe to our Lord, and a privilege we cannot afford to be lost to ourselves." At this, the congregation appointed two elders "to visit them at Cheam and assist in forming them into a Church."[131] Over the next few months, the church would continue to hear from the church at Cheam, expressing their gratitude to the Tabernacle for establishing a church in that place.[132]

A few observations can be made about Spurgeon's congregationalism when it came to his church planting. First, despite his influential position, Spurgeon preserved the congregational authority of each local church. While the minutes of the April 14, 1872 church meeting record Spurgeon pronouncing the group from Old Bailey a distinct Church, the record of the meeting shows that this signified two things: 1) given the Old Bailey group's successful examination, Spurgeon affirmed they were a church of like faith and order, and 2) once those members were dismissed from the Tabernacle and joined together in the right hand of fellowship, Spurgeon affirmed that they were indeed a church. In other words, this was not the pronouncement of a bishop, but the affirmation of a sister church

---

130. "Church Meeting May 13th, 1862," Ibid.

131. "Church Meeting July 7th, 1862," *MB 1861-1866*.

132. "Church Meeting September 22nd, 1862," Ibid.; "Church Meeting December 2nd, 1862," Ibid.

pastor. Once these churches were formed, Spurgeon played no authoritative role. Writing to the congregation at Drummond Road Chapel, upon their formal constitution as a church, he reminded them,

> In accordance with our principles, you will henceforth have the conduct of your affairs in your hands and, without constraint from any, be at liberty to adopt such means for extending the knowledge of the Savior's name in your locality, and such means for maintaining the discipline and purity of the Church as shall from time to time, in the fear of God, seem right to yourselves.[133]

Though these plants would remain in close association with the mother church, this relationship was purely voluntary, based on their existing relationship and common faith and order. As one historian observes, Spurgeon believed "churches ought to be self-supporting and self-governing.... no administrative hierarchy of a huge church planting organization emerged."[134]

Second, Spurgeon's elders played an important role in church planting. Once a group requested to be formed into a church, two elders were appointed by the congregation to inquire into the work of the preaching stations and examine the professions of faith of the new converts. Again, their role was not authoritative, but affirmative, examining the doctrine and order of these churches, and affirming their formation as a church. While the primary work of the elders at the Tabernacle was to shepherd their people, they also played an important role in the church planting ministry of the church. Also, given how a plurality of elders were uncommon among Baptists in Spurgeon's day, it is worth noting that these new churches followed the Tabernacle in appointing a plurality of elders to lead their congregations.[135]

Finally, the congregation also played an important role in church planting. They accepted into membership the new converts from the various preaching stations. Existing members

---

133. *Records of the Particular Baptist Congregational Church Meeting in Drummond Road Chapel, Bermondsey, London*, Angus Library, Oxford. 2.

134. Nicholls, "Spurgeon as a Church Planter," 44.

135. These churches also tended to hold to the other distinctives of the Metropolitan Tabernacle, especially open communion and strict membership.

who lived in those districts supported or participated in the work. It was not until the congregation granted the letters of dismission that members were free to form a new church. Though the congregation did not take the lead in this process, Spurgeon was committed to involving the congregation in the church planting efforts. The congregationalism of the Tabernacle knit the church relationally with all the new church plants, creating a network of churches throughout London and beyond.

Spurgeon's vision for kingdom growth was not that the Metropolitan Tabernacle would become the head of a new denomination, exercising authority over other churches. Rather, his hope was that through his pastoral training and church planting efforts, there would be separate and independent churches like the Tabernacle in all the major cities of England that would be responsible for planting many other independent churches through their regions.[136] Spurgeon's congregational polity was integral to his church planting strategy. At the same time, his church planting efforts also provide a picture of his "modified form of Episcopalian Presbyterian Independency" at work. Spurgeon acted as a pastor/bishop who trained up men to plant churches and mentored new pastors. His elders served as a presbytery who examined new churches and affirmed their constitution. And the congregation supported the work and authorized all that went on.

Conclusion

As a Baptist, Spurgeon was committed to congregational polity and once again, this is evident in his teaching and in the record of the *Church Meeting Minutes* of the Metropolitan Tabernacle. This was not a nominal or thin congregationalism. Rather, Spurgeon's robust congregationalism was based on the teaching of the New Testament. And it was carried out in the remarkable number of congregational meetings that his church held throughout his ministry. Even when thousands were coming forward for church membership, Spurgeon did not attempt to bypass the

---

136. *S&T* 1865:174.

congregation's role and authority in the membership process but continued to promote it as a regular (and frequent) part of the life of the church.

Though Spurgeon and the church officers played a significant role in the leadership of the church, they also respected and preserved the authority of the congregation. The relationship between the officers and the congregation was marked by affection and trust. However, Spurgeon was also careful to place certain limits on congregational authority. In the establishment of many institutions at the Metropolitan Tabernacle, only the Pastors' College was formally owned by the congregation. The other institutions were supported by the congregation, but were governed by their own boards and members of the church. And when it came to new churches, Spurgeon respected the independency of each local church and did not exercise authority over them.

At a time when churches were growing lax in their membership and disordered in their polity, Spurgeon provided a convictional approach to church polity. His commitment to regenerate church membership was grounded in the theological conviction that the church was to be distinct from the world. This led to the careful processes of receiving new members, maintaining an accurate membership roll, and disciplining the wayward. By laboring for a regenerate membership, Spurgeon was able to entrust the authority of the church to the congregation with confidence. The minute books of the church reveal the congregation's active involvement in receiving new members, church discipline, calling church leaders, overseeing pastoral training, planting churches, and more. At the same time, in all these matters, the congregation depended on the leadership that Spurgeon and the other church officers provided. This was not a pure democracy, but a modified congregationalism, where the congregation and the leaders operated together in a relationship of trust.

For Spurgeon, the purpose of a biblically-ordered church was connected to her mission. The fruitfulness of the Word preached was tied to the purity of the church. "Before we can do anything for Christ, we must first be right at home."[137] In the discipline of the church, Spurgeon ensured that only true soldiers of Christ were enlisted and that the army marched together under the leadership of her commanding officers into war.

---

137. *MTP* 7:367.

8

The Church Militant

Spurgeon's ministry was characterized by remarkable growth and activity. Throughout his pastorate, thousands joined his church, and at the height of his ministry, he was pastoring the largest church in the Christian world. Under his leadership, the congregation built a magnificent building and maintained an active ministry that had an impact on London and around the world, training and sending out hundreds of pastors and missionaries, and establishing numerous charitable institutions, church plants, publications, and more. With so much to commend it, Spurgeon's story is often told as a triumphant tale of success and accomplishment. But these triumphs alone do not tell the whole story.

From his arrival in London, Spurgeon's ministry was embattled.[1] In addition to major controversies, he also found himself engaged in many smaller conflicts. From the

---

1. For works that provide an extensive treatment of Spurgeon's controversies, see Larry J. Michaels, "The Effects of Controversy on the Evangelistic Ministry of C. H. Spurgeon" (PhD diss., The Southern Baptist Theological Seminary, 1989); Jeremy D. Jessen, "Mr. Valiant for Truth: The Polemic of Charles Haddon Spurgeon as Pastor-Theologian During the Downgrade Controversy (1887-1892)" (PhD diss., The Southern Baptist Theological Seminary, 2019); Iain H. Murray, *The Forgotten Spurgeon* (Edinburgh: Banner of Truth Trust, 2002); Tom Nettles, *Living by Revealed Truth: The Life and Pastoral Theology of Charles Haddon Spurgeon* (Fearn, UK: Christian Focus Publications, 2015), 471-578.

Rivulet controversy,[2] to controversies related to war,[3] slavery,[4] Darwinism,[5] hyper-Calvinism,[6] the temperance movement,[7] and many others, Spurgeon applied his biblical convictions to the issues of his day and did not hesitate to speak out. The nature of these controversies varied. Some he initiated, while others came to him because of his unique popularity. Some concerned biblical and theological matters, while others dealt with current events and denominational issues. What all these controversies reveal is that despite his tremendous "success," Spurgeon's ministry was simultaneously marked by steady conflict and opposition from beginning to end. Though modern readers marvel at all that he accomplished, Spurgeon saw things differently. He was grateful for all his accomplishments. He also recognized the limits of his efforts against the errors around him and regretted not being able to do more.[8]

Amid these many conflicts, two controversies stand out: the Baptismal Regeneration Controversy in 1864 and the Downgrade

---

2. For Spurgeon's account of this controversy, see *Autobiography* 2: 259-81.

3. For a summary of this conflict, see Nettles, *Living by Revealed Truth*, 500-05 and Geoff Chang, "Spurgeon and the Collision of Politics and Faith," *Reformation Today*, November 2022.

4. For an account of this controversy, see Thomas Kidd, "John Brown is immortal": Charles Spurgeon, the American press, and the ordeal of slavery, American Nineteenth Century History (2023), DOI: 10.1080/14664658.2023.2252647, and Nathan Rose, "Spurgeon and the Slavery Controversy of 1860: A Critical Analysis of the Anthropology of Charles Haddon Spurgeon, as it relates specifically to his Stance on Slavery," *Midwestern Journal of Theology* 16, no. 1 (2017): 21-28.

5. For Spurgeon's account of his Gorilla lectures and the subsequent exchanges, see *Autobiography* 2:51-58. See also Geoff Chang, "A Symbol of the Invisible": Spurgeon and the Animal World, *Andrew Fuller and Charles Spurgeon: A Theology of Animal Life: Reflections in the Eighteenth and Nineteenth Centuries,* Andrew Fuller Center for Baptist Studies at the Southern Baptist Theological Seminary, No. 13, 2021, 24-42.

6. For an account of this conflict, see Iain H. Murray, *Spurgeon v. Hyper-Calvinism: The Battle for Gospel Preaching* (Edinburgh: Banner of Truth Trust, 2010).

7. Geoff Chang, "Spurgeon, Temperance, and Christian Liberty," *Theologia Viatorum: The Journal of the London Lyceum*, No. 1, Vol. 1, 2023, 55-61.

8. "Being debarred from serving the Lord by my own public ministry, it has been laid upon my heart to endeavor to stir up my brother ministers to use increased diligence while they are permitted the great pleasure and privilege of preaching the word. It is a hard trial to be laid aside, and harder still if the heart be pierced with regrets for opportunities unimproved when health was in possession." *S&T* 1870:1.

Controversy in 1887–1888.[9] In the former conflict, Spurgeon battled the growing ritualism which arose from the Oxford Movement in the Church of England. In the latter conflict, Spurgeon confronted the increasing rationalism led by theological liberals within the Baptist Union. Speaking in 1857 in the "The War of Truth," Spurgeon foreshadowed these two conflicts:

> We have more to fear than some of us suppose from Rome; not from Rome openly... but I mean the Romanism that has crept into the Church of England under the name of Puseyism. Everywhere that has increased; they are beginning to light candles on the altar, which is only a prelude to those greater lights with which they would consume our Protestantism. Oh! that there were men who would unmask them! We have much to fear from them; but I would not care one whit for that if it were not for something which is even worse. We have to deal with a spirit, I know not how to denominate it, unless I call it a spirit of moderatism in the pulpits of Protestant churches. Men have begun to rub off the rough edges of truth, to give up the doctrines of Luther and Zwingli, and Calvin, and to endeavor to accommodate them to polished tastes.... There is creeping into the pulpits of Baptists and every other denomination, a lethargy and coldness, and with that a sort of nullification of all truth.[10]

Though the battle against ritualism and rationalism would come to a head in those two controversies, Spurgeon's willingness to confront these errors characterized his ministry from beginning to end. For his willingness to engage in these conflicts, Spurgeon would sacrifice many relationships, endure much heartache, and in the end, it would "cost him his life."[11]

Driving Spurgeon's choice to engage in these controversies was his understanding of the warfare of the Christian life. In this age

---

9. For a brief account of these two conflicts, see *Autobiography* 2:82-87; 4:253-64. Much more work has been done on the latter controversy. One of the fullest accounts and analysis of it is an unpublished manuscript by Ernest A. Payne entitled "The Down Grade Controversy," Spurgeon Collection, Regent's Park College, Oxford. Also, see Mark Hopkins, *Nonconformity's Romantic Generation: Evangelical and Liberal Theologies in Victorian England* (Eugene, OR: Wipf & Stock Publishers, 2006).

10. *NPSP* 3:44.

11. This was his Susannah's belief, having walked with her husband through the Downgrade Controversy. *Autobiography* 4:255.

before the return of Christ, the Christian lives in enemy territory. Therefore, it is no surprise that one of the primary images of the Christian found in Scripture was that of a soldier.

> The Christian is engaged throughout his whole life as a soldier—he is so called in Scripture—"A good soldier of Jesus Christ"; and if any of you take the trouble to write out the passages of Scripture in which the Christian is described as a soldier, and provision is made for his being armed, and directions given for his warfare, you will be surprised to find there are more of this character than concerning any other metaphor by which the Christian is described in the Word of God.[12]

The militant church, then, was a company of soldiers, banded together for the truth of the gospel. As evil and error abounded in both the Church of England and Dissenting churches, Spurgeon believed it was his duty as a preacher to be "a voice crying in the wilderness," even if he was the only voice.[13] He did not face these controversies alone, however. He had the support of the church, the army of God. When Spurgeon encountered slander and opposition, his congregation bore them with him. To be a member of the Metropolitan Tabernacle brought with it notoriety among the many who opposed their outspoken pastor, but this only strengthened the bond between the pastor and his people, uniting them in the fight.

> The love that exists between a Pastor and his converts is of a very special character, and I am sure that mine was so from the very beginning of my ministry. The bond that united me to the members at New Park Street was probably all the stronger because of the opposition and calumny that, for a time at least, they had to share with me. The attacks of our adversaries only united us more closely to one another; and, with whole-hearted devotion, the people willingly followed wherever I led them. I have never brought any project before them, or asked them to aid me in any holy enterprise, but they have been ready to respond

---

12. *MTP* 10:511.
13. *NPSP* 2:117.

to the call, no matter what amount of self-sacrifice might be required.[14]

Far from weakening the church, Spurgeon believed these controversies bound the church together and strengthened their devotion to the Lord's work. Spurgeon led his army forward as they battled the evils of his day together.

What is the Church Militant?

Spurgeon drew his doctrine of the church militant from the overarching story of Scripture. Ever since the arrival of the serpent in the Garden,[15] there has been "a deadly hereditary feud between the Christian and the powers of darkness."[16] This conflict has marked not only Christians, but all the people of God at every point of redemptive history. From Cain and Abel to Abraham's battles, to the Exodus, to Israel's march in the wilderness, the Canaanite conquest, and David's battles, and on through the rest of Israel's story, the theme of the war between the seed of the woman and the serpent runs through all of Scripture.[17] This war would culminate with the coming of Christ. Through his death, Christ "gave the death-blow to all his enemies. That hour when they thought they were treading on him, he was crushing them, and bruising the serpent's head."[18] By his resurrection, Christ triumphed over sin, Satan, and death, and now reigns as the King of God's armies.

> I see the champion awake, he unbinds the napkin from his head, he sees again the light—he rolls off the cerements of the tomb, rolls them up and places them by themselves. He has risen up; the stone has been rolled away; he comes forth into mid air and fires. O Hell, how didst thou shake! O Death, how wast thou

---

14. *Autobiography* 2:122.

15. Unlike the historical criticism of his day, Spurgeon held to a literal understanding of the events of Genesis 3, while also understanding those events to have a theological meaning. See Sermon 2165, "The Serpent's Sentence," *MTP* 36:517.

16. *MTP* 12:532.

17. Spurgeon traced this theme of conflict and warfare not only through Israel's history, but to the New Testament church, and into church history. *NPSP* 5:42-44.

18. *MTP* 7:164-65.

plagued!... He rises, and in that moment sin dies.... Nor was sin alone that day scattered. Did not all the hosts of hell fall before him?... Their hopes were gone, they were scattered indeed. As the wax melteth before the fire, so did their hopes melt away.[19]

Now, as the triumphant King, Christ has redeemed for himself a people, and he sends them out among the nations to rescue captives from their bondage through the proclamation of the gospel. What the Old Testament reveals is that Israel's deepest problem was not their slavery to other nations, but their spiritual bondage to sin. And just as God rescued Israel from slavery, God now saves sinners from their sin through Christ's finished work.[20] Now, as the redeemed people of God, Christians, like Israel, are called to engage in warfare, not over lands or possessions, but for the truth of the gospel. Though its nature has changed, the warfare remains. Every true Israelite is to follow the Son of David into battle, not against the nations, but for the sake of the nations, against the spiritual forces of darkness.

> Like the Spartans, every Christian is born a warrior. It is his destiny to be assaulted; it is his duty to attack.... He must be able to say with David, 'I come against thee in the name of the Lord of hosts, the God of the armies of Israel whom thou hast defied.' He must wrestle not with flesh and blood, but against principalities and powers. He must have weapons for his warfare—not carnal— but "mighty through God to the pulling down of strongholds."[21]

---

19. Ibid., 165.

20. "Observe, the children of Israel were emancipated from bondage, and had left Egypt behind, even as you and I have been rescued from our natural estate and are no longer the servants of sin. They had been redeemed by blood sprinkled upon the door posts and upon the lintel, and we too have had redemption applied to our souls, and have seen that God has looked upon the blood and has passed over us. They had feasted upon the paschal lamb as we have done, for Jesus has become to us our meat and our drink, and our soul is satisfied with him. They had been pursued by their enemies, even as we were pursued by our old sins, but they had seen these furious foes all drowned in the Red Sea, which they had passed through dry-shod; and we, too, have seen our past sins for ever buried in the Red Sea of atoning blood. Our iniquities, which threatened to drive us back into the Egypt of despair, are gone for ever; they sank like lead in the mighty waters, the depths have covered them—there is not one of them left." *MTP* 12:530.

21. *MTP* 7:545.

Spurgeon's understanding of spiritual warfare was also connected with his doctrine of sanctification. Soon after his conversion, Spurgeon encountered the Methodist teaching of Christian perfectionism, which taught "that no child of God [felt] any conflict within."[22] Though he heard this in the Primitive Methodist chapel in which he was converted, Spurgeon immediately walked out, rejecting any such teaching. His own experience taught him that, for the Christian, there would be "a daily struggle with the evil within."[23] Moreover, to accept perfectionism would be to deny Scripture's teaching on the reality of indwelling sin in the believer.

Related to this was Spurgeon's rejection of antinomianism, "that is, people who held that, because they believed themselves to be elect, they might live as they liked."[24] This was a view that was popular among High Calvinists and was particularly influential in the region where he first pastored. Antinomianism recognized the reality of indwelling sin but denied the need to battle that sin. Spurgeon certainly believed that salvation was a gift, based entirely on the finished work of Christ. But he also believed that true Christians who are filled with the Holy Spirit bear the necessary fruit of warring against sin.

> We cannot be saved *by* or *for* our good works, neither can we be saved *without* good works. Christ never will save any of His people *in* their sins; He saves His people *from* their sins. If a man is not desiring to live a holy life in the sight of God, with the help of the Holy Spirit, he is still "in the gall of bitterness, and in the bond of iniquity."[25]

Therefore, for Spurgeon, a proper doctrine of sanctification in the Christian meant life-long warfare against sin. "The moment of conversion is rather the commencement than the closing of spiritual warfare, and until the believer's head shall recline upon

---

22.   *MTP* 8:167.
23.   *Autobiography* 1.263.
24.   *Autobiography* 1:258.
25.   Ibid.

the pillow of death he will never have finished his conflicts."[26] At conversion, the Christian has received a new nature, but this does not change the old nature. Rather, the sign of the arrival of the new nature is that conflict now rages in every believer.[27] For Spurgeon, the mark of spiritual life was not perfection, but persistent struggle against sin. In this life, the Christian was, fundamentally, a soldier. "To be a Christian is to be a warrior. The good soldier of Jesus Christ must not expect to find ease in this world: it is a battle-field. Neither must he reckon upon the friendship of the world for that would be enmity against God. His occupation is war."[28]

This was true not only for the individual Christian but for the church also. Spurgeon saw his church as an army of soldiers, gathered for war against sin and for the spread of the gospel.[29] Even as engaging in spiritual warfare defined the individual Christian, so it was for the church. "In any one church there will be, there must be, if it be a church of God, earnest contention for the truth and against error."[30] This theme of conflict could be traced throughout church history, from the days of the apostles

---

26. *MTP* 12:602.

27. "Conversion and regeneration do not change the old nature; that remaineth still the same; but we have at our new birth infused into us a new nature, a new principle, and this new principle at once begins a contest with the old principle; hence the apostle tells us of the old man and of the new man; he speaks of the flesh lusting against the spirit, and the spirit striving against the flesh. I do not care what the doctrinal statement of any man may be upon the subject; I am sure that the experience of the most of us will prove to a demonstration that there are two natures within us, that only a complex description can describe us at all; we find a company of two armies within us, and the fight goes on, and, if anything, waxes hotter every day. We do trust that the right principle grows stronger, and we hope that through grace the evil principle is weakened and mortified; but, at present, it is with most of us a very sharp contest, and were it not for divine strength, we might throw down our weapons in hopelessness." *MTP* 12:531.

28. *MTP* 37:229. One of the more unique sermons that Spurgeon preached on this theme was Sermon No. 3188, "Discipline in Christ's Army," where he re-interprets Parliament's "Army Discipline and Regulation Bill" and applies it to the Christian life. *MTP* 56:121.

29. "I shall speak especially to the members of this Christian church. I exhort you, dear brethren, who are soldiers of Christ, to be good soldiers, because many of you have been so." *MTP* 16:368.

30. *MTP* 12:537.

to the present day.[31] For Spurgeon, church history confirmed what Scripture taught, namely, that "the church on earth has, and until the second advent must be, the church militant, the church armed, the church warring, the church conquering."[32]

The Mission of the Church

Spurgeon rejected a dispensationalist understanding of redemptive history, which he believed created too much discontinuity between Israel and the church. At the same time, on this side of Christ's finished work, before his return, Spurgeon saw the unique and central role of the church in God's redemptive purposes:

> To me, the one thought concerning all the kingdoms of the earth is this—how is the gospel advancing in Turkey, or in Afghanistan, or in other lands? I care for this world only for the sake of God's own people in it. The world is all scaffolding; the Church of Christ is the true building. The ultimate purpose of God is the gathering out of the world as many as he has given unto his Son, Jesus Christ, that they may have eternal life in him, and glorify him for ever.[33]

In other words, mission of the church is not to conquer the kingdoms of this world or to establish some kind of political "Christendom." In the scope of redemptive history, all the political kingdoms of the world are only so much scaffolding. Beneath and within that scaffolding is the true building, the church, which is being constructed. God's purpose during this period of redemptive history is to build his church. The day will one day come when the scaffolding will fall away, and the finished building of the church of Christ will be revealed. Until that day, the kingdoms of this world remain, as God gathers sinners from every tribe, tongue, and nation into the church. This understanding of redemptive history focused the mission of the church towards the building of the church through the salvation of sinners.

---

31   *MTP* 12:608-12.

32.   *NPSP* 5:41.

33.   *MTP* 48:473.

But the church is not only the goal of the mission. It is also the means. Though it is God who builds the church, Spurgeon believed that the earthly means that God used was the church itself. "The Church is the world's hope. As Christ is the hope of the Church, so the Church is the hope of the world. The saints become, under Christ, the world's saviors."[34] While the Christian's battle against indwelling sin is a necessary part of his warfare, it does not exhaust his mission on earth. After all, "sanctification might be completed in a moment."[35] Rather, as Christians battle indwelling sin, the church's mission is to bear witness to Christ and to advance the truth of the gospel for the salvation of the world. It is through the witness of the church that God accomplishes his purposes in redemptive history.

Though the outcome is secured, it is only through perseverance and suffering that the church will prevail. While the church lives in this world, it is constantly at war. "Let me just say, once more, concerning this war, that it is one that is to be of perpetual duration. Let us recollect, my beloved, that this war between right and wrong must be continued, and never must cease until truth has the victory."[36] In his teaching on the church militant, Spurgeon emphasized two wars in particular: the war against sin and the war against error.[37]

For all Christians, the battle began not out in the world but in the heart in the war against sin. Though their sins were forgiven and defeated in Christ, indwelling sin remained. Therefore, depending on God, each Christian was to declare their allegiance to Christ and seek to overcome all known sin. It was in this war against indwelling sin that the Christian was consecrated for

---

34. *MTP* 51:434.

35. Ibid.

36. *NPSP* 3:44.

37. In Sermon No. 250, "War! War! War!," Spurgeon describes three enemies: the war against sin, against error, and against strife with one another. *NPSP* 5:202-05. In Sermon No. 718, "The Standard Uplifted in the Face of the Foe," Spurgeon divides the war into two categories: battles in the inner man and battles without. *MTP* 12:602. In Sermon 3511, "The Battle of Life," Spurgeon uses the three categories of the world, the flesh, and the devil. *MTP* 62:219-21. In these sermons, the church's conflict against sin and error are prominent.

service.[38] But the church was not to be content in merely fighting against sin in themselves, but must also fight against sin out in the world.[39] Though Spurgeon supported the temperance movement and other efforts at social reform on a broader scale, his emphasis in the fight against sin was far more individualized, and focused on individual conversions.[40] He called Christians to live holy lives out in the world, bearing witness against sin and praying that the Holy Spirit would use their lives to convict others. God's army was to be clothed in holiness, not only as protection but as its weapon against evil. "Do you want to know the armor of that war? I will tell you. They are clothed in white linen, white and clean. Strange battle array this! And yet this is how they conquer, and how you must conquer, too. This is both armor and weapon. Holiness is our sword and our shield."[41] Moreover, Christians were to speak out about evil, no matter how unpopular. "Never let a sin pass under your eye without a rebuke."[42]

Preaching the gospel required being honest about the existence of sin in the world. As the pastor, Spurgeon modeled this in his preaching, condemning the popular vices of his day, from theatergoing to Sabbath-breaking, to corporate greed, to warfare,

---

38. "Oh! cry unto God your strength, and look unto the hills from whence cometh your help, and then fight on again, and as each sin is overcome, each evil habit broken off, each lust denied go on to the rooting up of another, and the destruction of more of them, until all being subdued, body soul and spirit shall be consecrated to Christ as a living sacrifice, purified by his Holy Spirit." *NPSP* 5:202-03.

39. "And while this battle is being fought, ay, and while it is still fighting, go out and fight with other men's sins. Smite them first with the weapon of holy example." *NPSP* 5:203.

40. While Spurgeon believed in the value of mercy ministries, his goal was ultimately to bring the gospel to those in need. His Sunday Schools were an example of this. Even while providing a basic education to poor children, Spurgeon emphasized the goal of teaching the gospel. "The Sunday School does not want a direct text for its institution or foundation. It is a marvel that it was not instituted long before it was, for the very spirit of Sabbath School work lies in the words here—'every creature.' You are not, in looking after the children, to include only some privileged classes and exclude the ragged and the depraved; the City Arab is at least a 'creature,' and you are as much bound to preach the gospel to him as to your own dear child, who is the object of your tenderest love.... Their poverty must never make us say that it is not worth while to teach them. It is the glory of the gospel that the poor should have the gospel preached to them." *MTP* 15:629-30.

41. *MTP* 25:23.

42. Ibid.

and much more. This was nevertheless to be done with wisdom and gentleness, not to wound the hearer, but to convict the heart. All such preaching existed to drive the sinner to the hope of the gospel, leading eventually to true societal reform. Through the holiness of the church, sin was defeated in the church and confronted out in the world.

The second great war of the church was the war against error. It was the church's mission to advance the truth of the gospel. But in this fallen world, errors abound, corrupting the truth. Spurgeon did not see error standing still, but ever-advancing. "The fact is that in such an age as this, if we do not attack error, error will eat us up."[43] Only the faithful teaching of the church could stem the tide of error. Some of these errors, like false religions and atheism, assaulted the church from the outside. Other errors, like ritualism and theological liberalism, assaulted the church from the inside. Whatever the shape or origin of the error, the church must fulfill its mission, not only by proclaiming the truth but also by confronting these errors. To remain silent in the face of this world's errors would be to forfeit the mission and cease to be the church. The church's identity depended on her clarity about the truth.

> The spotless purity of truth must always be at war with the blackness of heresy and lies. I say again, it would cast a suspicion upon its own nature; we should feel at once that it was not true, if it were not at enmity with the false. And so at this present time, the church of Christ, being in herself the only incarnation of truth left upon this world, must be at war with error of every kind of shape; or if she were not, we should at once conclude that she was not herself the church of the living God.[44]

In advocating this war against error, Spurgeon was not concerned about promoting particular denominational causes. As a Baptist, he disagreed with other denominations about baptism and church order and fought for those distinctives in his church planting and denominational involvement. But he placed those efforts

---

43. *MTP* 12:538.
44. *NPSP* 5:41.

in a different category, dealing more with church health than with gospel faithfulness. In the face of more serious errors, he understood that those issues were secondary. Against ritualism and rationalism, however, his primary concern was to defend those doctrines which related to the gospel. This was a battle not only of Baptists but for all Christian churches.

> I would always be very tender of the honor of the Christian body to which I belong, but I would rather see its honor stained, than that the glory of the entire church should be dimmed. Every soldier ought to love the peculiar legion in which he has enlisted, but better to see the colors of that legion rent to tatters, than to see the old standard of the cross trampled in the mire.[45]

As holiness protected the church against sin, so the clear proclamation of the gospel raised a banner for the church against error. Over and against the latitudinarianism of his day, Spurgeon called his church to proclaim its faith unashamedly and fully:

> There is a Christianity distinctive and distinguished from Ritualism, Rationalism, and Legalism, and let us make it known that we believe in it. Up with your banners, soldiers of the cross! This is not the time to be frightened by the cries against conscientious convictions, which are nowadays nicknamed sectarianism and bigotry. Believe in your hearts what you profess to believe; proclaim openly and zealously what you know to be the truth. Be not ashamed to say such-and-such things are true, and let men draw the inference that the opposite is false. Whatever the doctrines of the gospel may be to the rest of mankind, let them be your glory and boast. Display your banners, and let those banners be such as the church of old carried.[46]

Though Spurgeon used the language of warfare, he did not get carried away with the imagery as did William Booth and the Salvation Army. He found their use of drums, uniforms, military titles, and martial parades pretentious.[47] Such militant language pointed to a spiritual reality, but the Christian worker ought

---

45. *NPSP* 5:202.

46. *MTP* 17:195.

47. G. H. Pike, *The Life and Work of Charles Haddon Spurgeon*, Vol. 5 (London: Cassell & Company Ltd, 1892), 8.

to speak, dress, and act like any common person. Even more importantly, he was adamant that this never justified coercion or hatred of any kind by the church. Even as Christians opposed heresy and error, they were never to war with any persons. Even as they warred with heresy, they prayed for and loved the heretic.[48] On one occasion, Spurgeon listed a third war of the church, namely, the war against war itself. In other words, the church should strive to love and live at peace with all people, even while confronting sin and error.[49] Spurgeon rebuked those who turned religious controversies into opportunities to make personal attacks upon others. He warned his people about the temptation to think their personal battles were Christ's battles. The Christian's goal in speaking out should not be to defend himself but to uphold Christ's truth. When it came to defending his own honor, the Christian was called to look to their Master for vindication.

> Full often, when we get into little tempers, and our blood is roused, we are apt to think that we are fighting the cause of truth, when we are really maintaining our own pride. We imagine that we are defending our Master, but we are defending our own little selves. Too often the anger rises against an adversary not because his words reflect dishonor upon the glorious Christ, but because they dishonor us. Oh! let us not be so little as to fight our own battles.[50]

Spurgeon also condemned all violence in the name of religion. Historically, he condemned the violence of the medieval Catholic Church, which imprisoned and killed those who held to heretical ideas.[51] But even in his own day, Spurgeon also condemned

---

48. "We are at war with infidelity, but the persons of infidels we love and pray for; we are at warfare with any heresy, but we have no enmity against heretics; we are opposed to, and cry war to the knife with everything that opposes God and his truth: but towards every man we would still endeavor to carry out the holy maxim, 'Love your enemies, do good to them that hate you.'" *NPSP* 3:42.

49. *NPSP* 5:204-05.

50. *NPSP* 5:202.

51. "We fight not against the men, but against the things which we consider in God's sight to be wrong.... It is this mistake which has nailed martyrs to the stake and cast confessors into prison, because their opponents could not distinguish between

the violence of British "missionary" endeavors, which justified their oppression of foreign nations with the claim of gospel advancement.[52] Christ did not conquer with gun or sword, but with love. It was the sacrificial love of Christians laying their lives down for others that the Spirit used to convict people of their sin. Therefore, along with the proclamation of the truth, Spurgeon prayed, "Let love abound. Let it be all the weapons of our war."[53]

In the sermon, "The March!," on the eve of his congregation's relocation to the Metropolitan Tabernacle, Spurgeon recognized the many enemies occupying the neighborhood of Southwark. The Roman Catholic Church had recently established a cathedral nearby. There was a growing spirit of secularism and atheism among the working and upper classes of that neighborhood. And among the lower class, there was a general indifference towards religious matters. Amid all these errors, what was Spurgeon's solution?

> Will we bring in some Socialist system? Shall we preach up some new method of political economy? No! the cross, the old cross is enough.... We will but preach Christ as the sinner's Savior, the Spirit of God as applying Christ's truth to the soul, and God the Father in his infinite sovereignty saving whom he will, and in the bounty of his mercy willing to receive the vilest of the vile.[54]

Amid the many challenges, Spurgeon's focus for his church was singular: keep preaching the gospel; keep sending out evangelists; keep planting gospel-preaching churches; keep mobilizing the people for gospel-efforts. As the church battled sin and error, she needed to remember that these deconstructive efforts paved

---

the imaginary error and the man. While they spoke stoutly against the seeming error; in their ignorant bigotry they felt that they must also persecute the man, which they need not and ought not to have done." *NPSP* 3:42.

52. "Now, here comes another Christianity, which has lately displayed itself to many heathen nations. It comes with the Bible in its knapsack, and the Martini-Henry rifle in its hand. Is not this a fine combination for conversion? Jesus comes before the Zulu riding upon a Gattling gun. Of course, these poor heathen know nothing about our political combinations, but if they suppose that Christians are invading their land will they, therefore, love Christ?" *MTP* 25:264.

53. Ibid.

54. *MTP* 7:167.

the way for the constructive message of the gospel. Through the preaching of the gospel, the saints were strengthened, sinners were converted, and the mission of the church advanced. "The reason for a church being a church lies in its mutual edification and in the conversion of sinners; and if these two ends are not really answered by a church, it is a mere name, a hindrance, an evil, a nuisance."[55]

In Spurgeon's day, church success was often measured by numerical and financial growth. With larger buildings and institutions came increased pressure for positive reports of successes. But so often these triumphalist views of the church missed an important reality: the church on earth is ever at war. The victories we may experience are only partial and never perfect. Therefore, numerical increase will not always be the best indicator of success. Rather, the militant church's success should be measured by its faithfulness to the mission. "The duty of the Church is not to be measured by her [earthly] success.... The church has to do her duty, even though that duty should bring her no present reward."[56] Only by holding on to the gospel and faithfully proclaiming it, would a church accomplish its mission.

The Army Engaged

The preacher had a special role to play in the church's war. "It is the preacher's business Sabbath after Sabbath, and week-day after week-day, to preach the whole gospel of God and to vindicate the truth as it is in Jesus from the opposition of man."[57] In calling a man to preach, the congregation entrusted to the preacher the high calling of making the gospel known week after week in the gatherings of the church. Yet this battle could not be left to one man alone.

> Those of us who are specially called to preach the gospel must take our part, and go on preaching it with all our might. Oh! it is blessed employment, and angels might well envy us, that we

55. *MTP* 17:196.

56. *NPSP* 6:86.

57. *NPSP* 5:203.

have such an office committed to us as to preach the gospel. But, brethren, you must not lay all the labor or all the responsibility on one man. A one-man ministry is, indeed, a curse to any church, if that be the only ministry of the church. All ministries must be used.[58]

Spurgeon believed that a fundamental weakness of the Church of England was its inordinately high view of the clergy, which resulted in a minimization of the work of the church. Though he was glad to stand shoulder-to-shoulder with evangelical ministers in the Church of England, he had little expectation that their congregations would do much by way of gospel ministry. "However evangelical the Church of England may become, it will never be able to compete with Dissenting churches either in piety or usefulness until it gives due honor and scope to what it has been pleased to call lay agency."[59]

On the other hand, the strength of the congregational vision of the church was about more than just church meetings and governance. Rather, it was a vision for the entire membership of the church engaged in the fight. Spurgeon believed that the church was the army of God. Therefore, the way to enter into the fight was by joining a church. By joining a church, a Christian comes alongside his leaders and links arms with other soldiers. New recruits are trained in God's Word and equipped for battle. Most of all, in the church, the Christian declares his allegiance to Christ and makes clear to the world that he marches under his banner. In an age where there was so much confusion as to what it meant to be a Christian, this kind of clarity was especially important.

The church unfurls her ensign to the breeze that all may know whose she is and whom she serves. This is of the utmost importance at this present, when crafty men are endeavoring to palm off their inventions. Every Christian church should know what it believes, and publicly avow what it maintains. It is our duty to make a clear and distinct declaration of our principles,

58. *MTP* 15:633-34.
59. *S&T* 1866:428.

that our members may know to what intent they have come together, and that the world also may know what we mean.[60]

Spurgeon longed to see truly active churches. Too often, churches were marked by pointless activities: endless meetings, fruitless resolutions, territorialism, and very little real action. Thus in his church, Spurgeon urged all his members to do something in the war for truth. This was the point of all church order, not to hinder the work of the church, but to facilitate the members' ability to engage in the work.

> As in the ranks each man has his place, and each rank has its particular phase in the battalion, so in every rightly constituted church each man, each woman, will have, for himself or herself, his or her own particular form of service, and each form of service will link in with every other, and the whole combined will constitute a force which cannot be broken.[61]

Under the leadership of the Tabernacle, the church organized numerous ministries. For many members, this meant serving as a Sunday School teacher and bringing the gospel to poor children. For others, it was participating in the various mission stations and supporting the work of the college students. With all the publishing happening out of the Tabernacle, many members looked for ways to distribute gospel literature. Still others took on all kinds of creative evangelistic efforts, like distributing fresh flowers to poor urban neighborhoods as a means for evangelistic conversations, or stocking coffee shops with gospel tracts, or organizing an outreach to policemen. Some members even joined in cross-cultural mission work, taking the gospel to lands that had no witness. Spurgeon did not limit what efforts one might take, nor did he try to micro-manage it all. Rather, he encouraged his people to be entrepreneurial. The most important thing was that everyone attempted *something*.

> We have each an allotted work to do, if we are the Lord's elect; let us take care that we do it. You are a tract distributor; go on with your work, do it earnestly. You are a Sunday-school teacher;

---

60. *MTP* 17:194.
61. *MTP* 17:195.

go on, do not stay in that blessed work, do it as unto God, and not as unto man. You are a preacher; preach as God giveth you ability, remembering that he requireth of no man more than he hath given to him; therefore, be not discouraged if you have little success, still go on. Are you like Zebulon, one that can handle the pen? Handle it wisely; and you shall smite through the loins of kings therewith. And if you can do but little, at least furnish the shot for others, that so you may help them in their works of faith and their labors of love. But let us all do something for Christ. I will never believe there is a Christian in the world who cannot do something.[62]

In all these efforts, the goal was ultimately to proclaim the gospel. This was the duty not only of the pastors but of all Christians. Spurgeon believed that a view of ministry that limited preaching only to the clergy was "the invention of Satan." And yet, this was not only a problem among Roman Catholics or in the Church of England, but Spurgeon saw many Dissenting church members adopting the same attitude, believing they could serve God by proxy, by merely supporting their ministers.[63] Against such a view, Spurgeon taught that it was the duty of all Christians, men and women, to preach the gospel wherever God had placed them. Though women were not to preach in the worship gathering of the church,[64] Spurgeon urged lay men and women in all kinds of other settings to proclaim the gospel to the lost and participate in the mission of the church.

> It is sometimes asked, "Ought laymen to preach?" Nonsense! any man may preach if he has the ability. I do not believe, in my soul, that there is authority for saying, "These men are to preach, and these people are to talk of Christ; and all the rest of you are to hold your tongues, and listen." No, no, no! Let, every man of you preach; let every woman among you, in her own sphere, talk, and tell of what the Lord has done for her soul. I do believe it is the invention of Satan to lift up some few men above the rest, and

---

62. *NPSP* 3:45-46.

63. *NPSP* 5:205-06.

64. "Women are best when they are quiet. I share the apostle Paul's feelings when he bade women be silent in the assembly. Yet there is work for holy women, and we read of Peter's wife's mother that she arose and ministered to Christ." *MTP* 31:225.

say, "Only some of you are to fight the Lord's battles".... Christ expects every man—not here and there one, that is paid for doing it—the minister—but every man—to tell what God has done, for his soul. Do this, and who can tell what good may come of it?[65]

Consequently, the preacher's job was not only to wield the sword of the Spirit in preaching the gospel, but also to equip his people to handle the sword themselves. Whether young or old, man or woman, "this sword suits every hand," and the Word of God was to be wielded by every member of the church.[66] Though the church was to be focused on the proclamation of the gospel and the salvation of sinners, Spurgeon did not see this as being in conflict with the edification of the saints. Rather, one of the primary ways to build up the church in maturity and strength was to deploy the members in gospel ministry.

> There is nothing healthier for the sick, there is nothing more encouraging for the desponding, there is nothing more strengthening for the weak, there is nothing more soul-enriching for the poor in spirit, than for every Christian man among us to gird himself to do something for his Lord and Master.... I charge you, therefore, my beloved flock, let not a single one of you stay back at this time, when every king should go forth to the battle.[67]

As the congregation participated in the work of proclaiming the gospel, the church would become the best means for preserving the gospel. Too often, Christians attempted to preserve biblical orthodoxy through universities, denominational structures, or other para-church agencies. Yet, again and again, Spurgeon saw these efforts that by-passed the church fail.[68] Others believed that the way to preserve biblical fidelity was by entrusting authority to ministers. Yet repeatedly, Spurgeon saw cases where

---

65. *MTP* 51:443.

66. *MTP* 37:237.

67. *MTP* 15:572-73.

68. "We have been wondering why our societies have not greater success. I believe the reason is because there is not a single word in the Book of God about anything of the kind. The Church of God is the pillar and ground of the truth, not a society. The Church of God never ought to have delegated to any society whatever, a work which it behoved her to have done herself." *MTP* 7:363.

preachers deceived their congregations and led them into heresy.[69] In some of these churches, these preachers would override the congregationalism of the church in order to put down any opposition.[70]

Instead of these alternatives, Spurgeon believed that the church alone, namely the congregation, was the true guardian of the gospel.

> Hence the truth is not trusted to the ministry, it is based and pillared upon the whole church. The poor old bedridden sister who sings of Jesus' everlasting love is quite as much a defender of the faith as an archbishop, and perhaps more; the unlettered peasant, who knows the doctrines of grace by deep experience, and hence will never let them go, is as true a guardian of the gospel treasure as the most profound scholar, and perhaps far more so. The whole of you who really love God are set for the maintenance of the truth in the world. Under God the Holy Spirit the cause of truth depends upon you; you are its pillar and its basement.[71]

Spurgeon, as the pastor of the Metropolitan Tabernacle, played an important role in defending the gospel. Yet in time he would be gone, and there was no guarantee that future pastors would follow in his footsteps. Thus, even in his own case, he understood that the preservation of the gospel could not be left to ministers. As much as his congregation looked to him, Spurgeon impressed upon them their responsibility in the fight for the truth. The congregational nature of the church had to be preserved, and each member of the congregation must play their role in preserving and proclaiming the truth of the gospel.

---

69. "Many have thought, however, that the truth would be quite safe in the hands of ministers. If we could not leave its preaching to the society, at least let the minister, so intimately connected with the Church, become the pillar and ground of the truth. It is a melancholy fact that heresy never began with the people yet, but with the minister." Ibid.

70. "If the people could but speak so as to be heard we should not have one half the heresy which now defiles the house of God. The people are very often put on one side, as if they were not at all to be considered, but were to be managed and catered for by their spiritual lords. Then, alas! these great ones betray the cause, and sell Christ as cheaply as Judas did." *MTP* 24:547-48.

71. *MTP* 24:548.

The Army United

But the Metropolitan Tabernacle was only one church. Spurgeon envisioned the universal church, all true, gospel-preaching churches spread over the earth, as one massive army.[72] Though Dissenting churches had divided into various denominations with differing convictions regarding second-order issues, all true churches gathered under the banner of Christ and his gospel.[73] In other words, at the heart of the unity of the universal church was a spiritual unity in the gospel. While denominational or associational unity could be useful to a certain extent, this did not replace the spiritual unity of the universal church grounded in the gospel. The attempt by the Roman Catholic Church or even certain Protestant denominations to bring about wider institutional unity at the expense of biblical fidelity only led to the weakening of local churches. Instead, Spurgeon believed that in strengthening the independence and fidelity of each church, the universal church was also strengthened. It was only as churches conscientiously submitted to the authority of God's Word that they could work together under the rule of Christ.

> The only Christian unity which you and I may ever expect to see and to seek after is, not the amalgamation of all churches into one colossal scheme of government, but the spiritual union of all the churches in working for the Lord, each church exercising its discipline within its own bounds, and carrying out of Christ's commands within its own walls, and at the same time recognising all other truly Christian churches as being parts of the one body of Christ. Instead of attempting to destroy all these separate churches in order to create unity, we should

---

72. "That she is an army is true enough, for the church is one, but many; and consists of men who march in order under a common leader, with one design in view and that design a conflict and a victory." *MTP* 17:194.

73. "Display your banners, and let those banners be such as the church of old carried. Unfurl the old primitive standard, the all-victorious standard of the cross of Christ. In very deed and truth—*in hoc signo vinces*—the atonement is the conquering truth. Let others believe as they may, or deny as they will, for you the truth as it is in Jesus is the one thing that has won your heart and made you a soldier of the cross." *MTP* 17:195.

build up the walls of each house so that the whole city may be compact together.[74]

It was this vision of the universal church as the army of God that drove Spurgeon's concern for churches in other denominations. While he worked to promote Baptist convictions, he did not see the Baptists in competition with the Presbyterians, or Congregationalists, or other denominations. Rather, he supported their work, partnered with them, and prayed for them.

> Let it never be a joy to a Baptist if he hears that some Congregational Church does not prosper. Let it always be a joy to a Presbyterian when he hears that a Wesleyan is doing good. Let it be a great joy to us if any part of the Church of God prosper, and if in any place there be decay or decline, let us bear in our prayers that particular portion of the Church of God, and pray him to strengthen that part of the city wall against the foe.[75]

Even as he believed that Baptists held their conviction according to Scripture, he still recognized that different denominations each had their distinctive emphases and strengths, both theologically and ecclesiologically.[76] Only in working together with all the churches of Christ would the militant church advance in its mission.

Since associations were made up of local churches, Spurgeon did not see his emphasis on local churches in conflict with his work for denominational health. No matter how well organized or financially sound denominational structures were, they were only as healthy as their local churches. Speaking at the inaugural meeting of the London Baptist Association held at the Metropolitan Tabernacle, Spurgeon urged the attendants first to

---

74. *MTP* 12:537.

75. *MTP* 60:434.

76. "Why, I believe that different denominations are sent on purpose to set out different truths. There are some of our brethren a little too high, they bring out better than any other people, the grand old truths of sovereign grace. There are some, on the other hand, a little too low; they bring out with great clearness the great and truthful doctrines of man's responsibility. So that two truths that might have been neglected, either the one or the other, if only one form of Christianity existed, are both brought out, both made resplendent, by the different denominations of God's people, who are alike chosen of God, and precious to him." *NPSP* 4:212.

consider how they have worked for unity within their churches before being concerned for broader unity.[77] Even as the universal church gathered under the banner of the gospel, each local church represented a regiment within the larger army, holding its own banner aloft under the gospel.

Each local church, then, was to be marked by unity in the gospel. Membership and participation at the Lord's table was an expression of the unity among believers in life and doctrine. Here was the strength of Christian witness: not a solitary soldier proclaiming the truth, but an entire army holding to the truth and working together for its advancement. "Here is the secret of strength. Split us into fractions and we are conquered; unite us into a steady phalanx, and we become invincible, knit us together as one man, and Satan himself can never rend us asunder."[78] Unity in the local church was more important than her numbers, or wealth, or talents.

> Oh, my brethren, the smallest church in the world is potent for good when it hath but one heart and one soul; when pastor, elders, deacons, and members, are bound together by a threefold cord that cannot be broken. Then are they mighty against every attack. But however great their numbers, however enormous their wealth, however splendid may be the talents with which they are gifted, they are powerless for good the moment that they become divided amongst themselves. Union is strength. Blessed is the army of the living God, in that day when it goeth forth to battle with one mind, and its soldiers as with the tramp of one man, in undivided march, go onwards towards the attack.[79]

Practically, this drove Spurgeon's concern for regenerate church membership. False soldiers, though they increased the church's numbers, actually only weakened the unity of the church. "We must watch lest the Church be adulterated by additions which are not an increase to her strength…. Hitherto you have been as one man—undivided and indivisible. This is actually necessary in the Church for the carrying out of any of her purposes. Divided

---

77. *S&T* 1866:39.

78. *NPSP* 2:75.

79. *NPSP* 5:409-10.

we should utterly fail."[80] But this unity was more than just an institutional unity. Because the church was made up of those who had been transformed by the love of Christ, they would also be marked by love for one another. Together they served, and together they suffered.[81] In this loving unity, the church demonstrated to the world something that could be found nowhere else. Even though Spurgeon used the language of warfare, it was the church members' love for one another and for the lost that provided the most powerful apologetic for the truth and power of the gospel, "infinitely [surpassing] all the books of analogy and evidence which have ever been written."

> Oh, my brethren, only fancy a church of the size of this, put down in this south of London, made up of holy men and holy women like Christ, who, with all their imperfections, as to the general bent and current of their lives are living unto God and for the glory of Christ, and for the good of their fellow-men; picture such a church in perfect unity, and I tell you it would present an argument for Christianity which would infinitely surpass all the books of analogy and evidence which have ever been written. This would be a nut, which the adversary could not crack: it would baffle all his criticisms and syllogisms.... By the phalanx of unity in Christ the battle must be won.[82]

The Army's Confidence

The doctrine of the church militant taught that as long as the church lived on earth before the return of Christ, it would be in constant war. Even as the gospel advanced in certain times and places, no victory was ever final. Every generation of Christians had to do their part in fighting against sin and error. From without and from within, the militant church has no rest until it joins the King and becomes the church triumphant. As Spurgeon charged his congregation, "Be always at it, all at it, constantly at it, with

---

80. *MTP* 7:367.

81. "Whatevear is said of one of us, let it be said of all of us." *NPSP* 2:75.

82. *MTP* 25:262-63.

all your might at it. No rest. Your resting time is to come, in the grave. Be always fighting the enemy."[83]

As a pastor, Spurgeon understood that the prospect of engaging in a life-long war against a seemingly undefeatable enemy was daunting. Like Israel, the church often grew faint-hearted and was tempted to turn back in the day of battle.[84] Here was where the church had to be reminded that as important as its role was, it was only an instrument. The true warrior was God. Therefore, the church's strength did not come from itself or its efforts, but from God.

> The power of the army of the Lord does not lie in connection with any one of his soldiers, in the man himself—the Lord is their strength. They may differ in many respects, but this is true of every single warrior in the host of the Lord, that the Lord is his strength. He has no strength in the flesh, he cannot find anything there which can assist him; all his springs are in his God, and he draws all his supplies for power in spiritual conflicts, from God and from God alone.[85]

Therefore, the church did not fight alone, but rested securely in God's presence, knowing salvation was secure. Rather than fighting from a posture of fear or defeat, God's soldiers ought ever to be marked by confidence and optimism, knowing that the Spirit dwelt in the church, and God surrounded his people.[86] It was this perspective of God's presence that changed how Christians were to view their obstacles and opposition. As fearsome and daunting as they might be, they were nothing before the power of the omnipotent God.

---

83. *NPSP* 5:206.

84. "This faint-heartedness is so common that it has been the plague of Israel from her first day until now." *MTP* 32:485.

85. *MTP* 13:481.

86. "Now, how comforting is this text to the believer who recognizes himself as a soldier, and the whole church as an army! The church has its van-guard: 'Jehovah will go before you.' The church is also in danger behind; enemies may attack her in her hinder part, 'and the God of Israel shall be her rereward.' So that the army is safe from enemies in front—and God alone knoweth their strength, and it is also perfectly secure from any foes behind, however malicious and powerful they may be; for Jehovah is in the van, and the covenant God of Israel is behind: therefore the whole army is safe." *NPSP* 5:42.

All the foes of the Church with all their battlements behind which they are intrenched, are nothing. They but seem to be. They are shadows, emptiness, nothing. Do you in confidence cry to your God—"Lord, do but rise; do but stand up; do but manifest thy power in any way whatever, and thine enemies are scattered at once, and those that hate thee must flee before thee for evermore."[87]

Spurgeon believed God's power was made most evident during times of darkness and defeat, and he urged his congregation to persevere in hope.

If the church's power came from God, this changed the church's attitude. Even while the church was to be active and engaged, it was to depend entirely on God and not on itself. This dependence was demonstrated in two ways. First, the church's confidence had to be in the gospel, not in the church. Rather than relying on entertaining innovations, business strategies, or church structures, the church was to be confident in the power of the gospel to change lives. Though the world despised the church and sought to overthrow it, yet "the gospel is the voice of the eternal God, and has in it the same power as that which brought the world out of nothing, and which shall raise the dead from their graves at the coming of the Son of Man."[88] Whether the gospel was preached by a polished preacher or an uneducated deacon, God accomplished his work through his Word, sometimes even in spite of the instrument. Such dependence, rather than creating uncertainty, fostered confidence in each soldier as they proclaimed the gospel.[89]

A second way the church demonstrated dependence on God was through prayer. Behind Spurgeon's prominent preaching

---

87. *MTP* 7:164.

88. *MTP* 17:198.

89. One story illustrates this confidence. Of a conversation with T. W. Medhurst, his first student, Spurgeon recalled: "One day, with a very sad countenance, he said to me, 'I have been preaching for three months, and I don't know of a single soul having been converted.' Meaning to catch him by guile, and at the same time to teach him a lesson he would never forget, I asked, 'Do you expect the Lord to save souls every time you open your mouth? 'Oh, no, sir! he replied. 'Then,' I said, 'that is just the reason why you have not had conversions: According to your faith be it unto you.'" *Autobiography* 2:151.

ministry was a praying church. Because the battle belonged to the Lord, Spurgeon believed that the true battle was not in the preaching, but in the praying. In many churches, the battle was lost not in the preaching, but in the lack of prayer. He envisioned himself as Joshua on the battlefield, and the church as Moses holding up his staff in prayer. Just as Moses grew tired, so the church and the preacher often grew weary in prayer. And as soon as prayer wanes, the preaching will cease to go forth.

> You are not so likely to fail in your efforts as in your prayers. We never read that Joshua's hand was weary with wielding the sword, but Moses' hand was weary with holding the rod. The more spiritual the duty, the more apt we are to tire of it. We could stand and preach all day, but we could not pray all day. We could go forth to see the sick all day, but we could not be in our closets all day one-half so easily. To spend a night with God in prayer would be far more difficult than to spend a night with man in preaching. Oh! take care, take care, church of Christ, that thou dost not cease thy prayers! Above all, I speak to my own much loved church, my own people. You have loved me, and I have loved you, and God has given us great success, and blessed us. But, mark, I trace all of it to your prayers.[90]

While the church prays, the victory will be won. Yet this prayer was intended not only for the pastor, but for all the ministries of the church and all the ways the gospel went out from its members. Here, even the feeblest members had a vital work to do, namely, praying for the power of God to accompany his Word. "If you can neither teach in the classes or in the Sunday school, nor preach in the streets and so fight, you can at least be much in the closet and much in prayer. Oh the untold benefits that come to a Christian church from the quiet prayerful members!"[91]

In all its faithful ministry and prayer, the church draws comfort from its King. Communion with Christ is the soldier's privilege amid the conflict:

---

90. *NPSP* 3:47.

91. *MTP* 12:538-39.

In every conflict which the child of God has to wage, it is not the private person who goeth to the warfare, it virtually is Christ fighting—Christ contending. It is a member of Christ's body laboring against Christ's enemy for the glory of the Head. Christ the Head has an intense feeling of sympathy with every member, no matter how humble. Since there is a vital union between Christ and every member, there is also an undying sympathy; and whenever, brother, thou contendest for the faith till thou growest weary, Jesus Christ will be sure to give thee some proof of His close communion with thee.[92]

Here is the true joy of the soldier—not the vanquishing of opponents or the grandeur of his exploits, but the presence and love of his Lord. This is how the church battled pride amid her accomplishments: by communion with its King. "The true secret of a Christian's joy is not to be his conquest over sin or over error, but the person of his Lord Jesus Christ.... I am persuaded, beloved, that the best cure for pride is a sight of Christ."[93] In faithful obedience to the mission, the church did not blaze its own trail but followed in the footsteps of the King. All that the church faces, the King has already faced and defeated. In this way, Spurgeon framed the journey of the militant church not as suffering, but as fellowship with Christ, both in his suffering and his victory.[94]

Because Christ the Head has triumphed, victory is ultimately guaranteed for his Body. Though the church militant is ever besieged and persecuted, the eyes of faith reveal something different: the gates of hell will not prevail against the church. Because God is at work in the church and his presence goes with it, the church militant is confident that the end will not be defeat but victory when the King returns.

---

92. *MTP* 10:514.

93. Ibid.

94. "Cheer up now thou faint-hearted warrior. Not only has Christ traveled the road, but he has slain thine enemies. Dost thou dread sin? he has nailed it to his cross. Dost thou dread death? he has been the death of Death. Art thou afraid of hell? he has barred it against the advent of any of his children; they shall never see the gulf of perdition. Whatever foes may be before the Christian, they are all overcome.... Well then, the army may safely march on and you may go joyously along your journey, for all your enemies are conquered beforehand. What shall you do but march on to take the prey?" *NPSP* 5:47.

Even so hath it been with the Church of God in all ages; her march has been that of one who is fair as the moon, clear as the sun, and terrible as an army with banners. Let but her silvery trumpet sound, and the echo shakes the vaults of hell. Let but her warriors unsheath their sword, and their enemies fly before them like thin clouds before a Biscay gale. Her path is the pathway of a conqueror; her march has been a procession of triumph. Wherever she has put her foot, the Lord hath given her that land to be her heritage for ever and ever, and as it was in the beginning it is now, and ever shall be till this world shall end. Amen.[95]

Conclusion

Spurgeon's vision of the militant church can be traced throughout his preaching ministry, from his early sermons at Waterbeach to the very last sermon he preached at the Metropolitan Tabernacle. This was not an image that he employed only during times of controversy in order to stir his people to action. Rather, whether in seeming popularity or persecution, Spurgeon understood that in this period of redemptive history, the church was to be marked by a willingness to fight for the truth, even as it fulfilled its mission to take the gospel to the ends of the earth.

This vision of the militant church did not replace Spurgeon's Reformed ecclesiology and Baptist church polity. Rather, it colored those theological and practical ideas, revealing their importance. Spurgeon used his understanding of the militant church to teach his people why ecclesiology and church polity mattered. A proper understanding of the congregational nature of the church revealed that the army of God was not made up merely of clergy, but of every member of the church. With its regulative principle, the army follows the commands of its Captain, rather than compromising with the enemy. Prayer meetings were to be marked by wartime urgency, rather than peacetime leisure. Regenerate church membership was not just about maintaining an accurate roll; it meant enlisting Christians in the fight for the truth and mobilizing them for action.

---

95. *MTP* 7:162.

Ultimately, Spurgeon's convictional approach to ecclesiology and church polity mattered because he understood that the church was in a fight and the truth of the gospel was at stake. He pursued a faithful understanding and practice of the church because this was how the church preserved and advanced the gospel.

9

The Army at War

Of the many errors that abounded in his day, there were two that Spurgeon saw as particularly formidable:

> Just now two armies have encamped against the host of God, opposed to each other, but confederates against the church of God. Ritualism, with its superstition, its priestcraft, its sacramental efficacy, its hatred of the doctrines of grace; and on the other side Rationalism, with its sneering unbelief and absurd speculations. These, like Herod and Pilate, agree in nothing but in opposition to Christ.[1]

They were particularly dangerous because rather than coming from the outside, they were promoting their teachings from within the church, drawing Christians away from historic Protestant orthodoxy. Ritualism had infiltrated the Church of England through the Oxford Movement and was rapidly gaining influence throughout the land. Likewise, rationalism was growing in influence in Nonconformist churches, particularly in the form of German higher criticism. Spurgeon recognized the teaching of both movements as utterly incompatible with the gospel.

Living in England in the nineteenth century, Spurgeon did not face martyrdom or imprisonment for his Christianity. Nonetheless, he and his congregation experienced persecution through opposition and slander. Ritualism and rationalism did not aim so much for dominance as they did for compromise and acceptance. Those who rejected their teaching were deemed narrow-minded and intolerant.

---

1. *MTP* 17:200.

When it came to differences over secondary or tertiary doctrines, Spurgeon modeled a large-heartedness towards all who held to the gospel. As we've already seen, he frequently cooperated with Congregationalists, Presbyterians, and even Anglicans in missions, evangelism, and mercy ministries. He once lectured for a meeting of Quakers commending George Fox in his fight against merely external religion. He admired and supported the work of Plymouth Brethren like George Mueller and Hudson Taylor. When his students asked him about evolution, he stated his opposition to the theory but left room for disagreement. In these and many other ways, Spurgeon showed impressive generosity for all who held to Christ.

However, when it came to errors that touched on primary doctrines and compromised the gospel, there could be no compromise. Regardless of the consequences, Spurgeon believed that any tolerance of such errors would be a betrayal of his Captain and the church's mission. The temptation, of course, was that, through compromise, a larger unity could be had between churches, leading to greater accomplishments for Christ. But in doing so, they disobeyed Christ's clear orders to wield the sword of the Spirit, which is the word of God (Eph. 6:17). Preaching on that verse, Spurgeon stated:

> It is clear from our text that our defense and our conquest must be obtained by sheer fighting. Many try compromise; but if you are a true Christian, you can never do this business well. The language of deceit fits not a holy tongue. The adversary is the father of lies, and those that are with him understand the art of equivocation; but saints abhor it. If we discuss terms of peace, and attempt to gain something by policy, we have entered upon a course from which we shall return in disgrace. We have no order from our Captain to patch up a truce, and get as good terms as we can. We are not sent out to offer concessions. It is said that if we yield a little, perhaps the world will yield a little also, and good may come of it. If we are not too strict and narrow, perhaps sin will kindly consent to be more decent. Our association with it will prevent its being so barefaced and atrocious. If we are not narrow-minded, our broad doctrine will go down with the

world, and those on the other side will not be so greedy of error as they now are. No such thing. Assuredly this is not the order which our Captain has issued. When peace is to be made, he will make it himself, or he will tell us how to behave to that end; but at present our orders are very different.[2]

The mission of the militant church was not to negotiate terms of peace with the world, but to confront the world's errors with the truth of the gospel.

Thus, Spurgeon led his church into war through two methods in particular: his sermons and his magazine, *The Sword and the Trowel*. Through his sermons, Spurgeon had the opportunity to speak to his congregation of several thousand week after week to mobilize them for action. Though his congregation was his primary audience, these sermons would also have a far reach as they were published, distributed throughout the world, and read by tens of thousands. Similarly, in *The Sword and the Trowel*, Spurgeon had a monthly opportunity to speak to the growing network of churches that was arising out of the Pastors' College. But its impact was felt throughout the evangelical world, giving Christians in every denomination not only a vision for the gospel, but also for the church.[3]

In particular, four themes of the militant church stand out: action, purity, mission, and faithfulness. These four themes are prominently reflected in Spurgeon's four sermons from the Baptismal Regeneration controversy, but they also are reflected in his sermons and articles for his other controversies. In calling for action, Spurgeon promoted his congregational vision of the church with an active and working membership where every soldier is engaged. In calling for purity, Spurgeon reflected his commitment to the church's holiness, particularly in its associations, but also in its membership. In calling for evangelism, Spurgeon charged the church with the mission of proclaiming and preserving the

---

2. *MTP* 37:229-30.

3. The church was central to Spurgeon's vision for *The Sword and the Trowel*. In the opening article, he writes, "Our Magazine is intended to report the efforts of those Churches and Associations, which are more or less intimately connected with the Lord's work at the Metropolitan Tabernacle, and to advocate those views of doctrine and Church order which are most certainly received among us." *S&T* 1865:1.

gospel. Finally, in calling for faithfulness, Spurgeon called the church to build on the foundation of the Word of God. Through his sermons and *The Sword and the Trowel*, Spurgeon thus advanced his militant ecclesiology and church polity amid controversy.

The Baptismal Regeneration Controversy[4]

Beginning in the early nineteenth century, in response to the "quiet worldliness" of the church, the rationalism of the Enlightenment, and the inactivity of evangelical churchmen,[5] a movement arose out of Oxford that sought to bring the English Church back to its former glory before the Reformation. Led by John Henry Newman (1801-1890) and Edward B. Pusey (1800-1882), the Oxford Movement was driven by a series of publications, the *Tracts for the Times*.[6] In these tracts, the authors argued for the recovery of an older understanding of the Church, for apostolic succession, a sacramental view of salvation, the authority of tradition alongside the Scriptures, the use of the confessional, and other doctrines associated with Roman Catholic teaching. Though the movement was initially condemned, its writings continued to be distributed and discussed among the rising generation of Anglican priests. By the mid-1800s, the Church of England was reinvigorated, in no small part owing to the Oxford Movement, resulting in advances in literature, hymns, art, and architecture,[7] the founding of new schools, and the building of hundreds of new churches,[8] not

---

4. This section draws from an article I wrote on Spurgeon's use of Martin Luther against the Oxford Movement. Geoffrey Chang, "Spurgeon's Use of Luther against the Oxford Movement," *Themelios*, Vol. 43, Issue 1.

5. For a description of the condition of the Church of England prior to the Oxford Movement, see R.W. Church, *The Oxford Movement: Twelve Years 1833-1845* (London: MacMillan and Co., 1891), 2-17.

6. The Oxford Movement was also known as Tractarianism, after the ninety tracts they published, or Puseyism, after Edward Pusey their leader. The tracts can be accessed here: "Tracts for the Times," Project Canterbury, cdli:wiki, http://anglicanhistory.org/tracts/. Accessed on January 21, 2020.

7. S. L. Ollard, *A Short History of the Oxford Movement* (London: A. R. Mowbray & Co., 1915), 204-39.

8. G. H. F. Nye, *The Story of the Oxford Movement* (London: Bemrose & Sons, 1899), 144-49.

only in England but throughout the British empire.[9] It was in this context that Spurgeon began his pastoral ministry in 1854 at the New Park Street Chapel, later to become the Metropolitan Tabernacle.[10]

In the first ten years of his ministry, Spurgeon was regularly outspoken about the growth of Roman Catholic theology within the Church of England. But on the Sunday after the 300th anniversary of John Calvin's death,[11] the conflict exploded. On June 5, 1864, Spurgeon preached the sermon "Baptismal Regeneration,"[12] condemning the doctrine of baptismal regeneration found in the *Book of Common Prayer*. Spurgeon warned his publishers about the risk that this sermon would pose for the sale of his books. He was also deeply aware how this would expose him to the slander of his enemies and even some allies. And yet for the sake of his conscience, he felt compelled to speak out about something he considered a serious error.[13]

In the next three months, Spurgeon would preach three more sermons confronting the Church of England.[14] These four sermons would be published together in one volume and sold to the public.[15] After 1864, Spurgeon would continue his attacks through *The Sword and the Trowel*, publishing articles against Roman Catholicism and the Oxford Movement up to the end of his ministry. In all this, Spurgeon ignited a firestorm

---

9.   See Steward J. Brown and Peter B. Nockles, eds. *The Oxford Movement: Europe and the Wider World 1830-1930* (Cambridge: Cambridge University Press, 2012).

10.   Spurgeon preached against the Oxford Movement as early as August 1851. *LS* 1:191.

11.   Evangelicals throughout London gathered that week for various commemorations to celebrate the occasion. See G. Holden Pike, *The Life and Work of Charles Haddon Spurgeon* (Edinburgh: Banner of Truth Trust, 1991), Vol. 3, 92.

12.   *MTP* 10:313.

13.   "Among my hearers and readers, a considerable number will censure if not condemn me, but I cannot help it. If I forfeit your love for truth's sake I am grieved for you, but I cannot, I dare not, do otherwise. It is as much as my soul is worth to hold my peace any longer, and whether you approve or not I must speak out." Ibid., 314-15.

14.   Sermon No. 577, "Let Us Go Forth," *MTP* 10:365; Sermon No. 581, "Children Brought to Christ, and Not to the Font," *MTP* 10:413; Sermon No. 591, "'Thus Saith the Lord.' Or, the Book of Common Prayer Weighed in the Balances of the Sanctuary" *MTP* 10:533.

15.   *MTP* 10:548.

of controversy. Hundreds of articles, tracts, and sermons were written against him. Many of Spurgeon's former allies turned against him, forcing him to resign from the Evangelical Alliance. Yet, because of Spurgeon's leadership, many pastors also joined him in this fight, along with their churches.[16]

Militant Church Sermons during the Baptismal Regeneration Controversy

Though Spurgeon addressed the growth of Roman Catholicism in the Church of England in his sermons throughout his ministry, there were four sermons in particular that were devoted to this subject. While these sermons cover a range of theological topics, they also demonstrate Spurgeon's strategy for engaging the church militant. The following summaries each focus on a different theme of Spurgeon's four-part strategy, though they all contain multiple themes.

Sermon No. 573, "Baptismal Regeneration" – A Call to Action.

Preached on Sunday morning, June 5, 1864, this is the sermon that ignited the controversy and from which the controversy was named. Here in this sermon, Spurgeon drew from the language of the *Book of Common Prayer* to show that the liturgy of the Church of England promoted a view of baptism as effectually regenerating the recipients apart from faith, even in the case of infants. To be clear, Spurgeon's concern was not against infant baptism or the mode of sprinkling. Rather, it was the doctrine of baptismal regeneration, namely, that a person can be regenerated apart from faith, through the church's practice of baptism. Though the Church's *Thirty-Nine Articles* nowhere taught baptismal regeneration, the official liturgy in the *Book of Common Prayer* confused the issue, giving those in the Oxford Movement support for their position. For example, after the baptism of the infant, the priest is to offer this thanksgiving: "We yield thee hearty thanks, most merciful Father, that it hath pleased thee to regenerate this infant with thy Holy Spirit, to receive him for thine own child by adoption, and to incorporate him into thy holy Church."

---

16. *Autobiography* 3:84-85.

As a Baptist, Spurgeon found such language utterly offensive in the Church of England context. There, baptism and church membership was not based on a credible profession of faith but on citizenship. In his own church, with a rigorous membership process in place, Spurgeon could refer to the members of his church as regenerated, adopted, and members of Christ's church. But apart from this understanding and practice of regenerate church membership, to apply the promises of the gospel so definitively to any citizen of England was to undermine the gospel itself.

Spurgeon's goal, then, was not merely to expose the language of baptismal regeneration in the *Book of Common Prayer*. Rather, this sermon was a call to action. He sought to awaken the indignation of his hearers and provoke a response.[17] At the heart of the sermon, he sought to expose how baptismal regeneration contradicted and made a mockery of the gospel. The baptismal liturgy of the Church assured all baptized infants that they had been regenerated and saved. This, in essence, inoculated sinners from the gospel, thus removing the need for repentance and faith.[18] Even as the church was called to preach the gospel for the salvation of sinners, this liturgy undermined the church's mission.

---

17. "My brethren, do not think I speak severely here. Really I think there is something here to make mockery for devils. Let every honest man lament, that ever God's Church should tolerate such a thing as this, and that there should be found gracious people who will feel grieved because I, in all kindness of heart, rebuke the atrocity. Unregenerate sinners promising for a poor babe that he shall keep all God's holy commandments which they themselves wantonly break every day! How can anything but the longsuffering of God endure this? What! not speak against it?" *MTP* 10:321.

18. "How can any man stand up in his pulpit and say Ye must be born again to his congregation, when he has already assured them, by his own 'unfeigned assent and consent' to it, that they are themselves, every one of them, born again in baptism. What is he to do with them? Why, my dear friends, the gospel then has no voice; they have rammed this ceremony down its throat and it cannot speak to rebuke sin. The man who has been baptized or sprinkled says, 'I *am* saved, I *am* a member of Christ, a child of God, and an inheritor of the kingdom of heaven. Who are you, that you should rebuke *me*? Call *me* to repentance? Call *me* to a new life? What better life can I have? for I *am* a member of Christ—a part of Christ's body. What! rebuke *me*? I am a child of God. Cannot you see it in my face? No matter what my walk and conversation is, I am a child of God.'" *MTP* 10:321.

Spurgeon also sought to arouse indignation by showing how baptismal regeneration made a mockery of the body of Christ. Thousands of those who had received baptism as infants went on to live profligate lives, yet the Established Church did not excommunicate them, but continued to affirm their regeneration and salvation. Spurgeon found this intolerable:

> Am I untruthful if I say that thousands of those who were baptized in their infancy are now in our gaols? You can ascertain the fact if you please, by application to prison authorities. Do you believe that these men, many of whom have been living by plunder, felony, burglary, or forgery, are regenerate? If so, the Lord deliver us from such regeneration. Are these villains members of Christ? If so, Christ has sadly altered since the day when he was holy, harmless, undefiled, separate from sinners. Has he really taken baptized drunkards and harlots to be members of his body?[19]

In calling such people regenerate and members of Christ, the name of Christ was being blasphemed among the nations.

For every Christian who treasured salvation by grace alone, through faith alone, and in Christ alone, this sermon aroused their indignation and called them to action. Here was Spurgeon's congregational vision for the conflict. He would not write academic treatises to engage the universities against baptismal regeneration. Instead, he preached sermons to engage his church and the wider Protestant community into action.

Sermon No. 577, "Let Us Go Forth," A Call to Holiness.
The second sermon of the controversy was preached just three weeks later, on Sunday morning, June 26, 1864. Having aroused the indignation of his hearers, what was Spurgeon calling them to do? He made it clear in this sermon: "The divine command is not, 'Let us stop in the camp and try to reform it—things are not anywhere quite perfect, let us therefore stop and make matters right;' but the Christian's watch cry is, 'Let us go forth.'"[20] The basis for this call to separation was the holiness of the church.

19. Ibid., 318.
20. Ibid., 367.

In all her associations, the church was to reflect the purity of the gospel and her distinction from the world. "The Church of God is to be distinct and separate from all other corporations or communities."[21]

This sermon was primarily aimed at the evangelicals, both ministers and church members, who remained in the Church of England, seeking to reform it from the inside. Though Spurgeon believed in the genuineness of their faith, he especially rebuked the ministers for their dishonesty in promising to believe and uphold the teaching and liturgy of the Church.[22] In this matter, Spurgeon argued that those in the Oxford Movement had more integrity than the evangelicals because they believed in the teaching of the *Book of Common Prayer*. By remaining in the Church, evangelicals undermined not only their integrity but the truthfulness of their own words, inviting scoffing from the world.

> When worldly men hear ministers denouncing the very things which their own Prayer Book teaches, they imagine that words have no meaning among ecclesiastics, and that vital differences in religion are merely a matter of tweedle-dee and tweedle-dum, and that it does not much matter what a man does believe so long as he is charitable towards other people.[23]

He thus called all honest Christians to leave the Church of England and form a pure church, which held honestly to its doctrines and practices.[24] His concern was not for them to join his denomination. He would have been thrilled to see a new denomination of free Episcopal churches. Rather, his desire was to see Anglican evangelicals take a stand for the holiness of the church by separating from those who compromised the gospel.

---

21. Ibid.

22. "For clergymen to swear or say that they give their solemn assent and consent to what they do not believe is one of the grossest pieces of immorality perpetrated in England, and is most pestilential in its influence, since it directly teaches men to lie whenever it seems necessary to do so in order to get a living or increase their supposed usefulness." *MTP* 10:316-17.

23. Ibid., 317.

24. "Where union and friendship are not cemented by truth, they are an unhallowed confederacy. It is time that there should be an end put to the flirtations of honest men with those who believe one way and swear another." Ibid.

But this call to evangelicals in the Church of England was no different than the call given to every Christian. It was every Christian's duty to come out of the world and join the church. Every member of the Tabernacle took this step when they professed faith in Christ, were baptized, and joined the church. And those who refused to take that step of public separation from the world did not receive the church's affirmation.

> Every Christian is to go forth *by an open profession of his faith.* You that love the Lord are to say so. You must come out and avow yourselves on his side. You may be Christians and make no profession, but I cannot be sure of that, nor can any other man... since you do not acknowledge yourselves to be a part of Christ's Church, we are compelled to adjudge you as not a part of that Church.[25]

Rather than conforming to the errors and immorality of the world, a Christian stood for the truth and lived in obedience to God. And in that struggle, the Christian encountered Christ and communed with him. "Christ reveals himself as a sweet refreshment to the warrior after the battle, and so blessed is the vision, that the warrior feels more calm and peace in the day of strife than in his hours of rest. Believe me, the highway of holiness is the highway of communion."[26] The holiness of the church fueled Spurgeon's call for separation.

Sermon No. 581, "Children Brought to Christ, and not to the Font," A Call to Evangelism.

The next sermon was preached a month later, on Sunday morning, July 24, 1864, as a response to some of the arguments that were being raised against Spurgeon for the "Baptismal Regeneration" sermon. Some opponents had cited Mark 10:13-16, where children were brought to Jesus for his blessing, as a defense for infant baptism. Yet in this text, Spurgeon saw a call to the church for greater zeal in evangelism. Rather than interposing the church's

---

25. Ibid., 367-68.
26. *MTP* 10:375.

baptism between Christ and sinners, this text rebuked anyone who would prevent sinners from coming *directly* to Christ.

> Still hundreds will catch at this straw, and cry, "Did not Jesus say, 'Suffer the little children to come unto me?'" To these we give this one word, see that ye read the Word as it is written, and you will find no water in it but Jesus only. Are the water and Christ the same thing? Is bringing a child to a font bringing the child to Christ? Nay, here is a wide difference, as wide as between Rome and Jerusalem, as wide as between Antichrist and Christ, between false doctrine and the gospel of our Lord Jesus Christ.[27]

Rather than bringing children to be baptized, the proper method for bringing children to Christ was by praying earnestly for their salvation and using all means to teach them the gospel. Spurgeon saw his Sunday school teachers engaged in a noble effort at bringing children directly to Christ. The faithful evangelism of children was far more important than any baptismal practice.

> This pleading with them for God and with God for them is the true way to bring children to Christ. Sunday-school teachers! You have a high and noble work, press forward in it. In our schools you do not try to bring children to the baptistry for regeneration, you point them away from ceremonies; if I know the teachers of this school aright, I know you are trying to bring your classes to Christ. Let Christ be the sum and substance of your teaching in the school.[28]

While Spurgeon denied that infants could be regenerated, he certainly believed that children could be saved, even very little ones. At the Tabernacle, there was no rule regarding the age of baptism, and the congregation was willing to baptize and receive into membership any children who gave a credible profession of faith. Spurgeon once gave this clarification:

> We have never as a church thought that a certain number of years must have passed over a child before it can confess its faith in Christ and be received into the church. It is sometimes said that we teach adult baptism. We do nothing of the sort. We

27. Ibid., 416.
28. *MTP* 10:418.

practice believer's baptism, and baptize all who confess faith in the Lord Jesus Christ, whether they are children or adults. Our enquiry as to fitness does not refer to age, but to faith.

The number or the fewness of days or years is no consideration whatever with us. Our question is, "Dost thou believe in the Lord Jesus Christ?" If that be fairly answered we say at once, "What doth hinder you to be baptized?" However young a believer may be he should make an open confession of his faith, and be folded with the rest of the flock of Christ.[29]

Such children with credible professions of faith were brought through the normal membership process into membership. In my own research, I have found a record of someone as young as ten joining the church,[30] though such cases are not common.

Fervent prayer and evangelism were needed not only for children but all sinners. The church was to be fully engaged in bringing men and women to Christ. Jesus' rebuke of his disciples in the passage and his willingness to receive children should prompt Christians to pursue even the worst of sinners. But by making it the instrument of regeneration, the Church of England had placed baptism before evangelism, and had thus made a mockery of both the church and the gospel.[31] Faithful evangelism meant calling people to repentance and faith in Christ, not to baptism. Spurgeon's battle against baptismal regeneration was aimed at preserving a right understanding of the evangelistic mission of the church.

---

29. *MTP* 28:568.

30. "Denominational Intelligence—Baptism," *The Baptist Messenger: An Evangelical Treasury and Chronicle of the Churches from January to June, 1856 with Portraits of Ten Baptist Ministers.* Magazine D (London: James Paul, 1856), 72.

31. "The font is a mockery and an imposition if it be put before Christ. If you have baptism after you have come to Christ, well and good, but to point you to it either as being Christ, or as being inevitably connected with Christ, or as being the place to find Christ, is nothing better than to go back to the beggarly elements of the old Romish harlot, instead of standing in the 'liberty wherewith Christ hath made us free,' and bidding the sinner to come as a sinner to Christ Jesus, and to Christ Jesus alone." *MTP* 10:421.

Sermon No. 591, "'Thus Saith the Lord:' Or, the Book of
Common Prayer Weighed in the Balances of the Sanctuary,"
A Call to Faithfulness.

Two months later, on Sunday morning, September 25, 1864, Spurgeon delivered his final sermon in this series.[32] Here, he raised the central objection against the *Book of Common Prayer*, namely, the authority of Scripture. It was by the Word of God that God's people were made, and it is by the Word of God that his people are sustained. Christ's reign over the church was maintained insofar as the church submitted to his Word. The church "ought therefore to bow with reverence to that which is truly the Word of God, since it contains within itself the highest degree of power, and is ever how divine omnipotence manifests itself."[33] This sermon was a call to faithfulness in the church.

In particular, God's Word ought to reign in two areas: the teaching of the church,[34] and the worship of the church.[35] Rather than tradition, or councils, or aesthetics, or pragmatism, the church was to be ruled by God's Word in all that it taught and did. Here was Spurgeon's reformed commitment to the regulative principle. Any worship, no matter how historic or popular or beautiful, if it is not grounded in the gospel and Christ's commands, is to be rejected.

> You may further plead, in addition to all this venerable authority, the beauty of the ceremony and its usefulness to those who partake therein, but this is all foreign to the point, for to the true Church of God the only question is this, is there 'Thus saith the

---

32. In the next two years, Spurgeon would preach two more sermons on this topic. See Sermon No. 653, "A Blow for Puseyism," *MTP* 11:553; Sermon No. 695, "The Axe at the Root: A Testimony Against Puseyite Idolatry," *MTP* 12:325.

33. *MTP* 10:534.

34. "If he be God's minister he does not found his teaching upon his own authority, for then his message would be only that of himself and not to be esteemed; but he shows the authority of his Master, and none can gainsay him." Ibid.

35. "'Thus saith the Lord' *is the only authority in God's Church.* When the tabernacle was pitched in the wilderness, what was the authority for its length and breadth? Why was the altar of incense to be placed here, and the brazen laver there? Why so many lambs or bullocks to be offered on a certain day? Why must the passover be roasted whole and not sodden? Simply and only because God had shown all these things to Moses in the holy mount; and thus had Jehovah spoken." *MTP* 10:535.

Lord' for it? And if divine authority be not forthcoming, faithful men thrust forth the intruder as the cunning craftiness of men.[36]

Given the sole authority of God's Word in the church, all the various liturgies of the *Book of Common Prayer* ought to be tested against the Word. Whether infant baptism, confirmation, burial rites, ordination, or any other liturgical element, every aspect of the church's worship ought to be tested by this one question: is there a "Thus saith the Lord"? Is there warrant for the practice in Christ's Word? This was Spurgeon's challenge, not only to the Church of England, but to all Christian churches. In an age when the churches were increasingly pursuing new methods and entertainments to attract people, Spurgeon challenged them to faithfulness to God's Word. The regulative principle, then, was an expression of the church's submission to and hope in Christ's reign.

> Have any of you a hope of heaven which will not stand the test of 'Thus saith the Lord[?]' What are you resting upon? Are you resting upon something which you felt when excited at a prayer-meeting or under a sermon? Remember you will not have that excitement to bear you up in death, and the religion of excitement will not suffice in the day of judgment. Are you building upon your own works? Are you depending upon your own feelings? Do you rely upon sacraments? Are you placing your trust upon the word of man? If so, remember that when God shakes all things he will shake these false foundations; but O, build upon the Word of my Lord and Master; trust your soul with Jesus.[37]

The Sword and the Trowel during the Baptismal Regeneration Controversy

Spurgeon's four sermons in the Baptismal Regeneration Controversy were preached over four months. Though they would be published and have an impact well beyond those months, Spurgeon's battle against the Church of England would continue through his magazine. Begun in January 1865, six months after the "Baptismal Regeneration" sermon, *The Sword and the Trowel*

---

36. Ibid., 535-36.
37. Ibid., 547-48.

provided Spurgeon a means of continuing the war, engaging not only his congregation, but a wider evangelical readership. Though Spurgeon would continue to write against Puseyism until the end of his ministry, the first five years (1865–1869) of *The Sword and the Trowel* are particularly focused on this issue, with twenty-two different articles addressing the challenge of ritualism. In the preface to the 1868 volume, Spurgeon writes:

> We have waged determined war with Popery, for ours is pre-eminently
> A PROTESTANT MAGAZINE,
> But we fight against doctrinal Popery, not in Rome alone, but at Oxford too. To us the sacramentarianism of the English Church is not a thing to be winked at. We hold that he who hates Popery because of its antichristian teaching, will never stay his hand because it assumes a Protestant dress. The English Church is so Popish in its catechism, its baptismal service, and much of its ritualism, that it must not so much be reformed as transformed. These are not times to keep this matter in the background, and we have not done so.[38]

Though his original goal for his magazine was to promote a Baptist understanding of the church,[39] in light of the challenge of the Oxford Movement, it also became a rallying point for evangelicals and a Protestant understanding of the church, rejecting the sacramentarianism and ritualism of Rome, and preserving the truth of the gospel.

A Call to Action

The articles in those first five years expand on the themes of the four sermons. Spurgeon continued to call the church to action, with one of his primary strategies exposing the darkness of Roman Catholicism. In "The Inquisition"[40] and "The Massacre of St. Bartholomew,"[41] he recounted the horrors perpetrated by the Roman Catholic Church in torturing and slaughtering those

38. *S&T* 1868:iv.
39. *S&T* 1865:1.
40. *S&T* 1868:341.
41. *S&T* 1866:147.

they deemed heretics. Despite the Church of England's dignified and religious exterior, he warned his readers how Catholic ritualism had been enforced throughout history through violence and injustice. A few articles also featured his travels to Roman Catholic lands.[42] More than providing entertainment, he warned his readers of the current spiritual darkness and superstition covering the lands under Roman Catholic rule. In telling these stories, he did not hesitate to equate the Roman Catholic Church with the Church of England. "The distinction between the Popery of Rome and the Popery of Oxford is only the difference between prussic acid and arsenic: they are both equally deadly, and are equally to be abhorred."[43] This is the direction in which the Church of England was heading.

In response to all these dangers, Spurgeon called his readers to action. In perhaps the most significant article of these years, "The Holy War of the Present Hour," Spurgeon charged all believers to join him in the fight against error. "Let a crusade against Puseyism and all other error be proclaimed, and let all faithful souls enlist in the great war.... The gospel of Jesus is assailed by its ancient enemies, let every true man come to the front and face the foe."[44] Here, Spurgeon expands the fight beyond his own church or denomination, to all those who held the gospel. In response to this article, the Colportage Association and the Stockwell Orphanage would be founded as evangelical efforts to promote the Protestant faith in the countryside and among the poor.

A Call to Holiness

Spurgeon also continued to call for greater holiness in the church through his magazine. In "Anglican Ministers in Papist's Clothing," Spurgeon continued his scathing condemnation of evangelicals for remaining in the Church of England and pleaded for them to come out.[45] Rather than reforming the Church, their presence actually hindered any chance at reformation and

---

42. See S&T 1865:312; S&T 1868:102.
43. S&T 1868:203-04.
44. S&T 1866:340.
45. S&T 1865:210.

protected those who support ritualism.[46] In "Against Romish Anglicanism," Spurgeon not only called evangelical churchmen to leave the Church, he rebuked those Dissenters who tolerated its growing ritualism:

> Protestant Dissenters, how can you so often truckle to a Church which is assuming the rags of the old harlot more and more openly every day?... Protestantism owed much to you in the past ages, will you not now raise your voice and show the ignorant and the priest-ridden tendencies of all these mummeries, and the detestable errors of the Romish Church and of its Anglican sister?[47]

As a Baptist, Spurgeon believed that part of the worldliness of the Church of England was not only in its alliance with Rome but also with the state. Spurgeon believed that the existence of a state church was at the heart of all religious persecutions. "The dogma of union between church and state... is the essence of Antichrist and the germ of persecution: an injustice to man, and an impertinence to God."[48] To be sure, his goal was not for the government to extend patronage towards any denomination, not even his own. To accept such an arrangement would be to go the way of Rome.[49] Rather, Spurgeon sought to stir the hearts of all people, even those outside the church, to call for the abolishing of the state church.

> Against her common humanity is up in arms as much as evangelical religion. Her confessional is as dangerous to the mere moralist as to the Christian; her inquisition would be as ruinous to mercantile prosperity as to spiritual activity. Men of

---

46. "When will you come out? How far is the corrupt element to prevail before you will separate from it? *You* are mainly responsible for the growth of all this Popery, for your piety is the mainstay and salt of what would otherwise soon become too foul to be endured, and would then most readily be swept from the earth. You hinder reformation!" *S&T* 1865:210.

47. *S&T* 1865:357.

48. *S&T* 1868:342.

49. "To act as Rome has acted is to unprotestantise ourselves... is to degrade ourselves to their level by handling their weapons." Ibid.

all religions and of no religion should deprecate the growth of a system which rendered the Inquisition possible.[50]

The purity of the church had to be preserved.

A Call to Mission

In these articles, Spurgeon also sought to preserve a proper understanding of the gospel and call the church to evangelistic mission. By interposing baptism and other mediators, the ritualism and theology of the Church of England continued to take away from Christ's unique redemptive role. This, Spurgeon sought to expose and combat.

For example, in "Dr. Pusey on the Worship of Mary in the Church of Rome," Spurgeon exposed Pusey's support of the worship of Mary, and his teaching of Mary as a co-redemptress alongside Christ.[51] In "Priestism brought to the Touchstone," Spurgeon challenged the office of priest in the Church, stating that Christ is himself the final High Priest. "Having so great a High Priest as Jesus the Son of God... what need we of any earthly priest?"[52] Rather than going to a priest for confession, or absolution, or intercession, sinners are to look to Christ alone for salvation. Though Spurgeon held a high view of the church, he refused to make the church so high as to require the church's intercession for salvation, whether through its ordinances or anything else.

In preserving a proper understanding of the gospel, Spurgeon used his magazine to call all Christians to fulfill their mission. Evangelism was the task of every Christian. The conversion of the lost depended not on the clergy and their sacramental responsibilities but on the initiative of Christian men and women to speak of Christ to their neighbors.

Personal effort must also be used to propagate the truth upon the matters now assailed. There must be no time-serving, no vacillation; we must let all around us know what we believe, and

---

50. Spurgeon saw this as a concern not only for Christians, but for all English citizens. Ibid., 341.

51. *S&T* 1866:161.

52. *S&T* 1867:165.

why we believe it. Not alone the first rudimentary truths of the gospel must be taught, but the whole circle of revelation; we must conceal no distinctive doctrine, and withhold no unpalatable dogma. In the parlor and the kitchen, in the shop and in the field, we must lift up the cross and abase the crucifix, magnify the gospel and ridicule superstition, glorify the Lord Jesus and expose priest-craft. If England expects every man to do his duty, much more does God expect it at the hands of his people.[53]

Christ alone is the High Priest, and through union with Christ, the church became a holy and a royal priesthood called to represent God and proclaim the saving work of Christ to a lost world.[54]

A Call to Faithfulness

Spurgeon continued to call the churches to greater faithfulness to God's Word. Though the Oxford Movement appealed to a tradition older than the English Reformation, Spurgeon appealed to an even older authority, the teaching of the prophets and apostles in the Word of God. Whereas Roman Catholicism had built a doctrinal fortress, Spurgeon envisioned Scripture as a battering ram, capable of pulling down "piece by piece the mischievous system of falsehood, be it never so great or high."[55] Thus Spurgeon continued to fight against the extra-biblical practices of the church by pointing people to God's Word. In his article, "Notes on Ritualism," Spurgeon quoted Bishop Hooper's warning to those who implement the "inventions of men" in the church, rather than the pure worship of God based on his Word. Though defenders of ritualism argued that such practices were *adiaphora*, Hooper warned that as the church maintained those things "contrary to God's word... as the *candles, vestments, crosses, altars*, for if they be kept in the church as things indifferent, at length they will be maintained as things necessary."[56] Here was a warning to all churches that failed to keep to the regulative principle: extra-biblical inventions may seem useful and aesthetically pleasing

53. *S&T* 1866:343.
54. *S&T* 1867:165.
55. *S&T* 1866:123.
56. *S&T* 1869:277.

for a time, but eventually they overthrow the authority of God's Word in the church.

As in all battles, the fight against ritualism would be costly and would require sacrifice. Spurgeon knew this well. In "The Holy War of the Present Hour," he told the story of Arnold von Winkelried, a Swiss soldier who sacrificed his life, absorbing all the enemy spears and crashing through the ranks of the Austrian phalanx, allowing his comrades to burst through the gap and defeat their enemies. In a way, this is what Spurgeon had done with his sermons and writings. But then he drew this lesson:

> Is it needful to remind private Christians that when Arnold broke the ranks of the Austrians it would have been a useless waste of life if his fellow-Swiss had not followed up the advantage? There was the gap in that dreadful thorn-hedge of spears; his corpse had split the phalanx, and now over his body his grateful countrymen must dash to victory. Suppose they had all shrunk back; imagine that they had begun to criticize his action in the usual style,—" a very imprudent, rash man, very! He has acted very indiscreetly; we should have done so and so." Of course such critics would have done nothing at all; everybody knows that; but people who do not mean to do a thing, and who could not do it, are always saying, after it is done, that it should have been far better managed. But no, instead of wasting time in empty discussion the Swiss patriots asked no questions, but, seeing the opportunity made for them, they took immediate advantage of it. We do not doubt but that many a time the Christian church might have won great victories if it had been prepared to dash into the gap which some brave man, by God's grace, had been enabled to make. If it be inquired in the present instance, What can private Christians do in cases where such bold leadership has been granted them? our reply is, Let every spiritual weapon be used, let mighty prayer be kept ever waving like a two edged sword, and let holy earnestness in teaching the word prove the sincerity of the supplication. God is with us, and will manifest his power when we are all thoroughly intent upon stirring up his strength. We do not cry unto him as we should, nor feel enough the imminence of our peril; else should we soon see the making bare of his arm. Let united prayer be put up by all believers

concerning the present state of religion in England, and we shall not be many months before a change shall pass over the land.[57]

This is how Spurgeon envisioned himself in the Baptist Regeneration Controversy. Through his "Baptismal Regeneration" sermon, he had sacrificed himself to the spears of public scorn, not only from the established Church and its supporters, but also from Dissenters who did not want trouble. Yet his strategy for this war was never merely in his solitary sacrifice. Rather, in exposing the growing Roman Catholicism in the Church of England, he raised the public's concern and created a gap, as it were, in the enemy ranks. Now he called his congregation and all other Protestants to fill in the gap and join him in this war, by fighting for the purity of the church and the truth of the gospel.

The Downgrade Controversy

The nineteenth century marked the rise of German higher criticism, which aimed to look "behind the text" to determine the historical circumstances referred to in the text and out of which the text arose.[58] Protestants in the seventeenth and eighteenth centuries increasingly turned to a historical approach in their hermeneutic as part of their battle against Rome, to settle internal doctrinal disputes, and to respond to the subjectivism of pietism. In many ways, this approach coincided with the rationalist demands of the Enlightenment. But as society secularized, there was also a rise in skepticism about the historicity of the biblical narratives. Over time, due to advances in historical scholarship and an ever-increasing abundance of information about the past, scholars grew confident in their ability to figure out the historical circumstances of a text. Over time, this academic discipline of looking "behind the text" took priority over the text itself. Rather than discerning the meaning of the text, scholars reduced

---

57. *S&T* 1866:342-43.

58. See I. H. Marshall, *New Testament Interpretation*, ed. I. H. Marshall (Grand Rapids, MI: Eerdmans, 1977), 126; Stanley E. Porter and Beth M. Stovell, eds., *Biblical Hermeneutics: Five Views* (Downers Grove, IL: InterVarsity, 2012), 17–16; Richard F. Burnett, "Historical Criticism," in *Dictionary for Theological Interpretation of the Bible*, ed. Kevin J. Vanhoozer (Grand Rapids, MI: Baker, 2005), 291.

the meaning of the text to the socio-historical context or the psychological state of the authors.

Through the growing influence of German theologians such as F. Schleiermacher, F. C. Baur, and D. F. Strauss, this hermeneutic began to be translated and published in England in the early nineteenth century.[59] Far from leading to an interpretive consensus, higher criticism led to division, not only in the academy but also among pastors and churches.[60] On the liberal, or modernist, end of the division, adherents denied any belief in the supernatural, rejected the inspiration and infallibility of Scripture, adopted a progressive understanding of theology, and employed a hermeneutic of suspicion when it came to the biblical text. On the conservative end were evangelicals like Spurgeon, who continued to hold to orthodox positions even in the face of growing liberal scholarship.

Spurgeon believed that, at the root of historical criticism, was a disregard for the Bible as the infallible Word of God, which led to every facet of orthodox theology being challenged.[61] In their rejection of sin, the atonement, the resurrection, eternal punishment, and other historic doctrines, Spurgeon understood this to be a new religion, distinct from historic Christianity.[62] There could be no fundamental union between evangelicals and theological liberals. Yet these modernists, by reinterpreting the meaning of these doctrines, understood themselves as belonging to the Christian faith. Many were members of churches, supported mission and benevolent work at home and abroad, and continued to participate in denominational causes.

---

59.   In 1741, Johann David Michaelis (1717-91) traveled to England to form a bridge between English and German scholarship, and thus the influence of German theology began in the previous century. Anthony C. Thiselton, *Hermeneutics* (Grand Rapids, MI: Eerdmans, 2009), 140-41. For a work on the influence of Michaelis, see Michael C. Legaspi, *The Death of Scripture and the Rise of Biblical Studies* (Oxford: Oxford University Press, 2010).

60.   "Atomistic preoccupation with individual parts of the biblical witness, especially the various historical-psychological circumstances from which it arose, contributed to confusion over what the biblical witness as a whole is about: its actual content, subject matter, and theme." Burnett, "Historical Criticism," 291.

61.   *S&T* 1887:170.

62.   Ibid., 397.

By Spurgeon's arrival in London, historical criticism would have begun influencing all denominations.[63] But his sharpest conflict would be with the Baptist Union. One of the earliest conflicts came in 1883, when Spurgeon expressed his disapproval of the presence of a Unitarian minister at a Baptist meeting in Leicester. In 1884, the London Baptist Association sent four ministers to examine the Universalist teaching of a pastor and cleared him of any wrong. In 1885, the Baptist Missionary Society invited James Thew to preach at their meetings, where Thew dismissed the doctrine of eternal punishment.[64] In his correspondence with the secretary of the Baptist Union in 1885, Spurgeon expressed his concern: "The Baptist Union means, I suppose, to drive out the orthodox. What is to be done I know not, I would enter my earnest protest against the dubious notes which are continually put forth at its gatherings."[65]

Given his convictions and their refusal to act, from 1883 to 1887, there was an uneasy relationship between Spurgeon and the Baptist Union. He did not attend any association meetings, although he remained involved in the activities of the Union. During those years, the leadership tried to accommodate Spurgeon by avoiding the selection of any controversial topics for papers read at Baptist Union meetings, but this proved insufficient.[66]

Early in 1887, two articles on "The Down Grade," or infiltration of liberal theology, were published in *The Sword and the Trowel*. Then, between August and October, these were followed by three more articles from Spurgeon himself, condemning the new theology and lamenting the decline of Baptist and other Dissenting churches.

> A new religion has been initiated, which is no more Christianity than chalk is cheese; and this religion, being destitute of moral

---

63. For a brief catalog of the denominations influenced by higher criticism, see Murray, *The Forgotten Spurgeon*, 140-42.

64. Ernest A. Payne, "The Down Grade Controversy: A Postscript," *Baptist Quarterly* 28, no. 4 (April 1979): 149-50.

65. Ibid., 151.

66. Mark T. E. Hopkins, "Spurgeon's Opponents in the Downgrade Controversy," *Baptist Quarterly* 32, no. 6 (April 1988): 275.

honesty, palms itself off as the old faith with slight improvements, and on this plea usurps pulpits which were erected for gospel preaching. The Atonement is scouted, the inspiration of Scripture is derided, the Holy Spirit is degraded into an influence, the punishment of sin is turned into fiction, and the resurrection into a myth, and yet these enemies of our faith expect us to call them brethren, and maintain a confederacy with them![67]

Spurgeon had hoped that these articles would spark a conversation at the October meeting of the Baptist Union, but to his disappointment, the leadership refused to address the issue. This culminated in Spurgeon's withdrawal from the Union on October 28, 1887. The secretary of the Union, who was a friend of Spurgeon's, responded to his withdrawal with surprise and disappointment.[68] Given Spurgeon's prominence and the scathing language of his articles, this set off a massive press debate. Throughout this period, Spurgeon once again saw many of his former allies turn on him and attack him for his inflammatory comments regarding the state of the church.

Following Spurgeon's withdrawal, the Baptist Union formed a Council to address the situation. They first attempted to appease Spurgeon by sending him a delegation of four officials. But these conversations proved to be fruitless. Rather than discussing the need for an evangelical basis for the Union, they demanded that he name those who had abandoned evangelical beliefs. Spurgeon refused to do this knowing that it would only raise charges of slander against him, and that there was no doctrinal basis by which to judge his claims. In the end, this meeting only demonstrated the theological gulf between Spurgeon and the Union.

The delegation reported the impasse to the Council, and in response, they passed a "vote of censure," a public rebuke, against Spurgeon in January 1888. The following month, Spurgeon published another inflammatory response in *The Sword and*

---

67. *S&T* 1887:397.

68. Spurgeon claimed that he had corresponded frequently with Booth, the secretary, regarding these issues in the months prior, but those letters have never been produced. See Ernest A. Payne, *The Baptist Union: A Short History* (London: The Carey Kingsgate Press, 1959), 143.

the Trowel. In response, some in the Council wanted to censure Spurgeon further, but their motion was voted down. Through these months, however, his church stood by his side, and in January of 1888, passed the following resolution:

> That the church worshipping at the Metropolitan Tabernacle in annual meeting assembled, desires to express its hearty sympathy with its beloved pastor, C. H. Spurgeon, in the testimony for truth he has recently borne by his articles upon "The Down Grade," endorses his action in withdrawing from the Baptist Union, follows him in the course he has taken, and pledges itself to support him by believing prayer and devoted service in his earnest contention for the faith once for all delivered to the saints—enthusiastically carried unanimously.[69]

Spurgeon was not alone, but his church, the largest in the Baptist Union, unanimously expressed their support and resigned their membership in the Union along with him.

From late February to April 1888, the Baptist Union sought to vindicate its evangelical character by establishing a theological declaration. However, this declaration was viewed as historical, rather than legislative or creedal. Furthermore, it did not provide a clear theological statement on difficult issues. Articles on the Fall and Eternal Punishment were challenged and softened, much to the disappointment of Spurgeon's supporters, including his brother. James Spurgeon sought to amend the declaration, in a way that would make it much more conservative theologically, but his motion was tabled. This was his main concern going into the April meeting of the Baptist Union. But without his brother present, James was outmaneuvered diplomatically and none of his motions were accepted. In the end, the assembly passed the motion approving a declaration which gave no creedal basis to the Union, nor provided any theological clarity on controversial issues. Most discouraging of all, the approval for this motion was

---

69. "Annual Church Meeting January 31st, 1888," *MB* 1887-1894. The minutes show that the phrase "follows him in the course he has taken" was originally omitted but written in at a later time, perhaps by the person who verified the minutes. It appears that the original motion from J. A. Spurgeon and B. W. Carr did not include the church's resignation from the Baptist Union, but the congregation called for it and it was included.

seconded by James Spurgeon.[70] In a personal letter to a friend, Spurgeon wrote, "My brother thinks he has gained a great victory, but I believe we are hopelessly sold. I feel heartbroken. Certainly he has done the very opposite of what I should have done. Yet he is not to be blamed, for he followed his best judgment. Pray for me, that my faith will fail not."[71] While the Union celebrated their achievement as a vindication of their evangelical character, Spurgeon was solidified in his conviction that he had made the right decision.[72] Though many hoped that the declaration would pave the way for Spurgeon's return, this would never happen. The wounds incurred on both sides during the controversy were too deep for quick reconciliation.

The Sword and the Trowel during the Downgrade Controversy

While the Baptismal Regeneration Controversy was launched by a series of sermons, the Downgrade Controversy began through Spurgeon's magazine. Between the publication of the first article, "The Down Grade," in the spring of 1887 and the Baptist Union's declaration in the early summer of 1888, Spurgeon published nine articles and six personal notes dealing with the controversy. These pieces make up the bulk of Spurgeon's public engagement with the issue in *The Sword and the Trowel*. He would continue to write brief notes and publish a few more articles on the controversy in the following years, but by then the main conflict had already taken place.

A Call to Action

In these articles, Spurgeon once again called the churches to action by raising the alarm about the progress of liberal theology. The two opening articles of the controversy, entitled "The Down Grade,"

---

70. It is not entirely clear why J. A. Spurgeon seconded this motion. It is possible that he was so preoccupied with the amendment to the declaration that he did not fully realize the implications in doing so. See Hopkins, "Spurgeon's Opponents," 289. It should also be noted that, as a graduate of Stepney College, James' connection with Joseph Angus, who was the head of the college and helped draft the declaration, might have influenced him.

71. W. Y. Fullerton, *Charles Spurgeon: A Biography* (London: Williams and Norgate, 1920), 236.

72. *S&T* 1888:339.

written by Robert Shindler, detailed the rise of liberal theology and the resulting theological decline of various denominations. The pattern that Shindler observed was the move away from Calvinism, first towards Arminianism, then eventually towards Arianism or Socinianism.[73] Such a slide could be traced among Presbyterians,[74] the Church of England,[75] Independents,[76] and even certain Baptists.[77] In other words, theological liberalism was not contained to any one group but had infiltrated all of society.

Often, this slide happened as congregations and older ministers called young ministers who had received this new theology in their colleges. As a Congregationalist minister reported: "College… continues to pour forth men to take charge of our churches who do not believe, in any proper sense, in the inspiration of the Scriptures, who deny the vicarious sacrifice on the cross, and hold that, if sinners are not saved on this side the grave, they may, can, or must be on the other. And the worst of it is, the people love it."[78] In discovering their theological differences with this new assistant pastor, rather than taking action and putting them out, the people tolerated their ministries.[79] Over time, when the older minister died, these churches would allow these ministers to be their main preachers, and it would only be a matter of time before they were taken over by liberal theology. As a result, Shindler observed that many of these churches were "in a wretched state," attended only

---

73. *S&T* 1887:122.

74. Ibid., 123-26.

75. Ibid., 166.

76. Ibid., 166-68.

77. Ibid., 169.

78. Ibid., 464.

79. "Those who were really orthodox in their sentiments were too often lax and unfaithful as to the introduction of heretical ministers into their pulpits, either as assistants or occasional preachers.... The old ministers preached evangelical doctrine, but they complied all too readily with the wishes of their new colleague, and ceased to require a declaration of faith in the divinity of Christ in those who sought admission to the Lord's table. Sad to say, they continued to labor on in peace, the older men dealing out the 'wine of the kingdom,' and the 'Living Bread,' while the younger minister intermixed his rationalistic concoctions and his Socinian leaven." *S&T* 1887:125-26.

by a handful. Even in those churches that were still full, there was still "a fatal deadness spread over the congregation."[80]

Spurgeon recognized that the heart of the controversy was theological. At the same time, he believed it was the passivity of congregations that made room for such false teaching. "That the evil leaven is working in the churches as well as among the ministers, is also sadly certain. A heterodox party exists in many congregations, and those who compose it are causing trouble to the faithful, and sadly influencing the more timid towards a vacillating policy."[81] Rather than the congregation recognizing their responsibility to guard the gospel, they timidly adopted "a vacillating policy," leaving the doctrine of the church to be altered by unfaithful ministers.

A Call to Holiness

In these articles, Spurgeon also repeated his call for purity among the churches. Primarily, this call centered on the need for churches to disassociate with those who held to errors that compromised the gospel.[82] Once again, Spurgeon was not concerned about second-order denominational issues. This separation was over first-order gospel issues.

> The largest charity towards those who are loyal to the Lord Jesus, and yet do not see with us on secondary matters, is the duty of all true Christians. But how are we to act towards those who deny his vicarious sacrifice, and ridicule the great truth of justification by his righteousness? These are not mistaken friends, but enemies of the cross of Christ. There is no use in employing circumlocutions and polite terms of expression:—where Christ is not received as to the cleansing power of his blood and the justifying merit of his righteousness, he is not received at all.[83]

---

80. Ibid., 171.

81. Ibid., 465.

82. Though a secondary matter, Spurgeon was also concerned about the growing worldliness in the church that compromised its purity. "Our lament was not, however, confined to vital doctrines; we mentioned a decline of spiritual life, and the growth of worldliness, and gave as two outward signs thereof the falling-off in prayer-meetings, and ministers attending the theater." Ibid., 513-14.

83. *S&T* 1887:559.

Just as Spurgeon called evangelicals to leave the Church of England because of its ritualism, now he was faced with the need to leave the Baptist Union for its unwillingness to address theological liberalism. Had Spurgeon been in the leadership of the Union, he would have borne a particular responsibility to use his leadership to work for reform.[84] But as a member of the Union, to remain would be a betrayal of the gospel.

As the most influential pastor of the denomination, his strongest course of action and protest was to resign and to lead his congregation to do the same.[85] To do so was entirely in line with his congregational convictions. No matter how large and influential the Baptist Union had become, it had no authority over any minister or church, and therefore, any participation was strictly voluntary. Defending his resignation, Spurgeon wrote: "We retire at once and distinctly from the Baptist Union. The Baptist Churches are each one of them self-contained and independent. The Baptist Union is only a voluntary association of such churches, and it is a simple matter for a church or an individual to withdraw from it."[86] For Spurgeon, the independency of each church meant that each church had a responsibility to only pursue associations which were faithful to the gospel.

---

84. Although Spurgeon was disappointed in the leaders' unwillingness to act, he nonetheless sought to be sympathetic and charitable towards them, at least initially. "Brethren who have been officials of a denomination have a paternal partiality about them which is so natural, and so sacred, that we have not the heart to censure it. Above all things, these prudent brethren feel bound to preserve the prestige of 'the body,' and the peace of the committee. Our Unions, Boards, and Associations are so justly dear to the fathers, that quite unconsciously and innocently, they grow oblivious of evils which, to the unofficial mind, are as manifest as the sun in the heavens." Ibid., 510.

85. "One thing is clear to us: we cannot be expected to meet in any Union which comprehends those whose teaching is upon fundamental points exactly the reverse of that which we hold dear. Those who can do so will, no doubt, have weighty reasons with which to justify their action, and we will not sit in judgment upon those reasons: they may judge that a minority should not drive them out. To us it appears that there are many things upon which compromise is possible, but there are others in which it would be an act of treason to pretend to fellowship. With deep regret we abstain from assembling with those whom we dearly love and heartily respect, since it would involve us in a confederacy with those with whom we can have no communion in the Lord." Ibid., 515.

86. S&T 1887:560.

But even in disassociating with error, the fight for purity was not finished. Churches also needed to work for purity within. Shindler points out that the decline in Presbyterian churches was exacerbated due "to their rule of admitting to the privileges of Church membership... [those who were] unregenerate, and strangers to the work of renewing grace."[87] Spurgeon's teaching on purity in church associations applied as much to the "association" of church membership. Those in the church who refused to hold to gospel doctrines should be removed from the fellowship.[88] The purity of the church must not be compromised.

A Call to Mission
In the Downgrade Controversy, Spurgeon also continued his call to the church's evangelistic mission. His dominant emphasis in these articles was calling evangelicals to uphold orthodoxy and defend the truths of the gospel. He warned his readers that this controversy was not merely about denominational affairs, but about the truth of the inspiration of Scripture, substitutionary atonement, justification by faith, eternal punishment, and other gospel truths.

> Those who hold the eternal verities of salvation, and yet do not see all that we believe and embrace, are by no means the objects of our opposition: warfare is with men who are giving up the atoning sacrifice, denying the inspiration of Holy Scripture, and casting slurs upon justification by faith. The present struggle is not a debate upon the question of Calvinism or Arminianism, but of the truth of God versus the inventions of men. All who believe the gospel should unite against that 'modern thought' which is its deadly enemy.[89]

In other words, Spurgeon's call to disassociate was about more than just the holiness of the church. It was about the repudiation

---

87. Ibid., 126.

88. "Neither when we have chosen our way can we keep company with those who go the other way. There must come with decision for truth a corresponding protest against error. Let those who will keep the narrow way keep it, and suffer for their choice; but to hope to follow the broad road at the same time is an absurdity. What communion hath Christ with Belial?" Ibid., 465.

89. Ibid., 195-96.

of error and the preservation of the gospel.[90] Only in doing so, would the church remain faithful to its mission and preserve a gospel worth sharing. As so many turned away to a false gospel that could not save,[91] Spurgeon urged his readers all the more to greater faithfulness in personal evangelism. Though he was personally engaged in this theological controversy, Spurgeon remained devoted to the task of proclaiming the gospel.

> Deeply do we agree with the call of the more devout among the letter-writers for a more determined effort to spread the gospel. Wherever more can be done, let it be done at once, in dependence upon the Spirit of God…. those of us who raise these questions are not among the idlers, nor are we a whit behind the very chief of those who seek to win souls.[92]

A Call to Faithfulness

Spurgeon trumpeted his call to the church for greater faithfulness to God's Word. At its root, he believed that theological liberalism was a rejection of the inspiration, infallibility, and authority of Scripture.[93] By this one error, all other doctrinal errors were made possible. But in exalting human reason over Scripture, the church was left also defenseless against the latest fads and innovations of the day. The result could be seen in the abandonment of the regulative principle in Dissenting places of worship. "There

---

90. *"Are brethren who remain orthodox prepared to endorse such sentiments by remaining in union with those who hold and teach them?* These gentlemen have full liberty to think as they like; but, on the other hand, those who love the old gospel have equally the liberty to dissociate themselves from them, and that liberty also involves a responsibility from which there is no escaping. If we do not believe in Universalism, or in Purgatory, and if we do believe in the inspiration of Scripture, the Fall, and the great sacrifice of Christ for sin, it behoves us to see that we do not become accomplices with those who teach another gospel, and as it would seem from one writer, have avowedly another God." Ibid., 513.

91. "Assuredly the New Theology can do no good towards God or man; it, has no adaptation for it. If it were preached for a thousand years by all the most earnest men of the school, it would never renew a soul, nor overcome pride in a single human heart." Ibid., iii.

92. *S&T* 1887:515.

93. "What is the first step astray? Is it doubting this doctrine, or questioning that sentiment, or being skeptical as to the other article of orthodox belief? We think not…. The first step astray is a want of adequate faith in the divine inspiration of the sacred Scriptures." *S&T* 1887:170.

can be no doubt that all sorts of entertainments, as nearly as possible approximating to stage-plays, have been carried on in connection with places of worship, and are, at this present time, in high favor."[94]

But "where ministers and Christian churches have held fast to the truth that the Holy Scriptures have been given by God as an authoritative and infallible rule of faith and practice, they have never wandered very seriously out of the right way."[95] Therefore, Spurgeon urged churches to adopt evangelical confessions of faith, making clear the church's grounding in the Word of God. Apart from such a confession, churches remained defenseless against this false teaching. "Those bodies of men which hold no settled doctrines, and make no profession of believing anything definite, are like houses with open doors, inviting the unclean spirit to enter, and take up his abode."[96] And this would be true, not only for churches, but for any Christian institution. No longer could Christians merely assume that those who shared the name "Christian" believed the same things as they did. Faithfulness to God's Word meant making one's faith explicit in a creed and being accountable to that creed. Going forward, every association that Spurgeon would join, following the Downgrade Controversy, needed to have an evangelical confession of faith as a basis for their union.[97]

The Militant Church in Spurgeon's Sermons during the Downgrade Controversy

During the months of the Downgrade Controversy from August 1887 to April 1888, Spurgeon continued to preach every week to his congregation. While his articles in *The Sword and the*

---

94. Ibid., 606.

95. Ibid., 170.

96. *S&T* 1888:160.

97. There were at least three associations that Spurgeon joined after the Downgrade Controversy: the Fraternal Union in London, the Surrey and Middlesex Association, and The Pastors' College Evangelical Association. Each had their own confession of faith. See Geoffrey Chang, "Spurgeon's Associationalism after the Downgrade Controversy," https://www.spurgeon.org/resource-library/articles/spurgeons-associationalism-after-the-downgrade-controversy/

Trowel engaged in polemics against theological liberalism, week-by-week his sermons focused on preaching God's Word to his congregation.[98] Throughout the controversy, Spurgeon alluded to the growing challenge of this new theology and called his people to action. One sermon in particular was devoted entirely to the controversy, namely, sermon no. 1990, "A Sermon for the Time Present," preached on October 30, 1887, the Sunday after his resignation from the Baptist Union.[99] Unlike the Baptismal Regeneration Controversy, Spurgeon's sermons in this controversy were not primarily aimed at exposing and correcting the errors of the enemy. Rather, they were aimed at the edification and encouragement of his congregation during a time of uncertainty. Spurgeon continued to draw on his doctrine of the militant church, but this image now took on a new significance in the Downgrade Controversy. In his final address to the Pastors' College Evangelical Conference, entitled "The Greatest Fight in the World," Spurgeon reminded his students and pastors that the battle must be fought through the church. The church was the army of God.

> What can individual men do in a great crusade? We are associated with all the people of the Lord. We need for comrades the members of our churches; these must go out and win souls for Christ. We need the co-operation of the entire brotherhood and sisterhood. What is to be accomplished unless the saved ones go forth, all of them, for the salvation of others?[100]

Though many allies and students turned away from Spurgeon, he knew that he was not alone. His church was yet filled with those who would battle with him.

A Call to Action

The Downgrade Controversy marked a period of decline for evangelical churches in Britain. In the first sermon after his

---

98. For a theological evaluation of Spurgeon's sermons to his congregation during the Downgrade Controversy, see Jessen, "Mr. Valiant for Truth," 162-96.

99. *MTP* 33:601.

100. C. H. Spurgeon, *The Greatest Fight in the World* (Fearn, UK: Christian Heritage, 2014), 89.

resignation, Spurgeon opened with a survey of the churches of his day. Though Spurgeon pastored the largest Baptist church of his time, he considered the wider church to be in poor condition. Though they continued to be well-attended and active, Spurgeon knew that appearances could be deceiving. He compared the churches of his day to the church of Laodicea, which gloried in its wealth, and yet had closed the door to its Lord.[101]

Spurgeon lamented the lifelessness of these churches, where "the vitality of religion is despised, and gatherings for prayer are neglected." He grieved over the worldliness of the churches, "so that the vain amusements of the world are shared in by the saints." And yet these marks were symptoms of a deeper problem:

> It is a sad affliction when in our solemn assemblies the brilliance of the Gospel light is dimmed by error. The clearness of the testimony is spoiled when doubtful voices are scattered among the people, and those who ought to preach the truth, the whole truth, and nothing but the truth, are telling out for doctrines the imaginations of men, and the inventions of the age. Instead of revelation, we have philosophy, falsely so-called; instead of divine infallibility, we have surmises and larger hopes. The Gospel of Jesus Christ, which is the same yesterday, today, and forever is taught as the production of progress, a growth, a thing to be amended and corrected year by year. It is an ill day, both for the church and the world, when the trumpet does not give a certain sound; for who shall prepare himself for the battle?[102]

Spurgeon understood that the spiritual health of the church was a barometer to the quality of the theology that was being preached, and in his day the church was in poor health. He was not interested in downplaying the errors of liberal theology. Such theology muted the trumpet of the Gospel and caused the army of the church to grow lazy and unprepared for battle.

As for his own church, Spurgeon called his people to action. More than simply arousing their indignation, Spurgeon prepared them to suffer. Just as the Downgrade Controversy proved to be the most painful episode of his life, Spurgeon called his people

---

101. *MTP* 33:602.
102. *MTP* 33:602.

to join him in the fight and experience the opposition of the world. He warned his people, "When the world pretends to love, understand that it now hates you more cordially than ever, and is carefully baiting its trap to catch you and ruin you. Beware of the Judas kiss with which the Christ was betrayed, and with which you will be betrayed unless you are well upon your guard."[103] Rather than seeking this world's approval, Christ's army was made up of pilgrims willing to bear the cross.

> The Christian is not of the world, even as Christ is not of the world.... He is an alien. He is a pilgrim. Can he expect the comforts of home while he tarries here?... This world is a foe to grace, and not a friend to it; and hence the gracious man must have tribulation. If he is to be like his Lord he certainly will have it; and if he is to be like the Lord's people, he will have it, for they are a line of crossbearers.[104]

While traveling in this world, the church militant will suffer and face setbacks. And yet, there is hope. In the church's faithful suffering, God accomplishes his purposes.

> Probably the church of God has never had better times, certainly she has never had happier times, than during periods of persecution. These were the days of her purity, and consequently her glory. When she has been in the dark, God has been her light; and when she has been driven to and fro by the cruelties of men, then has she most effectually rested under the shadow of the Almighty.[105]

In other words, times of persecution were not pointless. In dark times, God continues to refine the church and purify her witness. Therefore, Christ's soldiers should not shrink from battle but remain in the conflict, whatever the cost.

A Call to Holiness
Spurgeon's desire in the Downgrade Controversy was to establish an evangelical basis for membership in the Baptist Union. In this,

---

103. Ibid., 656.
104. Ibid., 657.
105. *MTP* 33:687-88.

he failed. But in his church, things were different. Here, Spurgeon could pursue a confessional and regenerate church membership. This was not only something he practiced; he continued to teach his people what it meant to be distinct from the world.

> A church is an assembly called out. An ecclesia is not any and every "assembly": a mixed crowd of unauthorized persons, having no special right to come together would not be an ecclesia, or church. In a real ecclesia the herald summoned the citizens and burgesses by trumpet or by name, and it consisted of certain persons called out from among the common multitude. The true church consists of men who are called, and faithful, and chosen. They are redeemed from among men, and called out from among their fellows by effectual grace. God the Holy Spirit continues to call out, and bring to the Lord Jesus, those who are chosen of God according to the good pleasure of his will. Practically, conversion is the result of the call.[106]

Unlike the "mixed crowd of unauthorized persons," the church is to be a regenerate assembly, called out of the world, and converted by the Holy Spirit. In saying this, Spurgeon was likely thinking of the Baptist Union's refusal to regulate its membership, as later in the sermon he imagines Abram's companions tempting him to remain in Haran:

> Abram is very sincere, but he must not be bigoted. Surely he will not be so foolish as to believe in verbal inspiration, and insist upon Canaan, when Haran quite meets the spirit of the command. There is no doubt that Haran answers every purpose, and we mean to stay here, and Abram must stay with us.[107]

Before the church can engage in a fight for truth out in the world, it first has to fight for the purity of its own membership.[108]

---

106. *MTP* 34:122.

107. *MTP* 34:124.

108. "When the soldiers of Christ shall have included in their ranks all the banditti of the adversary, will there be any army for Christ at all? Is it not distinctly a capitulation at the very beginning of the war? So I take it to be." Spurgeon, *The Greatest Fight*, 90.

Only as the church remains pure can it be "the pillar and ground of the truth" and "a home for [the] Gospel."[109] Unlike the evangelicals who were unwilling to fight for the truth, the church should be made up of those willing to contend for it. One of the most important ways believers were to contend for the faith was by publicly joining churches that preached the truth. This was Spurgeon's emphasis in April 1888 as the Baptist Union was getting ready to meet for the first time after his withdrawal. In his sermon, "She Was Not Hid," Spurgeon compared the healed woman coming forward with the responsibility Christians had to identify with Christ by joining a church.

> Many argue, "To confess Christ and join with his people is not necessary to my salvation." Who said it was? Open confession is not necessary, nay, is not permitted, till you are saved. How could this woman have made any confession of a cure till she was cured? But being cured, it then became necessary that she should confess it: not necessary to the cure, that is clear, but necessary because of the cure. It is always necessary for a disciple to do what his Lord bids him. It is essential for a soldier of the cross to follow his Captain's orders. Jesus bids us let our light shine; dare we hide it away?[110]

To claim to be a soldier of the cross, but refuse to join Christ's army, the church, was to be in direct disobedience to the Captain. As Christians joined the church, their lives gave credence to the truth and power of the Gospel. Apart from people owning up to the Gospel by their membership in the local churches, Gospel ordinances would cease, preachers would languish, and the world would be left without a witness.

> It will not do, brethren, if we consider what the Lord Jesus Christ deserves of us, and how an open confession tends to certify his mission. The change wrought in the spiritual and moral condition of the saved is God's attestation of the Gospel; and if this is not to be spoken of, how is the world to know that God has sent the Gospel at all?[111]

---

109. *MTP* 34:123.
110. *MTP* 33:220.
111. Ibid., 221.

The best witness for the gospel was a church made distinct from the world through its faithful practice of church membership.

A Call to Mission

The preaching of the gospel is what characterized Spurgeon's ministry, and this was no different during the Downgrade Controversy. From August to October 1887, when Spurgeon was publishing scathing articles on the controversy, he preached sermons such as "The Blind Beggar of the Temple and His Wonderful Cure";[112] "Love at its Utmost";[113] and "How Hearts are Softened,"[114] all of which focused on the message of God's saving grace in Jesus Christ. In July 1887, rather than being distracted by the theological and ecclesiological decline happening around him, he continued to preach expositionally and proclaim the same gospel, like a soldier remaining at his post.

> Dear friends, I am going to preach to you again upon the corner-stone of the gospel. How many times will this make, I wonder? The doctrine of Christ crucified is always with me. As the Roman sentinel in Pompeii stood to his post even when the city was destroyed, so do I stand to the truth of the atonement though the church is being buried beneath the boiling mudshowers of modern heresy. Everything else can wait, but this one truth must be proclaimed with a voice of thunder. Others may preach as they will, but as for this pulpit, it shall always resound with the substitution of Christ.[115]

At the height of the controversy in October, Spurgeon finally referred more explicitly to the dispute, but only to point out his distaste for controversy and his relief at being able to declare the Gospel clearly and plainly.

> There is more joy in one sermon than in years of disputation. Oh, that every one in this congregation might believe in Jesus and live! What a refreshment it is to the preacher's mind to get to his message at last, to get away from the bamboozlement of those

---

112. Ibid., 445.
113. *MTP* 33:505.
114. Ibid., 517.
115. Ibid., 374.

who confound plain truth, and to come to matter-of-fact dealing with eternal salvation. There, let them question and quibble—the blood of Jesus Christ, the Son of God, cleanseth us from all sin.[116]

While Spurgeon did not shrink from defending the Gospel, his much greater preference was to declare it. In a sermon towards the end of 1887, he confessed, "I regret that I have been forced into controversy for which I have no taste, and in which I have no pleasure.... To spread the Gospel I should choose the gentler method: it is only to defend it that I have to draw the sword."[117] Even while his opponents accused Spurgeon of inciting trouble and relishing the conflict, he made it clear that he took no joy in it. Instead, the proclamation of the gospel, not the deconstruction of theological liberalism, remained at the center of his preaching throughout the controversy.

Amid this controversy, Spurgeon spoke as earnestly as ever to fellow pastors. For years, he had told his students that the pulpit was the Thermopylae of Christendom. Now, amid so much error, churches needed faithful pastors to stand in their pulpits and proclaim the truth.

> The church will never make any great advance until once more God sends here and there, and in fifty places, men with burning hearts and with trumpet voices to proclaim the truth, the whole truth, and nothing but the truth. We need men that will not yield to the current of the times, nor care one jot about it; but will hold their own and hold their Master's Word against all comers, because the Lord of hosts is with them, and the Spirit of God resteth upon them.[118]

The urgent need of the day was for faithfulness. The sword of the Spirit was meant to be "sharp and cutting." Therefore, any attempts to "blunt the word, or try to cover its edge" would be treason.[119] Preaching God's Word meant being willing to offend modern sensibilities with the truth.

---

116. Ibid., 575.
117. Ibid., 699.
118. *MTP* 33:439.
119. Ibid., 441.

This battle for the Gospel affected not only pulpits but pews also. The members of the church were to be just as engaged in this mission to spread the Gospel. Spurgeon feared that the claims of this New Theology only distracted people from their mission of evangelizing the lost.

> Let us come down from those high matters to common-place affairs. Let us quit clouds and skies, and condescend to men of low estate. Let us come down from communing with the philosophers of culture, and the apostles of a new theology, to the ordinary people who live around us, and cannot comprehend these fine fictions. Let us come down to the streets and lanes, and do what we can for the poor, the fallen, the ignorant.[120]

While the main players of the Downgrade Controversy were church leaders, Spurgeon understood its effects would ripple out to congregations, and then to the world. If Christians did not hold fast to the true Gospel, then the lost around them would not have a chance to hear about Christ.

> God grant us faithfulness, for the sake of the souls around us! How is the world to be saved if the church is false to her Lord? How are we to lift the masses if our fulcrum is removed? If our Gospel is uncertain, what remains but increasing misery and despair? Stand fast, my beloved, in the name of God! I, your brother in Christ, entreat you to abide in the truth. Quit yourselves like men, be strong.[121]

Spurgeon understood the church to be in a fight. From pastor to people, the church's mission was to contend for the message of the Gospel and proclaim it to a dying world. Despite opposition or distractions, the church was to stand fast and remain strong in the truth.

A Call to Faithfulness

Though Spurgeon lamented the state of the church in his day, Christians could be confident that God's Word had not changed. Though churches all around struggled with coldness, error,

---

120. Ibid., 708.
121. *MTP* 34:84.

hypocrisy, and other evils, the Word remained ever pure and ever true.

> "Oh, but the worker is so feeble!" The word of God is not feeble. "But the worker feels so stupid." But the word of God is not stupid. "But the worker is so unfit." But the word of God is not unfit. You see it all comes to this: the preacher is bound, but the word of God is not bound: the worker is feeble, but the word of God is not feeble. You are nothing and nobody, but the word of God cannot be said to be nothing and nobody: it is everything and everybody: it is girt about with all power.... "But they say they have disproved the faith." Yes, they have disproved their own faith, but they have not disproved the word of God for all that. The word of God is not affected by the falsehood of men. "If we believe not, he abideth faithful; he cannot deny himself;" and till he denies himself we need not make much account of who else denies him. [122]

At the height of the controversy, Spurgeon called his congregation to have confidence in God and his Word. The gospel has not changed and God remained ever sovereign and triumphant against all evil.[123]

Therefore, even as Spurgeon called his people to depend on God's Word, he made clear that this was to be demonstrated by their faithfulness to prayer. One of the signs that churches had abandoned God's Word was their prayerlessness. Though many challenged Spurgeon's theological arguments, his opponents had little to say about his observation that prayer meetings were declining.[124]

> At the back of doctrinal falsehood comes a natural decline of spiritual life, evidenced by a taste for questionable amusements, and a weariness of devotional meetings. At a certain meeting

---

122. *MTP* 33:695.

123. "All his wisdom, all his foresight, all his power, all his immutability—all himself is yours. All for the church of God, when she is in her lowest estate she is still established and endowed in the best possible sense—established by the divine decree, and endowed by the possession of God all-sufficient. The gates of hell shall not prevail against her.... Therefore in the name of Jehovah we will set up our banners, and march onward to the battle." *MTP* 33:606.

124. Ibid., 513-14.

of ministers and church-officers, one after another doubted the value of prayer-meetings; all confessed that they had a very small attendance, and several acknowledged without the slightest compunction that they had quite given them up. What means this? Are churches in a right condition when they have only one meeting for prayer in a week, and that a mere skeleton?[125]

A true belief in the power of God's Word resulted not only in action, but in prayer. In the face of all discouragements, the church remained confident in God's power and turned to him in prayer.

Let us pray, then, that he will save; that he will save his own church from lukewarmness and from deadly error; that he will save her from her worldliness and formalism; save her from unconverted ministers and ungodly members. Let us lift up our eyes and behold the power which is ready to save; and let us go on to pray that the Lord may save the unconverted by thousands and millions.[126]

Apart from God's power, the army was powerless on its own. Behind all its activity was faithfulness in prayer.

But for prayer to be effective, it had to be grounded in the truth of the Word. In "The Secret Power in Prayer," Spurgeon reminded his congregation that the power of prayer did not lie in their merit, but in their union with Christ in the gospel:

Christ is the vine, and the vine includes the branches. The branches are a part of the vine. God, therefore, looks upon us as part of Christ – members of his body, of his flesh, and of his bones. Such is the Father's love to Jesus that he denies him nothing... when you and I are in real union to Christ, the Lord God looks upon us in the same way as he looks on Jesus, and says to us, "I will deny you nothing; ye shall ask what ye will, and it shall be done unto you."[127]

Here, the church was not only the army of God, but also the body of Christ. As those who are united to Christ, they could pray in

---

125.   *S&T* 1887:397-98, 513-14.
126.   *MTP* 33:607.
127.   *MTP* 34:23.

confidence according to God's will, knowing that he would look upon them as he looked upon his Son. Far from having a spirit of defeat, Spurgeon reminded the church militant of its riches in Christ. "When we speak of the privileges of the Church of God on earth it is impossible to exaggerate."[128] It was in this confidence that he called the church to pray. Spurgeon desired something more than individual prayers or scattered prayer meetings. Rather, he saw something especially powerful when the entire church gathered together as an army to lift their prayers to God.

> What a church we should be, if you were all mighty in prayer! Dear children of God, do you want to be half starved? Beloved brethren, do you desire to be poor, little, puny, drivelling children, who will never grow into men? I pray you, aspire to be strong in the Lord, and to enjoy this exceedingly high privilege. What an army would you be if you all had this power with God in prayer![129]

During the darkness of the Downgrade Controversy, faithfulness to God's Word meant faithfulness in prayer, believing God's promises and trusting him to bring revival to the church. Behind all the preaching, evangelism, church planting, ministerial training, and all the other ministries of the Tabernacle was an army of prayer warriors, bringing their requests before their God and pleading for his powerful work.

For all his efforts, Spurgeon would never see the Baptist Union restored to an evangelical basis.[130] According to Susannah, his wife, the Downgrade Controversy was "the deepest grief of his

---

128. Ibid., 157.

129. *MTP* 34:23.

130. W. Y. Fullerton, one of Spurgeon's associates and early biographers, attributes Spurgeon's failure to reform the Baptist Union to his impatience and pugnaciousness. "Spurgeon was too earnest, too intent on the eternal meaning of things, too sure of his standing, to be a good controversialist. His instinct led him to conclusions that others approached only by logic, and he was therefore not apt to be too patient with those who debated every step of the way, or lost themselves in details." Fullerton, *Charles Spurgeon*, 229. While Fullerton's conclusions are debatable, it is clear that while Spurgeon's strong personality and leadership worked well in his own adoring church context, that same strong personality and leadership was not always so well-received in associational settings with other church leaders.

life," and it "cost him his life."[131] Yet Spurgeon believed that the associations were not at the center of God's purposes. Rather, it was the church. The greatest weapon against error was not any para-church organization, but the local church, where the gospel was preached, and the people were engaged in gospel ministry. If there is to be any mechanism for bringing widespread change, it would have to begin with faithful churches holding fast to the gospel and biblical convictions.[132] Writing in 1890, two years after the painful events of the Downgrade Controversy, Spurgeon revealed the heart of his apologetic strategy for the gospel, namely, the militant church:

> We, being assured of the gospel, go on to prove its working character. More than ever must we cause the light of the Word to shine forth.... If sinners are converted in great numbers, and the churches are maintained in purity, unity, and zeal, evangelical principles will be supplied with their best arguments. A ministry which, year by year, builds up a living church, and arms it with a complete array of evangelistic and benevolent institutions, will do more by way of apology for the gospel than the most learned pens, or the most labored orations.[133]

Though Spurgeon would never publish a textbook on hermeneutics or a scholarly defense of the inspiration of Scripture, he would give his life to combating ritualism and rationalism in the best way he knew how: by preaching the gospel, pastoring an active and faithful Baptist church, and planting and influencing many more similar churches.

---

131. *Autobiography* 4:255. Thomas Spurgeon, his son, once said to Archibald Brown, "The Baptist Union almost killed my father." Brown responded, "Yes, and your father almost killed The Baptist Union." Drummond, *Spurgeon*, 719.

132. Spurgeon rarely spoke of trying to bring reform to the Baptist Union. His resignation was primarily a protest for their toleration of theological error. But he did give a hint as to how he might pursue reform if he ever wanted to, namely, by working through faithful churches. Writing to a pastor in December 1887, Spurgeon confided, "Surely the churches will yet speak out. I believe the Council does not know the true desire of the great bulk of the Baptist people. If I were seeking to return to the Union, I would appeal from the Council to the whole body." Pike, *The Life and Work of Charles Haddon Spurgeon*, Vol. 6, 293.

133. *S&T* 1890:3.

Conclusion

Church associations were an important component of Spurgeon's ecclesiology. He understood that the Metropolitan Tabernacle did not alone make up the universal church, but rather all faithful churches that held to the gospel also belonged to Christ's army. Therefore, he prioritized church associations on a local and national level, whether within his own Baptist denomination, or more broadly among evangelicals. In these associations, Spurgeon partnered with other pastors and churches for evangelism, church planting, tract distribution, social causes, and more.

However, what these controversies reveal is that church associations were not primary, but secondary in Spurgeon's mind. When church associations compromised the truth of the gospel, then each local church must remain faithful to its mission and prioritize the gospel over any association. The theme of disassociation is evident in both the Baptismal Regeneration Controversy and in the Downgrade Controversy. In the former, Spurgeon repeatedly called the evangelicals in the Church of England to come out of the established church, because their presence legitimized and protected the teaching of the Oxford Movement. In the latter, Spurgeon himself resigned from the Baptist Union because of their unwillingness to require an explicitly evangelical basis in light of the growing theological liberalism. Spurgeon's understanding of the militant church taught him that he must be ready to fight for the truth of the gospel even among those who were in church association with him.

At the same time, these controversies also reveal that Spurgeon did not fight alone but engaged the wider evangelical community. In his sermons and articles during these controversies, he called his hearers and readers to four priorities: to take action against error, to maintain the holiness of the church, to pursue their evangelistic mission, and to be faithful to the Word. During these controversies, Spurgeon did not emphasize his Baptist distinctives, but instead prioritized evangelical convictions. Even as he called for disassociation and was himself willing to disassociate, Spurgeon knew that this fight could not be won by his, or even his church's, solitary efforts, but required all those who held the gospel, who belonged to the universal church, to come forward and join him the fight.

Living in a religious society that promoted a nominal and passive Christianity under the Established Church, Spurgeon sought to stir Christians into gospel warfare. One of the primary doctrines he used was the teaching of the church militant. While on earth before the return of Christ, the church was an army at war. Drawing on the storyline of conflict in the Bible and the New Testament's teaching on spiritual warfare, Spurgeon sought to give his congregation a vision for the Christian life as a battle against sin and the errors of this world. To be sure, Spurgeon rejected all forms of violence or coercion when it came to the church. Rather, the mission of the church was declaratory. The church was called to protect and proclaim the truth of the gospel in every age and to every person. This was not merely the job of the minister but of the entire congregation, every soldier fighting for the truth in whatever capacity they had. Church membership was not a country club for people to enjoy their spiritual privileges. Rather, it was how Christ organized and united his people for war against evil. As the church presented a united front against evil, it became a formidable weapon in God's hand. In the end, the church's confidence was not in itself, but in the power of God. In prayer and the Word, the church marched with hope in God even amid the darkest times.

In taking a stand for the gospel, Spurgeon experienced much suffering, both emotionally and physically. Writing in March 1891, referring to the Downgrade Controversy, he wrote to a friend, "Good bye, Ellis; you will never see me again, *this fight is killing me.*"[134] Spurgeon had often called the pulpit the "Thermopylae of Christendom," which sounds thrilling and heroic, but don't forget that King Leonidas died in his stand against the Persians. Preaching the truth will require sacrifice and may very well cost you your life.

---

134. *Autobiography* 3:152.

But Spurgeon understood that his congregation also had experienced hardship. They too had left their historical association with the Baptist Union. They too had experienced the heartache of betrayal from some of their former students.[135] Amid the conflict, they watched their beloved pastor growing more infirm. But as the congregation faced uncertainty in the days ahead, Spurgeon reminded them of their identity as Christ's army and of their Captain. No matter how much they had suffered, serving Christ was worth whatever cost might come. In fact, no matter how much they had suffered, Christ, their Captain, had suffered infinitely more for their salvation, and he continues to bear their burdens. Therefore, amid the conflict, the church can trust him with their lives and follow him into battle. In his last sermon at the Metropolitan Tabernacle, Spurgeon concluded his preaching ministry with these words:

> He is the most magnanimous of captains. There never was his like among the choicest of princes. He is always to be found in the thickest part of the battle. When the wind blows cold he always takes the bleak side of the hill. The heaviest end of the cross lies ever on his shoulders. If he bids us carry a burden, he carries it also. If there is anything that is gracious, generous, kind, and tender, yea lavish and superabundant in love, you always find it in him. These forty years and more have I served him, blessed be his name! and I have had nothing but love from him. I would be glad to continue yet another forty years in the same dear service here below if so it pleased him. His service is life, peace, joy. Oh, that you would enter on it at once! God help you to enlist under the banner of Jesus even this day! Amen.[136]

Having fought the good fight, Spurgeon never ceased to pastor his congregation, pointing them to their "most magnanimous of captains" and urging them to continue in the fight.

---

135. For an account of the conflict that took place at the Pastors' College Conference following the Downgrade Controversy, see C. H. Spurgeon, *The Greatest Fight in the World: The Final Manifesto* (Fearn, UK: Christian Focus, 2014), 9–30.

136. *MTP* 37:324.

10

Conclusion

Spurgeon's ecclesiology flowed from the Reformed tradition in which he grew up and was converted. Whereas Roman Catholicism brought salvation and the church together, with salvation only available through the sacraments of the church, Reformed theology distinguished between salvation and the church. This was a distinction that Spurgeon held firmly throughout his life, especially as he countered the influence of the Oxford Movement. Participation in the church was only meaningful insofar as people held rightly to the gospel.

This careful distinction reinforced Spurgeon's congregational understanding of the church. This is how Spurgeon balanced the extremes of high-church Anglicans on the one hand and low-church evangelicals on the other. In rejecting a sacramental view of salvation, Spurgeon also rejected defining the church according to its structures or leadership. The local church was instead first and foremost the called-out congregation of believers, marked by the preaching of the gospel and the right observance of the ordinances. And yet, rather than resorting to societies or parachurch organizations, Spurgeon understood that the church was the focal point of God's redemptive purposes and held the promises of God.

Though Spurgeon devoted his ministry to serving his local church and strengthening other Baptist churches, he also believed in the universal church, composed of all true churches and Christians from every age. The unity that existed in the universal church was not institutional but spiritual, expressed in a doctrinal unity in the gospel. But this unity did not compromise the independence of every local church. Even as it cooperated with other churches for the work of the gospel, each congregation had the authority to govern itself under the Word of Christ. His fight against rationalism in the Baptist Union ultimately resulted in his withdrawal from the Union, a protest made possible because of his congregational convictions.

Christ's reign in the church was shown in Spurgeon's commitment to the regulative principle. In spite of the challenge of pastoring a church of several thousand, Spurgeon did not look for expedient solutions, but grounded his pastoral leadership in biblical convictions. In a day when revivalists and ritualists both were inventing all kinds of innovations in their gatherings, the worship of the Tabernacle was marked by simplicity, without any modern inventions or attractions. Each Lord's Day the church gathered to pray, to sing, and to hear Scripture read and preached. In the gatherings of the church, the congregation observed the ordinances of baptism and the Lord's Supper. As an open-communion Baptist, Spurgeon connected the Lord's Supper to the universal church as much as to the local church. Spurgeon emphasized the importance and necessity of the ordinances as a matter of discipleship and obedience, not salvation. When it came to baptism, however, Spurgeon rejected the increasing move towards open membership among Baptists and firmly wedded believers' baptism to membership in the local church.

Spurgeon's commitment to the regulative principle was also shown in his church polity. His transition from the Congregationalists to the Baptists brought a significant change to his understanding of the church, particularly concerning regenerate church membership. Rather than a "mixed multitude,"[1] Spurgeon believed that only those who believed the gospel and were regenerated by the Holy Spirit should be admitted into membership. It was through church membership that the church would be made distinct from the world. And yet, unlike the revivalists who were quick to count professions and dole out assurance, Spurgeon maintained a rigorous membership

---

1. *NPSP* 2:15-16.

process amid a revival. Rather than admitting people carelessly and *en masse*, candidates were considered individually, each going through a membership process that involved both the elders and the congregation. During his pastorate in London, the Metropolitan Tabernacle admitted over 13,000 people into church membership. However, this was only half the picture, as Spurgeon also believed that church membership should be meaningful. Those who had died, left the church, or departed the faith, were removed from the roll so that the membership of the church reflected only those who were attending and participating in the life of the church. Those who remained in membership were called to be engaged in prayer and active service for the Lord.

Spurgeon's commitment to regenerate church membership dovetailed with his commitment to congregational polity. As dissenting churches became more disorderly and pragmatic in their church governance, Spurgeon believed that elder and deacon-led congregationalism was the order prescribed by the New Testament. Only a congregation made up those who were filled with the Holy Spirit could exercise the authority of the church rightly. The congregation was the final authority in decisions regarding membership, discipline, church leaders, properties, and much more. However, this was not a pure democracy. According to what he saw in the New Testament, Spurgeon revived the office of elders in the church in 1859. These men served alongside Spurgeon in providing giving spiritual care and leadership to the congregation. The deacons, on the other hand, continued to oversee the practical and financial care of the church. Though Spurgeon served alongside these men and exercised leadership with them, he also played a unique role as the pastor. Certainly, his influence was unmatched in the church, and the church officers and the congregation looked to him for leadership. However, in decisions which involved the church, Spurgeon did not bypass congregational authority, but taught and led his people in the direction he believed they should go. It was this "modified form of Episcopalian Presbyterian Independency"[2] that Spurgeon taught from Scripture, practiced in his church, and promoted in his church plants.

In addition to his adherence to Reformed ecclesiology and Baptist church polity, Spurgeon's vision of the church was also colored and shaped by the various images of the church presented in Scripture. But out of all these images, the one that Spurgeon drew on the most was the church as the army of God, or the militant church. Amid the theological and ecclesiological decline all around him, Spurgeon believed that the battle depended not primarily on preachers or theologians, but on faithful churches.

Spurgeon's understanding of the militant church reinforced his ecclesiology. If the church was an army, then it was important not to limit its identity merely to the clergy or denominational structure. Rather, Spurgeon's congregational understanding of the church allowed him to call the entire church to join in the fight. Additionally, as an army, the church could not determine its own orders but needed to submit to the command of its Captain. Likewise, when it came to church polity, a well-ordered membership and the proper exercise of congregational authority meant a well-disciplined army, ready to fulfill the mission of proclaiming the gospel to the world. In its unity, not only was the church equipped to preach the gospel, but became itself a testimony to the truth and power of the gospel. Beyond his local church, Spurgeon desired all evangelical churches to see themselves as different regiments of the larger army of God, engaged in the fight against sin and error, and participating in the church's mission.

During times of controversy, Spurgeon drew on the doctrine of the church militant to call his congregation and evangelicals to join him in the fight for the truth. In the Baptismal Regeneration Controversy and the Downgrade Controversy, Spurgeon's writings and sermons reveal a fourfold strategy to engage the church militant. First, he sought to awaken the churches and call them to action by exposing the seriousness of the errors around them.

---

2. *MTP* 7:257.

Second, he called them to holiness by disassociating themselves from those who held to those errors, whether inside or outside their churches. Third, he called them to fulfill their evangelistic mission by protecting and proclaiming the gospel. Finally, he called them to remain faithful to their Captain by preserving the authority and infallibility of God's Word. For Spurgeon, the church militant was not an abstract theological concept. Rather, in times of controversy, a church's willingness to fight for the truth revealed whether it was a true church.

Concluding Reflections

More than a century has passed since his death, and yet Spurgeon remains remarkably relevant for modern-day pastors and church leaders. Much attention has been given to Spurgeon over the years as a preacher, evangelist, rhetorician, author, social activist, controversialist, philanthropist, and, in more recent days, theologian. But it must not be forgotten that most fundamentally, Spurgeon was a local church pastor. To say it another way, his pastorate was not the backdrop but the foundation that made all his other ministries possible. Moreover, his theological understanding and commitment to the local church undergirded his pastoral ministry. In a day when so much confusion exists about the local church, Spurgeon can serve as a helpful guide for pastors and church leaders in several ways.

First, Spurgeon provides a model for convictional ecclesiology and polity in a megachurch context. In an age where pragmatism and aesthetics so often drive decisions about church structure, the use of technology, the approach to corporate worship, and other aspects of church life, Spurgeon provides a bracing example of someone who was committed to following God's Word, not only when it came to the gospel, but also the church. Undoubtedly, Spurgeon was committed to the mission of the church in preaching the gospel. However, he refused to adopt methods or strategies that compromised Scripture's teaching on the church, even if such tactics might draw larger crowds and encourage more "decisions" for Christ. In a context marked by religious nominalism, Spurgeon saw simplicity of worship, lengthy prayers, solemn sermons, and a rigorous membership process as especially important for preserving the purity of the church. This is not to say that he was inflexible. As the church grew beyond his ability to pastor alone, he recognized the need to call elders to serve alongside him. In areas where Scripture was silent, Spurgeon refused to be bound by human tradition, but was willing to adopt new methods to shepherd his church better and reach the lost. He was one of the first to hold worship services in secular venues, such as Surrey Gardens Music Hall. His use of tickets at the Lord's Supper to track his membership was an important tool for pastoral care in a church so large. He adjusted church meetings to meet multiple times a month, to accommodate all those joining. Both in his commitment to Scripture and in his creative use of means where allowed, Spurgeon provides a model for pastors of large churches today to remain committed to the regulative principle even when it becomes difficult.

Second, Spurgeon provides a model for long-term, church-based ministry. In a day when pastors move from church to church or graduate from local church ministry into denominational or parachurch ministries, seeking to move into positions of greater prominence, Spurgeon provides an example of a pastor who stayed rooted in one church for thirty-eight years. Though he was beloved by his congregation upon his arrival, this affection and respect would only deepen over the years. Undoubtedly, Spurgeon's fruitfulness and his congregation's participation in his vision were, in large part, a result of his long-term ministry in the church. Additionally, even as his ministry and influence grew, Spurgeon's ministries also remained rooted in the local church. His publisher, Joseph Passmore, was a deacon in the church and one of his closest friends. Though he was active in pastoral training, these efforts were not out of a nearby college, but rooted in his local church. Similarly, his evangelistic and social ministries flowed out of the support and participation of his congregation. In all the ministries Spurgeon founded, he never moved beyond the umbrella of his local church.

Finally, Spurgeon's emphasis on the militant church provides a reminder to pastors of the church's context and mission. Here in the twenty-first century, especially in the West, themes related to spiritual warfare and the militant church have fallen out of use and are often seen as politically incorrect. Instead, church growth experts have emphasized the need for contextualization, adapting the church's doctrines and practices to the sensibilities of the world. Churches end up resembling shopping malls (or coffee shops, or rock concerts, or whatever trendy venue that attracts the target demographic), and Christians behave more like consumers than soldiers. Yet this is where church leaders need to recapture Spurgeon's vision of the militant church. Before the return of Christ, whether in times of prosperity or persecution, the church is ever in a spiritual war against sin and error. In this war, the church is never justified in any use of violence or coercion. Rather, in love, the church is called to proclaim the truth boldly and faithfully, even when it means suffering and rejection. The goal of the militant church is not the world's approval, but faithfulness to our Captain's orders and mission, whatever the cost. For someone who saw astonishing successes in his church, Spurgeon never lost sight of the church militant. In the triumphalism of our day, he stands as an important reminder to pastors and church leaders.

Spurgeon and the Church Triumphant

To the end of his life, Spurgeon saw himself in a war for the truth. His part in the war came to an end on Sunday, January 31, 1892, in Mentone, France. On that day, Spurgeon's membership at the Metropolitan Tabernacle came to an end, and his membership in the church triumphant began. The militant church lost a soldier, but the church triumphant gained a new singer. As much as Spurgeon loved his people at the Tabernacle, he had looked forward to joining this heavenly congregation all his life. All the joys of church life that he had experienced anticipated that moment when he would finally gather with the church triumphant.

> We leave the imperfect church on earth, but we claim membership with the perfect church in heaven. The church militant must know us no more, but of the church triumphant we shall be happy members. We may not see that honored men on earth who now serve Christ in the ministry, but we shall see Abraham, Isaac,

and Jacob, the noble army of martyrs, the goodly fellowship of the prophets, and the glorious company of the apostles. We shall be no losers, certainly, in the matter of society, but great gainers when we are introduced to the general assembly and the church of the first-born, whose names are written in heaven.

I said that we should be taken away from enjoyments. I spoke of Sabbath bells that would ring no longer, of communion tables at which we could not sit, and songs of holy mirth in which we could not join – ah, it is small loss compared with the gain unspeakable, for we shall hear the bells of heaven ring out an unending Sabbath, we shall join the songs that never have a pause, and which know no discord; we shall sit at the banqueting table where the King himself is present, where the symbols and the signs have vanished because the guests have found the substance, and the King eternal and immortal is visibly in their presence![3]

---

3.   *MTP* 12:646.

Bibliography

Primary Sources

Calvin, John. *Institutes of the Christian Religion*. Edited by John T. McNeil. Translated by Ford L. Battles. Philadelphia: Westminster Press, 1960.

_____. *Calvin: Theological Treatises*, LCC 22. Translated by J. K. S. Reid. Philadelphia: Westminster Press, 1961.

C.H. Spurgeon – Letters to his Father and Mother – 1850-84. Spurgeon Collection, Regent's Park College, Oxford.

Church Meeting Minutes 1719-1808 Horselydown & Carter Lane. Metropolitan Tabernacle Archives, London.

Church Meeting Minutes 1808-1854 Tooley Street & Carter Lane. Metropolitan Tabernacle Archives, London.

Church Meeting Minutes 1854-1861 New Park Street. Metropolitan Tabernacle Archives, London.

Church Meeting Minutes 1861-1866 Metropolitan Tabernacle. Metropolitan Tabernacle Archives, London.

Church Meeting Minutes 1866-1871 Metropolitan Tabernacle. Metropolitan Tabernacle Archives, London.

Church Meeting Minutes 1871-1876 Metropolitan Tabernacle. Metropolitan Tabernacle Archives, London.

Church Meeting Minutes 1876-1882 Metropolitan Tabernacle. Metropolitan Tabernacle Archives, London.

Church Meeting Minutes 1882-1889 Metropolitan Tabernacle. Metropolitan Tabernacle Archives, London.

Church Meeting Minutes 1889-1894 Metropolitan Tabernacle. Metropolitan Tabernacle Archives, London.

Cummings, Brian, ed. *The Book of Common Prayer: The Texts of 1549, 1559, and 1662.* Oxford: Oxford University Press, 2011.

Deacons Meetings 1861-1881 Metropolitan Tabernacle. Metropolitan Tabernacle Archives, London.

Elders Minutes 1876-1881 Metropolitan Tabernacle. Metropolitan Tabernacle Archives, London.

Luther, Martin. *Dr. Martin Luther's Small Catechism.* St. Louis, MO: Concordia Publishing House, 1971.

Newman, John Henry. *Lectures on the Doctrine of Justification.* London: Longmans, Green, and Co., 1908.

_____. "Tracts for the Times," Project Canterbury, cdli:wiki, http://anglicanhistory.org/tracts/.

Roberts, Alexander Roberts and James Donaldson, eds. *Ante-Nicene Fathers*, vol. 2, *Fathers of the Second Century: Hermas, Tatian, Athenagoras, Theophilus, and Clement of Alexandria.* Peabody, MA: Hendrickson Publishers, 2004.

_____. *Ante-Nicene Fathers*, vol. 5, *Hippolytus, Cyprian, Caius, Novatian, Appendix.* Peabody, MA: Hendrickson Publishers, 2004.

Spurgeon, Charles H. *Able to the Uttermost.* Pasadena, TX: Pilgrim Publications, 1985.

_____. *According to Promise: Or, the Method of the Lord's Dealings with His Chosen.* London: Passmore & Alabaster, 1887.

_____. *All of Grace: An Earnest Word with Those Who Are Seeking Salvation by the Lord Jesus Christ.* London: Passmore & Alabaster, 1886.

_____. *An All-Round Ministry.* Pasadena, TX: Pilgrim Publications, 1983.

_____. *Around the Wicket Gate: Or, a Friendly Talk with Seekers Concerning Faith in the Lord Jesus Christ.* Pasadena, TX: Pilgrim Publications, 1992.

_____. *C. H. Spurgeon Anecdotes.* London: Passmore & Alabaster, 1900.

_____. *C.H. Spurgeon's Autobiography: Compiled from His Diary, Letters, and Records, by His Wife, and His Private Secretary, Volumes 1-4*. London: Passmore & Alabaster, 1897.

_____. *C.H. Spurgeon's Forgotten College Addresses*. Leominster, UK: Day One Publications, 2016.

_____. *C.H. Spurgeon's Forgotten Early Sermons*. Leominster, UK: Day One Publications, 2010.

_____. *C.H. Spurgeon's Forgotten Prayer Meeting Addresses*. Leominster, UK: Day One Publications, 2011.

_____. *C. H. Spurgeon's Prayers*. Pasadena, TX: Pilgrim Publications, 1990.

_____. *C.H. Spurgeon's Sermons Beyond Volume 63*. Edited by Terence Crosby. Leominster, UK: Day One Publications, 2009.

_____. *C.H. Spurgeon's Works in His Magazine The Sword and the Trowel, Volumes 1-8*. Pasadena, TX: Pilgrim Publications, 2004.

_____. *"Come Ye Children."* Pasadena, TX: Pilgrim Publications, 1975.

_____. *Eccentric Preachers*. Pasadena, TX: Pilgrim Publications, 1978.

_____. *Farm Sermons*. Pasadena, TX: Pilgrim Publications, 1989.

_____. *Feathers for Arrows*. London: Passmore & Alabaster, 1891.

_____. *"George Fox": An Address Delivered to the Society of Friends*. San Bernardino, CA: Leopold Classic Library, 2016.

_____. *John Ploughman's Talk*. Philadelphia: Henry Altemus, 1896.

_____. *Lectures to My Students*. Pasadena, TX: Pilgrim Publications, 1990.

_____. *Memories of Stambourne*. Pasadena, TX: Pilgrim Publications, 1975.

_____. *Spurgeon Sermon Collection: The Metropolitan Tabernacle Pulpit*. Accordance electronic edition, version 1.5, 2 vols. Altamonte Springs, FL. OakTree Software, 2012.

_____. *"Only a Prayer Meeting!"* Fearn, UK: Christian Focus Publications, 2006.

_____. *Our Own Hymn Book: A Collection of Psalms and Hymns for Public, Social, and Private Worship.* London: Passmore and Alabaster, 1869.

_____. *Speeches at Home and Abroad.* Pasadena, TX: Pilgrim Publications, 1974.

_____. *Spurgeon's Sermons Preached on Unusual Occasions.* Pasadena, TX: Pilgrim Publications, 1978.

_____. *Teachings of Nature in the Kingdom of Grace.* Pasadena, TX: Pilgrim Publications, 1975.

_____. *The Clue of the Maze.* London: Passmore & Alabaster, 1892.

_____. *The "Down Grade" Controversy.* Pasadena, TX: Pilgrim Publications, 2009.

_____. *The Greatest Fight in the World: The Final Manifesto.* Fearn, UK: Christian Focus Publications, 2014.

_____. *The Gospel of the Kingdom: A Commentary on the Book of Matthew.* Pasadena, TX: Pilgrim Publications, 1996.

_____. *The Interpreter, or, Scripture for Family Worship: Being Selected Passages of the Word of God for Every Morning and Evening Throughout the year, Accompanied by a Running Comment and Suitable Hymns.* London: Passmore & Alabaster, n.d..

_____. *The Letters of Charles Haddon Spurgeon.* Edited by Iain H. Murray. Edinburgh: Banner of Truth Trust, 1992.

_____. *The Lost Sermons of C. H. Spurgeon.* 3 vols. Edited by Christian George. Nashville, TN: B&H Academic, 2016-2018.

_____. *The Metropolitan Tabernacle: Its History and Work.* Pasadena, TX: Pilgrim Publications, 1990.

_____. *The Metropolitan Tabernacle Pulpit: Sermons Preached and Revised by C. H. Spurgeon.* Vols. 7-63. Pasadena, TX: Pilgrim Publications, 1970-2006.

_____. *The New Park Street Pulpit: Containing Sermons Preached and Revised by the Rev. C. H. Spurgeon, Minister of the Chapel.* 6 vols. Pasadena, TX: Pilgrim Publications, 1975-1991.

_____. *The Salt-Cellars: Being a Collection of Proverbs Together with Homely Notes Thereon.* New York: A. C. Armstrong & Son, 1889.

_____. *The Soul Winner.* Pasadena, TX: Pilgrim Publications, 2007.

_____. *The Sword and the Trowel; A Record of Combat with Sin & Labour for the Lord.* 37 vols. London: Passmore & Alabaster, 1865–1902.

_____. *The Treasury of David: Containing an Original Exposition of the Book of Psalms; A Collection of Illustrative Extracts from the Whole Range of Literature; A Series of Homiletical Hints Upon Almost Every Verse; And Lists of Writers Upon Each Psalm.* 7 vols. Pasadena, TX: Pilgrim Publications, 1983.

_____. *"Till He Come:" Communion Meditations and Addresses.* Pasadena, TX: Pilgrim, 1971.

_____. *Types & Emblems: Being a Collection of Sermons Preached on Sunday and Thursday Evenings at the Metropolitan Tabernacle.* London: Passmore & Alabaster, 1875.

_____. *"We Endeavor," Helpful Words for Members of the Young People's Society of Christian Endeavor.* Pasadena, TX: Pilgrim Publications, 1975.

_____. *What the Stones Say: Or, Sermons in Stones.* Pasadena, TX: Pilgrim Publications, 1975.

_____. *Words of Cheer for Daily Life.* Pasadena, TX: Pilgrim Publications, 1978.

_____. *Words of Counsel for Christian Workers.* Pasadena, TX: Pilgrim Publications, 1985.

_____. *Words of Warning for Daily Life.* London: Passmore & Alabaster, 1895.

_____. *Words of Wisdom for Daily Life.* London: Passmore & Alabaster, 1892.

Spurgeon Memorabilia, Metropolitan Tabernacle Archives.

Spurgeon Sermon Outline Notebooks. 11 vols. Heritage Room, Spurgeon's College, London.

Testimony Book 1201 to 1600. Metropolitan Tabernacle Archives, London.

Wyncoll, Hannah, ed. *The Suffering Letters of C. H. Spurgeon.* London: The Wakeman Trust, 2016.

_____. *Wonders of Grace: Original Testimonies of Converts During Spurgeon's Early Years.* London: The Wakeman Trust, 2016.

Tracts for the Times; By Members of the University of Oxford. Vols. I-V 1833-40, London: J. G. & F. Rivington, 1839-40.

Turretin, Francis. *Institutes of Elenctic Theology.* Edited by James T. Dennison, Jr. Translated by George Musgrave Giger. Phillipsburg, NJ: P&R Publishing, 1997.

Secondary Sources: Articles and Papers

Briggs, J. H.Y. "Charles Haddon Spurgeon and the Baptist Denomination in Nineteenth Century Britain." *Baptist Quarterly* 31, no. 5 (January 1986): 218-40.

Chang, Geoffrey "New Insights into the Formative Influence of Spurgeon's Early Years," *Themelios*, Vol. 47, Issue 3.

_____. "A Symbol of the Invisible: Spurgeon and the Animal World," in Geoffrey Chang and C. Anthony Neel, *Andrew Fuller and Charles Spurgeon: A Theology of Animal Life: Reflections in the Eighteenth and Nineteenth Centuries.* Louisville, KY: The Andrew Fuller Center for Baptist Studies, 2021.

Chesterton, W. Ridley. "The Spurgeon Centenary. III. Social Life in Spurgeon's Day." *Baptist Quarterly* 6, no. 8 (October 1933): 337-345.

Dakin, Arthur. "The Spurgeon Centenary. II. The Preacher." *Baptist Quarterly* 6, no. 7 (July 1933): 289-295.

Glover, Willis B. "English Baptists at the Time of the Downgrade Controversy." *Foundations* 1, no. 3 (July 1958): 41-51.

Hatcher, William E. "Mr. Spurgeon as I Saw Him." in H. L. Wayland. *Charles H. Spurgeon: His Faith and Works.* Philadelphia: American Baptist Publication Society, 1892.

Hopkins, Mark T. E. "Spurgeon's Opponents in the Downgrade Controversy." *Baptist Quarterly* 32, no. 6 (April 1988): 274-294.

_____. "The Down Grade Controversy: New Evidence." *Baptist Quarterly* 35, no. 6 (April 1994): 262-278.

Lescelius, Robert. "Spurgeon and Revival." *Revival & Reformation* 3, no. 2 (Spring 1994): 61-83.

Lowe, Don and James Anderson. "A Tabular Comparison of the 1646 Westminster Confession of Faith, the 1658 Savoy Declaration of Faith, the 1677/1689 London Baptist Confession of Faith and the 1742 Philadelphia Confession of Faith." cdli:wiki, https://www.proginosko.com/docs/wcf_sdfo_lbcf.html.

Mohler, R. Albert. "A Call for Theological Triage and Christian Maturity." cldi:wiki, https://albertmohler.com/2005/07/12/a-call-for-theological-triage-and-christian-maturity/.

Morden, Peter J. "C. H. Spurgeon and Prayer." *Evangelical Quarterly* 84, no. 4 (October 2012): 323-344.

_____. "The Spirituality of C. H. Spurgeon 1: Establishing Communion: A Convertive Piety." *Baptistic Theologies* 4, no. 1 (Spring 2012): 1-26.

_____. "The Spirituality of C. H. Spurgeon 2: Maintaining Communion: The Lord's Supper." *Baptistic Theologies* 4, no. 1 (Spring 2012): 27-50.

_____. "The Spirituality of C. H. Spurgeon 3: The Outworking of Communion: Active Exertion." *Baptistic Theologies* 4, no. 1 (Spring 2012): 51-80.

Nicholls, Michael. "Mission Yesterday and Today: Charles Haddon Spurgeon 1834-1892." *Baptist Review of Theology* 2, no.1 (Spring 1992): 37-49.

_____. "Spurgeon as a Church Planter." *Baptist Review of Theology* 2, no. 1 (Spring 1992): 37-49

Norton, W. "Mister Spurgeon on Communion." *Gospel Herald: or Poor Christians Magazine* 26 (February 1858): 134.

Ort, Phillip, Timothy Gatewood, and Ed Romine. "Charles Spurgeon: The Quintessential Evangelical." *Midwestern Journal of Theology* 18, no. 1 (Spring 2019): 104-25.

Owens, Jesse F. "The Salters' Hall Controversy: Heresy, Subscription, or Both?" *Perichoresis* 20.1 (2022), 35-52.

Payne, Ernest A. "The Down Grade Controversy: A Postscript." *Baptist Quarterly* 28, no. 4 (April 1979): 146-58.

Price, Seymour J. "The Spurgeon Centenary. I. Gleanings from his Minute-books." *Baptist Quarterly* 6, no. 6 (April 1933): 241-54.

Quicke, Michael J. and Ian M. Randall. "Spurgeon's College." *American Baptist Quarterly* 18, no. 2 (June 1999): 118-30.

Rose, Nathan. "Spurgeon and the Slavery Controversy of 1860: A Critical Analysis of the Anthropology of Charles Haddon Spurgeon, as it Relates Specifically to his Stance on Slavery." *Midwestern Journal of Theology* 16, no. 1 (2017): 20-37.

Stanley, Brian. "Spurgeon and the Baptist Missionary Society." *Baptist Quarterly* 29, no. 7 (July 1982): 319-28.

Swanson, Dennis M. "The Millennial Position of Spurgeon." *The Master's Seminary Journal* 7, no. 2 (Fall 1996): 183-212.

Walker, Michael. "Charles Haddon Spurgeon and John Clifford on the Lord's Supper." *American Baptist Quarterly* 7, no. 2 (June 1988): 128-50.

Wills, Gregory. "The Ecclesiology of Charles H. Spurgeon: Unity, Orthodoxy, and Denominational Identity." *Midwestern Journal of Theology* 14, no. 2 (2015): 38-53.

Wolever, Terry. "William Hatcher's Conversations with C. H. Spurgeon on the Subject of Church Communion and the Strict Baptists of London (1888)." in Geoffrey R. Breed, *Calvinism & Communion in Victorian England: Studies in Nineteenth-Century Strict-Communion Baptist Ecclesiology*. Springfield, MO: Particular Baptist Press, 2008.

Secondary Sources: Dissertations

Ahn, Shinyul. "A Critical Examination of Selected Biographical Sermons of Charles Haddon Spurgeon." PhD diss., New Orleans Baptist Theological Seminary, 2017.

Brian, William A. "'When the Wind Blows Cold': The Spirituality of Suffering and Depression in the Life and Ministry of Charles Spurgeon." PhD diss., The Southern Baptist Theological Seminary, 2015.

Colquitt, Henry F. "The Soteriology of Charles Haddon Spurgeon Revealed in his Sermons and Controversial Writings." PhD diss., The University of Edinburgh, 1951.

Dickenson, Keeney R. "Preaching from the Overflow of Personal Piety: The Contribution of Prayer and Bible Intake to the Pulpit Ministry of Charles Spurgeon." DMin diss., The Southern Baptist Theological Seminary, 2017.

Earls, Rodney Douglas. "The Evangelistic Strategy of Charles Haddon Spurgeon for the Multiplication of Churches and Implications for Modern Church Extension Theory." PhD diss., Southwestern Baptist Theological Seminary, 1989.

Ellison, Robert H. "Orality-Literacy Theory and the Victorian Sermon." PhD diss., The University of North Texas, 1995.

Eswine, Zachary W. "The Role of the Holy Spirit in the Preaching Theory and Practice of Charles Haddon Spurgeon." PhD diss., Regent University, 2003.

George, Christian T. "Jesus Christ, the 'Prince of Pilgrims': A Critical Analysis of the Ontological, Functional, and Exegetical Christologies in the Sermons, Writings, and Lectures of Charles Haddon Spurgeon (1834-1892)." PhD diss., University of St. Andrews, 2012.

Jessen, Jeremy D. "Mr. Valiant for Truth: The Polemic of Charles Haddon Spurgeon as Pastor-Theologian During the Downgrade Controversy (1887-1892)." PhD diss., The Southern Baptist Theological Seminary, 2019.

Kruppa, Patricia S. "Charles Haddon Spurgeon: A Preacher's Progress." PhD diss., Columbia University, 1968.

Lewis, John W. "Insights from Charles Spurgeon's Christ-Centered Preaching for a Changing Culture." DMin diss., Liberty Baptist Theological Seminary, 2012.

McCoy, Timothy A. "The Evangelistic Ministry of C. H. Spurgeon: Implications for a Contemporary Model for Pastoral Evangelism." PhD diss., The Southern Baptist Theological Seminary, 1989.

Meredith, Albert R. "The Social and Political Views of Charles Haddon Spurgeon, 1834-1892." PhD diss., Michigan State University, 1973.

Michaels, Larry J. "The Effects of Controversy on the Evangelistic Ministry of C. H. Spurgeon." PhD diss., The Southern Baptist Theological Seminary, 1989.

Rice, Arthur G. "A Critical Examination of Charles Haddon Spurgeon's Theory and Practice of Sermon Illustrations." PhD diss., New Orleans Baptist Theological Seminary, 2012.

Rhodes, E. Ray. "The Role of Bible Intake and Prayer in the Marriage of Charles and Susannah Spurgeon." DMin diss., The Southern Baptist Theological Seminary, 2016.

Smith, Dale W. "The Victorian Preacher's Malady: The Metaphorical Usage of Gout in the Life of Charles Haddon Spurgeon." PhD diss., The University of Missouri – Kansas City, 2017.

Spyes, Louis E. "The Tie That Binds: Calvin, Spurgeon, and the Lord's Supper." ThM diss., Westminster Theological Seminary, 1995.

Strong, Robert. "A Study of the Factors of Persuasion in the Sermons of Charles Haddon Spurgeon." MA thesis, University of Southern California, 1933.

Sweatman, Kent E. "The Doctrines of Calvinism in the Preaching of Charles Haddon Spurgeon." PhD diss., Southwestern Baptist Theological Seminary, 1998.

Yap, Timothy. "Reading the Surrey Gardens Tragedy: Trauma, Ethos and the Rhetoric of Charles Haddon Spurgeon." PhD diss., Florida State University, 2002.

Zeluff, Daniel. "A Critique of English Speaking Preaching 1864-1964." PhD diss., The University of Aberdeen, 1964.

Secondary Sources: Eighteenth, Nineteenth, and early Twentieth Century Monographs

Adcock, E. F. *Charles H. Spurgeon: Prince of Preachers*. Anderson, IN: The Warner Press, 1925.

Breed, Geoffrey R. *Calvinism and Communion in Victorian England: Studies in Nineteenth-century Strict-communion Baptist Ecclesiology, Comprising the Minutes of the London Association of Strict Baptist Ministers and Churches, 1846-1855, and The Ramsgate Chapel Case, 1862*. Springfield, MO: Particular Baptist Press, 2008.

Brown, John. *Apostolical Succession in the Light of History and Fact*. London: Congregational Union of England and Wales, 1898.

Bunyan, John. *Grace Abounding to the Chief of Sinners*. London: Penguin Books, 1987.

_____. *The Pilgrim's Progress*. Edited by Roger Sharrock. London: Penguin Books, 1987.

Campbell, R. J. *A Spiritual Pilgrimage*, New York: D. Appleton and Company, 1917.

_____. *The New Theology*. New York: The Macmillan Company, 1907.

Christian, John T. *Close Communion, or Baptism as a Prerequisite to the Lord's Supper*. Louisville, KY: Baptist Book Concern, 1892.

Church, R. W. *The Oxford Movement: Twelve Years 1833-1845*. London: MacMillan, 1891.

Clifford, John. "The Place of Baptists in the Evolution of British Christianity," *Religious Systems of the World: A Contribution to the Study of Comparative Religion*, London: Swan Sonneschein & Co., Limited, 1905.

Conwell, Russell H. *Life of Charles Haddon Spurgeon, the World's Great Preacher*. Philadelphia: Edgewood Publishing, 1892.

Cramp, J. M. *Baptist History from the Foundation of the Christian Church to the Present Time*. London: Elliot Stock, 1871.

Creyton, Oliver. *Anecdotes and Stories of the Rev. C. H. Spurgeon*. London: Houlston and Wright, 1866.

Curwen, J. Spencer. *Studies in Worship-Music, Chiefly as Regards Congregational Singing*. London: J. Curwen & Sons, 1880.

Dale, R. W. *History of English Congregationalism*. New York: A. C. Armstrong and Son, 1907.

_____. *The Evangelical Revival and Other Sermons: with an Address on the Work of the Christian Ministry in a Period of Theological Decay and Transition*. London: Hodder and Stoughton, 1880.

Ellis, James. *Charles Haddon Spurgeon*. New York: Fleming H. Revell Co., 1892.

Fairbairn, A. M. *Catholicism: Roman and Anglican*. London: Hodder and Stoughton, 1899.

Finney, Charles G. *Lectures on the Revival of Religion*. New York: Leavitt, Lord, & Co., 1835.

Fulton, Justin D. *Charles H. Spurgeon: Our Ally*. Montreal: Pauline Propaganda, 1923.

Fullerton, W.Y. *Charles Spurgeon: A Biography*. London: Williams and Norgate, 1920.

Gill, John, *A Complete Body of Doctrinal and Practical Divinity; or, a System of Evangelical Truths, Deduced from the Sacred Scriptures*, Vol. III. London: W. Winterbotham, 1796.

Hall, Samuel. *A Short History of the Oxford Movement*. London: Longmans, Green, and Co.,1906.

Handford, Thomas W. *Spurgeon: Episodes and Anecdotes of his Busy Life*. Chicago: W. B. Conkey Company, 1892.

Hatcher, Eldridge B. *William E. Hatcher: A Biography*. Richmond, VA: W. C. Hill Printing, 1915.

Horton, Robert Forman. *An Autobiography*. London: George Allen & Unwin Ltd, 1918.

Magoon, E. L. *The Modern Whitfield: Sermons of the Rev. C. H. Spurgeon, of London; with an Introduction and Sketch of his Life*. New York: Sheldon, Blakeman & Co., 1856.

Marchant, James. *Dr. John Clifford: Life, Letters, and Reminiscences*. London: Cassell and Company, LTD, 1924.

Needham, George C. *Charles H. Spurgeon: His Life and Labors*. Boston: Bradley and Woodruff Publishers, 1892.

_____. *The Life and Labors of Charles H. Spurgeon: The Faithful Preacher, the Devoted Pastor, the Noble Philanthropist, the Beloved College President, and the Voluminous Author, Writer, Etc., Etc*. Boston: D. L. Guernsey, 1882.

Northrop, Henry D. *Life and Works of Rev. Charles H. Spurgeon* n.p.: Memorial Publishing Co., 1892.

Nye, G. H. F. *The Story of the Oxford Movement*. London: Bemrose & Sons. Ltd., 1899.

Ollard, S. L. *A Short History of the Oxford Movement*. London: A. R. Mowbray & Co. Ltd., 1915.

Pierson, Arthur T., ed. *From the Pulpit to the Palm Branch: A Memorial of Charles H. Spurgeon*. Birmingham, AL: Solid Ground Christian Books, 2006.

Pike, G. Holden. *The Life and Work of Charles Haddon Spurgeon, Volumes 1-2*. Edinburgh: Banner of Truth Trust, 1991.

_____. *The Metropolitan Tabernacle; or, an Historical Account of the Society*. Memphis, TN: General Books LLC, 2012.

Prime, Samuel. *Power of Prayer: The New York Revival of 1858*, Edinburgh: Banner of Truth, 1991.

Ray, Charles. *The Life of Charles Haddon Spurgeon*. London: Passmore & Alabaster, 1903.

Robinson, William. *Biblical Studies*. London: Longmans, Green, and Co., 1866.

Schindler, Robert. *From the Usher's Desk to the Tabernacle Pulpit*. New York: A. C. Armstrong and Son, 1892.

_____. *The Life and Labors of Charles Haddon Spurgeon*. New York: A. C. Armstrong and Son, 1892.

Scott, C. Anderson. *Evangelical Doctrine – Bible Truth*. London: Hodder and Stoughton, 1901.

Smith, J. Manton. *The Essex Lad Who Became England's Greatest Preacher: The Life of Charles Haddon Spurgeon for Young People*. New York: American Tract Society, 1892.

Stevenson, George J. *Sketch of the Life and Ministry of the Rev. C. H. Spurgeon from Original Documents*. New York: Sheldon, Blakeman & Co., 1857.

Stock, John. *A Handbook of Revealed Theology*. London: Elliot Stock, 1883.

"The Authors of 'The Life of General Gordon.'" *Spurgeon: The People's Preacher*. London: Walter Scott, n.d.

Ward, Wilfrid, *The Oxford Movement*. London: T. C. & E. C. Jack, 1889.

Wayland, H.L. *Charles H. Spurgeon: His Faith and Works*. Philadelphia: American Baptist Publication Society, 1892.

Williams, W. *Personal Reminiscences of Charles Haddon Spurgeon*. London: Passmore & Alabaster, 1895.

Secondary Sources: Mid Twentieth and Twenty-first Century Monographs

Avis, Paul D. L. *The Church in the Theology of the Reformers*. Eugene, OR: Wipf & Stock, 2002.

Bacon, Ernest W. *Spurgeon: Heir of the Puritans*. Arlington Heights, IL: Christian Liberty Press, 2001.

Bebbington David W. *Evangelicalism in Modern Britain: A History from the 1730s to the 1980s*. London: Routledge, 2000.

_____. *The Dominance of Evangelicalism: The Age of Spurgeon and Moody*. Leicester: Inter-Varsity Press, 2001, 2005.

Berkhof, Louis. *Systematic Theology*. Grand Rapids, MI: Eerdmans, 1996.

Bingham, Matthew. *Orthodox Radicals: Baptist Identity in the English Reformation*. Oxford: Oxford University Press, 2019.

Bray, Gerald. *The Church: A Theological and Historical Account*. Grand Rapids, MI: Baker Academic, 2016.

Briggs, J.H.Y. *The English Baptists of the 19th Century*. Didcot, UK: The Baptist Historical Society, 1994.

Chadwick, Owen. *The Victorian Church, Part One 1829-1859*. London: SCM Press, 1997.

_____. *The Victorian Church, Part Two 1860-1901*. London: SCM Press, 1997.

Cheyne, A. C. *The Transforming of the Kirk: Victorian Scotland's Religious Revolution*. Edinburgh: The Saint Andrew Press, 1983.

Chute, Anthony, Nathan A. Finn, and Michael A. G. Haykin, *The Baptist Story: From Sect to Global Movement*. Nashville, TN: B&H Academic, 2015.

Coffey, John and Paul C. H. Lim, eds. *The Cambridge Companion to Puritanism*. Cambridge: Cambridge University Press, 2008.

Curnow, Tim, Erroll Hulse, David Kingdon, and Geoff Thomas. *A Marvelous Ministry: How the All-round Ministry of Charles Haddon Spurgeon Speaks to us Today*. Ligonier, PA: Soli Deo Gloria Publications, 1993.

Dallimore, Arnold A. *Spurgeon: A Biography*. Edinburgh: Banner of Truth Trust, 2014.

Day, Richard Ellsworth. *The Shadow of the Broad Brim: The Life Story of C. H. Spurgeon*. Grand Rapids, MI: Baker Book House, 1976.

Deweese, Charles W. *Baptist Church Covenants*. Nashville, TN: Broadman Press, 1990.

Dever, Mark E., ed. *Polity: Biblical Arguments on How to Conduct Church Life*. Washington, DC: Nine Marks Ministries, 2001.

Drummond, Lewis. *Spurgeon: Prince of Preachers*. Grand Rapids, MI: Kregel Publications, 1992.

Duncan, J. Ligon III, Philip Graham Ryken, and Derek W. H. Thomas, eds. *Give Praise to God: A Vision for Reforming Worship*. Phillipsburg, NJ: P&R Publishing, 2003.

Elliot-Blnns, L. E *Religion in the Victorian Era*. Greenwich, CT: The Seabury Press, 1953.

Ellison, Robert H. *The Victorian Pulpit: Spoken and Written Sermons in Nineteenth-century Britain.* London: Associated University Press, 1998. 178 pages.

Estep, William R. *The Anabaptist Story: An Introduction to Sixteenth-Century Anabaptism.* Grand Rapids, MI: Eerdmans, 1996.

Findlay, James F. Jr. *Dwight L. Moody: American Evangelist 1837-1899.* Chicago: The University of Chicago Press, 1969.

Fish, Roy J. *When Heaven Touched Earth: The Awakening of 1858 and its Effects on Baptists,* Azle, TX: Need of the Times Publishers, 1996.

Garrett, James Leo. *Baptist Theology: A Four-Century Study.* Macon, GA: Mercer University Press, 2009.

George, Timothy. *Theology of the Reformers, 25th Anniversary Revised Edition.* Nashville, TN: B&H Academic, 2013.

George, Timothy and David S. Dockery, eds. *Theologians of the Baptist Tradition.* Nashville, TN: Broadman & Holman Publishers, 2001.

Grant, John W. *Free Churchmanship in England, 1870-1949: With Special Reference to Congregationalism.* London: Independent Press Ltd., 1955.

Hayden, Eric W. *A History of Spurgeon's Tabernacle.* Pasadena, TX: Pilgrim Publications, 1971.

_____. *He Won Them for Christ: 30 Conversions Under Spurgeon's Ministry.* Fearn, UK: Christian Focus Publications, 1993.

_____. *Highlights in the Life of C. H. Spurgeon.* Pasadena, TX: Pilgrim Publications, 1990.

_____. *Searchlight on Spurgeon: Spurgeon Speaks for Himself.* Pasadena, TX: Pilgrim Publications, 1973.

_____. *The Spurgeon Family.* Pasadena, TX: Pilgrim Publications, 1993.

_____. *The Unforgettable Spurgeon.* Greenville, SC: Emerald House Group, 1997.

Haykin, Michael A. G. and Terry Wolever, eds. *The British Particular Baptists, Volume I: A Series of Biographical Essays on Notable Figures.* Springfield, MO: Particular Baptist Press, 2019.

Höpfl, Harro. *The Christian Polity of John Calvin.* Cambridge: University of Cambridge Press, 1982.

Hopkins, Mark. *Nonconformity's Romantic Generation: Evangelical and Liberal Theologies in Victorian England.* Eugene, OR: Wipf & Stock, 2004.

Hoppen, K. Theodore. *The Mid-Victorian Generation 1846-1886.* Oxford: Clarenden Press, 2008.

Hylson-Smith, Kenneth. *Evangelicals in the Church of England 1734-1984.* Edinburgh: T. & T. Clark Ltd., 1988.

Janz, Denis R., ed. *A Reformation Reader: Primary Texts with Introductions.* Philadelphia: Fortress Press, 2008.

Jones, R. Tudur. *Congregationalism in England 1662-1962.* London: Independent Press Ltd., 1962.

Karkkainen, Veli-Matti. *An Introduction to Ecclesiology.* Downers Grove, IL: InterVarsity Press, 2002.

Klaassen, Walter, ed. *Anabaptism in Outline: Selected Primary Source.* Waterloo, ON: Herald Press, 1981.

Knight, Frances. *The Church in the Nineteenth Century: The I. B. Tauris History of the Christian Church.* London: I. B. Tauris, 2008.

Larsen, Timothy. *Contested Christianity: The Political and Social Contexts of Victorian Theology.* Waco, TX: Baylor University Press, 2004.

Leeman, Jonathan. *Don't Fire Your Church Members: The Case for Congregationalism.* Nashville, TN: B&H Academic, 2016.

Leith, John H. ed., *Creeds of the Churches: A Reader in Christian Doctrine from the Bible to the Present.* Louisville, KY: John Knox Press, 1982.

Lumpkin, William L. *Baptist Confessions of Faith,* Valley Forge, PA: Judson Press, 1969.

Marsh, P. T. *The Victorian Church in Decline: Archbishop Tait and the Church of England 1868-1882*, Pittsburgh, PA: University of Pittsburgh Press, 1969.

Merkle, Benjamin L. and Thomas R. Schreiner, eds. *Shepherding God's Flock: Biblical Leadership in the New Testament and Beyond.* Grand Rapids, MI: Kregel Publications, 2014.

Morden, Peter J. *Communion with Christ and His People: The Spirituality of C.H. Spurgeon.* Eugene, OR: Pickwick Publications, 2013.

Murray, Iain, H.J.C. Ryle: Prepared to Stand Alone. Edinburgh: Banner of Truth, 2016.

_____. *Spurgeon v. Hyper-Calvinism: The Battle for Gospel Preaching.* Edinburgh: Banner of Truth Trust, 2010.

_____. *The Forgotten Spurgeon.* Edinburgh: Banner of Truth Trust, 2002.

_____. *Revival and Revivalism: The Making and Marring of American Evangelicalism 1750-1858.* Edinburgh: Banner of Truth, 1994.

_____. *The Reformation of the Church: A Collection of Reformed and Puritan Documents on Church Issues.* Edinburgh: The Banner of Truth Trust, 1997.

Nettles, Tom. *Living by Revealed Truth: The Life and Pastoral Theology of Charles Haddon Spurgeon.* Fearn, UK: Christian Focus Publications, 2015.

Nicholls, Mike. *C. H. Spurgeon: The Pastor Evangelist.* Didcot, UK: Baptist Historical Society, 1992.

_____. *Lights to the World: A History of Spurgeon's College 1856-1992.* Harpenden, UK: Nuprint Ltd., 1994.

Oliver, Robert W. *History of the English Calvinistic Baptists 1771-1892: from John Gill to C.H. Spurgeon.* Edinburgh: Banner of Truth, 2006.

Orr, J. Edwin. *The Second Evangelical Awakening,* abridged reprint. NA: Enduring Word, 2018.

Payne, Ernest A. *The Baptist Union: A Short History*. London: The Carey Kingsgate Press Limited, 1959.

Pelikan, Jaroslav. *Reformation of Church and Dogma (1300-1700)*. Chicago: University of Chicago Press, 1984.

Ray, Charles. *A Marvellous Ministry: The Story of C.H. Spurgeon's Sermons 1855 to 1905*. Pasadena, TX: Pilgrim Publications, 1985.

Rhodes, Ray. *Susie: The Life and Legacy of Susannah Spurgeon, wife of Charles H. Spurgeon*. Chicago: Moody Publishers, 2018.

Rogers, Bennett W., *A Tender Lion: The Life, Ministry, and Message of J. C. Ryle,* Grand Rapids, MI: Reformation Heritage Books, 2019.

Rogers, Henry. *Puseyism; or The Oxford Tractarian School*. New Haven, CT: Yale University Library, 2010.

Ross, Bob L. *A Pictorial Biography of C.H. Spurgeon*. Pasadena, TX: Pilgrim Publications, 1981.

Schreiner, Thomas R. and Shawn D. Wright, eds. *Believer's Baptism: Sign of the New Covenant in Christ*. Nashville, TN: B&H Academic, 2006.

Schreiner, Thomas R. and Matthew R. Crawford. *The Lord's Supper: Remembering and Proclaiming Christ Until He Comes*. Nashville, TN: B&H Academic, 2010.

Skinner, Craig. *Lamplighter and Son: The Forgotten Story of Thomas Spurgeon and his Famous Father, Charles Haddon Spurgeon*. Nashville, TN: Broadman Press, 1984.

Torbet, Robert G. *A History of the Baptists*, Third Edition. Valley Forge, PA: The Judson Press, 1963.

Underwood, A. C. *A History of the English Baptists*. London: The Carey Kingsgate Press, 1961.

Walker, Michael. *Baptists at the Table*. Didcot, UK: Baptist Historical Society, 1992.

Wright, Stephen. *The Early English Baptists, 1603-1649*. Woodbridge, UK: The Boydell Press, 2006.

Index

Christian Focus Publications

Our mission statement –

STAYING FAITHFUL

In dependence upon God we seek to impact the world through literature faithful to His infallible Word, the Bible. Our aim is to ensure that the Lord Jesus Christ is presented as the only hope to obtain forgiveness of sin, live a useful life and look forward to heaven with Him.

Our books are published in four imprints:

CHRISTIAN
FOCUS

Popular works including biographies, commentaries, basic doctrine and Christian living.

CHRISTIAN
HERITAGE

Books representing some of the best material from the rich heritage of the church.

MENTOR

Books written at a level suitable for Bible College and seminary students, pastors, and other serious readers. The imprint includes commentaries, doctrinal studies, examination of current issues and church history.

CF4•K

Children's books for quality Bible teaching and for all age groups: Sunday school curriculum, puzzle and activity books; personal and family devotional titles, biographies and inspirational stories—because you are never too young to know Jesus!

Christian Focus Publications Ltd,
Geanies House, Fearn, Ross-shire,
IV20 1TW, Scotland, United Kingdom.
www.christianfocus.com